CW01506675

THE BIRTH OF A BOROUGH

AN ARCHAEOLOGICAL STUDY OF ANGLO-SAXON STAFFORD

The town of Stafford in the British midlands was founded in the early tenth century AD by Æthelflæd, King Alfred's daughter and leader of the western English armies. Explored in an intensive campaign of urban archaeology, including four major and some 30 minor excavations, Æthelflæd's foundation was revealed as a military garrison, making pots and provisioned with beef and bannocks. The site had been active in Iron Age and Roman times, but there was no evidence for its use in the Middle Saxon period (seventh-ninth centuries). After the Norman Conquest the place was virtually abandoned and not re-activated as a working town until the late twelfth century.

Re-examining the wider evidence for the origins of the Anglo-Saxon *burh* in Wessex and Mercia, the author concludes that all were new creations on sites chosen for strategic reasons, in which the previous existence of a royal centre or a minster was rarely determinant. Built as a fort and generally rectilinear in shape, the *burh* and its deployment were made in direct imitation of Rome in whose name England was being re-conquered from the Danes by Alfred and his successors. In the Midlands, this imitation extended not only to building of forts and the minting of coins, but the making of pottery in the local Roman model. Not until the later tenth or eleventh centuries did these foundations begin to function as towns, and many never did. The English borough, like the Roman *civitas,* was military and administrative in origin, and its purpose was control rather than commerce.

MARTIN CARVER is Professor Emeritus of Archaeology at the University of York

I Central Stafford from the air in 1982 (Aerofilms Ltd).

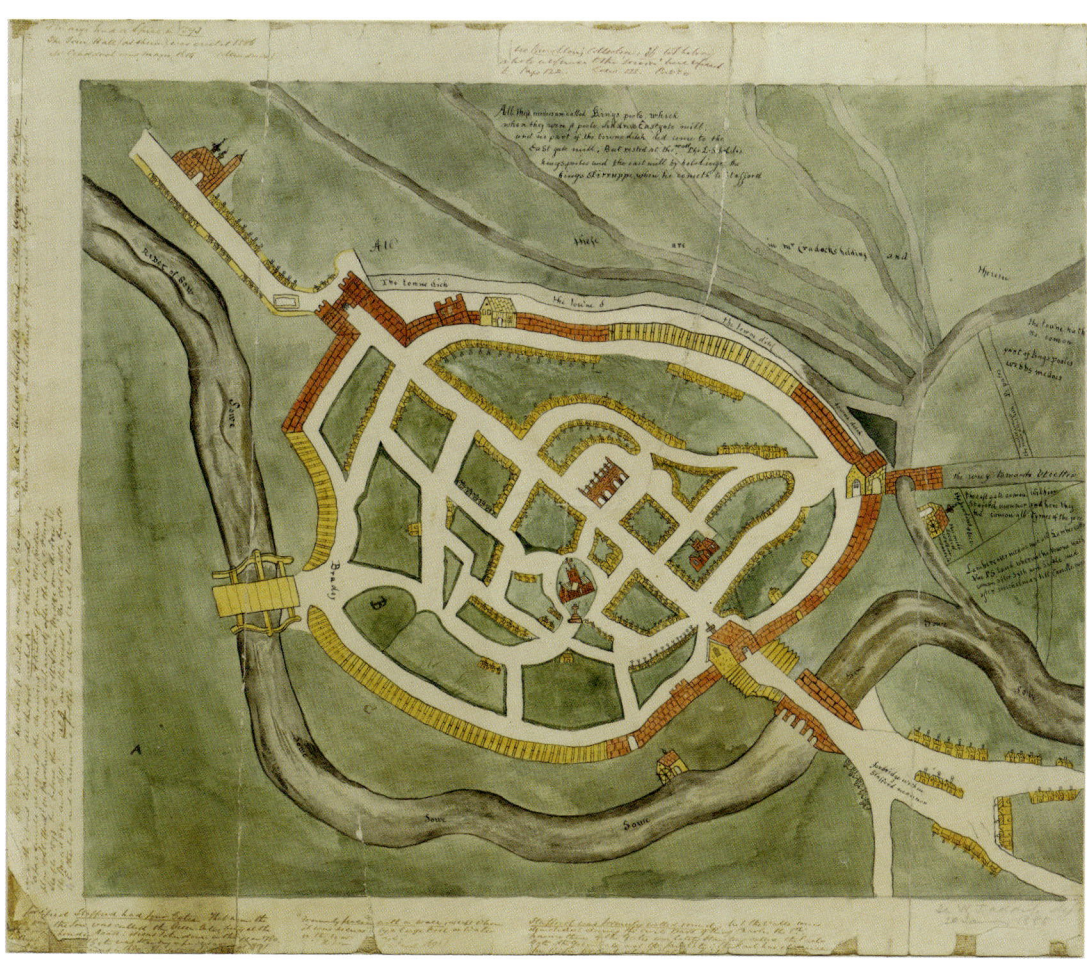

II The William Salt Map (William Salt Library, Plan 55/2/74; © William Salt Library).

III Stafford ware.

IV Stafford ware, a pedestalled cup or chalice.

THE BIRTH OF A BOROUGH

AN ARCHAEOLOGICAL STUDY OF ANGLO-SAXON STAFFORD

Martin Carver

Based on records and research by
Jon Cane, Charlotte Cane, Mark Taylor,
Jenny Glazebrook, Madeleine Hummler, Roy Barnes,
Lisa Moffett, James Greig, Steven Ashby,
Cecily Spall and Nicholas Thomas

THE BOYDELL PRESS

First published 2010
The Boydell Press, Woodbridge

ISBN 978 0 85115 623 1

The Boydell Press is an imprint of Boydell & Brewer Ltd
PO Box 9, Woodbridge, Suffolk IP12 3DF, UK
and of Boydell & Brewer Inc.
668 Mount Hope Ave, Rochester, NY 14620, USA
website: www.boydellandbrewer.com

A CIP catalogue record for this book is available
from the British Library

The publisher has no responsibility for
the continued existence or accuracy of URLs for
external or third-party internet websites referred to in this book,
and does not guarantee that any content on such websites
is, or will remain, accurate or appropriate

Papers used by Boydell & Brewer Ltd are natural, recyclable products
made from wood grown in sustainable forests

Printed in Great Britain by
CPI Antony Rowe, Chippenham and Eastbourne

Contents

Digests (of evidence)

Illustrations

All illustrations are © M. O. H. Carver except as marked.

Frontispieces

I   Central Stafford from the air in 1982 (Aerofilms Ltd)
II   The William Salt Map (© William Salt Library)
III   Stafford ware
IV   Stafford ware: a pedestalled cup or chalice

Figures

Preface

In 1974 – while I was busy doing something else – the telephone rang in the premises of our self-styled West Midlands Rescue Archaeology Committee (WEMRAC) at 25a The Tything, Worcester. On the phone was Ashley Carter, of the Stafford and Mid Staffordshire Archaeology Society, who had dug some test pits on the line of a proposed ring road at Clarke Street and found a great quantity of orange pottery. He thought it looked Roman – and yet. Soon I was Ashley's guest at his house near Stafford, where the potsherds were stacked high on the kitchen table. They were symmetrical, and orange or pink or grey in colour, smooth but very sandy, depositing a little weep of sand every time you picked one up. After some minutes I found what I was hunting for – a thin band of rouletting around the shoulder, like a row of marks from a toothed wheel. This pottery was not Roman, but tenth-century, the pottery of the earliest English towns. And Stafford was one of these: now the county town of Staffordshire, and long ago a foundation of one of England's few female generals: Alfred's daughter, Æthelflæd, Lady of the Mercians, who built her burh in a loop of the River Sow. Next year I excavated the Clarke Street site and began a ten-year campaign exploring Stafford. And the rest is history – or I would hope it to be.

This book offers an account of the campaign of 1975–1985, the discoveries made, the analyses undertaken and the conclusions drawn. The new information I offer is archaeological, but it is not presented here in the form of a conventional archaeological report of the kind intended only for other archaeologists. The archaeological records are held in Stoke-on-Trent Museum, where they are available for consultation. I recommend a visit anyway, to see one of the country's great collections, but it is not obligatory in order to access the archaeological evidence on which this book is based. That evidence has been sifted and digested and placed online as a publicly accessible archive in eleven volumes hosted by the Archaeological Data Service. There will be found texts, plans, sections, stratigraphic diagrams and photographs, relating to the fifty-five archaeological interventions recorded before and during the campaign, including the first excavation at St Bertelin's church and the four large set-piece excavations at Clarke Street, St Mary's Grove, Tipping Street and Bath Street.

This book by contrast is an attempt to use archaeology to write history, and my hope is that historians and those interested in English towns will find some sustenance here. Archaeology in towns has so far made some of its most useful contributions to the Late Saxon and Norman periods – the tenth to twelfth centuries – and it was here that the focus of our own research lay. We explored the fort founded by Æthelflæd and noted its highly organised and curiously Roman character. The centre of the town proved to have been dedicated to the collection of grain – rye, oats and wheat – and the baking of bread and bannocks on an industrial scale. The eastern edge of the town was dedicated to making copious quantities of pottery vessels known to us as Stafford ware and further east large numbers of cattle bones were tipped into the marsh that surrounded and defined the early site. This militaristic place flourished until the mid eleventh century when it was largely snuffed out, retreating into a small enclave around the church, while control was taken by two mighty castles, one by the River Sow and another on the road out of town to the west. The town itself started up again only in the late twelfth century, at first impoverished and servile and then flourishing with a full street plan studded with the tenements of residents and craftsmen. In the mid fourteenth century the greater part of the town was again abandoned and again the kernel of Stafford retreated into the area around St Mary's church. It was not to expand back into the full extent of the peninsula until the sixteenth century.

This extraordinary switchback ride of boom and bust is not perhaps what is expected of the conventional 'origins and development' of an urban history – but it does seem to be what happened on the ground. The marriage of history with the archaeological story is almost perfect: Æthelflaed built her burh at Stafford in 913, and this Late Saxon phase is archaeologically the most prominent and intriguing of all the periods unearthed. The Late Saxon town came to a dramatic end in the mid eleventh century. The Normans are known to have laid waste to the region with particular vigour and Stafford is recorded as the only borough that paid less after the Conquest than before it. There was a major new start on the ground in the late twelfth century. In 1206 Stafford acquired its charter from King John and became a free borough. The mid fourteenth-century hiatus aligns with the Black Death and the sixteenth-century resurgence with the visit of Elizabeth I, which took place in 1575.

To a continental reader it might seem that the people of the medieval Midlands never really got hold of the idea of living in towns. They remained places appropriate for the army, tax collectors or shopping, while sensible people lived in the countryside. This would be a slur on the constituency of Richard Brinsley Sheridan, and it would mask from us the extraordinary vision of the woman who founded it. Æthelflaed's dream, perhaps only approaching realisation today, was of a civilisation in the image of Rome.

Ellerton, 2009

Acknowledgements

This book is based on excavations and research that I initiated while Director of the West Midland Rescue Archaeology Committee (1974–1978) and Birmingham University Field Archaeology Unit (1978–1986). Our sponsors were Stafford Borough Council, Staffordshire County Council and the Ancient Monuments Inspectorate of the Department of the Environment, which became the Historic Buildings and Monuments Commission, and then English Heritage. After 1990 the project was brought to fruition through the good offices of the Department of Archaeology, University of York, and FAS Heritage Ltd. Publication was made possible by Richard Barber, Caroline Palmer and the Boydell Press with a grant from the Marc Fitch Fund.

Stafford ware was discovered by **Ashley Carter** at Clarke Street in 1974, an event that led directly to the research campaign. I directed the excavations at Clarke Street in 1975 (ST15, for WEMRAC), discovered the first Stafford-ware kiln at Tipping Street (south) in 1977 (ST17), designed and executed the evaluation of Stafford Town in 1979 (ST18–28) and directed the subsequent campaign 1980–1985.

The St Mary's Grove site (ST29) was supervised by **Jon Cane** who also oversaw the excavation at Tipping Street (ST32), supervised by **Mark Taylor**, and the excavation at Bath Street (ST34), supervised by **Roy Barnes** and analysed by **Jenny Glazebrook**. **Charlotte Cane** was Finds Supervisor 1980–1985 and reviewed finds from all interventions, creating the pottery typologies. Following my departure to York in 1986, Jon and Charlotte Cane also managed the post-excavation programme until 1988, when they left to pursue other careers.

The workforce in the field was dependent on volunteers from universities and the town, and in the early 1980s on a YOP (Youth Opportunity Programme) Scheme. The archaeological evidence has been edited and summarised and placed online by the Archaeological Data Service at the University of York. This vital operation to put the main reports in the public domain was funded by English Heritage. The data, styled 'Field Reports', are presented in eleven volumes FR1–11 (see Digest A6 for an index to the online archive).

Important special studies were carried out as follows:

Sarah Bazalgette, analysis of records from the Evaluation campaign [FR2]
Jon Cane, stratigraphic analysis of the sites at St Mary's Grove, Tipping Street and Bath Street [FR5, 6 and 7]
John Chadderton, study of Roman pottery from Stafford [FR8]
Charlotte Cane, study of Stafford ware and of medieval pottery [FR8]
Joanna Williams, bone comb [FR8]
Steve Ashby, bone comb [FR8]
Cecily Spall, cache of iron implements from Tipping Street [FR8]
Alison Cameron, study of human bone [FR9]
Madeleine Hummler and **James Rackham**, study of animal bone assemblages [FR9]
Lisa Moffett, study of plant macrofossils [FR10]
Susan Colledge and **James Greig** of the University of Birmingham, study of pollen sequence from the King's Pool [FR10]

Lawrence Bowkett, 'The Stafford Hinterland. An archaeological and historical review from the Roman Invasion to c. 850 AD' [FR11]

All these studies are available in the Stafford online archive at: http://ads.ahds. ac.uk/catalogue/archive/stafford_eh_2009
There were also three valuable dissertations:

John Darlington, 'Approaches to Iron Artefact Analysis: A Guide and Appraisal' (study of iron objects from Stafford) (MA dissertation, University of Birmingham, 1985)
Jenny Glazebrook, 'Stafford – A Survey of the Urban Fabric' (MA dissertation, University of Birmingham, 1983)
Alison Jill Walker, 'The Archaeology of Stafford to 1600 AD' (MA dissertation, University of Bradford, 1976)

My warmest thanks to Nicholas Brooks, Grenville Astill and Jon Cane for reviewing an earlier draft of the text. The book has profited greatly from their advice, though probably less than they hoped. Lastly I am very grateful to Jon and Charlotte Cane and all the other contributors to the original Stafford campaign whether archaeologists, specialists or volunteers. The present synthesis was only made possible by the research they did.

The publishers are grateful to the **Marc Fitch Fund** for a grant towards the cost of publication, and the author to Caroline Palmer, Rohais Haughton, Vanda Andrews, Cecily Spall, Pam Cope and Madeleine Hummler for their editing, advice and encouragement.

The spelling of names in this book follows that used in *The Anglo-Saxon Chronicle*, edited by Dorothy Whitelock (Whitelock 1961).

Abbreviations

References to the online excavation record

The full record of the archaeological evidence on which this book is based is available in the Stafford online archive at:
http://ads.ahds.ac.uk/catalogue/archive/stafford_eh_2009
References are made to this record, where prefixes have the following meanings:

C	Context: an ancient deposit, defined archaeologically, for example a layer of clay or a tumble of stones; contexts are always four-digit numbers and normally recognised without the C prefix, which has only been inserted at the first instance as an aid to explanation
cp	Cooking pot
Cu	Copper-alloy object
F	Feature: an ancient activity, defined archaeologically, for example a rubbish pit or pottery kiln
Fe	Iron object
FR	Field Report, the reports made in the field (see Digest A7 for a detailed list)
Int	Intervention number
KP	Site code for King's Pool which prefixes the King's Pool investigations
S	Structure: an ancient construction, defined archaeologically, for example a potter's building (see Digest A5 for a list of excavated structures)
ST	Site code for 'Stafford' followed by the intervention number, for example ST29 – St Mary's Grove excavations; all interventions have a ST number except the King's Pool investigations, which are prefixed KP (see Digest A1 for a list of archaeological interventions at Stafford to 1988)
sw	Spindle whorl
WS	Worked stone

A structure is a set of features. A feature is a set of contexts. See Carver 2009 for reference to this system of nomenclature.

Other abbreviations

BMC	British Museum Catalogue of English Coins, vols 1–5
BUFAU	Birmingham University Field Archaeology Unit (now Birmingham Archaeology). BUFAU 7 refers to the unit's annual report in 1984
SCoFE	Stafford College of Further Education
SMSAS	Stafford and Mid Staffordshire Archaeological Society
VCH	*Victoria County History of Staffordshire, Vol. VI: Stafford Town* (1979)
WEMRAC	West Midlands Rescue Archaeology Committee

1

Questions

In July AD 913 Æthelflæd, Lady of the Mercians, founded Stafford as part of a campaign for the recovery of England from the Danes. She was the commander of the left flank in the northward advance, while her brother Edward the Elder led the pincer movement on the right flank. Wessex had already been won, thanks to the persistence and ingenuity of their father, Alfred the Great.

The primary instrument of this war was the *burh*, a fortification with provision for residence and trade, which was garrisoned by levy or conscription from its local territory. In Wessex, some record of the procurement system has survived as the Burghal Hidage, which names the places and the human resources required to man them[1] (Fig. 1.1). The places chosen were broadly of three types: former Roman forts or fortified towns, like Winchester, Portchester and Chichester; new foundations that resembled Roman forts, like Wareham, Wallingford and Cricklade; and smaller sites of unknown form at promontories or river junctions, like Lydford and Lyng. Together these places are thought to have formed a defensive system, in which some fortified enclosure was, or was intended to be, in reach of all the people.

The choice of the Wessex sites has been argued to have been determined by the fact that they were already royal property, or the site of an ecclesiastical community, or both. The intention, as perceived from documentary records, was also to canalise trade through these places, and to concentrate the income stream from fines and taxes within them to the benefit of king and church. Such a concept may have been in experimental development at Canterbury, before the age of Alfred.[2] Even if the context of their creation was military, they thus appear as something more than forts, the first manifestation of the English borough. It is perhaps reasonable here to draw a distinction between the nature of places as observed in documents and on the ground. Burh and borough are documentary terms carrying a sense of the chartered town of the Middle Ages that might not be appropriate. On the ground we can define a fort by its fortifications, and a town by its artisan activity. Accordingly the terms used in this book are *burh* to denote the sites documented as burhs in the literature, *fort* for a defended site defined archaeologically, here generally of the ninth/tenth centuries, and *town* for sites with signs of dense occupation and commerce. In each case, the term need not imply the detailed reality of these places, and the question of their actual military, commercial, royal and ecclesiastical emphasis will need to be resolved locally.

Sites and purposes of the Anglo-Saxon towns

Archaeological, topographical and historical investigations have sought a general prescription for the Anglo-Saxon town that it may not have uniformly enjoyed. Studies of the Wessex *burhs* have led to the deduction that many of the larger ones were laid out with a street grid, which reinforces the idea that they were intended as towns, as opposed to merely forts, from the moment of their foundation.[3] Surprisingly, this picture has received little archaeological endorsement: several decades of intensive excavation have strengthened the conviction that in most cases it took another century or so for the more conventional trappings of town life – craft, trade and suburbs – to arrive.[4]

In the Midlands, the Anglo-Saxon towns have been less intensively investigated, but the expectation is that they will be similar in purpose and design to those of Wessex. However, the two military campaigns in south and north were consecutive and there was a difference in their context; while the first in Wessex was defensive, the second, north of the Thames, was largely aggressive. Burh-building in both territories are nevertheless likely to have been closely connected by strategy, origin and design. In 898, a conference was convened in London

---

1   Hill 1969, and see Brooks 1996.
2   Stenton 1971, 528–9.

3   Biddle and Hill 1971; Biddle 1976.
4   Vince 1994.

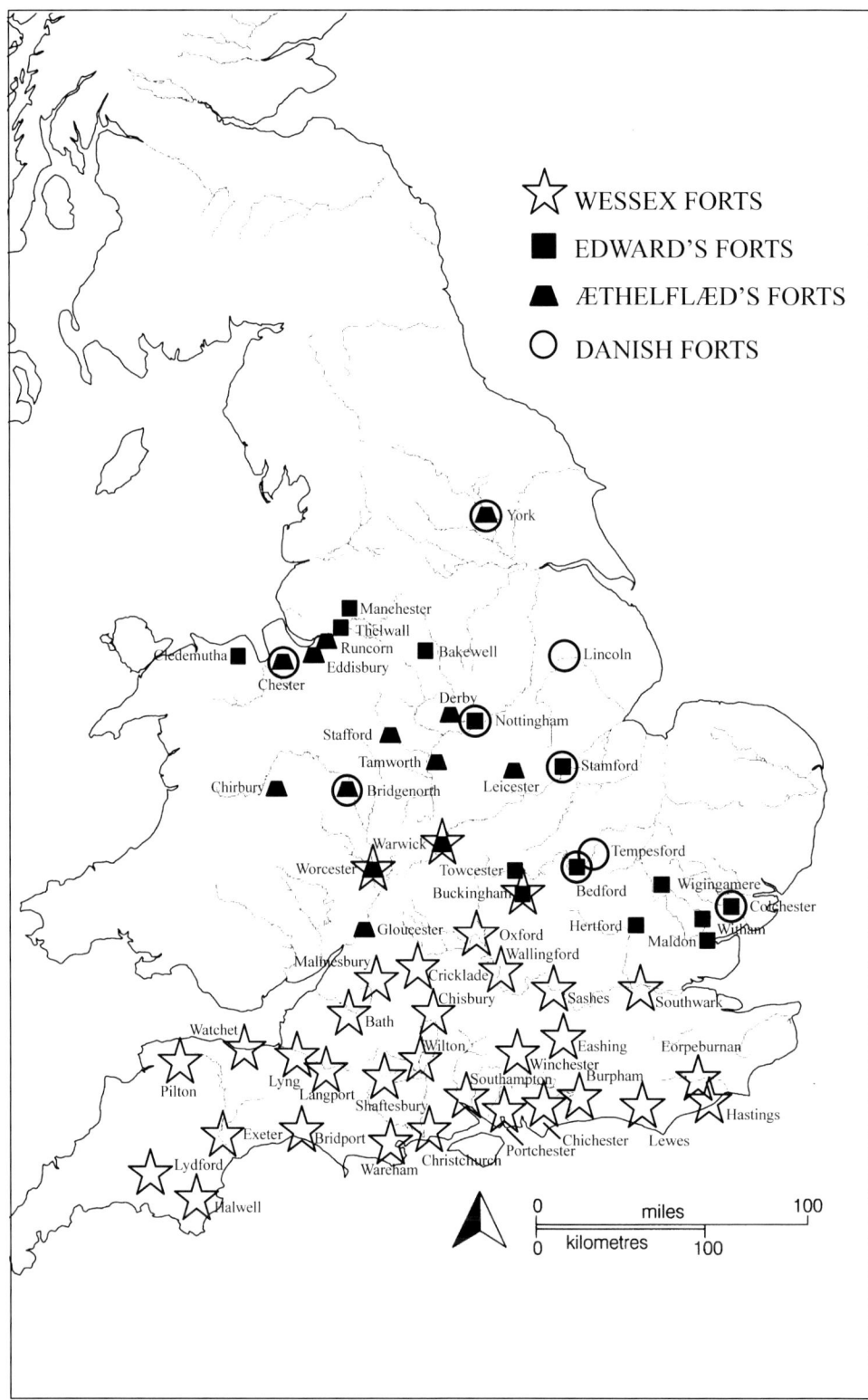

Fig. 1.1 The location of the burhs of Wessex, Mercia and eastern England.

attended by King Alfred, Edward the Elder, Archbishop Plegmund, Bishop Werferth, Earldorman Ethelred of Mercia and Æthelflæd, his lady and Alfred's daughter.[5] Since the purpose of the meeting was to discuss the layout of a street grid that would stretch from Thames Street to Cheapside, it could be considered a conference on town planning, attended by many of the principal players. Alfred died on 26 October 899 leaving Ethelred, Æthelflæd and her brother Edward to carry the banner of reconquest. On 5 August 910, the Wessex and Mercian army with Ethelred at its head routed the Danes at Wednesfield near Tettenhall. Ethelred died the following year, possibly from wounds received at the battle.[6] Æthelflæd died in 918 having taken the submission of Leicester and York and Edward in 924 after acceptance as overlord by the Northumbrians, Scots and Strathclyde Britons. Between them, this trio of aristocratic commanders had built at least twenty-eight forts (Table 1.1).

The known midland burhs are listed in the Anglo-Saxon Chronicle and the so-called Mercian Register, which gives brief notices of the foundations of Edward and of Ethelred and Æthelflæd respectively. The most detailed account of the purpose of any burh is provided for Worcester, devised by Ethelred and Æthelflæd together with the bishop, Werferth. The burh was for the protection of 'all the people' and was expected to generate income from the start, to cover the cost of its own defence, and to allow a share of the profits from tax and fines to the church and to the king.[7] The implication is that a number of pre-existing activities were to be centralised within a defended area, with a consequent reorganisation of benefits. Since he operated in former Danish territory, Edward often adapted former Danish forts in East Anglia, or built his own on the opposite side of the river. In the west, Ethelred and Æthelflæd chose both former Roman and non-Roman sites. The assumption is that, whatever their strategic rationale, all the places listed had or acquired at least some of the functions of military, economic and spiritual control.

Table 1.1 The forts of Edward and Æthelflæd

Edward's forts

912   Edward built the northern borough of Hertford. Edward camped at **Maldon** while the borough was being constructed at **Witham**. Edward constructed the southern borough of **Hertford**.

913   Edward fighting the Danish army round Luton.

914   Edward made boroughs at **Buckingham** either side of the river.

5   Brooks 1996, 143.

6   Walker 2000, 92.

7   Stenton 1971, 529.

915   Edward obtained the borough at **Bedford**, and built another on the south side of the river.

916   Edward built the borough at **Maldon**.

917   Edward ordered **Towcester** to be occupied and (repaired?), then built a borough at **Wigingamere**. Towcester resisted an all day attack by the Danes. Danes built a fort at Tempsford. Edward besieged and took Tempsford. Then a great English army besieged Colchester and took it. The Danes besieged Maldon but it was relieved by the English. Edward provided **Towcester** with a stone wall, and repaired **Colchester**, winning the allegiance of the East Angles who had gone Danish.

918   Edward went to **Stamford** and ordered the borough on the south side to be built. The northern borough surrendered and gave allegiance to Edward.

919   Edward built the borough at **Thelwall** and repaired **Manchester**. Ethelred (and Æthelflaed's) daughter Alfwyn was deprived of authority in Mercia and taken to Wessex.

920   Edward went to **Nottingham** and built another borough on the south side of the river, with a bridge between the two. Went to **Bakewell** and built a borough there. And the king of Scots, Ragnald, and the sons of Eadwulf and all who lived in Northumbria, including English, Danish, Norse and others, and the Strathclyde Britons accepted him as lord.

921   Edward built a borough at **Cledemutha** (mouth of Clwyd?, Rhuddlan?).

924   Edward died at Farndon in Mercia.

Æthelflæd's forts

890s?   Ethelred fortified **Gloucester**.

c.899   Ethelred and Æthelflæd built the borough at **Worcester**, towards the end of Alfred's reign.

907   Æthelflæd restored **Chester**.

910   Æthelflæd built the borough at *Bremesbyrig*.

912   Æthelflæd built a borough at *Scergeat* and at **Bridgenorth**.

913   Æthelflæd went with all the Mercians to **Tamworth** and built the borough there in early summer; and before Lammas (July) that at **Stafford**.

914   Æthelflæd built the borough at **Eddisbury** in early summer and at **Warwick** in the early autumn.

915   Æthelflæd made boroughs at **Runcorn** before Christmas and at **Chirbury** and *Weardbyrig* after Christmas.

916   Æthelflæd sent an army into Wales to revenge the killing of Abbot Egbert, destroying Brecenanmere (Llangorse) and capturing the king's wife (Danish or Welsh?).

917   Æthelflæd obtained **Derby** before Lammas. Four thegns dear to her were killed within the gates.

918   Æthelflæd took the submission of the Danish army of **Leicester**; beat Ragnald at the second battle of **Corbridge**, and the people of **York** pledged allegiance to her. But she died at Tamworth, twelve days before midsummer (9 June?) in the eighth year of her reign over the Mercians; she is buried at Gloucester.

Archaeological investigations

Since the largest foundations in the Midlands, as elsewhere, became towns and remained towns, archaeological access to the Late Saxon deposits has been piecemeal and interpretation difficult. Perhaps the most elusive aspect of the early town is the one most eagerly sought, that is the line of the defended enclosure. But in spite of the ingenious use of maps and church

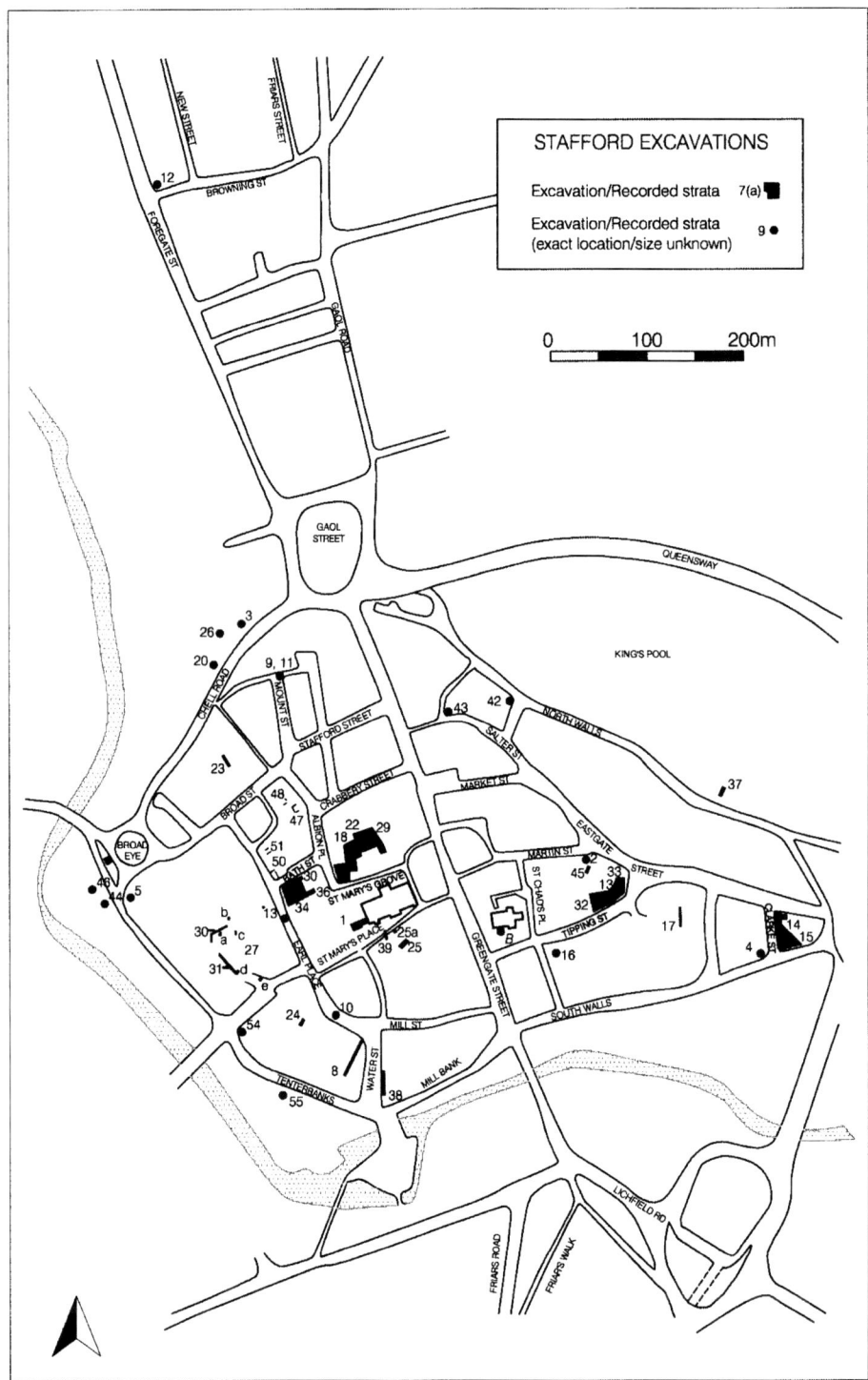

Fig. 1.2 Stafford town showing the location of archaeological interventions. For key to numbers see Digest A1.

records, the numerous attempts at inference rarely rise above the probable, so that it remains true that we do not know the form of a Mercian fort with the confidence of some examples from Wessex.

Archaeological investigations at Hereford have revealed burials of the Anglo-Saxon period at the cathedral and a length of defences, sealing an eighth-/ninth-century grain-dryer. Lengths of the defences have also been excavated at Worcester and Tamworth. Later Anglo-Saxon occupation has been confirmed in these places and the majority of all the named burhs. The problem has been to weave these intermittent and opportunistic interventions into a settlement with a credible shape, origin and history, comparable with that achieved in Wessex and Winchester in particular.[8]

Chance, aided by design, has allowed the emergence of the otherwise not-very-famous site of Stafford as the Mercian town that has seen one of the most intensive campaigns of archaeological research to date. The first investigation there was carried out by Adrian Oswald in 1954 at the site of St Bertelin's church in the town centre. Opportunist recording by members of the local archaeological societies then kept the torch burning until the discovery of Late Saxon Stafford-ware pottery in 1974. The site of its discovery, at Clarke Street, was excavated in 1975, and a watching brief in 1977 south of Tipping Street brought to light the first Stafford-ware kiln. In 1979, an evaluation of the whole historic core was undertaken, resulting in a map of the Late Saxon settlement and its deposits. In 1980–1985, three more area excavations followed, at St Mary's Grove, Bath Street and Tipping Street (north). Before 1985 Stafford had therefore been explored by five area excavations, stretching east-west across the Late Saxon town, as well as some thirty targeted trenches (Fig. 1.2).

The results of all these excavations and the assemblages recovered from them, and all the preliminary archaeological studies that were accessible, have been gathered, edited and placed in an online archive hosted by the Archaeological Data Service[9] (see Digest for the contents). Since a large team was involved, these reports do not always agree with each other, and the rival opinions are represented. The online archive is therefore itself a definitive resource that will hopefully be useful to future researchers.

The purpose of this book is to summarise what has been found at Stafford and reopen the debate on the Anglo-Saxon town. When I started writing it, I felt that its purpose should also be to help reawaken interest in a subject that seemed to have lost momentum since the

1970s; but the appearance of new initiatives in the last two years, for example the Burh to Borough project at Wallingford, gives cause for optimism.[10] This is another southern project, and the early midland towns continue to be less favoured in early urban research, so the present work should still have its uses. The investigation of Stafford was part of a wider inquiry of the 1970s that included Shrewsbury, Worcester, Lichfield, Hereford and Tamworth.[11] My original purpose as director of a regional research group at that time was to throw some light on the origins of places that became burhs, hoping in particular for some signs of pre-existing British centres of power and ritual. In practice, I found, as many have before and since, that the opportunities presented by a modern town rarely match our questions. This requires not so much that such questions be abandoned, but that they should be addressed over many years with great patience and eternal vigilance on the street.

What were these questions? In addition to the possible British origins of Late Saxon towns in the west and north, there were other matters relating to the choice of site. Were Late Saxon towns strategic or tactical and mainly military in their rationale? Were they meant to be forts or towns or both? What form did they take and why? Were they primarily foundations of the king and for the service of the kingdom? Was the presence of a Middle Saxon church community or a royal vill determinant? In what sense were these towns commercial and when did they become so? Why did they make coins and what were these used for? What happened to the Anglo-Saxon town at the Norman Conquest – and why?

As is often the way with archaeology, our answers to these general historical questions have proved somewhat oblique, while revelations about matters less formally previewed have sprung uninvited and evocatively into the light of day. The early site of Stafford lay in a peninsula formed by a loop in the River Sow and surrounded by marshland. It had been exploited in the Iron Age for storing grain and in the Roman period as arable land with some reclamation of the marsh. A north-south axial road, now Greengate Street, is argued to have had a Roman origin, and to have remained a crossing point through the otherwise blank centuries that followed. Although there are a few suggestive signals, there was no decisive archaeological evidence for occupation between the Roman period and the early tenth century, at which point there was an explosion of activity (Fig. 1.3). A chapel was constructed in the centre of the peninsula at St Bertelin's, with a central burial in

---

8 An attempt to address some of these matters is reserved until Chapter 6.

9 http://ads.ahds.ac.uk/catalogue/archive/stafford_eh_2009. The contents of the online archive will be found in Digest A6 at the end of this book.

10 http://www2.le.ac.uk/departments/archaeology/research/projects/wallingford (accessed 18 January 2010).

11 Carver 1978, 1980b, 1981; Shoesmith 1980, 1982; Rahtz 1977, Rahtz and Meeson 1992.

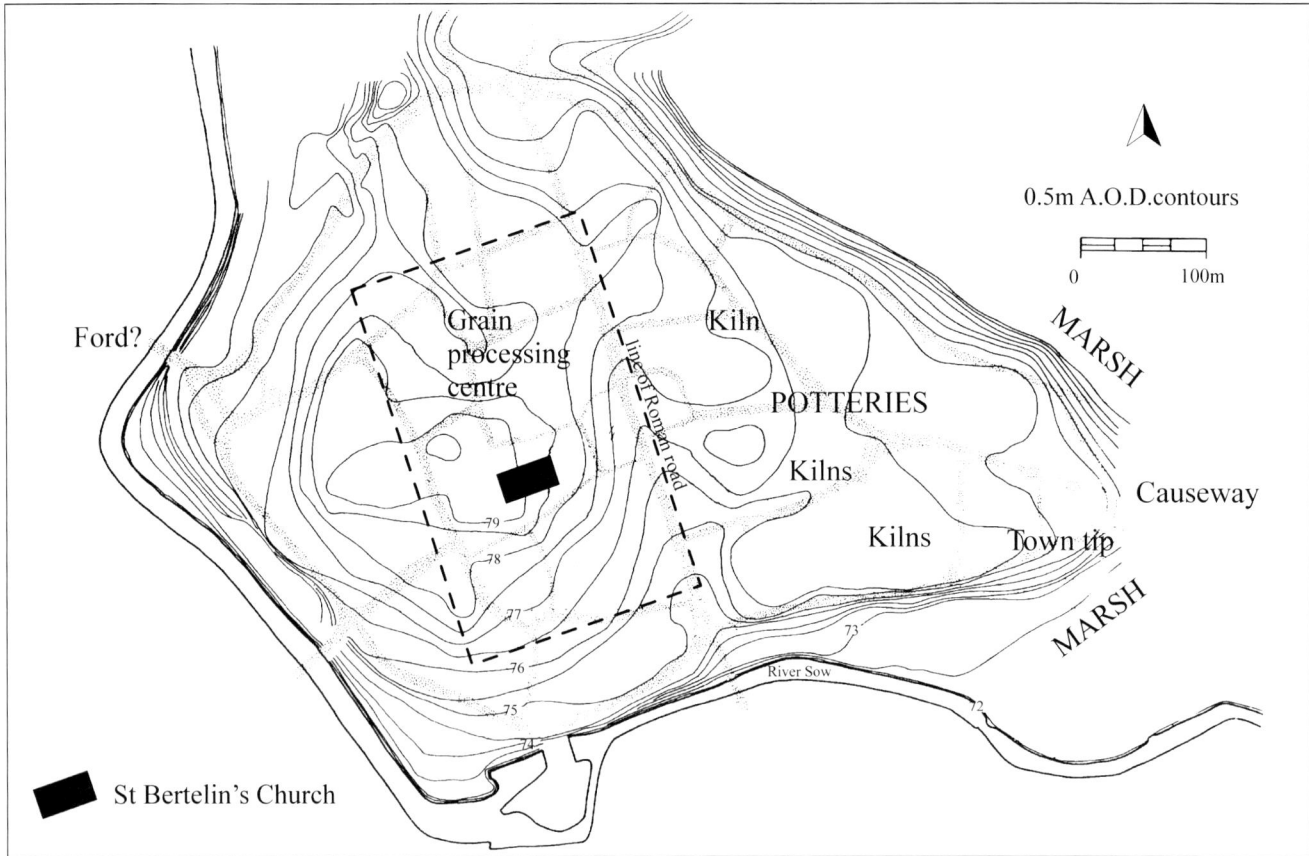

Fig. 1.3 Late Saxon Stafford, showing the location of St Bertelin's Church, the grain-processing industry, the potteries and the burh as argued in this book.

a tree trunk coffin.[12] North of the chapel was a large area dedicated to the processing of grain and the baking of loaves of bread and oatmeal bannocks. To the west was a smithy and stable block. To the east of the main axial road were the potters' workshops, producing a wide range of pots, pitchers, bowls and lamps as well as the ubiquitous Stafford-ware jar. Still further east at the marsh edge was the town dump, with piles of pottery wasters and butchered animal bone.

There was no convincing case for a pre-existing minster at Stafford, although it is not in the least improbable that there was one. The prime mover, as we have it, is the production of provender and pots on a large scale, presumably in support of some group of dependent persons, such as an army. The actual location of the defences remained unconfirmed, although such signs as we have, archaeological, documentary and topographical, converge on a rectangular area in the centre of the site that included both the church and the grain yard. The potteries and dumps to the east are outside this area, contained by a triangle of streets leading to the eastern causeway across the marshes.

12 A new interpretation; see Chapter 3.

Theme and structure of the book

The thesis that has been woven from these discoveries and their dating is consistent with the documentary record, that Æthelflæd, Lady of the Mercians, constructed a burh at Stafford in AD 913. The archaeological verdict is that the activities of the burh were highly regulated and inspired by an image of Rome. The basic form of settlement is hypothesised to be that of a Roman fort, with a *vicus* (a settlement outside a Roman fort) to the east. The processing of grain, the provision of beef and the production of pottery were organised, localised and standardised. The finds of three human skulls with pottery wasters perhaps gives an indication of the degree of regulation. This was a lady that meant business, and the business was winning a war.

The Roman references made by Alfred and his children have attracted various degrees of emphasis in earlier studies, although others have attributed the inspiration for pottery, and even the burhs to Carolingian France. The argument here is that the pottery made in the burhs of Æthelflæd and Edward deliberately resembles the Roman pottery previously

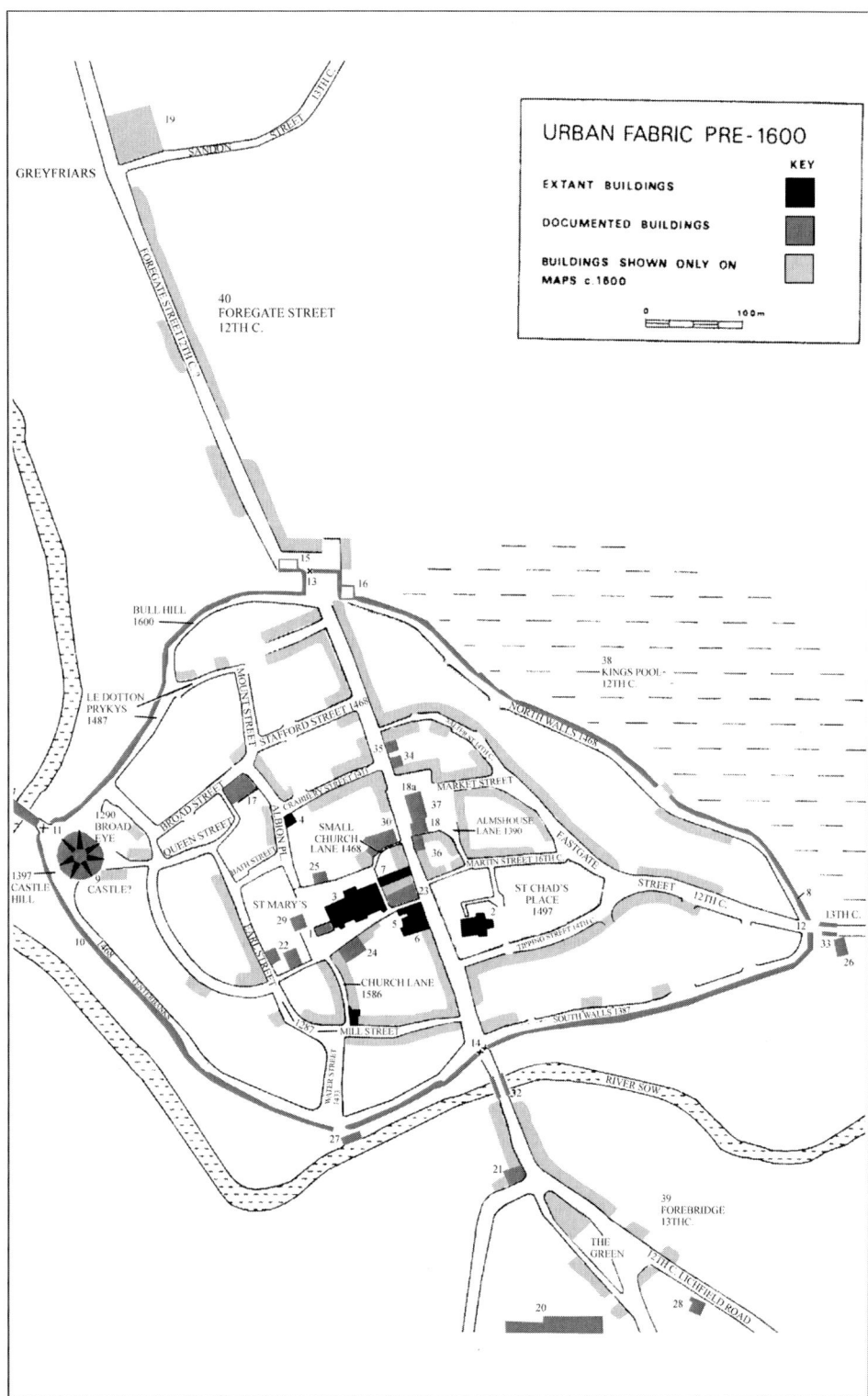

Fig. 1.4 Medieval Stafford. For key to numbers see FR2.3.4 (Glazebrook 1983).

made in the same region: Stafford ware imitates Severn Valley ware, Thetford ware imitates Black Burnished ware. To these we may add the more familiar Roman references: to Roman coinage, Roman forts, Roman street grids and perhaps even the Roman campaign of conquest. Æthelflæd's image of Rome was therefore from sources that were partly historical and partly archaeological in nature: the inherited story of the Roman conquest on the one hand and the plethora of Roman earthworks, walls, coins and pots on the other.

Anglo-Saxon Stafford has so far yielded evidence for coinage, pottery, butchery and grain processing, but no other crafts and no imports. However, the distribution of Stafford-ware pottery suggests that the whole of the peninsula was occupied, and by the time of Domesday Book was recognised as having 156 properties. Insofar as archaeological observation has allowed, the emphasis of the place remained administrative and military, with a fort, a church and an industrial *vicus*, until the Norman Conquest. A motte was then constructed on the western promontory of the peninsula, possibly overlooking a ford, looking also towards the site of the subsequent castle of Stafford, at Castle Church, some 2 kilometres from the town. The conquest here was particularly brutal, and resulted not only in the imposition of a castle, but in the destruction and suppression of every other activity except the intermittent minting of coins for about a hundred years.

Redevelopment began in the late twelfth century, maintaining the location of the church, the north–south axial street and routes through the Late Saxon industrial quarter to the east, but in other respects redrawing the town plan (Fig. 1.4). Tenements were laid out over the whole peninsula and crafts flourished in them until the early fourteenth century, when there was another hiatus, followed in the mid sixteenth century by another

revival. In spite of being designated as the shire town, Stafford was a place in need of continual resuscitation. From Æthelflæd to Elizabeth I, the enterprise required successive surges of external investment. Perhaps for this reason, it is at Stafford, a place unenthused by the urban project, that the intentions of the crown are particularly graphic.[13]

These ideas are discussed in their historical context in Chapter 6. But before then it has been my intention to lead the reader lightly through the process whereby our picture of Æthelflæd's town has seen the light of day. Chapter 2 recounts the archaeological exploration of Stafford and how the research project was designed. Chapter 3 summarises the seven 'windows' opened on the early medieval town – the four modern area excavations, the earlier unearthing of St Bertelin's, the more recent excavations at Broadeye and the environmental sequence from King's Pool. Chapter 4 brings together the evidence for Æthelflæd's burh and its experiences up to the Norman Conquest. Chapter 5 describes briefly the changes that the Conquest brought and Stafford's consequent middle age.

Even though this campaign ended twenty-five years ago, and is only now being rescued and brought to press, it was not a haphazard exercise and still invites judgement on its design, method, agenda, results and their interpretation. Every town in England has its own archaeological story to tell, but such stories may breed useful generalities. Those that have new light to offer on the tenth and eleventh centuries reflect on a period of English history of particular energy and brilliance.

---

13 Cf. Astill 2009b, 258. This vacillation reflects, with good archaeological precision, urban trajectories widely observed in northern Europe (Haase 1960).

2

Digging up Stafford: Evaluation and Design

History of the investigations

Stafford today is a busy urban place (Fig. 2.1) with shopping precincts, car parks and the headquarters of the municipality and the county. In 1975 it was under construction, a late-comer to the boom of the 1960s that had refashioned so many historic town centres and shocked the archaeological community into its 'rescue' response. Since it was only then beginning its redevelopment programme, large areas of Stafford lay open in 1975, unencumbered by buildings and awaiting planning decisions. There had been only one archaeological research investigation, the opening of a small area on the site of St Bertelin's church outside the west front of St Mary's, Stafford's principal church.[1] The excavator, Adrian Oswald of Birmingham City Museum, decided he had found St Bertelin's chapel and its predecessors, together with a lump of wood six foot long, which was interpreted as a wooden cross of the early Mercian period. The footings of the medieval chapel and a reconstruction of the early medieval 'cross' remain on display to this day (Fig. 2.2). Oswald's interpretation was made in the natural expectation that Stafford should have an early Anglo-Saxon church – as indeed it still may; but the archaeological sequence and its dates have proved to be unsafe (Chapter 3, p. 21).

Over the following twenty years there were intermittent observations and excavations in which the local archaeological society and the University of Keele were active, associated particularly with the names of Paul Robinson, Francis Celoria and Ashley Carter.[2] Talk of a ring road in 1974 led Ashley Carter to cut trenches and test pits on a car park site east of Clarke Street, unearthing copious quantities of orange pottery, later identified as Late Saxon Stafford ware.[3] The whole available site was excavated in 1975, revealing a marsh sequence from the first millennium BC to the Norman period. From the tenth century it had been used as a dump, but in the eleventh to thirteenth centuries the area was developed briefly as an urban tenement fronting on to Eastgate Street.[4] The Late Saxon pottery from Clarke Street consisted predominately of wasters, suggesting that it was made locally, a supposition confirmed in 1977 when a chance visit on a Sunday morning to a site south of Tipping Street on the eve of its redevelopment discovered a kiln in section, with numerous large fragments of good quality pottery, henceforward termed Stafford ware (Fig. 2.3; Frontispiece III, IV; see Chapter 4).[5]

At this point the potential of Stafford as a Late Saxon site was evident, as was the imminence of the redevelopment programme that would shortly disturb a large part of it. I had been responsible for the 1975 excavations and the 1977 observations and as Director of WEMRAC[6] and then of BUFAU[7] was pursuing an active programme of research into the origins of west midland towns. The Stafford opportunity was created thanks largely to enlightened staff at Stafford Borough (Brian Lambert), Staffordshire County (Ken Sheridan and Bob Meeson) and the Department of the Environment (Brian Davison and Anthony Fleming). In 1979, these agencies responded positively to a proposal for an evaluation of the whole historic site, to consist of a review of what was known from literature, a

---

1 FR2.3.2, no. 1, and FR3. References to the online archive are given in the form FR2.2, 3, where FR 2.2 (Field Report 2) is the file and subfile number and 3 is the number of the referenced item. For an index to the archive see Digest A6 below. Oswald 1955a and b for the excavation.

2 FR2.3.2, 2–13.

3 FR2.3.2, 14. See Preface above.

4 FR2.3.2, 15; and see pp. 47–53.

5 FR2.3.2, 17. The early literature refers to this pottery as west Midlands early medieval ware. See pp. 79–93.

6 West Midland Rescue Archaeology Committee formed in 1974 to undertake emergency recording, excavation and research in the West Midlands. In 1978 it was disbanded and the responsibility for rescue passed to the County Councils.

7 Birmingham University Field Archaeology Unit, now Birmingham Archaeology.

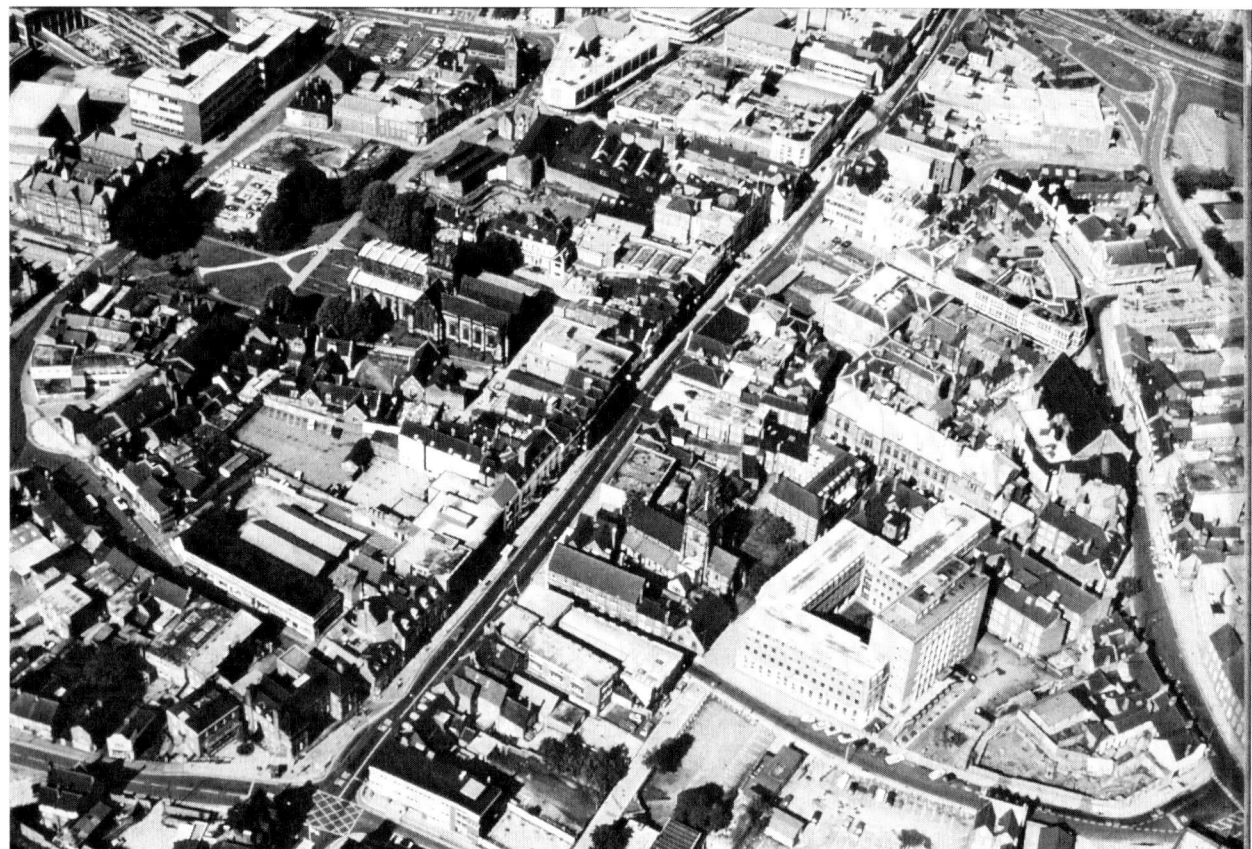

Fig. 2.1 Aerial view of Stafford showing excavations in progress in 1982, in (from left) Bath Street, St Mary's Grove and Tipping Street (north) (Aerofilms Ltd).

Fig. 2.2 St Mary's Church, west end, with the foundations of St Bertelin's Church and the reproduction of the 'cross' from the 1954 excavations. A picture taken in 2008.

Fig. 2.3 Salvage expedition at Tipping Street (south) in 1977. A general view looking east, and a whole Stafford-ware pot retrieved at the site.

topographical plan of the town, together with thirty new stratigraphic samples to be taken in trenches and pits from areas that currently lay open.[8] The resulting urban archaeological data base comprised a record of all archaeological interventions, archaeological contacts (i.e. casual observations), records of historically attested buildings of before 1600, documented places and medieval streets.[9] This material would be used to construct a resource model showing what Anglo-Saxon and medieval deposits lay where, how deep and to what degree of preservation. The work was carried out between 5 March and 22 April 1979, mainly by a team of students seconded to BUFAU (Figs 2.4, 2.5; for the location of all excavations, see Fig. 1.2).[10]

Model of the archaeological resource

The topographic model (Fig. 2.6) shows the form of the site, a peninsula in a loop of the River Sow, otherwise surrounded by marshland.[11] The highest point lies to the west and north of St Mary's church and an axial street (now Greengate Street) connects the neck of the peninsula in the north with a crossing point over the river in the south. To the east, routes leaving Greengate Street on the high ground converge on a causeway that leaves the peninsula between the river and King's Pool, and is presumed ancient (see Chapter 4).

The archaeological deposits are generally shallow, the subsoil being a metre or less from the modern surface (Fig. 2.7). They are in consequence very vulnerable to disturbance. Where they are intact, the earliest prehistoric and Roman strata are about 25 centimetres

8 FR2.3.2, nos 18–28.

9 See the online archive at FR2.3.1 to 2.3.6.

10 The results will be found in FR2.3.2. See also *BUFAU 2* (1979), 6–9.

11 FR2.4.

Fig. 2.4 Evaluation test pit (ST36, Bath Street, 1979).

Fig. 2.5 Evaluation trench (ST22, St Mary's Grove, 1979).

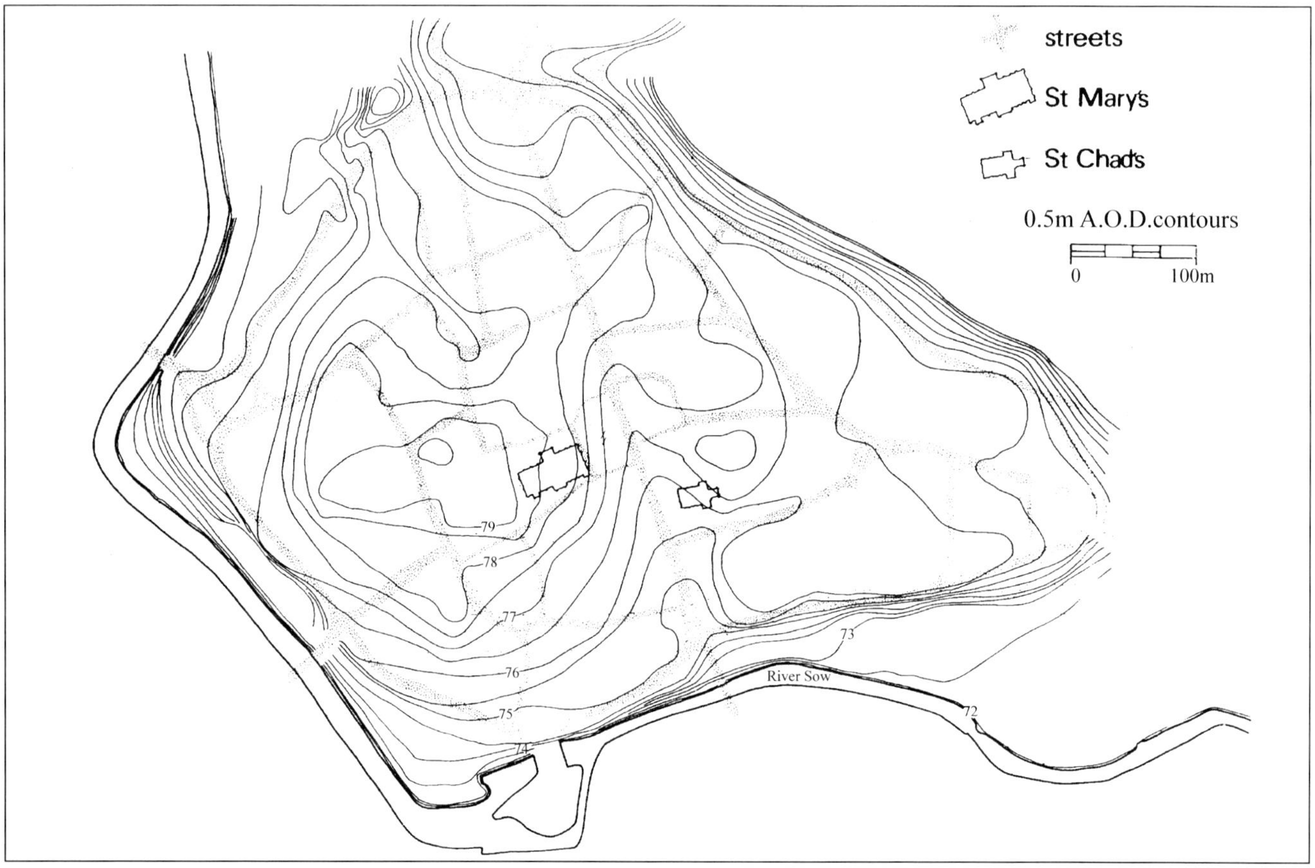

Fig. 2.6 Stafford: surface topography (J. Cane; FAS Heritage). The modern contours are owed to a survey by Madeleine Hummler (STAFFTOP).

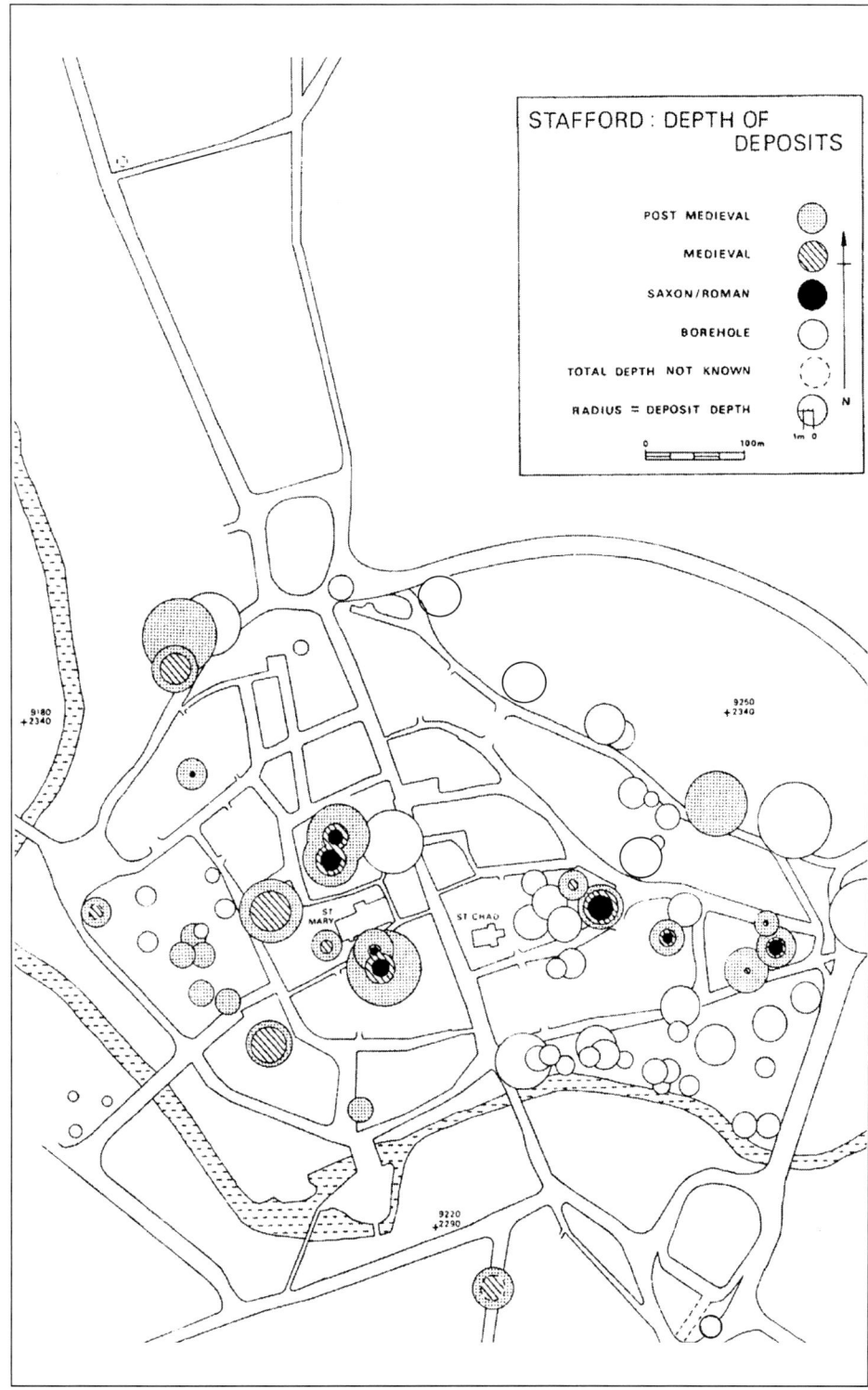

Fig. 2.7 Resource model: depths of deposit by date (Glazebrook 1983).

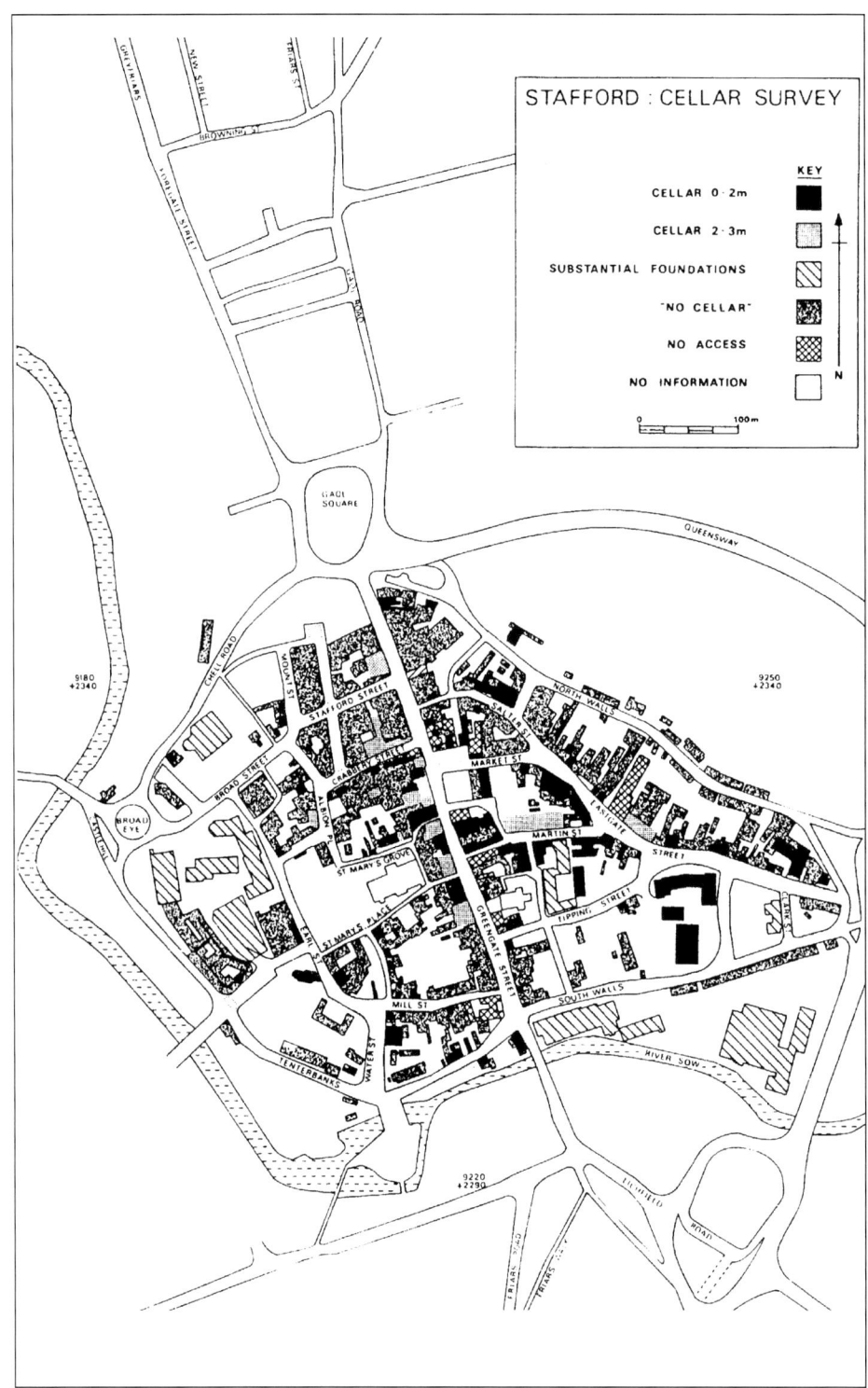

Fig. 2.8 Stafford cellar survey by depth (Glazebrook 1983).

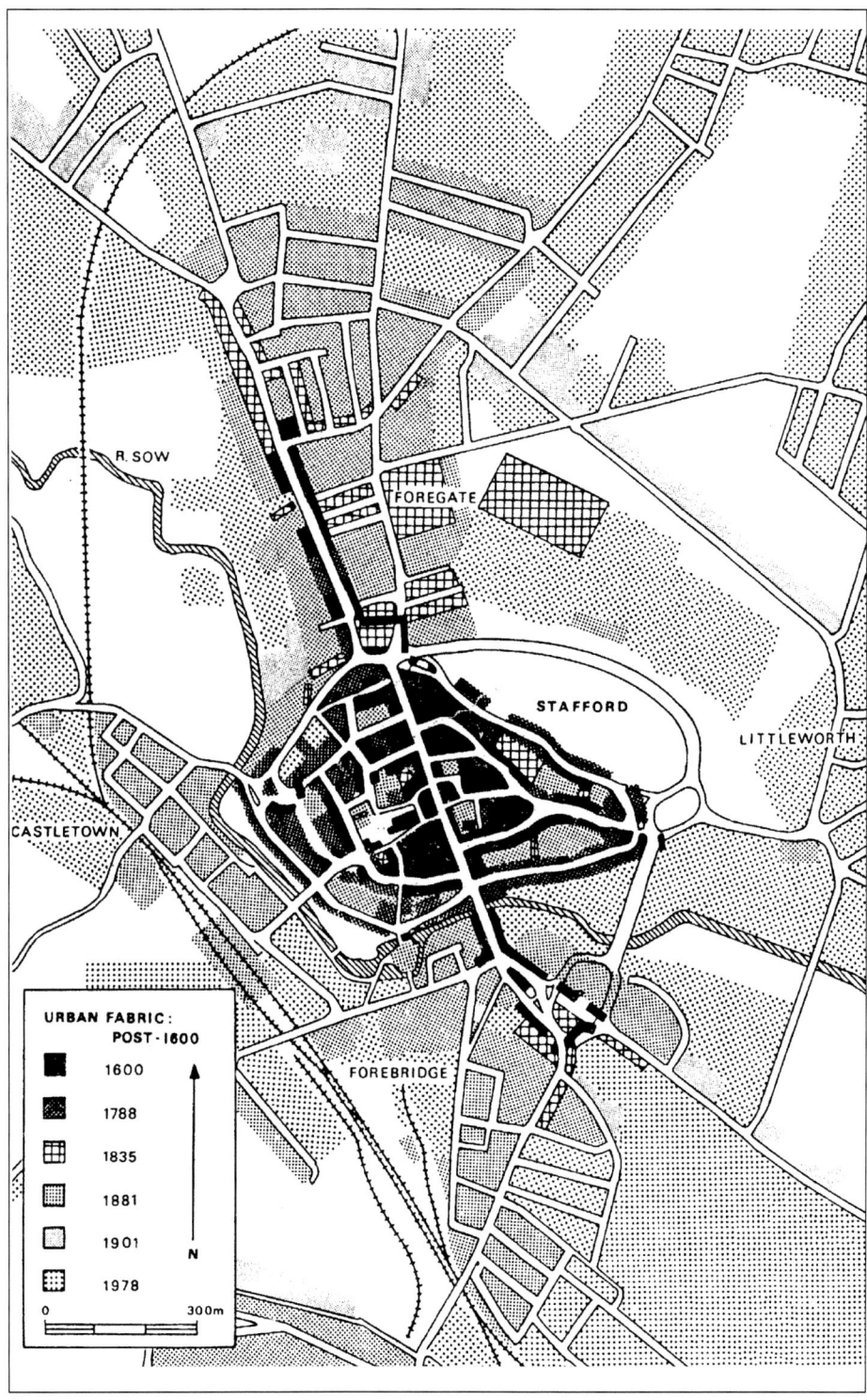

Fig. 2.9 Stafford: urban expansion (Glazebrook 1983).

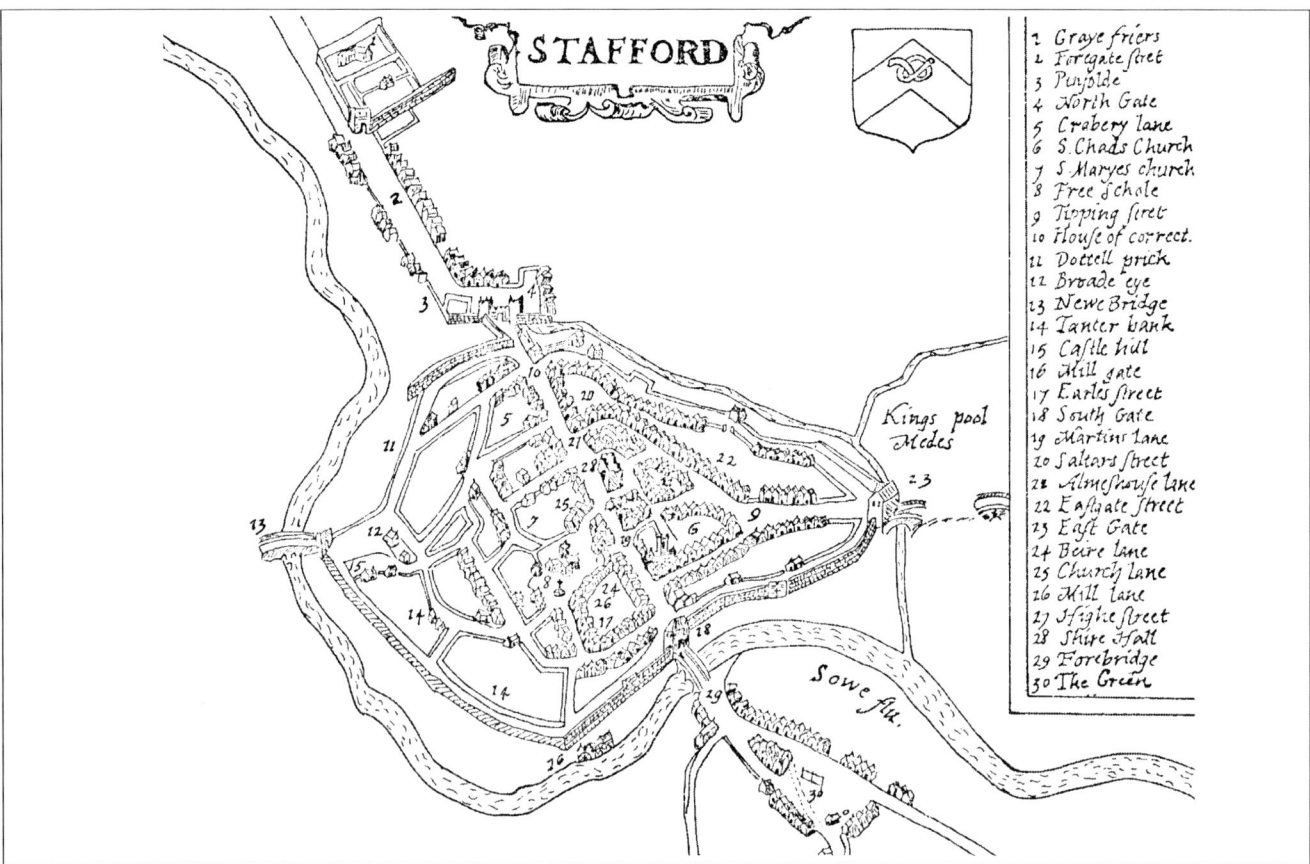

Fig. 2.10 John Speed's map of Stafford of c.1610.

thick[12] and are punctuated by Late Saxon pits, post-holes, wells and ovens. Late Saxon strata occasionally survive as surfaces of rammed pebbles. The impact of the Norman invasion was often disruptive, scattering Late Saxon assemblages of pottery, bone and burnt grain into new pits and those earlier features that remained open. In spite of this it has usually been possible to distinguish the Late Saxon from later medieval activities with a high level of confidence. Activity began again in the late twelfth century, in the form of pits, buildings, wells and a forge. The town declined in the fourteenth through to the sixteenth century with a result that it was spared the heavy domestic digging that reduces so many urban sequences to a featureless mass of black earth, caused by the cutting and recutting of rubbish and cess pits.

The degree of disturbance to the archaeological strata was partly predicted by the depths of existing cellars (Fig. 2.8). Architectural survivals and early maps provided a framework for the location and plan of the settlement into the Middle Ages and beyond (Frontispiece II, Figs. 2.9, 2.10 and 1.4).

Project design and programme

The resource model (or deposit model) forms one part of the three parts necessary for a Project Design, the others being the Research Agenda and the Social Context.[13] The research agenda to be applied to this deposit in 1979 was dominated by questions about the form and location of the Late Saxon burh, its function, its provision and the character of the pottery industry (Chapter 1). Nevertheless, the character of Late Saxon culture was still sufficiently unknown, at least in the West Midlands, for a more empirical approach to be valid. This was especially justifiable in the light of the development situation: three areas were open and awaiting planning permission in advance of construction. The deposit model predicted useful results in each case. There was no call to prioritise and each site would be completely eradicated by new construction. It made sense to make these areas the target of an intensive campaign of excavation. They were Bath Street (ST34), St Mary's Grove (ST29) and Tipping Street (north)

---

12 E.g. at St Mary's Grove and Clarke Street. See Chapter 3.

13 See Carver 2003, 2009.

(ST32, ST33), all excavated between 1980 and 1985 by BUFAU, and supervised on site by Jon and Charlotte Cane.

At the same time, two additional lines of inquiry were put in train. James Greig and Susan Colledge of Birmingham University took cores from peat underlying the King's Pool, from which they were able, by pollen analysis, to offer a sequence of the local environment from the pre-Roman to the modern period.[14] Lawrence Bowkett, then a student at Birmingham University, undertook a 'Hinterland Survey' designed to put Stafford in its geographical context during its period of occupation.[15]

In parallel with the three major area excavations, and after their completion, there were occasional small-scale opportunities for checking, verifying or probing key parts of the Anglo-Saxon fabric. Six trenches were cut between November 1983 and April 1984 in an attempt to locate the burh defences 'but none of them produced the hoped for evidence'.[16] Five interventions were designed to test the medieval circuit[17] and five others were in pursuit of a hypothetical smaller Late Saxon burh circuit containing St Mary's and Tipping Street.[18] In 1985, salvage recording in advance of development at Queen Street was undertaken by John Darlington (Stafford Castle archaeologist).[19] Excavations at Salter Street in 1994 found kilns of the eleventh and the fourteenth century.[20] Since 1994, interventions at Stafford have taken place under the PPG16 system.[21] In most cases, client reports have been generated, some or all of which have been placed in Stafford County's archaeological office.[22] Of these the investigation at

Broadeye is the one that bears most directly on the arguments presented in this book.[23]

Social context

The Social Context – the social, political, and economic situation presented to us – was not specifically integrated into the 1980 project design, but in retrospect it can be seen to have been influential and even crucial for the results that were achieved.[24] Typical factors contributing to the social context are the welcome afforded by local people, which determines access and ease of working, the attitude of their representatives in local government and the resources that it was possible to gather to execute fieldwork, and therefore the constitution of the workforce. These all affect the feasibility of completing effective research.

The local people were markedly hostile to archaeology in the mid 1970s, seeing it as a middle-class indulgence in a deprived area. This attitude changed in the late 70s as local people became involved in fieldwork and the down-to-earth character of the team (in all senses) was appreciated. The presence of young students and the success of two local employment schemes (MSC and YOP)[25] were also helpful in earning the acceptance of the project (Figs. 2.11, 2.12). For our part, a charm offensive was mounted, consisting of frequent open days and site tours, school visits and formal exhibitions designed and mounted by Charlotte Cane, supported by MSC employment of would-be artists (Fig. 2.13). The Borough and County council officials were supportive all the way through, organising access, providing priming funds, and lending property that could be used as accommodation and workspace (Fig. 2.14).

But even for their day, the resources that were available to carry out the ambitious programme were unusually meagre. From 1975 to 1980 there was only one professional archaeologist (M. Carver), the remaining staff being volunteers or students on Birmingham University's intercalated year of archaeological practice. Two of the students engaged in the 1979 evaluation campaign, Jon Cane and Charlotte Cane (née Hilton), were promoted to the position of supervisor the following year. Their workforce was mainly provided by the Youth Opportunity Scheme for those leaving school at sixteen. The Manpower Services Scheme meanwhile provided funds for two additional supervisors (Roy Barnes and Mark Taylor). Thus the principal workforce

---

14 FR10.2; and see Chapter 3.

15 FR11.

16 FR2.3.2, 39, 42, 43, 44, 45, 46; *BUFAU* 7, 13.

17 FR2.3.2, 37 (1981), 42 (1983), 44 (1984), 46 (1984), 55 (1988).

18 FR2.3.2, 38 (1982), 39 (1983), 43 (1984), 45 (1984), 54 (1988); *BUFAU* 7, map on p. 12.

19 FR2.3.2, 47–52.

20 FR2.3.2, 56.

21 Planning Policy Guidance Note 16 put local authorities under a moral obligation to make developers pay for archaeological investigation before planning permission was granted.

22 Among interventions known to have taken place are: Dodd 2000 at Broad Street. Earthworks Archaeological Services E310, February 2000; Foundations Archaeology 2001, 2002, 2003; Sheridan Centre Report 188, 240, 285; Krawiec 2003 at Earl Street, Birmingham Archaeology 11101.01; Ramsey 2004 at North Walls. Birmingham Archaeology 1221; Dodd 2004 at Gaolgate Street. Earthworks Archaeological Services E286, July 2004; Colls, Cuttler and Hunt at Broadeye 2003–2007 (continuing from Krawiec 2003). Birmingham Archaeology. These have not been given ST numbers, but details should be available via the Staffordshire County Council HER: http://www.staffordshire.gov.uk/environment/e-land/ CulturalEnvironment/HistoricEnvironmentRecord

23 Cuttler et al. 2009; and see pp. 39–41; 99.

24 See FR2.6 for this section.

25 The Manpower Services Scheme and the Youth Opportunities Project were government-funded schemes to counter unemployment.

Fig. 2.11 Members of the Youth Opportunities Programme in action, 1982 (J. Cane).

Fig. 2.12 The team opening the excavation at St Mary's Grove on a winter day (J. Cane).

Fig. 2.13 The mayor of Stafford welcomed to the public on-site exhibition by Andrew Brooker-Carey, manager of BUFAU.

Fig. 2.14 St Mary's Grove: derelict properties on loan to the project team as temporary residence.

at Stafford was under twenty-five and much of it under eighteen. It was remarkable that such an inexperienced team achieved so much.

Publication

In general the Stafford excavations took place before the application of PPG16 or in most cases before the establishment of English Heritage in 1983. As a consequence, although it may seem surprising today, there has been no pressure or encouragement and no financial assistance from developers, local authorities or central government to realise the rewards of the investment that was made in excavation.[26] The grant for Clarke Street was £3,000 in all, and did not include post-excavation. The 1979 campaign had no post-excavation grant, but the post-excavation was largely achieved nonetheless by Sarah Bazalgette, Jenny Glazebrook and other students during their practical 'year out'.[27] English Heritage subsequently supported a post-excavation programme from 1985 to 1988, and considerable progress was then made by Jon and Charlotte Cane. Reports and drawings were prepared for the four main excavations, and the Urban Archaeological Data Base was enhanced. The Canes also carried out experiments on making Stafford ware and drying grain. Plant remains were studied and reported by Lisa Moffett, pollen by James Greig and Susan Colledge, and animal bone by James Rackham and Madeleine Hummler (FR9, FR10).[28]

The task of bringing this large campaign to publication was daunting, and in 1989 Jon and Charlotte Cane left BUFAU to pursue other careers. I was subsequently approached by BUFAU and asked to help complete the task. There were, however, to be no grants from English Heritage either to complete the post-excavation or to support the publication, and subsequent applications to major research sponsors all failed.[29] These

matters naturally affected what it was possible to do. The default strategy was to create an online archive so that the work of BUFAU and the archaeological data collected over the years could at least be placed in the public domain. The appropriate vehicle to achieve this now existed at York in the form of the Archaeological Data Service.[30] This would be followed by a synthesis that offered a description of the major findings and their significance in the context of early medieval England – this book.

Archaeological readers should note the imperfections of this exercise in advance. First, it is based on analyses of pottery, animal bones and botanical remains that date from the 1980s and were in some cases preliminary even then. They have undoubted value but I have tried to avoid leaning too heavily on conclusions that were provisional. The pottery is probably the most crucial element of the material, and has been subject to later refinements of date and provenance, especially by Debbie Ford of the Potteries Museum at Stoke-on-Trent.[31] I have attempted to reflect these updates in my synthesis, but specialists will become aware how much could and should be done to enhance and modernise the conclusions presented here. One update that was undertaken was the calibration of the radiocarbon dates, which has led to their reappraisal and in particular the revision of date brackets considered in the 1980s to prove an occupation of Stafford in the ninth century.[32]

I also thought it prudent to re-examine all the stratigraphic sequences on all five major sites, to ensure they were internally consistent, and to attempt a concordance between them.[33] In general, the result has been to define unequivocal Late Saxon phases at all sites. This new reading should not be seen as a deficiency of the excavators, but as the result of someone being able to review and compare all the results in a single exercise of synthesis.

26 Interim results and interpretations were published in *West Midlands Archaeology* (Barnes et al. 1982, Cane et al. 1981, Cane et al. 1983, Carver 1975, 1977, 1979, 1980a).

27 Officially the 'intercalated year' between years two and four of a four-year degree course.

28 The analysis of animal bone was confined to primary contexts of the Late Saxon and medieval periods, which comprise a sequence of pits in ST29 and 32, and a sequence of dumps on ST15. The largest assemblage (355 identified bones from Dump 4 on ST15) is still small for any statistical analysis, and the majority of the other groups are very much smaller (see FR9.2).

29 English Heritage (twice), Society of Antiquaries of London, Headley Trust, AHRC, and Leverhulme Emeritus fund.

30 See Digest A6 for a list of contents, and enter www.http://ads.ahds.ac.uk/catalogue/archive/stafford_eh_2009/index.cfm on the internet to go online. The creation of the onlive archive was made possible by the completion of a basic portfolio of publication drawings by FAS Heritage Ltd, funded by English Heritage. I am most grateful to Cecily Spall of FAS and Barney Sloane of EH for their professional services in this regard.

31 Ford 1995, 1999.

32 See pp 26, 31, 45, 61 below.

33 All the sequences have been revised and updated since their interim reports, but these reports and the first-hand interpretations of the excavators that they represent have been included in archive, even where I do not believe them to be correct.

3

Seven Windows on Early Stafford:
The Principal Investigations

The sum of all the observations made to date offers a rough guide to the occupation of the Stafford peninsula and the legibility of its strata (Chapter 2). However, the type of intimate sequence that new history demands is only available from targeted excavation and sampling. Accepting that these need to encompass major questions and produce accessible results, it can be argued that there have been seven of them to date: excavations at St Bertelin's church (ST01), excavations in the town centre at Bath Street (ST34) and St Mary's Grove (ST29), excavations in the industrial area at Tipping Street (north) (ST32), excavations in 1975 on the periphery of the peninsula at Clarke Street (ST15) and investigations of the pollen sequence in the former King's Pool. To these we may now add the 2003–2006 rescue excavation at Broadeye, which is also summarised below[1] (Fig. 3.1).

That is not say that other observations and excavations have no value; on the contrary, every well-recorded archaeological intervention in every town has the capacity to illuminate the past, just as the painting of a landscape is composed from a thousand brush-strokes. But for history we require actors, or the archaeological equivalent: dated activities in context. And for this we need excavation on a broad scale, especially when, as here, very little was previously known of the period or the place. Accordingly I propose to summarise and review here the basic sequence of events dug up at each of these interventions, leaving evocations of the Late Saxon and medieval towns until Chapters 4 and 5 respectively.

St Bertelin's (FR3; 1 on Fig. 3.1)

Excavations by Adrian Oswald (then of Birmingham City Museum) were undertaken in 1954 at the west end of St Mary's church. Here he found a set of stone foundations interpreted as belonging to the documented medieval chapel of St Bertelin, and among them a set of post-holes with a central grave-shaped pit containing a large lump of oak (Figs 3.2, 3.3, 3.4). The latter object was interpreted as a wooden cross of the Anglian period (seventh–ninth centuries) and was reconstructed as such at the site and on the cover of the report (Fig. 3.5). C. A. Ralegh Radford saw the object as a preaching-cross that had preceded the construction of a timber chapel.[2] The digging of the burial pit, and by extension the construction of the timber building, took place before the year 1000, as indicated by a farthing of Ethelred II in a layer above the pit.[3] After a period of disuse, and after 1000, the chapel, that is the chapel of St Bertelin, was reconstructed with stone footings. Subsequent reconstructions – attributed to the thirteenth, fourteenth, fifteenth and seventeenth centuries – were also defined (Fig. 3.2). The latest version of the chapel stood until its demolition in 1801.

Samples thought to originate from the 'cross' were submitted for radiocarbon dating in 1971, by which time it had become a 'cruciform coffin'.[4] In 1984, the stratification of the earliest phases of Adrian Oswald's excavation was re-examined in the light of our own experiences of digging in Stafford, also taking into account the radiocarbon dates, which were unavailable to the excavator (not least because the excavation took place before radiocarbon dating had been invented). The descriptions of features and contexts were redefined and numbered for greater clarity[5] and then reassembled in a sequence diagram, divided into four main periods (Fig. 3.6). The effect of this re-examination has been to strengthen the Late Saxon phase, but to leave the question

---

1 Cuttler et al 2009. I am most grateful to the authors for discussion and sight of a draft in advance of their own publication.

2 Oswald 1955a, 26–7.

3 Dolley in Oswald 1955a.

4 Shotton and Williams 1971, 152.

5 FR3.4. The context numbers add 1000 to the Oswald numbers. The feature numbers are new.

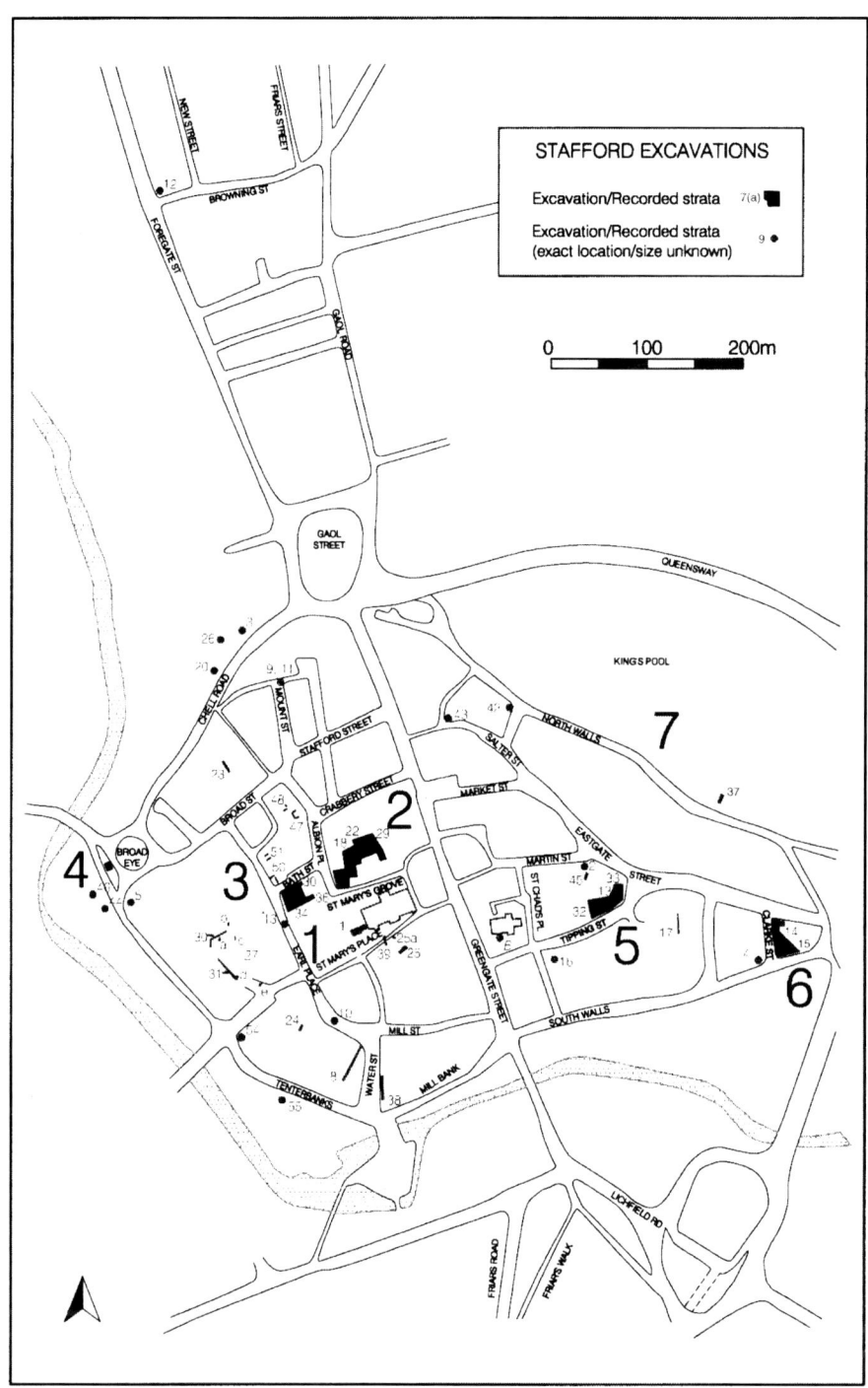

Fig. 3.1 The locations of the 'seven windows': 1 St Bertelin's, 2 St Mary's Grove, 3 Bath Street, 4 Broadeye, 5 Tipping Street, 6 Clarke Street, 7 King's Pool.

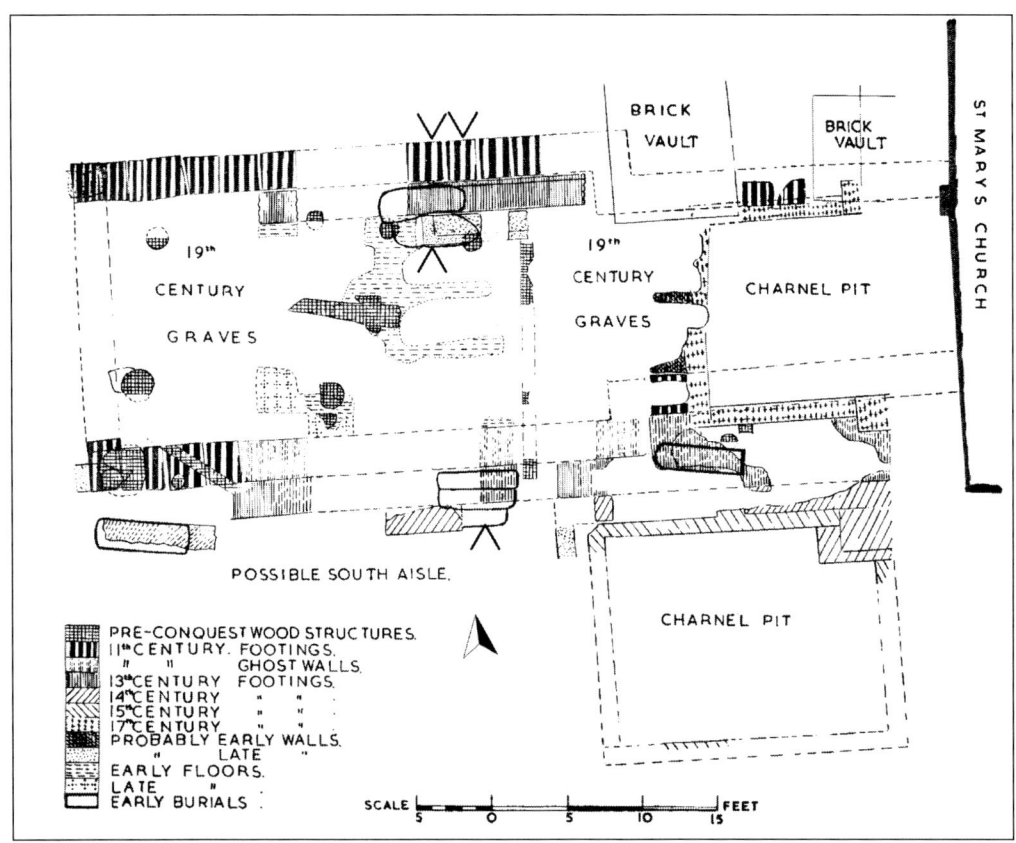

Fig. 3.2 St Bertelin's: excavation plan (Oswald 1955a).

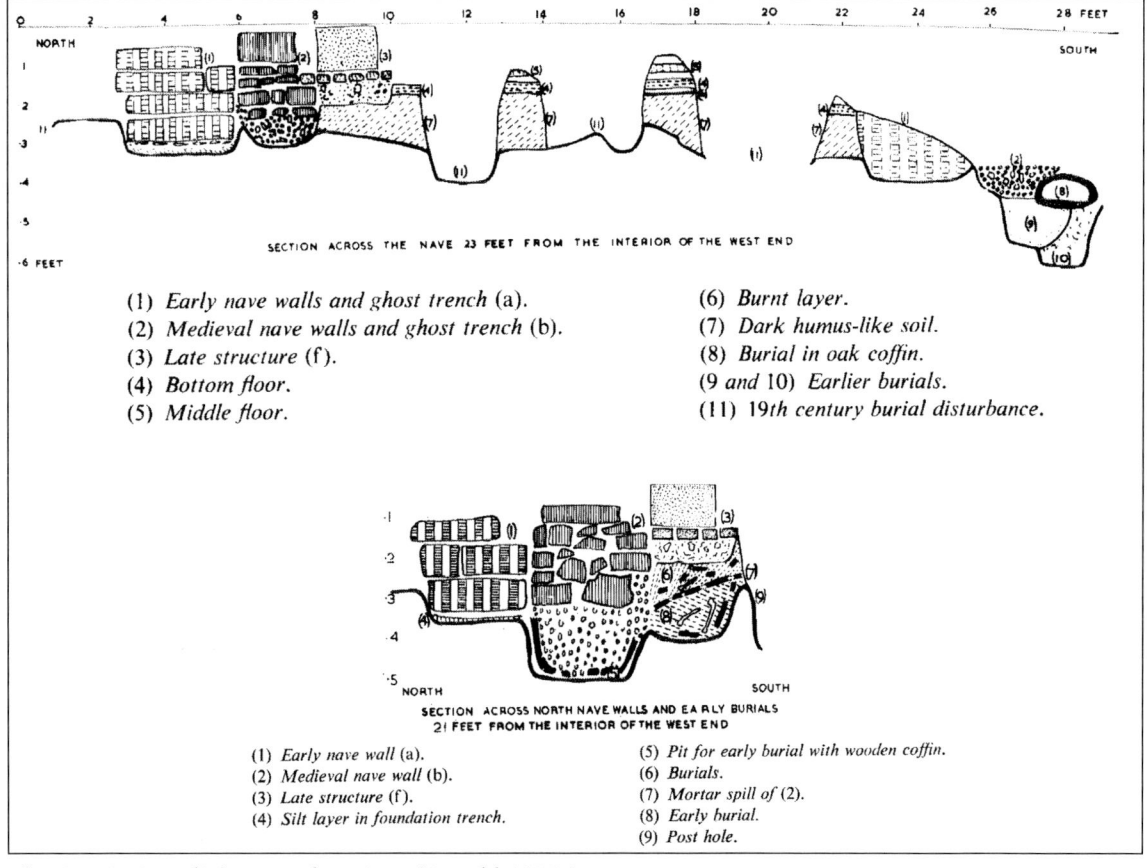

(1) *Early nave walls and ghost trench (a).*
(2) *Medieval nave walls and ghost trench (b).*
(3) *Late structure (f).*
(4) *Bottom floor.*
(5) *Middle floor.*

(6) *Burnt layer.*
(7) *Dark humus-like soil.*
(8) *Burial in oak coffin.*
(9 and 10) *Earlier burials.*
(11) *19th century burial disturbance.*

(1) *Early nave wall (a).*
(2) *Medieval nave wall (b).*
(3) *Late structure (f).*
(4) *Silt layer in foundation trench.*

(5) *Pit for early burial with wooden coffin.*
(6) *Burials.*
(7) *Mortar spill of (2).*
(8) *Early burial.*
(9) *Post hole.*

Fig. 3.3 St Bertelin's: general sections (Oswald 1955a).

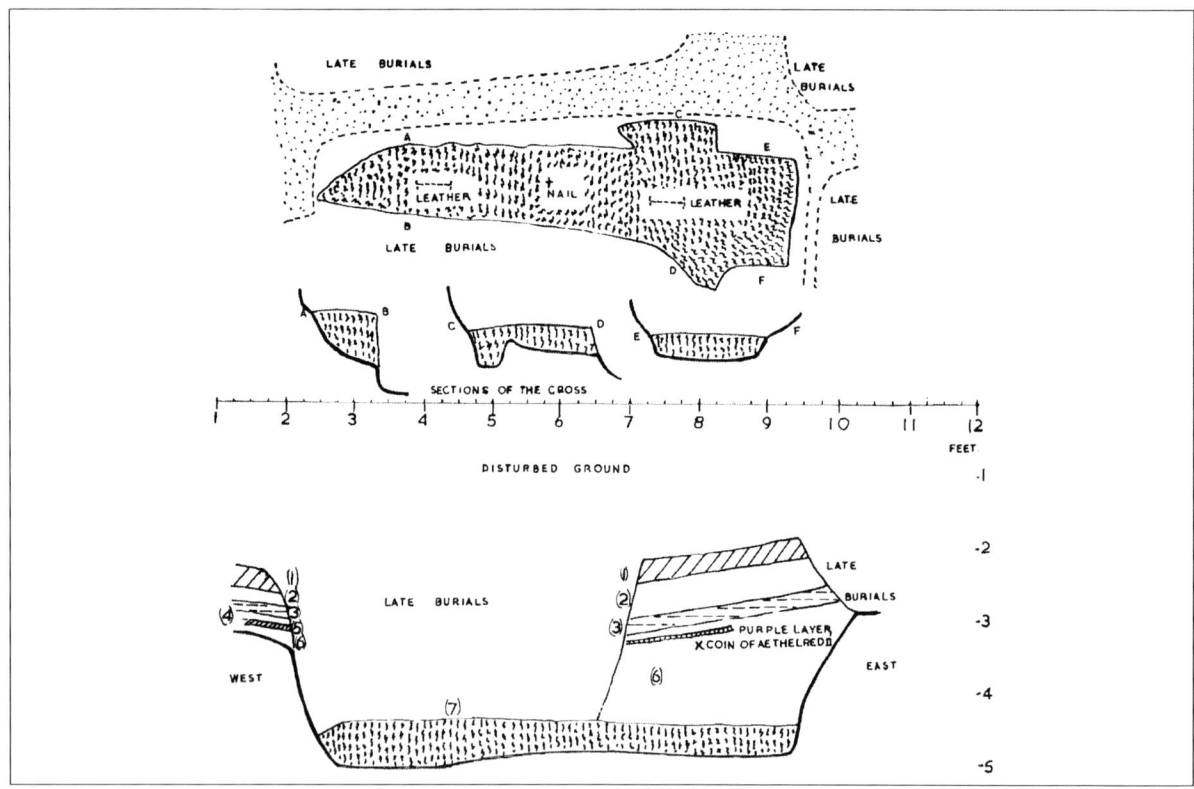

Fig. 3.4 St Bertelin's: section across the 'cross-pit' F13 (Oswald 1955a).
In the text the contexts are numbered 1001–1007.

Fig. 3.5 Artist's impression of the
St Bertelin's cross (Oswald 1955a).

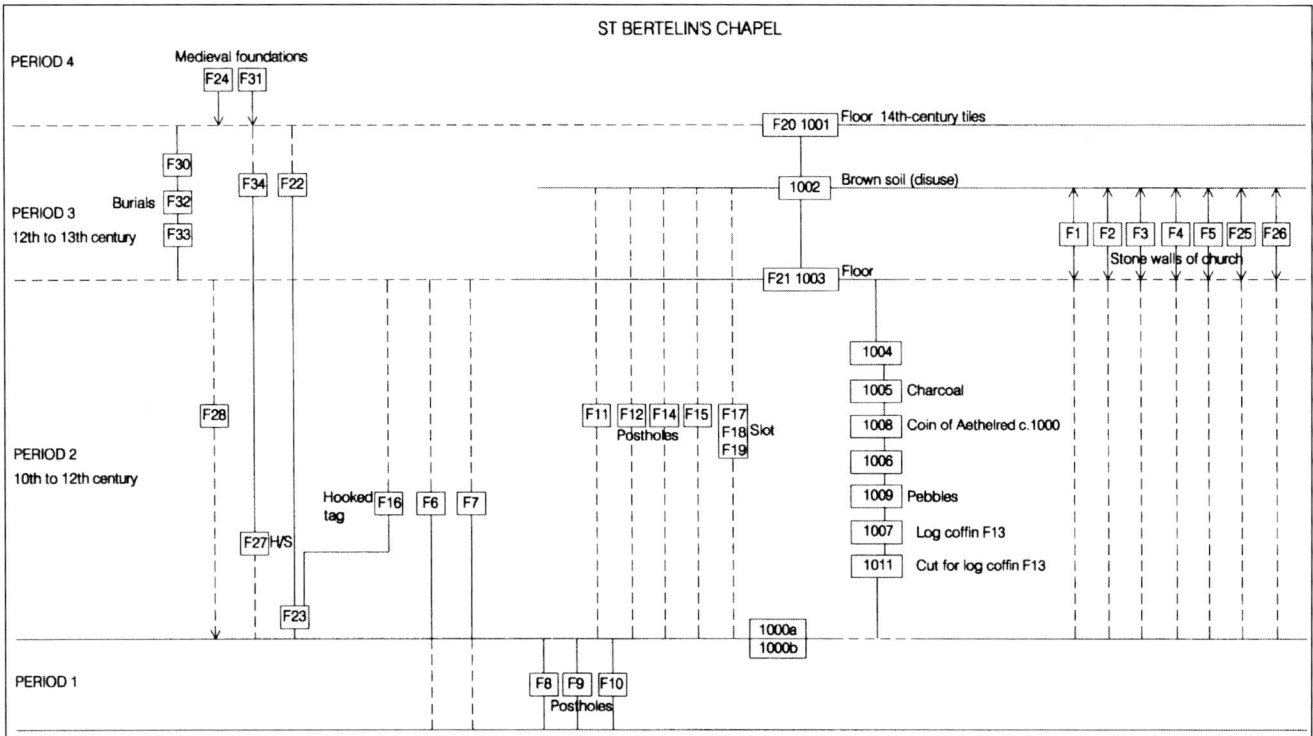

Fig. 3.6 St Bertelin's: stratigraphy, 2009.

of an Anglian (seventh–ninth centuries) phase even less certain than before.

The argument for the sequence depends on the stratigraphy and the few indications of date. The site had been largely destroyed by nineteenth-century graves, leaving only patches of wall and floor and a few early graves definable. The surface of the natural sand lay 5 feet (1.52m) below the modern ground surface and 'fell away' to the south.[6] No Roman pottery was reported.[7] The conditions of the excavation were difficult, being 'carried on in the wettest period of the rainiest summer in living memory'.[8]

For the excavator, the question of an Anglo-Saxon phase at St Bertelin's depended mainly on 'quite the most remarkable and interesting feature of the whole excavation', namely the supposed cross.[9] This object lay in an east-west pit cut some 16 inches (41cm) into subsoil. To the excavator it appeared 'as a thick layer of carbonised wood and in the initial stage of uncovering was thought to be the remains of a wooden coffin, although even at this stage the absence of any bones was remarked ... The carbonised wood of the shaft varied in thickness from 6 to 8in. [15–20 cm] and the underside

was markedly semi-circular. In the bottom half, the point at the west end showed well in section, and the hook-shaped arm went deeper into the natural soil than the shaft. Fragments of leather were found in two places, and a nail was discovered in the centre of the shaft.'[10] The lump was subsequently said to measure 8 x 3.5 feet (2.4 x 1.07m) in plan, to come to a point at the west end and to feature two flaps at the east end. The thickness and shape led to its identification as a circular cross shaft, and the flap 'with its peculiar hooked outline' was argued to be an arm and compared to the short arms of crosses from Carlisle, Burnsal and Bridekirk.[11]

While there is nothing improbable about a wooden cross belonging to the first (or second) millennium AD, the proposed example is unusually crude and squat – especially if the 'sharpened' west end is held to imply that this part had been planted in the ground. The length and width of the object, its discovery in a grave-shaped pit, the leather attached to the top (i.e. inside) and the nail, all revive the possibility that it was a coffin, not a cross. Its description, especially the curved base, recalls the tree-trunk coffins known from the seventh century onwards in East Anglia. Poor bone preservation and collapsed sides are common in heavy timber coffins in sandy soils.[12] Attempting to appreciate the shape of the objects, we have to take note of the excavator's comment

6 This southward slope was also found in the evaluation campaign, ST25, 25c (FR 2.3).

7 Although Mr Horne spoke of a large ditch with Roman material (pers. comm. in 1975), this was not confirmed by Adrian Oswald (lunch meeting at the Athenaeum, 1981).

8 Archdeacon Parker in Oswald 1955a, 3.

9 Oswald 1955a, 15.

10 Ibid., 17

11 Oswald 1955a, 18; Collingwood 1927, 87, 89, 94.

12 Carver 2005, 292–8.

on the experience of lifting the wood in the prevailing conditions: 'Owing to the continuous rain it began, despite protection, to disintegrate rapidly … it was taken up piecemeal.'[13]

The dating and phasing of the St Bertelin's sequence depends mainly on the observed relationship of graves, walls and pits to a layer of dark brown humic soil with no finds, which lay on the sand subsoil (C1000). With three undiagnostic exceptions, all the features, whether walls, pits, post-holes or graves, were cut through this layer.[14] The 'cross' pit (F13) was either cut through it, or contained the equivalent material redeposited as fill (1006). The section reproduced in Fig. 3.4 is equivocal, in that layers supposedly within the pit are not distinguished from those cut by it or over it. The cross-pit sequence can best be reconciled with the written descriptions by supposing that all the layers 1006, 1008, 1005 and 1004 were deposited in that order, on top of and sagging into, a pit (F13) already containing the wood lump 1007 (Fig. 3.4). In this case all these layers, including that containing the coin of Ethelred II, are later than the deposition of the cross, and this is the basis of Oswald's argument that the cross-pit is Anglo-Saxon. However, if the coin was shovelled in as part of a backfill, then the pit and its cross are later, and can be much later, than AD 1000.

The sequence has been further complicated by the radiocarbon dates, which were obtained from two samples:

Birm 137 First Sample: 'oak believed part of cruciform coffin of St. Bertelin'
    770 ± 78 BP ie. 1180 AD uncalib.

Birm 136a, b Second Sample: 'charcoal associated with wood remains believed cruciform coffin of St Bertelin'
    2 parts: a. 1105 ± 90 BP = 845 AD uncalib.
              b. 1120 ± 120 BP = 830 AD uncalib.

Judging by their description, the 'First Sample', oak (twelfth-century) would appear to be from 1007 in F13, and the 'Second Sample', charcoal (ninth-century) would appear to be from 1005. The earliest dates are thus at the top and the latest at the bottom. Between 1007 and 1005 comes 1008 which contained the farthing of Ethelred II (971–1016), said by Dolley to have been deposited c. AD 1000.[15] On the face of it, the layers are inverted. An oak coffin dated to 1180 was placed in a pit around that date and subsequently covered by a layer containing an eleventh-century coin and then a layer with residual

ninth-century charcoal. This is a not improbable interpretation of the sequence encountered.

The samples for radiocarbon dating were obtained from material in store at Birmingham Museum, some years after the excavation. Even so the Birmingham Laboratory that dated the samples should have been ready to distinguish wood from charcoal. Shotton and Williams comment: 'Close correspondence of Birm 136a and 136b suggests validity of date. It could have been a wooden object from a Saxon church, for such material was burnt when no longer required. Unless contaminated, Birm 137 which is probably wood of a coffin, must be later and not connected with St Bertelin.'[16]

Of course, the two samples rediscovered at Birmingham may have come from two different contexts, or had been confused, and this would leave us free to accept that the date of the wood in the cross-pit (1007) is ninth-century or later. Maybe both the samples came from 1007, but gave very different dates because the wood was oak, and included old heartwood. Or both the samples came from 1007, but this context had originally included charcoal in a wooden coffin.[17] Alternatively, the charcoal deposited in context 1005 may have derived from timbers felled and used in construction in the ninth century but burnt down after AD 1000.

The 'cross' was presumably old and possibly broken when buried, so whatever motives can be surmised for its disposal, it may have been older than the timber chapel in which it was laid to rest. If the cross was actually a tree-trunk burial, the context of deposition requires a less contrived explanation – the burial of a dead person, although such an act can still signal the construction of a church, and/or the translation and use of an ancient coffin, carrying with it the sanctity of a supposed association with a legendary saint. Such an establishment, and the adoption of an earlier St Bertelin to sanctify it, could find a context in either the Anglo-Saxon or the medieval period.[18] If we accept the excavator's argument that a timber church was separated from a stone church by a period of disuse, and that nothing lay beneath, then the initiation of Christian sanctity on this spot was the burial of a coffin in a timber building. If we can further ignore the twelfth-century radiocarbon date and accept

---

13 Oswald 1955a.

14 The exceptions are F8, F9, F10; but since these relate to the other post-holes in plan, they may simply have escaped observation until the subsoil was reached (see Fig. 3.7).

15 Dolley in Oswald 1955a.

16 Shotton and Williams 1971, 153. The possible provenances for these dated samples are (a) the wood of the supposed cross (1007; Fig.3.4, layer 7); (b) the charcoal layer recorded over the pit (1005; Fig. 3.4, layer 5; Fig. 3.3, layer 6; these are assumed to be the same); (c) another wooden coffin (F27, F28 and F30 all had wooden coffins). Birm 137 (twelfth-century) was wood and should have come from the cross, 1007 or a wooden coffin. Birm 136 (ninth-century) was charcoal and should have come from 1005 (layer 5).

17 I originally thought that the St Bertelin 'cross' was a charcoal burial, but now prefer a tree-trunk coffin from the shape. It still could be both. See also Biddle 1986, 10, nn. 49, 50.

18 Thacker 1985; see Chapter 6 below.

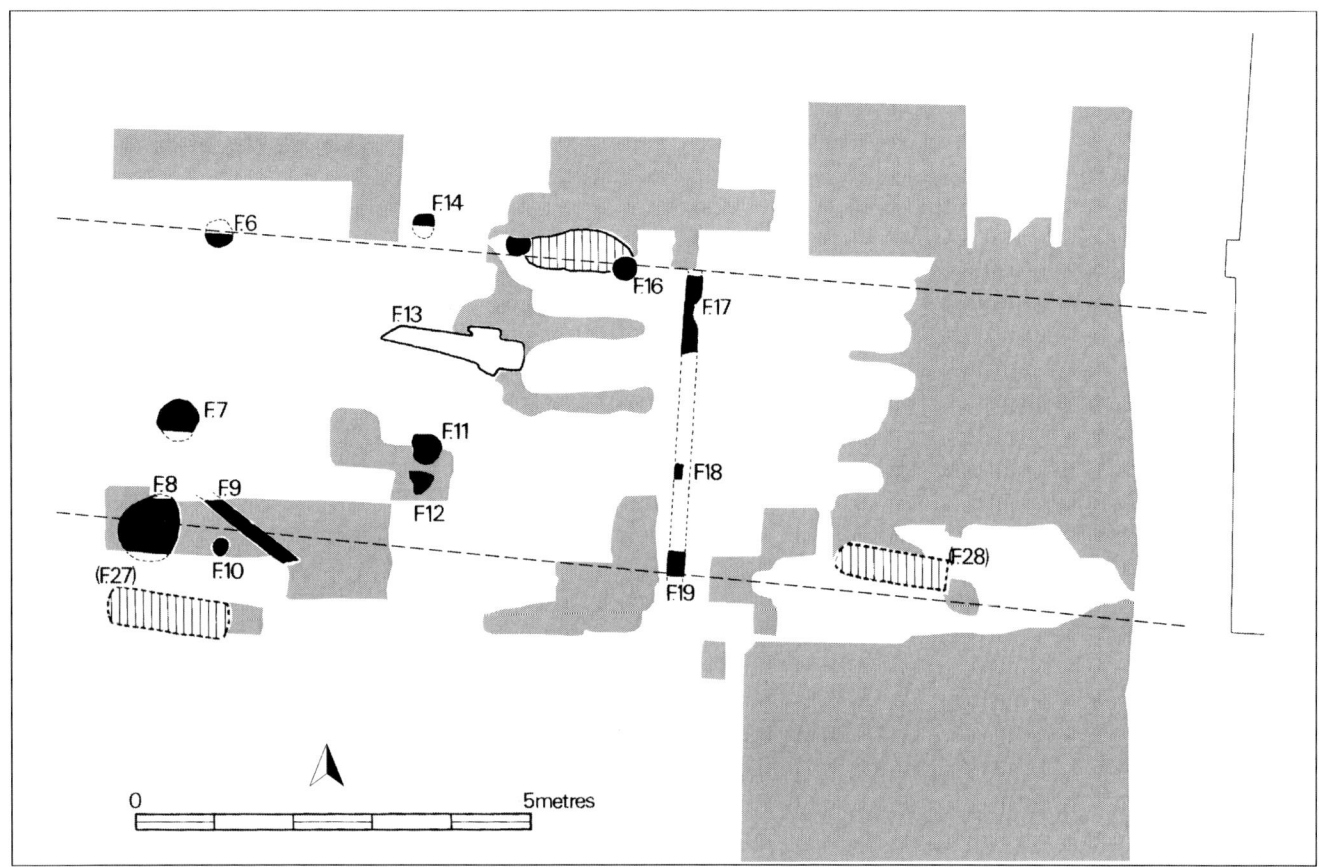

Fig. 3.7 St Bertelin's: Period 2 (Late Saxon). Timber features marked in black.

all the other evidence, then the wood from pit F13, the cross, becomes the earliest object. If it, or its timber building, can be dated to the ninth century, then we must suppose some Christian activity in the neighbourhood at least from then, with the timber chapel itself erected after an unspecified interval, at which point the cross was buried.

Unfortunately, even if the pit with its cargo of a cross or a tree-trunk burial is accepted as the earliest activity encountered, it does not date with any certainty from before the time of Æthelflæd. The 1971 dates were not calibrated. Judging from other dates collected for Stafford (see Digest A2) a date of 1120 BP would calibrate to around 880–980 (1sig.) or 800–1000 (2sig.) cal. AD (cf. Tipping Street, Har 8240). Thus even the earliest dates, those from the samples of 'charcoal associated with wood', fit comfortably within the expected Late Saxon occupation for Stafford.

There are possibly too many uncertainties here to be confident of the stratigraphic sequence or the exact context of the radiocarbon samples. The options are to accept the ninth- to eleventh-century date for the coffin/cross and timber building and ignore the twelfth-century date, seeing it as relating to another coffin (option 1); or to accept the twelfth-century date and allow the charcoal and the coin to be residual in a foundation which

essentially belongs to the Middle Ages (option 2). Either is possible, but three objects found in the excavations tip the balance in favour of option 1: the coin, deposited c. 1000, and a dress-hook and a fragment of book clasp both of which could be Anglo-Saxon in date (see Chapter 4, p. 73).

We are now ready to attempt a revision of the principal elements of the sequence at St Bertelin's (Fig. 3.6). The earliest activity is represented by the dark brown layers (1000a and b) which resemble in their description, and in their situation above the natural sand, layers 2238 and 2239 at St Mary's Grove (p. 29), namely components of an Iron Age and Roman cultivated soil (*PERIOD 1*). No features or finds are assigned to this period (see above).

The timber structure defined at the west end of St Mary's, and its central pit, came into being between AD 800 and 1000 (*PERIOD 2*; Fig. 3.7). The building can therefore be a construction of Æthelflæd in the early tenth century, sanctified by the interment of a coffin, perhaps declared to contain the remains or relics of St Bertelin. This does not preclude the presence of other earlier churches elsewhere, or even of a seventh- to eighth-century minster; but we are obliged to acknowledge that such a desirable quarry remains elusive.

This timber chapel or mortuary house may have burnt

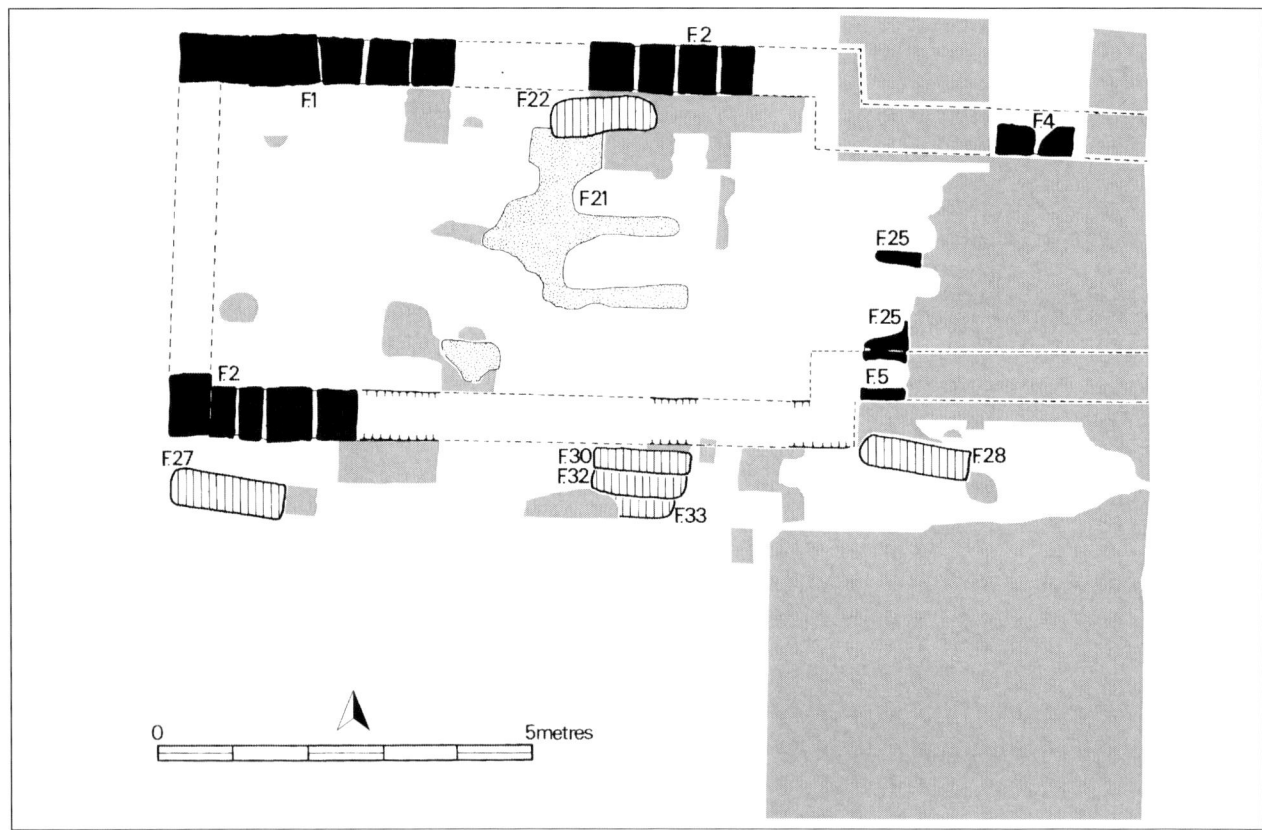

Fig. 3.8 St Bertelin's: Period 3 (thirteenth century).

Fig. 3.9 St Bertelin's: Period 4 (fourteenth century).

down after AD 1000, accounting for the charcoal layer (1005) stratified above the coin of Ethelred II. After a period of disuse, it was superseded by a stone chapel, which had a truer east-west alignment, a nave, a narrower chancel and a floor (F21/1003). Graves 22 and 30–34 align with its walls. We have to suppose that the 1180 radiocarbon date no longer applies, since we can no longer be sure to what it refers. However, given the plan of Church 2, a date in the twelfth century would seem acceptable (*PERIOD 3*; Fig. 3.8).

A brown soil (1002), interpreted as another layer of disuse, appears to separate the floor of stone Church 2 (1003), from the floor of a new stone Church 3 (20/1001) (*PERIOD 4*; Fig. 3.9). This rebuilt chapel is offset to the south, so a refoundation from scratch seems likely. The new floor was associated with floor tiles, which were dated to the later fourteenth century. The Anglo-Saxon church proposed here is placed in its context in Chapter 4 and its medieval successor in Chapter 5.

St Mary's Grove (FR5; 2 on Fig. 3.1)

Moving a hundred metres to the north of St Bertelin's, we arrive at the site of the largest excavations so far conducted in Stafford, which targeted a then open space within the quadrilateral defined by St Mary's Grove, Greengate Sreet, Crabbery Street and Albion Place (Fig. 3.10). In 1979, much of the area was occupied by the large brick building of St John's indoor market, while the frontage of St Mary's Grove was lined with eighteenth-century and later residences. All the buildings were scheduled for demolition to make way for a new market complex, but there was no obligation to allow time for excavation after demolition and before construction – when the whole site would have been accessible. Planning Policy Guidance note 16, which pressured local authorities to make time for archaeological investigation, was still ten years away. The site available for investigation was therefore that area unencumbered at the time, essentially the back gardens of the St Mary's Grove houses.

The area was tested during the evaluation campaign of 1979 with two trenches, which found a depth of up to 1 metre of garden soil above a metre of stratified deposit.[19] The more easterly of the two test trenches (ST22) contacted what was predicted and later confirmed to be a Late Saxon bread oven, cut into a buried soil, sealed by a layer (1026) containing Stafford ware. This layer was cut in turn by thirteenth-century pits and sealed by medieval

and later cultivation soils and twentieth-century builders' rubbish (1012, 1014, 1002).

These test trenches promised a useful sequence, and excavation began in 1980. A 2-metre wide baulk was left against the base of standing buildings but otherwise the maximum area was opened. The awkward-shaped site provided an area roughly 20 x 40 metres towards the centre of the quadrilateral of streets, with a tongue about 10 x 15 metres which reached to the corner of St Mary's churchyard where the two streets, St Mary's Grove and Albion Place, met.[20] Guided by the evaluation trenches, the site was lowered by up to a metre by machine, mainly through modern garden soil, and the spoil taken away by lorry. The site was then excavated to subsoil by hand, mainly at recovery level D.[21]

The overall distribution plan of all the features may be seen in the composite plan in Fig. 3.11. Due to their relative positions with respect to the Saxon and medieval geography of the town, the north-east, central and south-west parts of the area had experienced rather different deposit histories. Important horizons for phasing were provided by the subsoil (2240), the Iron Age and Romano-British buried soil (2239), a Late Saxon occupation layer (1607) and a massive levelling operation (approximately of the sixteenth century, 1341/1710).[22] In the *north-east* part of the site, the Iron Age to Saxon sequence had survived well to a depth of 25 centimetres. The Late Saxon features that were eventually defined (a pebble surface and four ovens) were located here. The *central* area had been largely destroyed in the twelfth century by a massive quarrying operation of the twelfth century (F435, 480), and these quarry pits were subsequently truncated by the sixteenth-century levelling operation (here 1710, the equivalent of 1341). The *south-west* part offered no Roman or Saxon phases. It had also been visited by quarrying in the twelfth century (F290), but subsequently enjoyed a long medieval sequence, of post-hole buildings and pits. At a given moment, between the thirteenth and sixteenth centuries, a boundary ditch (F298) with a sequence of burials south of it, showed that the graveyard of St Mary's had once encroached this far north (or rather that the development of St Mary's Grove had encroached onto the medieval churchyard). This ditch marked the southern limit of the medieval development, which was dominated by a stone-built barn S7 and dryer S8. There was no sighting of any medieval street. Post-medieval development, following the levelling operation, took the form of gardens in the south-west, and a

---

19 FR2.3; ST18, measuring 4 x 1.5m, reported quarries containing Stafford ware cut into natural sand at 76.63m AOD, a depth of about 2.10m below GS, succeeded by post-medieval pits. ST22 located the natural subsoil 2.83m down at 75.53m AOD. The cultivated buried soil had no pottery but some slag.

20 The excavation was led by Jon Cane, with a small team of archaeologists (Charlotte Cane, Roy Barnes, Nina Skippon-Cook, Mark Taylor) employed through the Manpower Services Scheme and a larger team of volunteers and young people provided by the Youth Opportunities Programme.

21 A high intensity excavation level; see Carver 2009, 124–8.

22 As can be observed in the sections, FR5.3, figs 5/25–30.

Fig. 3.10 Excavations in progress at St Mary's Grove (J. Cane).

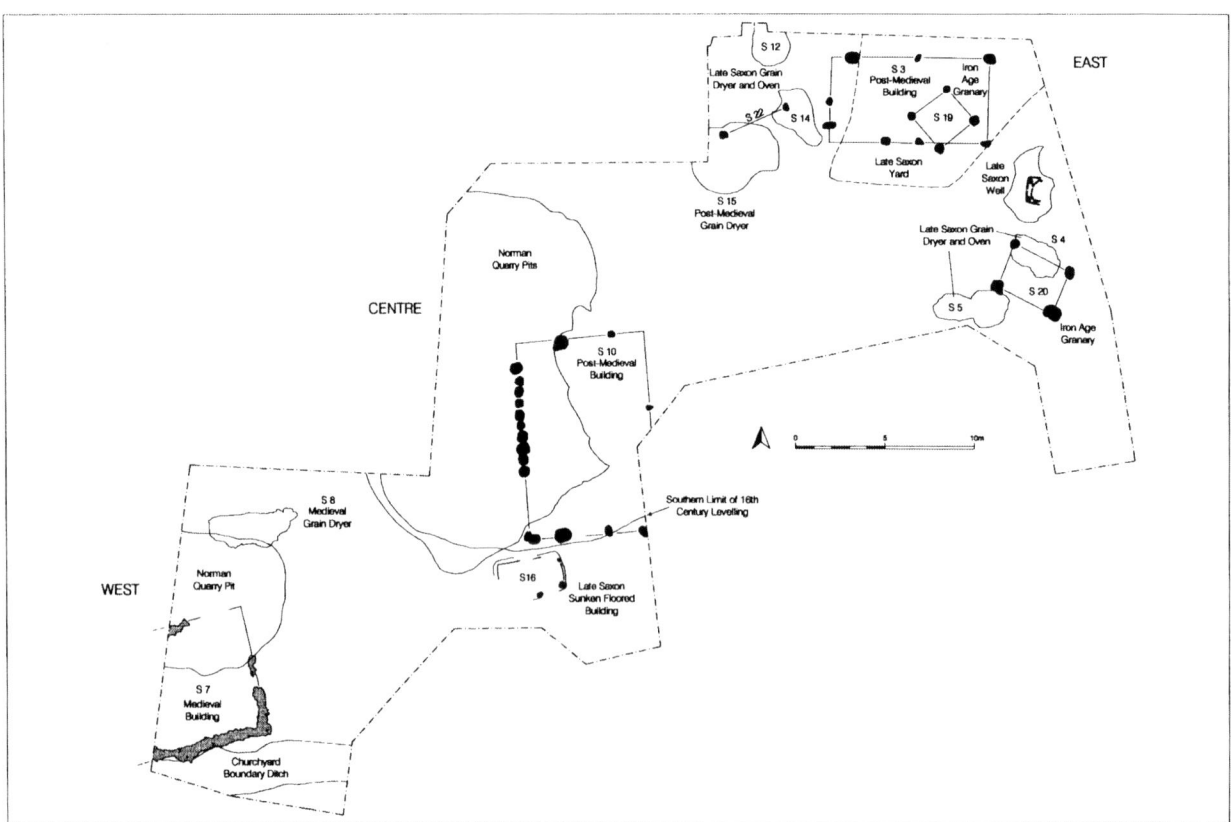

Fig. 3.11 St Mary's Grove: composite plan (J. Cane).

number of structures (e.g. S3, S10) and a kiln (S15) in the north-east. All parts of the site were covered by recent garden soil, 40–60 centimetres thick at the south-west and up to 1.2 metres thick at the north-east. This soil was punctuated with eighteenth- to twentieth-century drains, brick and concrete foundations.

As can be seen, the sequence was distributed over the site in period packages: the Iron Age to Saxon only in the north-east, the twelfth-century quarrying in the centre and south-west, the medieval sequence only in the south-west and the post-medieval largely in the north-east. This is likely to represent the real land-use for the medieval period, which would have declared itself from pits and pottery in the north-east, had it been there. In contrast, Late Saxon activities in the centre and south-west are likely to have been once present and since lost. Quantities of Stafford ware and charred grain were redeposited in the central quarries (F435, F426), showing that a major area of Late Saxon grain processing had been effaced.

The dated sequence
The work undertaken by Jon and Charlotte Cane on completion of the excavation in 1984 included the context-by-context modelling of the stratification, the typing of all Saxon, medieval and post-medieval pottery and the analysis of the small finds.[23] This was revised in 2007, by applying a pottery seriation using pottery typologies published by Deborah Ford,[24] and integration with the radiocarbon and dendrochronological dates (see Digest A3).

The radiocarbon dates for St Mary's Grove were taken from two contexts, one from a post in an Iron Age granary, which gave a sixth to second century BC date, and one from a Late Saxon bread oven (2247 from F584), from which three dates were measured (Digest A2). For the Late Saxon oven, as can be seen, one of these dates differs markedly from the other two, and although it might be tempting to conflate all three into the tighter bracket AD 720–890, the context does not really allow this, since it is essentially a mixture of wood used to fire an oven, potentially including heartwood. The most legitimate of the three then becomes the latest, 720–1020, although this date range is not particularly helpful. In any event, taking the three together does not justify the dating of this oven (and by extension the others) to the ninth century (and thus before the foundation of the burh) as proposed by J. Cane, quoted by Moffett and cited elsewhere.[25] There were two dates from dendrochronology: the lining of the well F608,

made from timbers felled in the late spring of AD 1007, and of a cess pit F404, from timbers felled after 1173, and probably after 1183.

The integrated sequence model is seen in Fig. 3.12, divided into seven periods. In *PERIOD 1* (Iron Age, late first millennium BC; Fig. 3.13) the land was used to store grain in four-post granaries (S19, S20, S22). There were two fragments of pottery, and a small assemblage of mixed burnt grain (Chapter 4, p. 58).[26] At some point in *PERIOD 2* (Roman, first–fourth century AD) the land was under cultivation.[27]

Redevelopment began again in *PERIOD 3* (tenth–eleventh centuries; Fig. 3.14), certainly in the east, and probably all over the site.[28] A pebbled hard-standing (F134) was constructed, serving grain dryers and baking ovens making bread, bannocks or oatcakes (see report on burnt grain, Chapter 4, pp. 66–73). Activity areas were regulated and demarcated by fences (S4, S5 and S18; S12, S14 and S17). Well F608 was relined in AD 1007, and thus had probably been already working in the tenth century. A sunken-floored plank-lined cellar (S16) in the central area probably also served the grain processing industry as a store. The animal bones, such as they were, indicated a community mainly consuming beef supplied in pre-butchered joints often as shoulders. The community appears to have had virtually no access to game, either in the Anglo-Saxon period or later.[29]

In *PERIOD 4* (Norman, eleventh–twelfth centuries; Fig. 3.15) the grain industry gave way to quarrying and spasmodic occupation. In the eleventh century, a fire occurred in S16 and residual heaps of burnt grain signal the end of grain-processing. By the twelfth century, ten large quarry-pits had been dug, presumably to extract sand, and subsequently backfilled with the detritus of the Late Saxon industrial quarter – Stafford-ware pottery and burnt grain. Cess pits (F443, F449 and F404) and a scatter of post-holes show continuous if reduced levels of occupation.[30] Sheep/goat and pig are minor components throughout, although arguably of slightly greater significance than in the preceding and following periods. F404 was a rare example of a deposit numerically dominated by pigs, and included two young ones. This, and the bone component profile as a whole, suggests that pigs were kept and butchered locally, in

---

23 FR8.2–8.5.

24 Ford 1995; Ford 1999; see FR8.2 and below.

25 FR5.2; Moffett 1994; Blair 2005, 309, n. 91: 'At Stafford, crop-processing was occurring next to the church in the mid ninth century, well before Æthelflæd fortified the site in 913.' Citing Moffett 1994, see FR1.5).

26 S19, S20, S22. Dated by C14 from wood in a post-hole: 520–190 cal. BC.

27 Dated by twenty-seven sherds of Roman pottery. FR8.2.2.

28 Dated by Late Saxon pottery (Stafford ware), dendrochronology (1007 for the well) and a radiocarbon date of 720–1020 cal. AD for fuel in a bread oven.

29 The early animal bone assemblages were small: 4kg (about 86 bones) from Late Saxon primary contexts and a slightly larger medieval assemblage mainly from six pits (FR9.2).

30 Dated by Stafford-ware pottery, with twelfth-century pottery in upper backfills. Cess pit F404 was lined in the later twelfth century (dendrochronology). See p. 149.

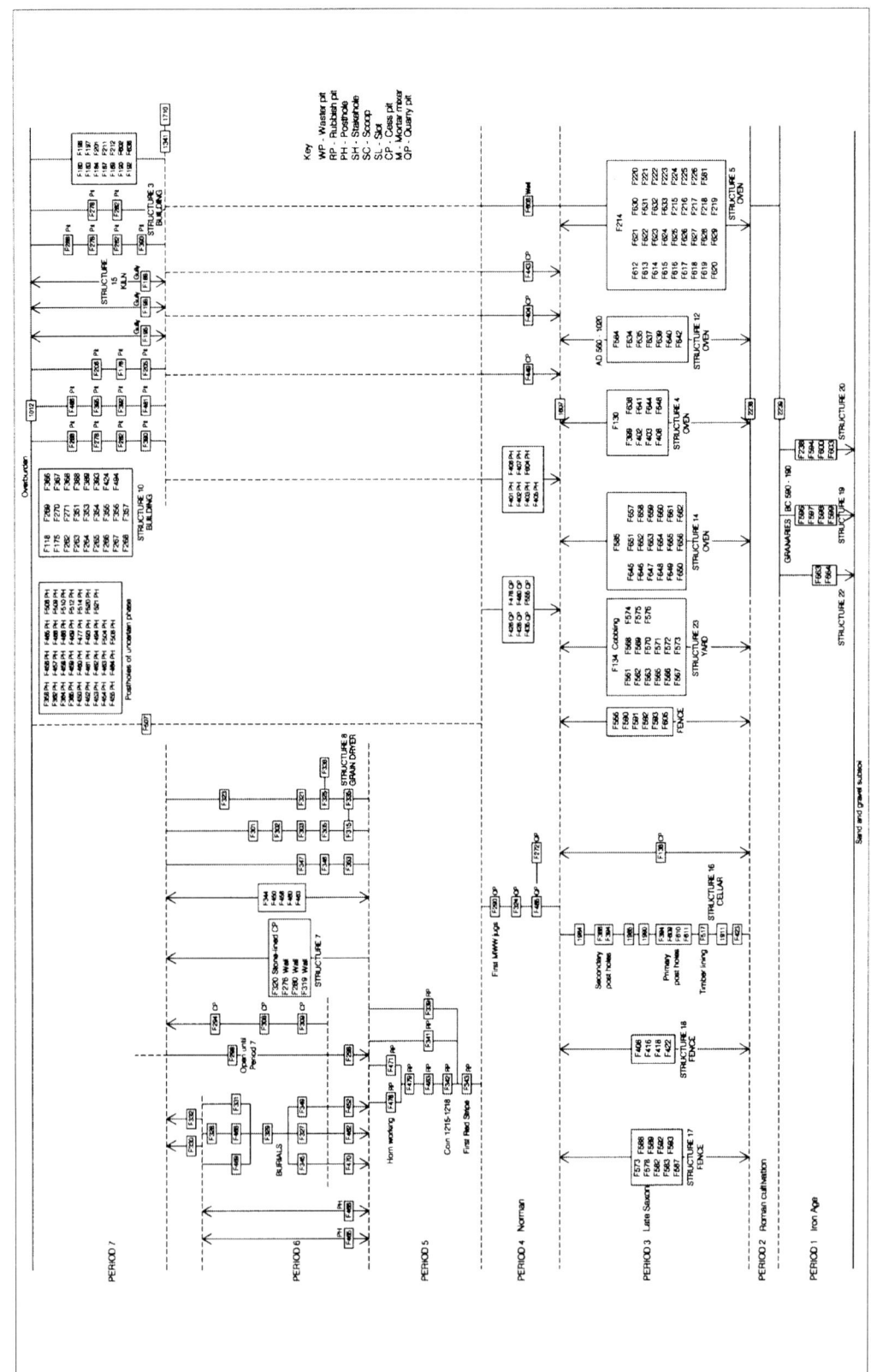

Fig. 3.12 St Mary's Grove: stratigraphy, 2009 (Cane/Carver).

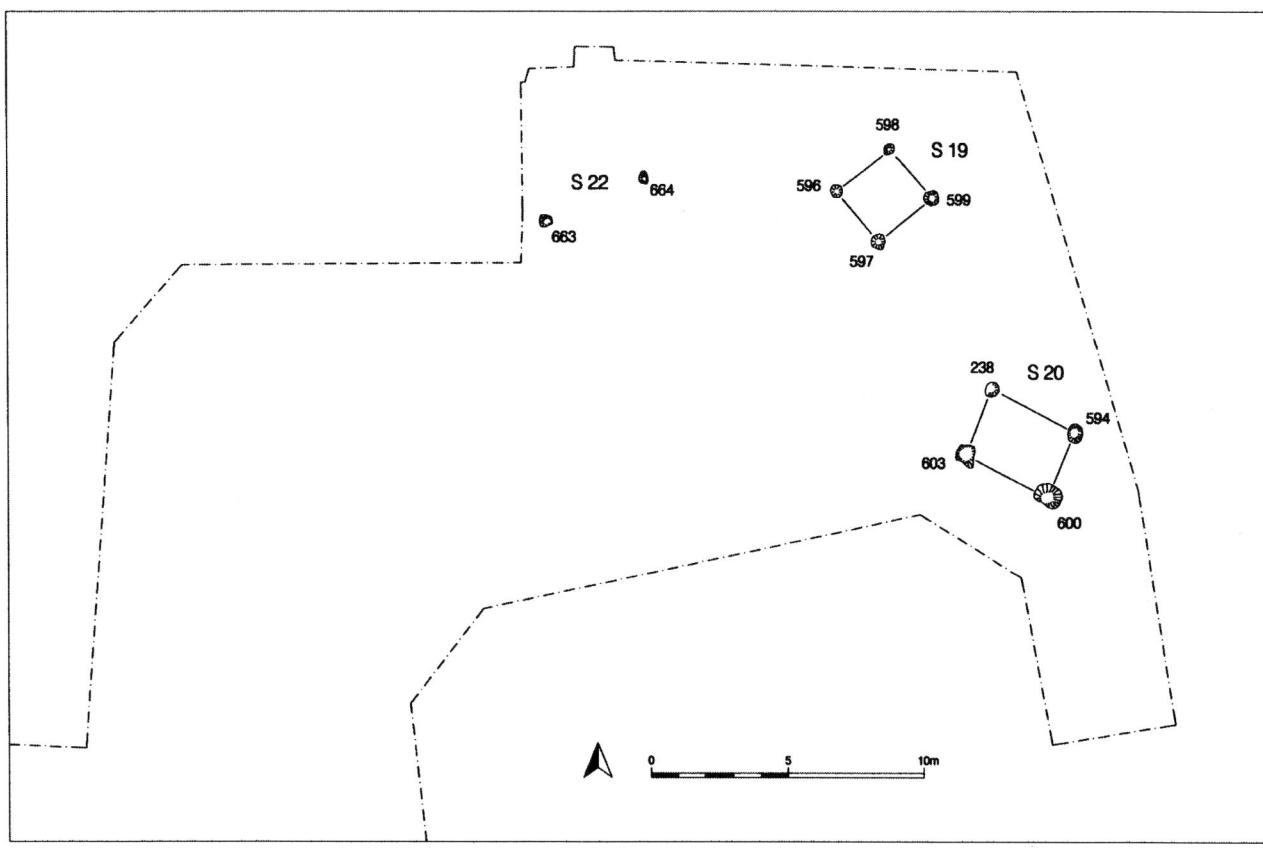

Fig. 3.13 St Mary's Grove: Period 1 (Iron Age) (J. Cane).

Fig. 3.14 St Mary's Grove: Period 3 (Late Saxon) (J. Cane).

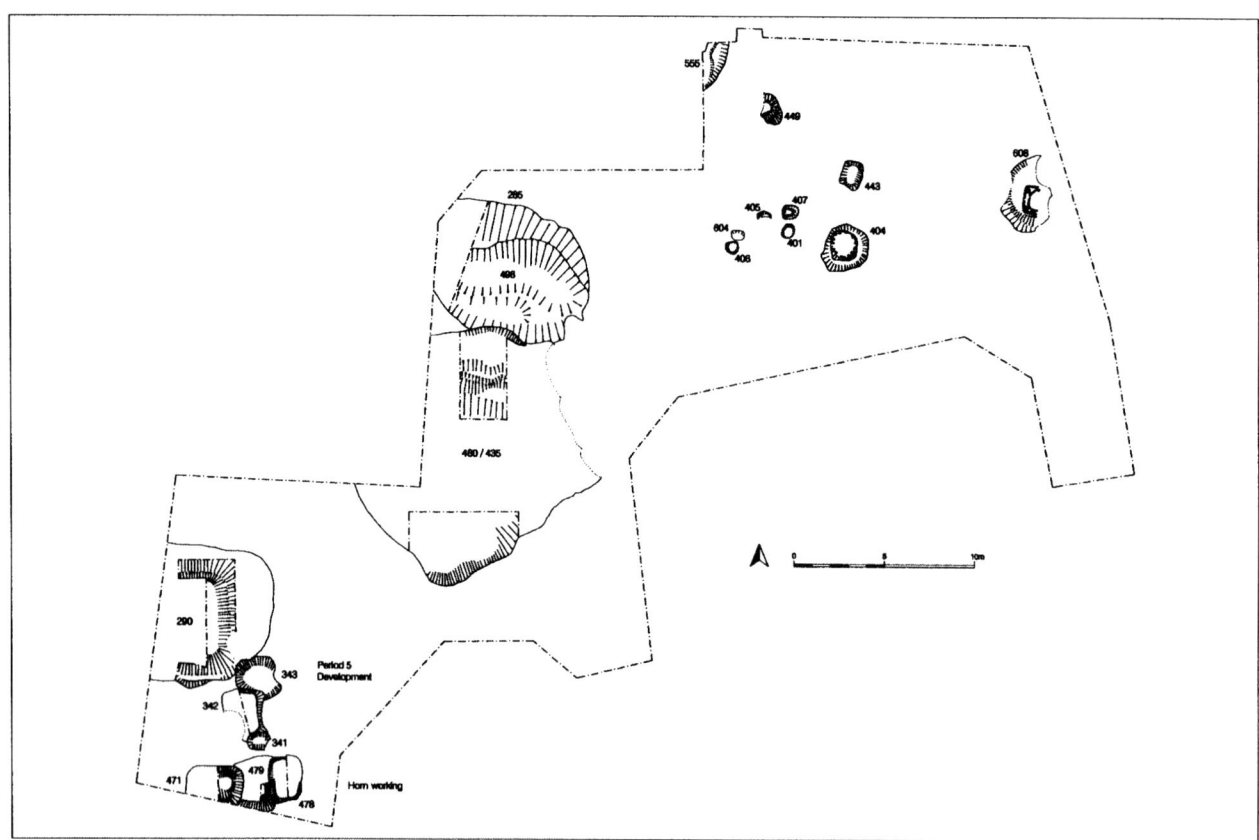

Fig. 3.15 St Mary's Grove: Periods 4–5 (twelfth–thirteenth centuries) (J. Cane).

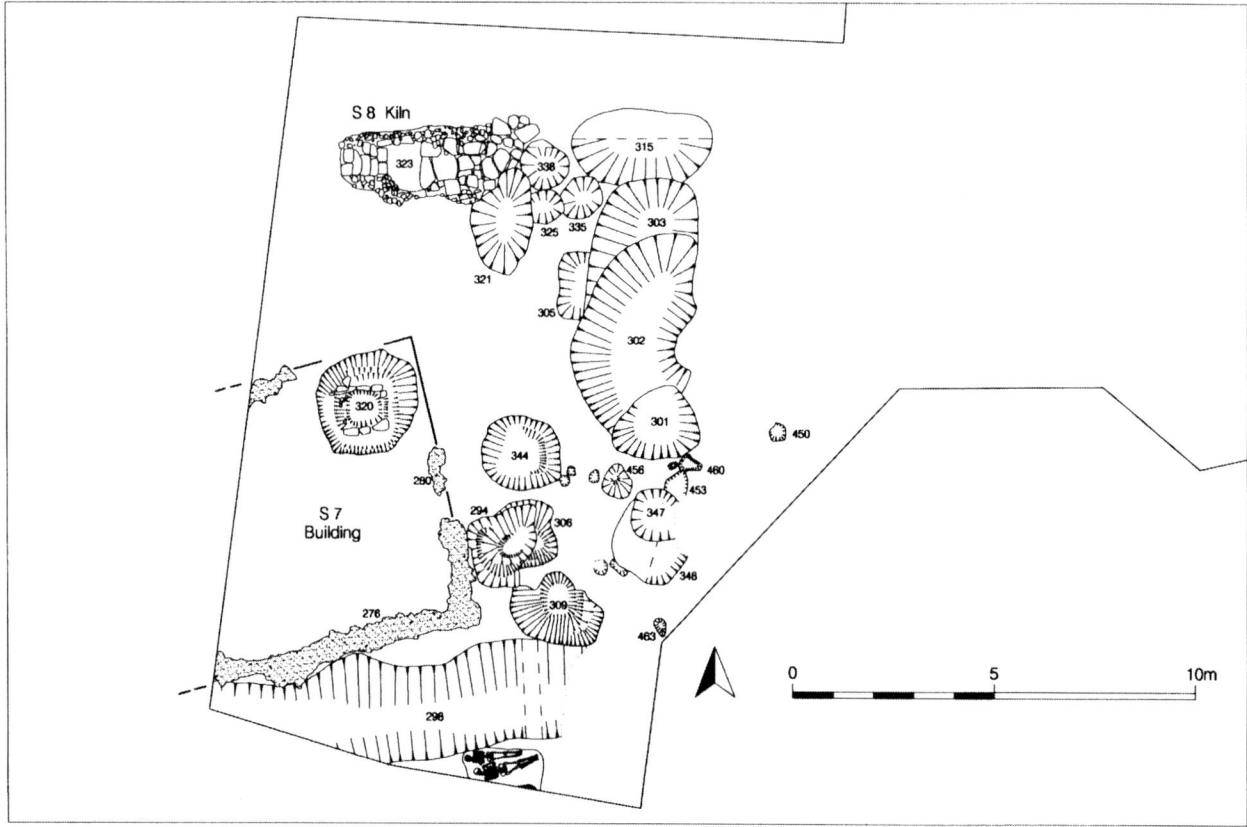

Fig. 3.16 St Mary's Grove: Period 6 (fourteenth–sixteenth centuries) (J. Cane).

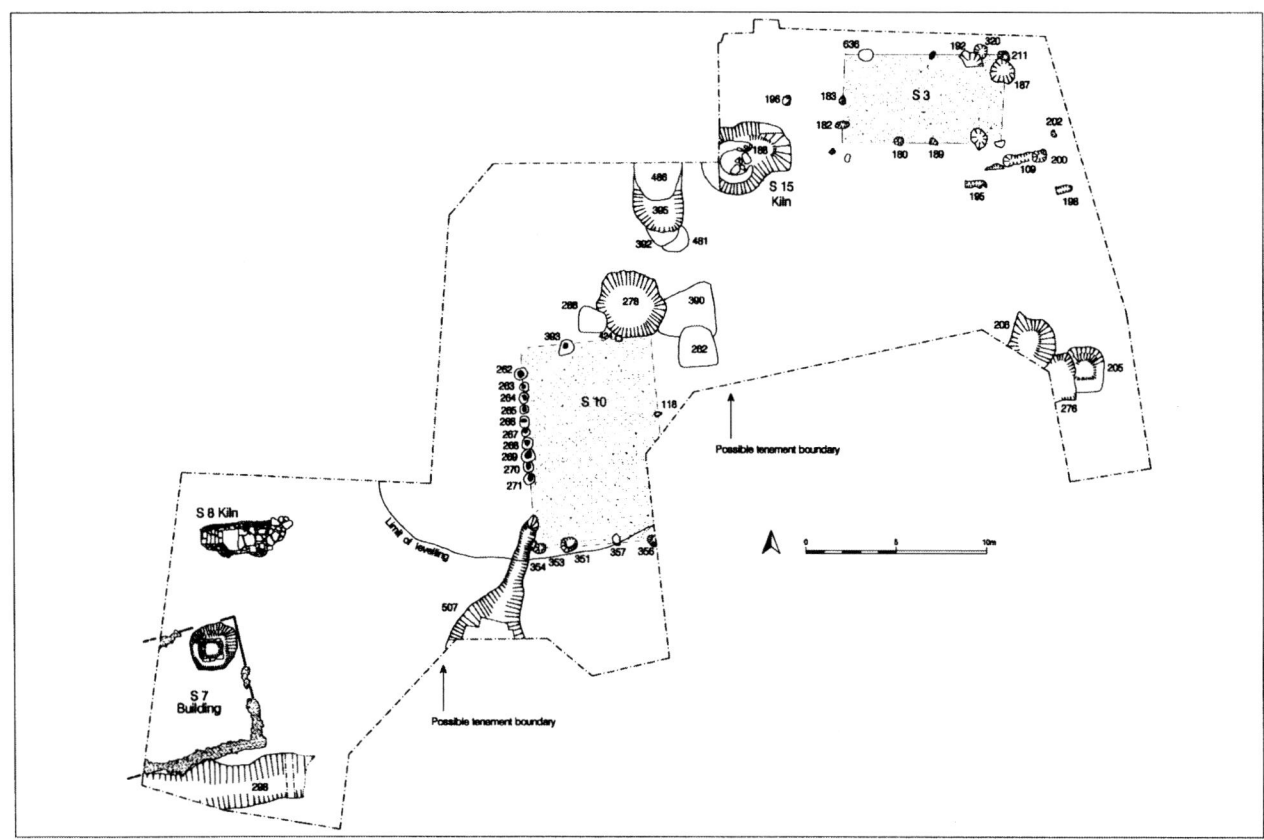

Fig. 3.17 St Mary's Grove: Period 7 (post-medieval) (J. Cane).

contrast to the cattle. There was only one example of deer (F435, Period 4) from the whole assemblage. Rabbit or young hare was present in the Saxo-Norman well F608 (Periods 3–4) and thereafter. Production picked up again in *PERIOD 5* (late twelfth – thirteenth centuries; Fig. 3.15). A series of rubbish pits in the south-west indicates the recommencement of craft including horn-working (F478).[31]

In *PERIOD 6* (thirteenth–sixteenth centuries; Fig. 3.16), industrial activity increased, and the grain-processing theme returned. In the south-west part of the site, a stone-founded barn (S7) and stone-built grain dryer or kiln (S8) were constructed. On the south side, a boundary ditch (F298) marked the medieval edge of St Mary's churchyard.[32] Cattle bones dominate the assemblage of domestic meat animals (cattle, sheep, pig) throughout the Middle Ages. Where quantities and context were significant (Period 6), adult cattle represent 80% of the total remains of meat species. No bones below the metatarsals are present (no feet or hooves), and it is suggested that the waste represents joints obtained after preparation by butchers and consumed nearby. Of other species, it can be noted that cats were present throughout the Anglo-Saxon and medieval

sequence, and cats and dogs were being disposed of locally in Period 6. Birds represented in the medieval context overall included 16 goose, 8 domestic fowl, 3 duck, 3 woodcock and 1 carrion crow.

In *PERIOD 7* (post-medieval, sixteenth century and later; Fig. 3.17) the construction of a rectangular building (S3) and a malting kiln (S15) suggest a brewery on the north-east side. In the centre there were fences or other timber structures (S10, S23, S24). In the south-west, pits were dug. There was a large animal bone assemblage, implying both consumption and craft.[33]

Bath Street (FR7; 3 on Fig. 3.1)

Immediately to the west of St Mary's Grove another research opportunity presented itself in what had been the car park of the Police Social Club (Fig. 3.18a). This

31 Dated by pottery and a coin of King John (in F342).
32 Dated by pottery seriation.

33 This sixteenth-century assemblage has not been included in the current appraisal, but it has great potential. Post-medieval contexts totalled 3,858 bone fragments of which 2,486 could be identified. These included a large group of cattle bones in F102 (495 bones, mainly metapodials), a sizeable group of pig bones in F146 (108), numerous dogs (298 dog bones in F115 alone). Other species represented are deer (fallow deer, possibly also red deer), cat, rabbit, fish and frog. Amongst birds, domestic geese dominate (48 bones), followed by domestic fowl (43 bones), with duck, woodcock, jackdaw and heron also represented.

Fig. 3.18 Bath Street: (above) opening of the excavations; (below) the site on completion (both J. Cane).

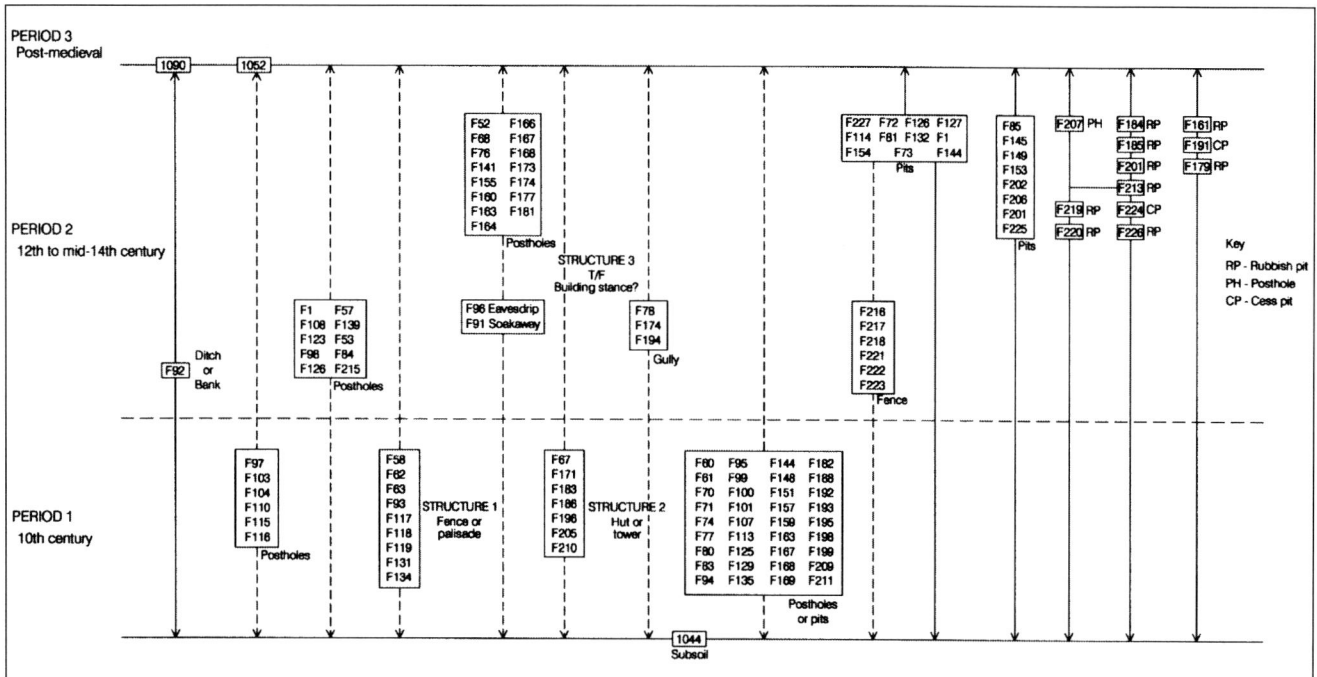

Fig. 3.19 Bath Street: stratigraphy, 2009.

site occupies the highest point in the town, where the natural sands and gravels, identical to those encountered on most sites in the town, rise to about 80 metres above sea level. Bath Street and Earl Street are shown on the earliest maps of Stafford (c. 1600) their courses having remained essentially the same, but neither is shown as having built-up frontage at this time.

The area was tested by two machine-dug trial trenches early in 1981, which suggested the survival of medieval deposits under a considerable depth of later overburden.[34] Area excavation, supervised by Roy Barnes, began in November 1981 covering an area of about 325 square metres south-east of the junction of Bath Street and Earl Street. The upper layers, judged to be the result of late and post-medieval cultivation, were removed by machine. This conscious decision – to destroy without full record the later deposit – was taken because at that time the threat was considered imminent. The operation left only a small amount of soil sealing features cut into the natural sand and gravels. Later features cut through this remaining deposit were excavated at recovery level C prior to the exposure of the natural subsoil. All features cut into the natural were then fully excavated at recovery level C or D[35] (Fig. 3.18b).

Post-excavation analysis was undertaken in three programmes. Jenny Glazebrook incorporated an account of the sequence in her MA dissertation.[36] Jon Cane reconsidered the sequence, which was reconsidered and

revised again in 2007 by Carver, using pottery seriation (Digest A3; Fig. 3.19). The main problem in establishing a sequence was either that there was no stratification, or that what there was had been truncated by cultivation or removed by over-machining.[37] The great majority of features excavated was defined against subsoil, with only the pit cluster on the east side offering a sequence of cuts. In reality, the phasing was thus dependent on the presence or absence of Stafford ware, medieval and post-medieval pottery, all easily distinguishable. The seriation showed that occupation was more or less continuous, with some features, notably ditch F92, remaining open over a long period.

The principal objective was to determine which features, if any, could be assigned to a Late Saxon phase, since the quantity of Stafford ware leaves little doubt that there was one. No wasters were reported, so we must assume that pottery was not being made here. The location of the site would also lead to the supposition that it lay at the heart of the burh. Apart from Stafford ware, features produced slag and iron fragments, said to be of horseshoes. The slag and the iron fragments are both found in features otherwise innocent of pottery – so could belong to an initial phase. After excluding all features that contained medieval or later pottery, we were left with six pits, fifty-six post-holes and six stake-holes that were eligible for inclusion in the earliest phase. Fifteen of these features contained slag without pottery, and virtually all later features also contained slag. This implies a major smithing activity and an early one, the

34 ST35 and ST36 supervisor: M. Taylor; see FR2.3.

35 For recovery levels, see Carver 2009, 124.

36 Glazebrook 1983, 17–25.

37 FR7.2.

Fig. 3.20 Bath Street: Period 1 (Late Saxon).

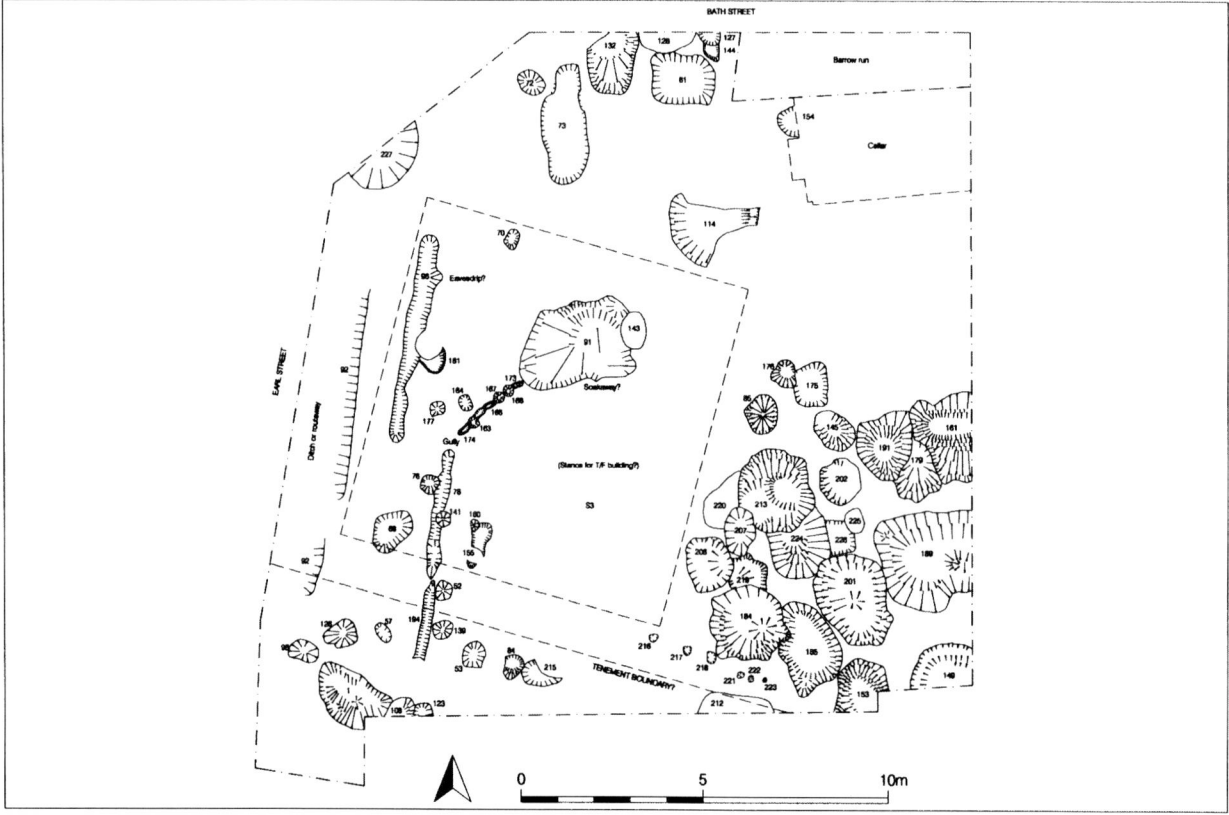

Fig. 3.21 Bath Street: Period 2 (medieval).

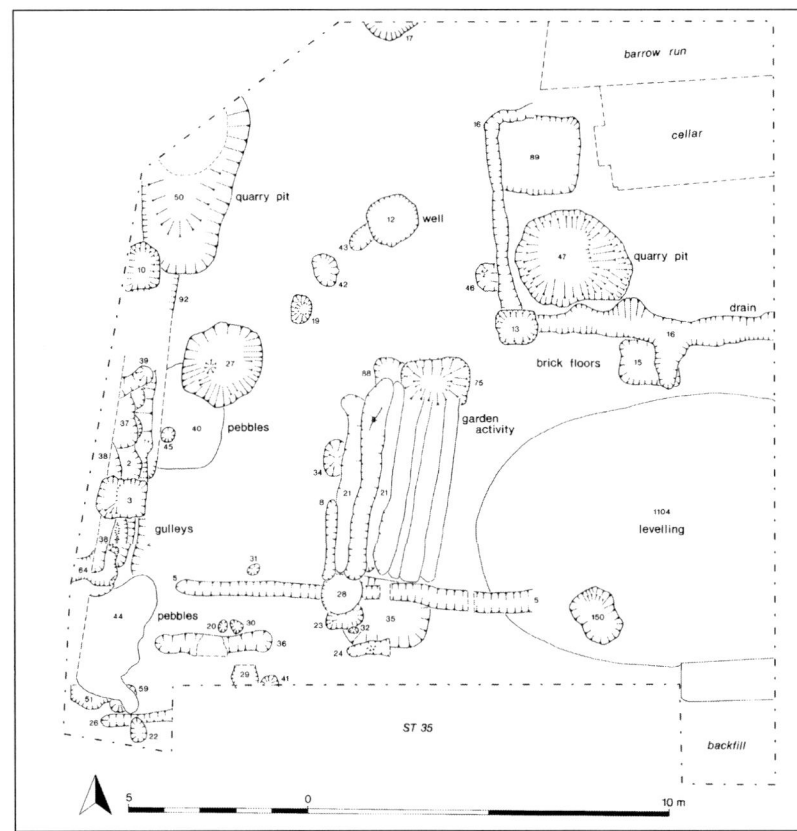

Fig. 3.22 Bath Street: Period 3 (post-medieval).

products of which had been dispersed. Late Saxon discard seemed to have involved the whole area. A radiocarbon date was taken from one post-hole (F58) which gave a measure of AD 600–880. While certainly Anglo-Saxon, the presence in the sample of oak heartwood raises doubts that its deposition was that early (Digest A2).

The sloping edge F92 ran along the Earl Street frontage, and is assumed to indicate a wide ditch, known only from fills against its eastern shoulder, the rest of which lies beneath Earl Street. It contained some of the earliest medieval contexts on the seriation diagram (Digest A3). The features that it had cut contained only insignificant or early pottery. Its earliest backfill layer (1090) was extensive in section, running nearly the length of the west edge, and provided an interface with the natural sand and gravel along the whole of its length. The Late Saxon post-holes, if we believe them, mark the edge of Earl Street too. This provides endorsement for the idea that Earl Street is a boundary of some antiquity, perhaps even dating to the time of the burh. This ditch was being backfilled in the twelfth/thirteenth centuries and later.

The sequence of events was otherwise grouped into three periods.[38] In *PERIOD 1* (tenth–eleventh centuries; Fig. 3.20), there was a structure involving smithying and

using Stafford ware. A boundary, perhaps consisting of a palisade and ditch, ran north–south along the western edge of the site, the eastern edge of what would become Earl Street.[39]

In *PERIOD 2* (twelfth–fifteenth centuries; Fig. 3.21), the basic geography is given by gullies and post-holes to the west and pits to the east. The pits are notably constrained in the south-east corner, which implies that Earl Street is still the frontage. The blank space implies that there was probably a timber-frame building with soak-away between the pit group and Earl Street.

In *PERIOD 3* (sixteenth–twentieth centuries; Fig. 3.22), the few post-holes, the cultivation marks, the drains and the well strongly suggest a post-medieval garden. The Speed map of 1600 does not indicate a built-up frontage on either Earl Street or Bath Street (Fig. 2.10).

Broadeye (4 on Fig. 3.1)

Commercial excavations by Birmingham Archaeology in 2003 and 2006 found a wide ditch with recuts encircling the probable site of a Norman motte[40] (Fig. 3.23). The excavators make a good documentary case

---

38 The detailed contents for each period are inventoried in FR7.4.2.

39 Dated by Stafford ware or absence of later pottery.
40 Cuttler et al. 2009.

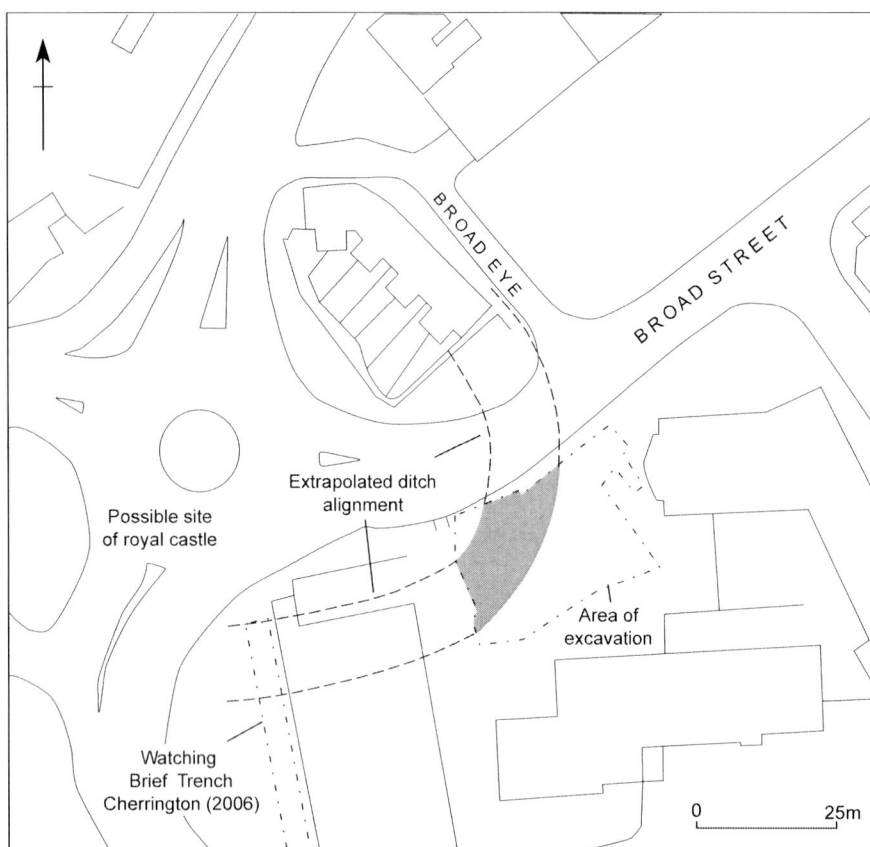

Fig. 3.23 Broadeye: plan (Cuttler et al. 2009, fig. 5).

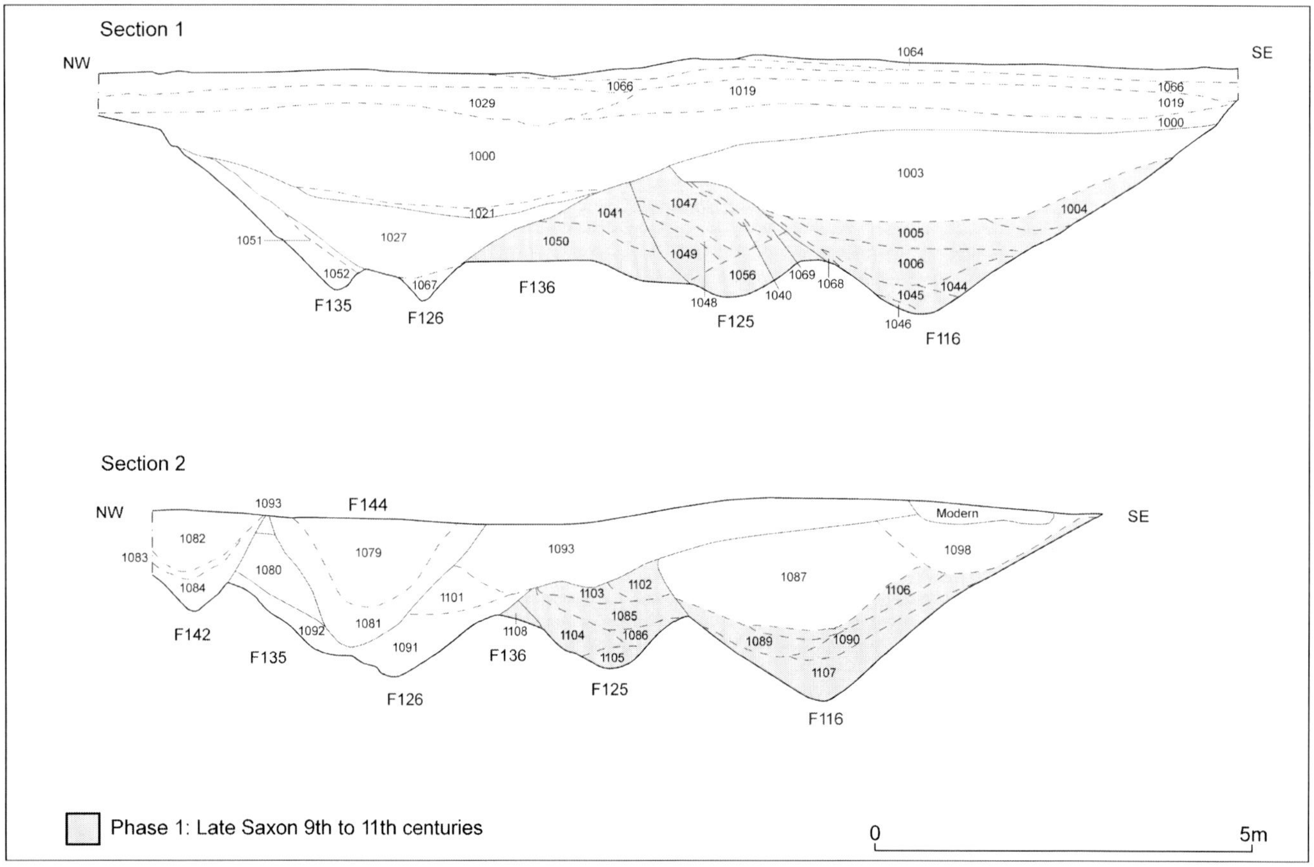

Fig. 3.24 Broadeye: section (Cuttler et al. 2009, fig. 7).

Fig. 3.25 Tipping Street (north): overview of the excavation (J. Cane).

for a Norman castle at this point (in addition to the one at Castle Church, west of the town), built in 1070 and demolished by 1086 but apparently surviving as a ruin all the way through the Middle Ages (see pp. 99, 107 below).[41]

The ditch system was complex (Fig. 3.24). The ditch-cuts F135 and F136 contained only Stafford ware, and F116 had only Stafford ware at the bottom (1046, 1087), and a small number of post-Conquest sherds in its latest fill (1003), leading the excavators to believe they had found a Late Saxon defence. But an early Norman motte or bailey ditch could also contain only Late Saxon pottery in its primary layers. The ditch contained smithing slag in F136, eight fragments of human skull and, from its continuation (F100), intentionally dumped charred debris from crop-processing.

These results align well with the construction of a Norman motte or bailey disturbing a Late Saxon occupation area in which both smithing (as at Bath Street) and crop-processing (as at St Mary's Grove) were prevalent.

Tipping Street (north) (FR6.4; 5 on Fig. 3.1)

The next two area excavations were situated to the east of the axial street (Greengate Street) that bisects the peninsula. The sites were Tipping Street (north) adjacent to St Chad's church, and Clarke Street at the south-eastern periphery adjacent to the marsh.

The area available for excavation at Tipping Street comprised the frontage area on the north side of Tipping Street where it meets Eastgate Street (Fig. 3.25). Across the road was the large open space where the first Stafford-ware pottery kiln had been found in 1977 (ST17, Tipping Street (south), an area also known as Pitcher Bank).[42]

Tipping Street (north) was tested archaeologically in 1979 as part of the site evaluation programme, with a small trench (ST19) running north-south which suggested a tenth-century phase connected with the Stafford-ware pottery industry. This was sealed by twelfth-/thirteenth-

41 See also Youngs and Morgan in Darlington 2001, 33.

42 This area was the subject of renewed investigations at the time of writing, in which more pottery kilns were found. Pers. comm. Andy Norton, Oxford Archaeology.

Fig. 3.26 Tipping Street (north): (above) Int 32 subsoil surface; (below) Int 33 on completion (Cane/Taylor).

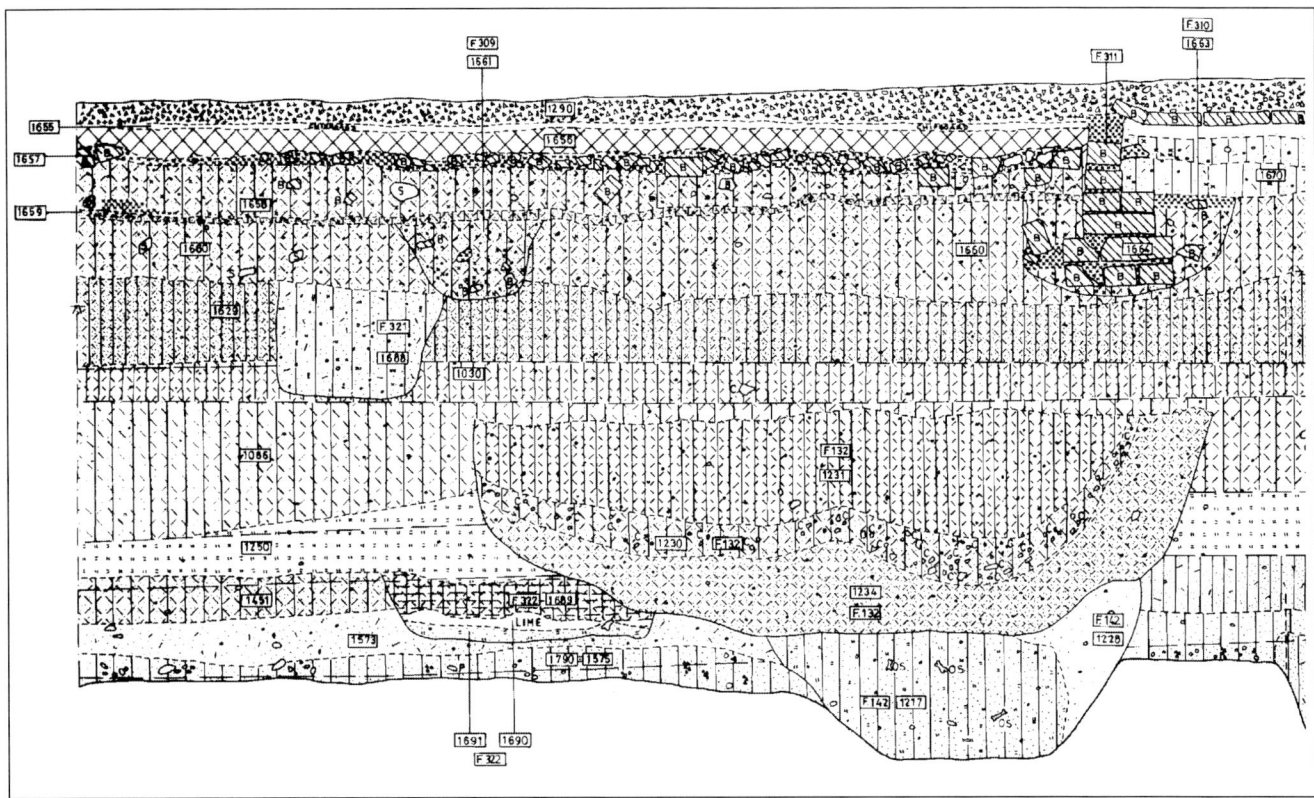

Fig. 3.27 Tipping Street (north): principal horizons as seen in section D (east facing) (Taylor).

century activity and a substantial post-medieval built-up.[43] Excavation began on 1 February 1982 under the supervision of Mark Taylor in two adjacent interventions: the main area (Int 32) lay north of the street (Figs 3.25, 3.26a), and the smaller area (Int 33) lay on the corner (Fig. 3.26b). The excavations were completed in October 1983.

The deposit was relatively shallow, the overburden at half a metre deep or less giving on to sand and gravel subsoil, which was cut by numerous pits, post-holes and two pottery kilns. The quantity of Stafford-ware wasters left no doubt that this was a potters' workshop. The number of features and the apparent lack of legible stratification led to the generation of a number of interpretations of the sequence, promoting the idea that there were two Saxon phases, and that most of the post-holes belonged to medieval buildings.[44]

In 2007, the stratigraphy was revisited in order to resolve the question of how many of the post-holes might belong to the Late Saxon period. In practice the inquiry was greatly simplified by the discovery of five persistent soil horizons in section, represented on the field drawing reproduced here as horizontal clayey soils between 10 and 30 centimetres thick, which could be interpreted as

episodes of cultivation and/or discontinuity (Fig. 3.27).[45] All features were then placed in the stratification diagram according to whether they cut or were sealed by these five consecutive horizons, or equivalent contexts (Fig. 3.28). Post-holes are notoriously difficult to place stratigraphically, since some show before their correct phase through the rotting of the post, the creation of a void and the subsequent collapse of higher layers, while others remain invisible until seen against the subsoil. Many of the remaining ambiguities in the sequence were resolved through the association of post-holes in plan. Horizon 1 (1790 etc.), which separated Anglo-Saxon from later activity, was particularly strong and widespread, with a banded structure suggesting abandon and subsequent cultivation. This had sealed a convincing single Late Saxon phase with the lion's share of the post-holes, forming a fenced enclosure (see Chapter 4).[46]

Similarly the exercise endorsed the co-existence of a medieval timber-frame building (S7) and its forge (S3) on the south-west side, blank in the Stafford-ware distribution, following the deposition of the cultivated soil of Horizon 1. Although Horizon 2 (1451 etc.) does

43 FR2.3.

44 FR6.2, 6.4.

45 1790, 1573, 1250, 1030. See also Fig.3.28.

46 See Chapter 4. Debbie Ford conjectured the existence of some structures in her Stafford-ware article (1999, 16), based on an unfinished plan at Stoke museum.

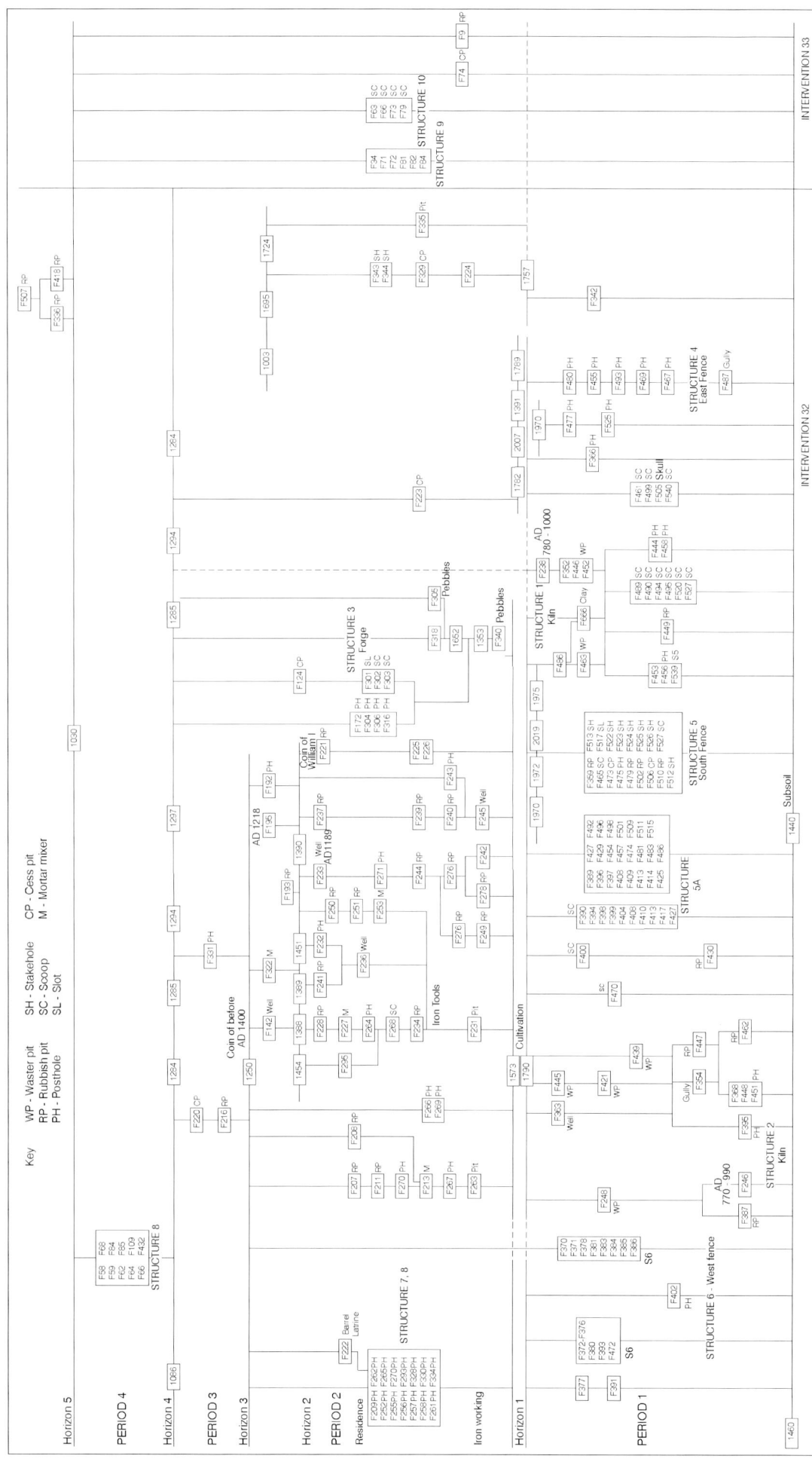

Fig. 3.28 Tipping Street (north): stratigraphy, 2009 (Cane/Taylor/Carver).

also provide a hiatus, it refers only to a limited number of features – wells and the pit associated with the discard of metal tools (F234). The remaining features are contained only between Horizon 1 and Horizon 3 (1250). Moreover all features in this phase seriate to the same period, which already has jugs, but does not yet have Midlands purple ware. All the recorded features cutting Horizon 1 thus seem to belong to a relatively short period from the late twelfth to before the mid fourteenth century (see below).

Radiocarbon measures were taken from pottery kilns F246 (770–990) and F238 (780–1000), both dates likely to be later rather than earlier in their range due to the presence of oak heartwood in the samples. An archaeomagnetic date was obtained for the forge (c. AD 1170), and dendrochronology dates of after AD 1189 for well F233, and of 1255/6 for well F142.[47] Rubbish pit F221 contained a coin of William I (residual), pit F195 a coin of John (before 1218), and F216 a coin of Edward I or II (before 1400). The seriation undertaken for Tipping Street (north) found that all pottery before Horizon 1 was Stafford ware and all other types of pottery cited had occurred in contexts before Horizon 2 (Digest A3). There appeared to be no orange wares. The seriation was thus useful in showing that all the medieval pottery from Tipping Street belonged to a relatively short-lived phase from the late twelfth to mid fourteenth century. The seriation was less useful for the stratigraphy since the features it focussed on were already very well stratified. In fact this good stratification confirmed the general impression that Cane's medieval types (61 of them) were mostly variations on the two or three more basic types define by Ford.[48]

The sequence (Fig. 3.28)

The result of this analysis was to simplify the sequence into two major developments, Period 1, broadly tenth/ eleventh century, and Period 2, broadly the twelfth/ thirteenth century, with a gap between them. These are followed by post-medieval phases but not in any great intensity. The features defined in Int 33 belong to Int 32's Period 2.

Apart from a small group of flints in the south part of the site, and Roman pottery residual in later features, there is no evidence for any occupation before the Late Saxon period (*PERIOD 1*, tenth–eleventh centuries; Fig. 3.29). The radiocarbon dates (above) allow the initial development to have taken place in the tenth century, consistent with the Æthelflædan foundation. The site was laid out as a single operation with three fences containing an area of land beside Tipping Street or its predecessor, namely the road leading to the east. Inside this enclosure

were two pottery kilns, one early (S2) and possibly experimental, the other long-lived and surrounded by scoops and waster pits (S1). Two human skulls were found with wasters (in scoops F342, F505). Water was supplied at first by a gulley (F354) and then by a well (F363) (see Chapter 4, pp. 76–92).

PERIOD 2 (late twelfth – early fourteenth centuries; Fig. 3.30) embraces events taking place between Horizon 1 and Horizon 3. The Late Saxon pottery workshop was abandoned and the kilns truncated by ploughing (Horizon 1). Development did not apparently start up again until the late twelfth century in the form of a building (S7) parallel to the street, accompanied to the east by a forge (S3) comprising a U-shaped furnace and a pebble surface adjacent to it to the north. Immediately north of S7 (i.e. outside its back door) was a barrel stance, which may represent either a latrine or a water butt. Beyond that were four wells which succeeded each other, and a number of contemporary rubbish pits, among them one (F234) with a rich assemblage of iron tools (described in Chapter 5, pp. 108–17). There were five other pits containing debris from mortar mixing. Further to the east was a pebble surface (F224), sealing Late Saxon pits, and cut by cess pit F329. Further still to the east, in Int 33, an adjacent tenement seems to be under development at the same time. It consisted of a fence S9, a building of wooden posts parallel to Pitcher Bank (S10), two cess pits and five rubbish pits (Fig. 3.30).

The evidence from archaeomagnetic and radiocarbon dating, dendrochronology and seriated pottery place all these events in the late twelfth to early fourteenth centuries. There is some stratigraphic evidence that the forge and its wells represent the primary development on the west side, diversifying at a given moment into mortar mixing. The east side appears to have been more residential.

Evidence for activity after the mid fourteenth century (*PERIOD 3*) was thin. The site was abandoned and/or cultivated (Horizon 3), and development was subsequently spasmodic until the early modern period.[49]

Identification of animal bone groups from Tipping Street was undertaken only for targeted features, altogether totalling 1,302 bones or bone fragments, of which 369 could be identified. For *PERIOD 1* the groups proved too small to be informative; only in *PERIOD 2* did a single pit (F234) produce a large enough assemblage – which was, however, smashed into very small fragments and splinters, thus accounting for

---

47 A radiocarbon date was obtained from the same context of 1220–1400.

48 FR8.2.6 and Digest A3.

---

49 It could fairly be said that only Periods 1 and 2 have been reported at Tipping Street, that is from the appearance of Stafford ware to the non-appearance of orange wares, i.e. sometime before the later fourteenth century. There are no plans that refer to Period 3 and later. However, J. Cane notes that the area reverted to cultivation in the fourteenth century until the sixteenth (FR6.3).

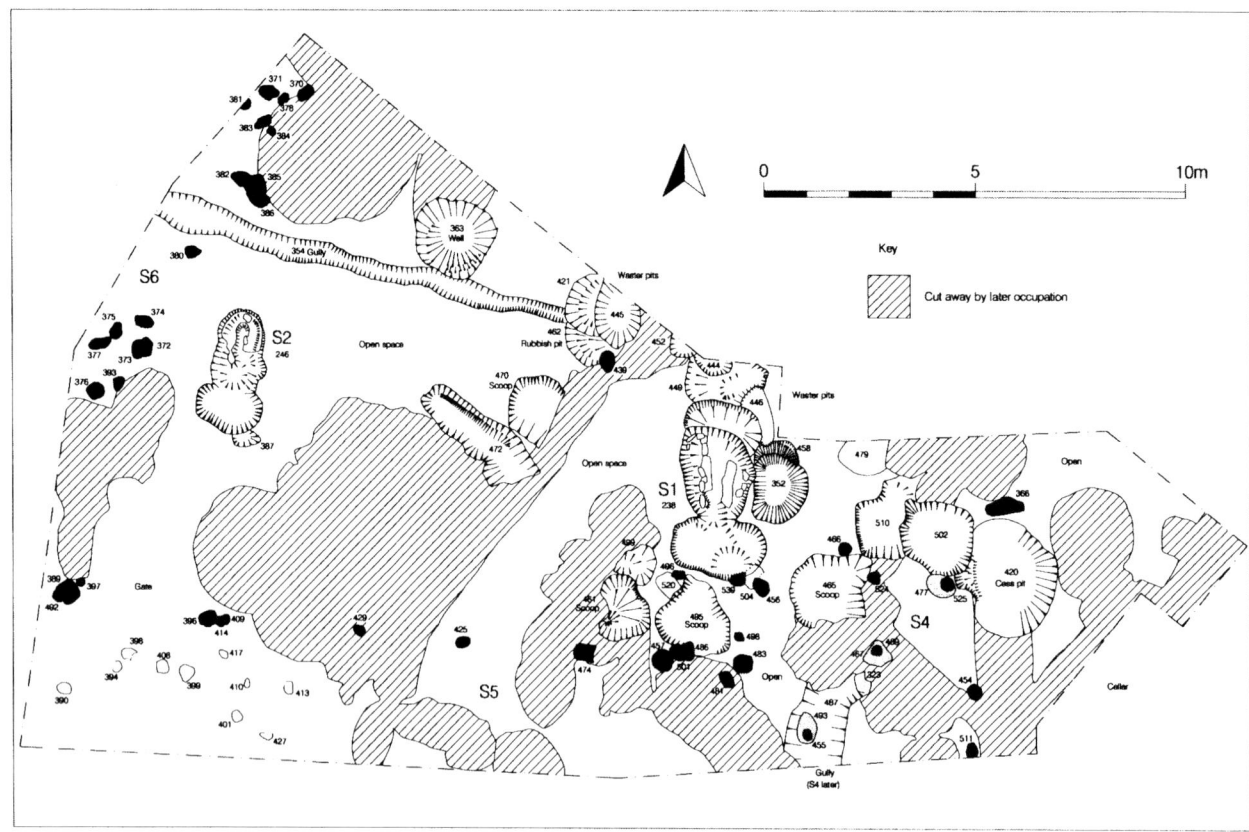

Fig. 3.29 Tipping Street (north): Period 1 (Late Saxon).

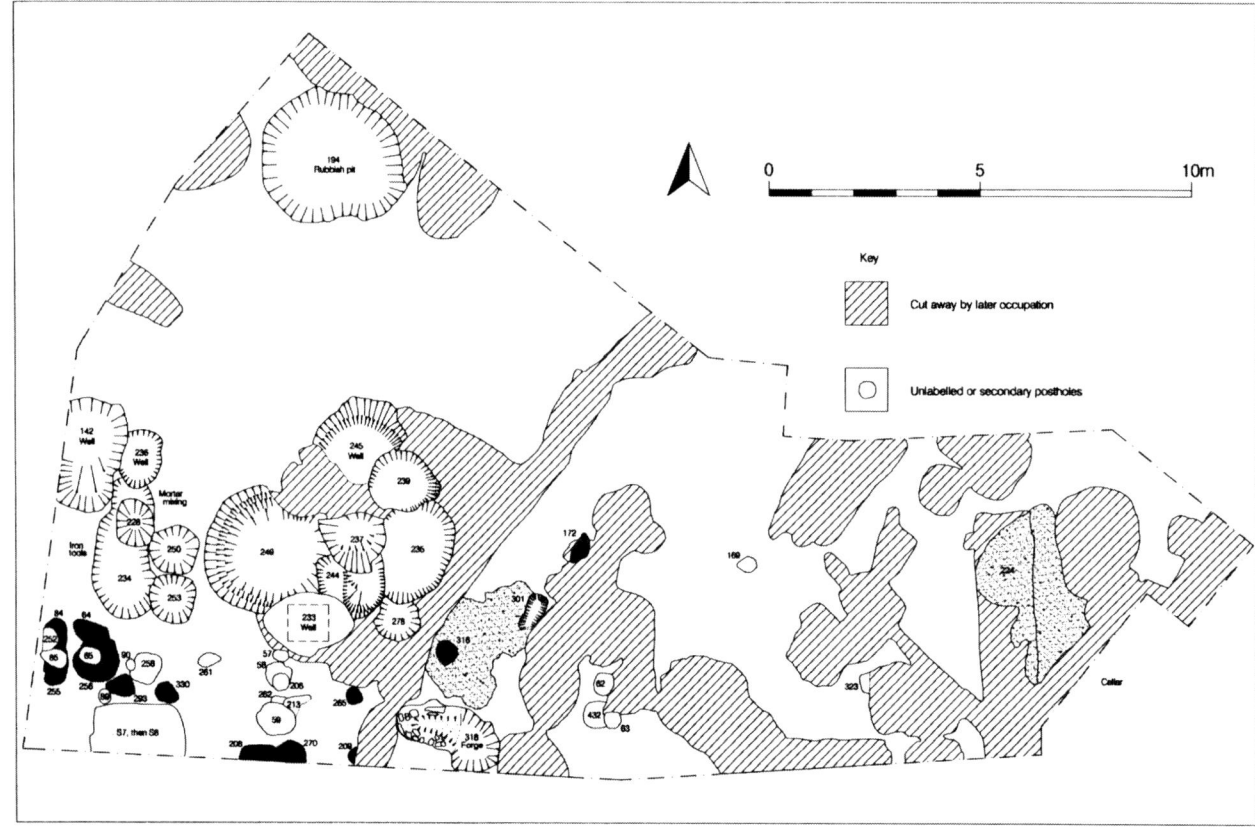

Fig. 3.30 Tipping Street (north): Period 2 (twelfth–fourtenth centuries).

the greater proportion of unidentified bone (858 or 78% of the total).

Unlike Clarke Street (ST15) and St Mary's (ST29), Tipping Street yielded very few cattle bones, compared with the other two domesticates, sheep and pig. Sheep/goat dominates Period 2 and pig accounts for a sizable part of the assemblage in Periods 1 and 2. However, numbers of bones or percentages have little meaning in the case of Tipping Street, as the samples are too uneven. An example is provided by the more or less complete skeleton of a piglet discarded in the disused Period 1 well F363, thus artificially pushing up the percentage of pig bones. It would be invalid to interpret the Tipping Street data as showing a decrease of cattle versus sheep/goat versus pig through time. Apart from the main meat-bearing species, the medieval period at Tipping Street produced a few bird bones (mainly domestic fowl, a few bones of geese and smaller birds), some fish bones and two cat bones (from well F233).

Clarke Street (FR 4; 6 on Fig. 3.1)

The available site ran along the eastern side of Clarke Street, a narrow thoroughfare running north-south between Eastgate Street and South Walls on the eastern edge of the town (Fig. 3.31). The area had been explored by Ashley Carter for Stafford and Mid Staffordshire Archaeological Society in 1970, when two trenches were dug by the north frontage. Trench 1, nearest to Eastgate Street, located post-medieval foundations and a 'possibly medieval' round clay structure; and Trench 2 located a late wall parallel to the street.[50]

In 1974, as part of a response to the proposed construction of a new inner relief road, scheduled to start in January 1976, Carter dug a series of ten sondages side by side on the south side of the site. Sondage 1 contacted builders' rubble at 3 feet down; Sondage 5 and 8 contacted drains with leaking sewage. Sondage 9, 7 and 3 contacted medieval deposits at depths of 5–6 feet.[51] The finds included some 3,000 sherds of sandy pottery at first thought to be Roman, and later identified as Late Saxon. It was this find that led to the investigation of the Clarke Street site in area, and ultimately to the full Stafford campaign (see Chapter 2).

The 1975 excavation took place on the eastern side of Clarke Street and covered virtually the whole frontage, including the areas already tested. The area was limited to the east by standing buildings and existing property boundaries. The need to accommodate the spoil heap on site reduced the investigated area further to around 260 square metres. The operation began on 1 June 1975

and was completed six weeks later in mid July of that year. After initial cleaning of the site (then a temporary car-park), the 1970 trenches and 1974 test pits were identified and re-excavated below subsoil level. Assessment of the sections revealed by this operation resulted in the decision to remove the upper layers by machine (at recovery level A). This was done with a Drott (front bucket), with tidying up and final scraping by JCB (back-actor).

The preliminary clearing (Level A) and subsequent definition at Level B and C revealed the foundations of three cellars (I, II and III) along the west edge, pits on the north side, and in the large southern area cultivation marks running north-south (Fig. 3.32). The subsoil sloped strongly to the south-east: natural gravel and eleventh- to thirteenth-century levels had already been reached on the west side, while some remaining post-medieval soils remained on the south side. A series of charcoal spreads was defined along the western edge of the area, and it later became apparent that they were the destruction levels of timber structures in this area (S2 and 3). At the north end the features originally exposed by Trench 1 in 1970 were re-examined. A second circular clay foundation was found (1008) and the two interpreted as stances for barrels (perhaps for latrines) of the post-medieval phase.

On the south-east side the cultivation soils eventually gave way to pits containing Late Saxon material, but continued to descend into marshland on the south side. A halt was called when the southern section (section 3) stood 2 metres deep, and the marsh layers were then sampled in two trenches 5 metres back from the excavation edge (sections 6 and 7). The deposit proved to consist of interleaving sloping layers representing marsh reclamation and occupation deposits forming successive edges to the marsh itself. The uppermost parts of this deposit contained copious quantities of animal bones and Stafford-ware wasters, evidently dumped into the marsh at the edge of the peninsula.

In general, retrieval was achieved at recovery level C, with level D applied to the house platform on the west side. The excavation was recorded using contexts only, which proved inadequate for analysis, and features were later identified and recorded. The stratigraphy (Fig. 3.33) first prepared in 1975 was subsequently revisited and dated with the aid of a seriation diagram (Digest A3).

The sequence
The lowest deposits on the south-east side belonging to *PERIOD 1* (pre-tenth century) suggested there had been some management of the water in the Roman period, but whatever drainage had been put in place failed during the post-Roman period and the area reverted to stagnant marsh. The Late Saxons appear to have found the marsh as open water, at least in winter. They consolidated its edge with gravel (1177A) and used the area to dispose of badly fired Stafford ware. This represents the earliest

---

50 ST06; FR4; the barrel stance survived as 1019 in ST15

51 ST14; FR4. Sondage 10 was reopened prior to excavation in 1975.

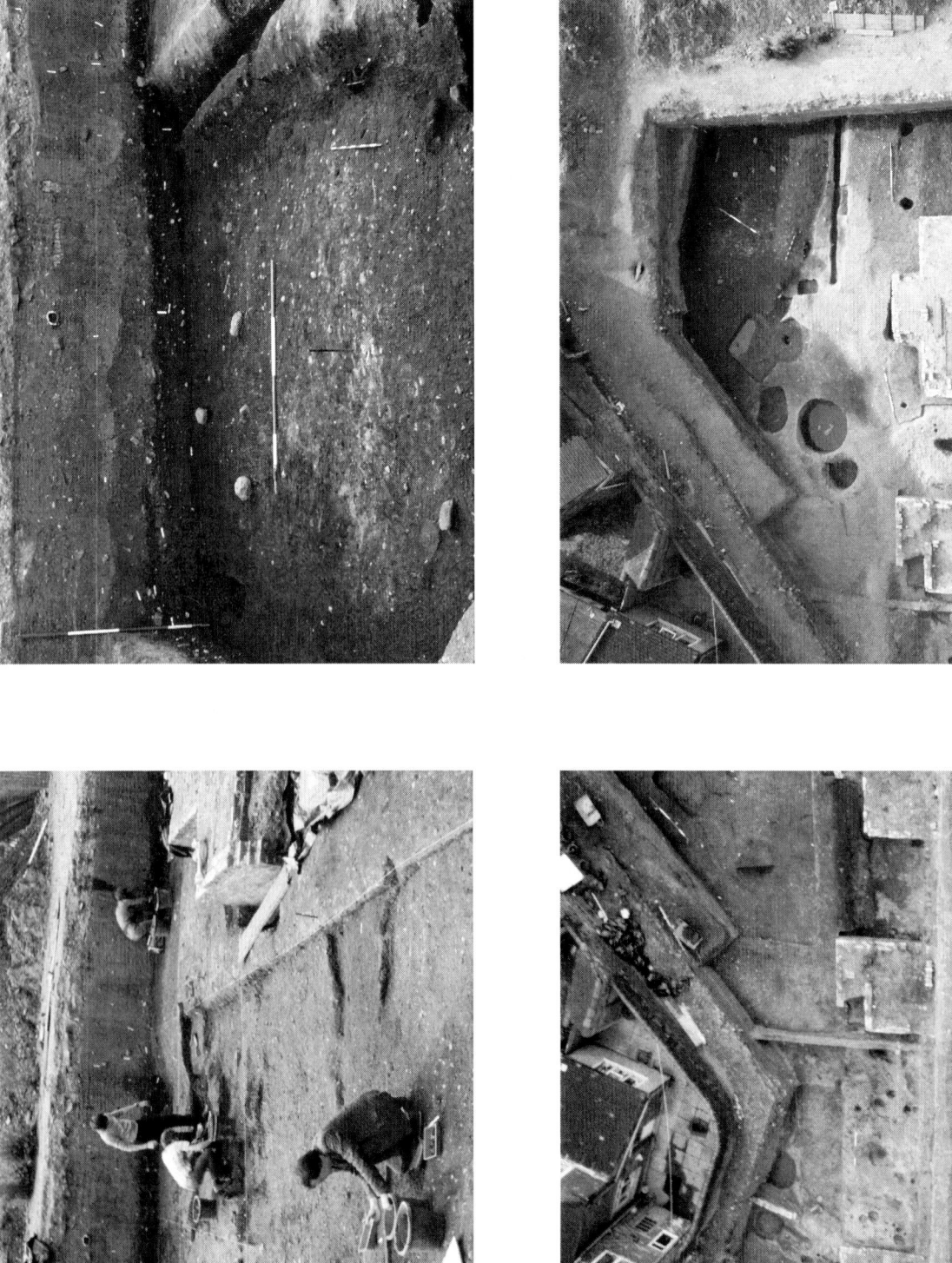

Fig. 3.31 Clarke Street: clockwise from top left: (a) excavations in progress; (b) the marsh; (c) overhead (south); (d) overhead (north).

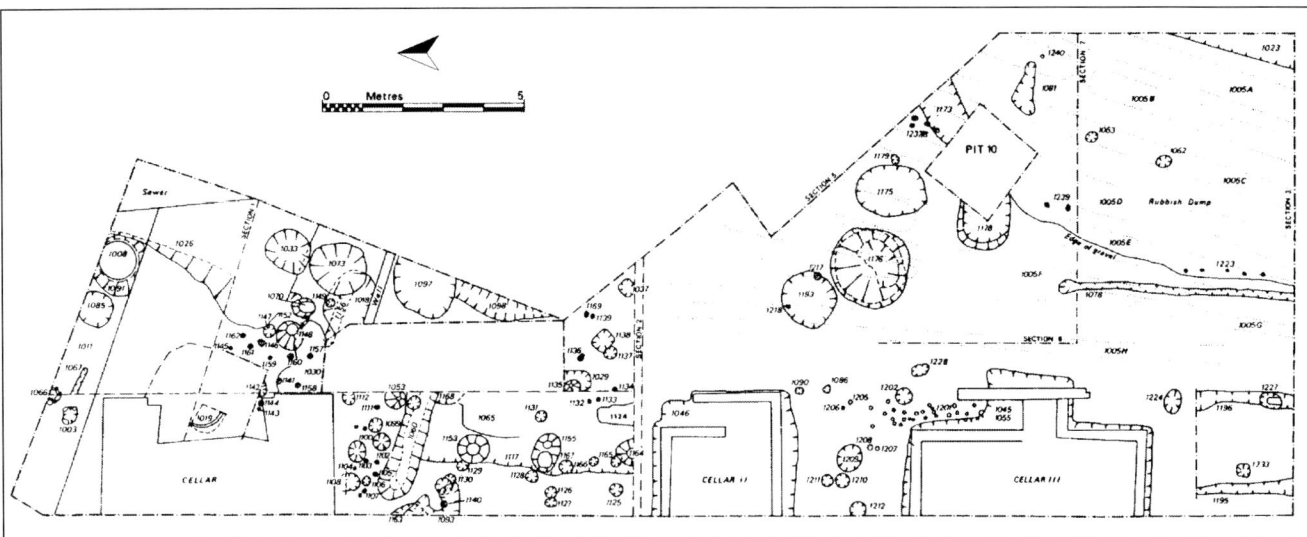

Fig. 3.32 Clarke Street: composite plan.

activity at the Clarke Street site (*PERIOD 2*: tenth–eleventh centuries; Fig. 3.34).

The area continued as a tip into *PERIOD 3A* (twelfth into early thirteenth century; Fig. 3.35), Dumps 2 and 3 being rich in Stafford ware perhaps representing a clearing operation from somewhere in the town. Cattle were watered there, and a little group of latrine pits (F1175 etc.) suggests frequentation by people. In a new development in *PERIOD 3B* (thirteenth century), the marsh area was sealed with clay (1123). Buildings were constructed on the west side, consisting of a shack (S3) and a more substantial post-hole structure with a hearth (S2). They appear to occupy a tenement facing onto Eastgate Street and separated from the dump area by a fence (F1078). The dumping continued, especially of animal bone (Dump 4).

The Eastgate appears in documents in the twelfth century, and its name implies that defences were also in place by this time. If the interpretation of the Clarke Street sequence is correct, at least part of the south-eastern part of the defensive circuit and possibly the Eastgate itself were built on reclaimed land. This may have been done in order to bring the Eastgate as close as possible to the bridge over the King's Pool dam, and to the Eastgate Mill, to make them easier to defend.

The buildings were burnt down and broken jugs associated with the extensive layer of burning (1020 etc.) suggests that this had occurred by the mid fourteenth century (*PERIOD 3C*). Following the fire, the majority of the Clarke Street site remained under cultivation from the late fourteenth century to the eighteenth or later (*PERIOD 4*; Fig. 3.36). The redevelopment of the Eastgate Street frontage comprised the installation of two barrels on clay stands. These may have been beer barrels, and imply a pub, but the late medieval re-use of barrels as

emptyable latrines means that this could be a residential dwelling. Map evidence cites this part of Eastgate Street as residential by 1600. The cellars exposed on the site belonged to a row of dwellings built along the newly laid out Clarke Street in the mid to late nineteenth century.

The animal bones from all Roman, Anglo-Saxon, medieval and post-medieval contexts at Clarke Street were examined in a preliminary exercise following excavations in 1975. They amounted to 2,613 bones or fragments of bones of which 1,339 were identified to species (51%). The activity at Clarke Street consisted mainly of consecutive dumpings of domestic and industrial waste into the edge of the marsh surrounding the Stafford peninsula, from the tenth to thirteenth centuries. The bone groups selected for further study were only those from primary contexts. They amount to 1,492 bones of which 661 (44%) were identified to species. Over half of these were recovered from *PERIOD 3B*, the ultimate dumping episode, which ceased during the thirteenth century.

The tenth-century dumping assemblage was numerically dominated by maxilla, mandible and skull bones of cattle and sheep and ought to represent waste from the preparation of carcasses for food. No young animals were recorded. The numerical dominance of butchers' waste (heads, feet) continued in the twelfth- and thirteenth-century dumps, but the medieval waste also included a slightly increased proportion of femur, humerus and scapula, i.e. meat-bearing bones. This profile probably means that whereas the marsh edge was used to dump waste products from butchery throughout the tenth to thirteenth centuries, in the later period (from the late twelfth century) the midden also began to receive local waste from the adjacent residential buildings then erected along Eastgate Street.

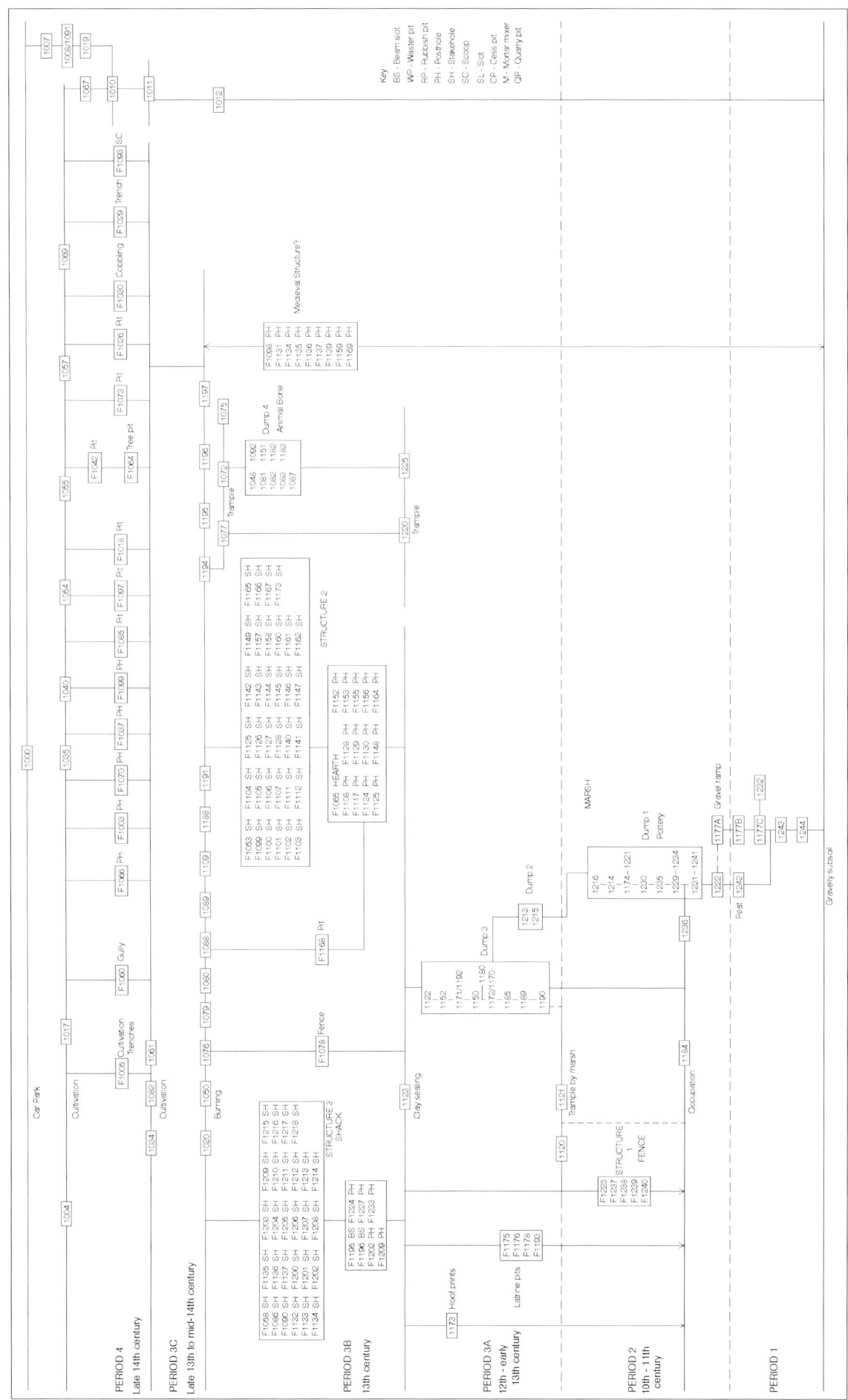

Fig. 3.33 Clarke Street: stratigraphy, 2009.

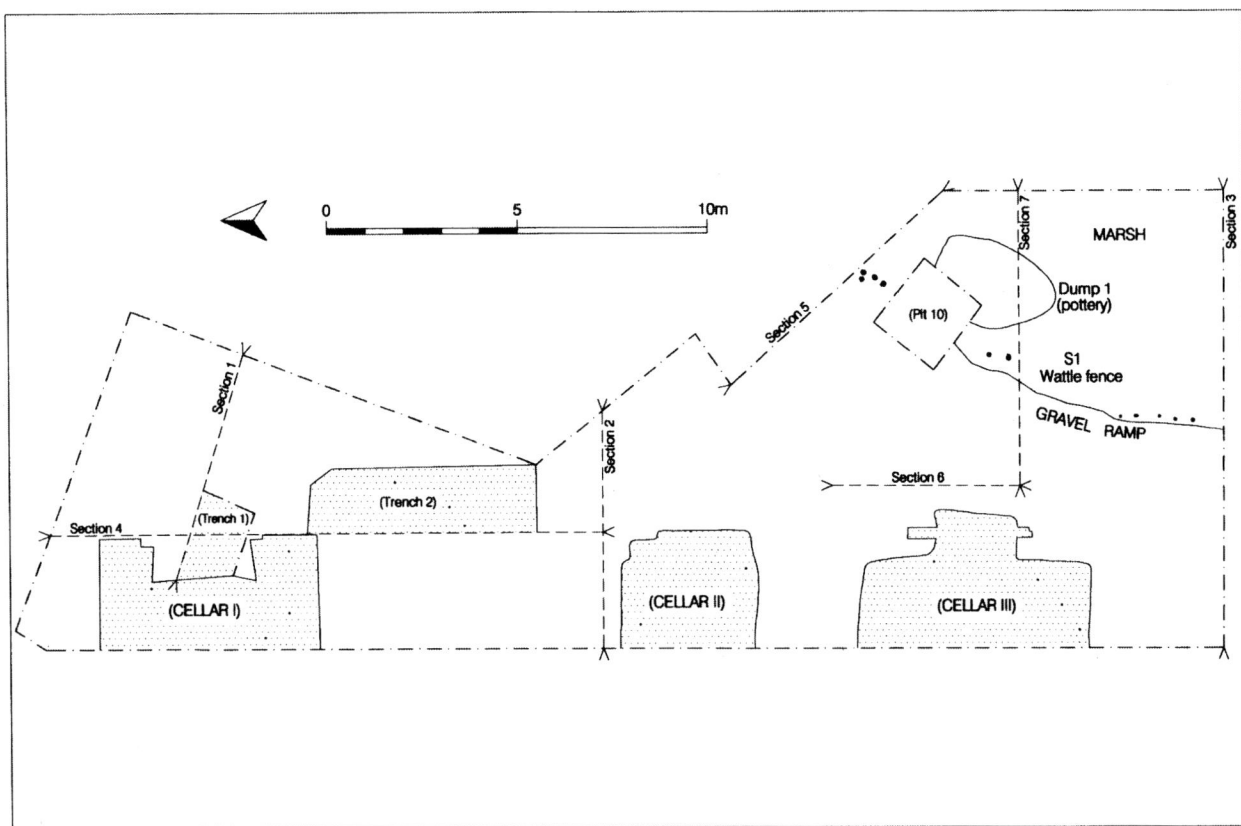

Fig. 3.34 Clarke Street: Period 2 (Late Saxon).

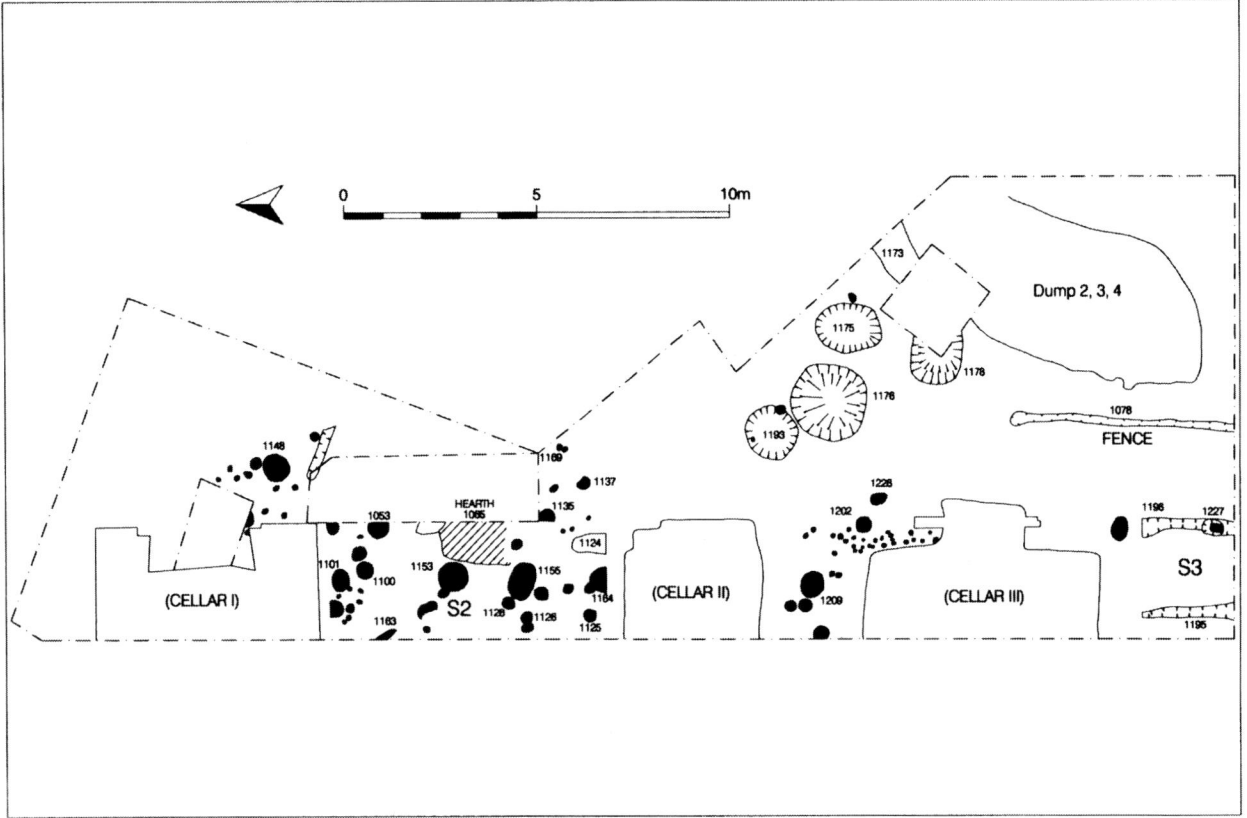

Fig. 3.35 Clarke Street: Period 3 (twelfth–fourteenth centuries).

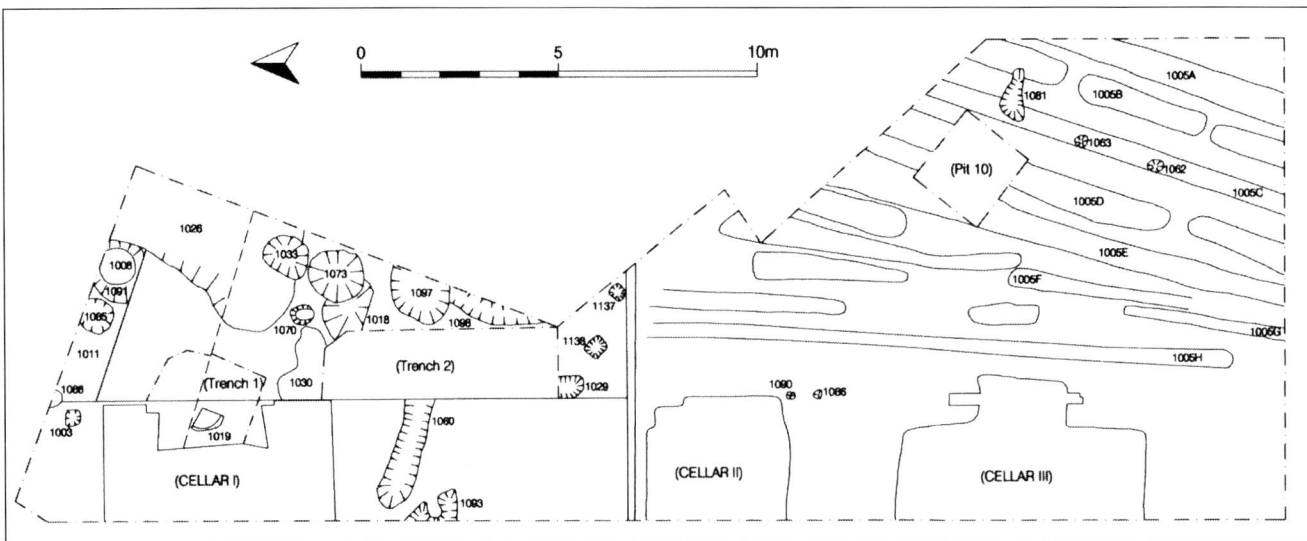

Fig. 3.36 Clarke Street: Period 4 (post-medieval).

Fig. 3.37 King's Pool: (above) the King's Pool surface in the 1970s; (below) using the Russian borer (Carver/Greig).

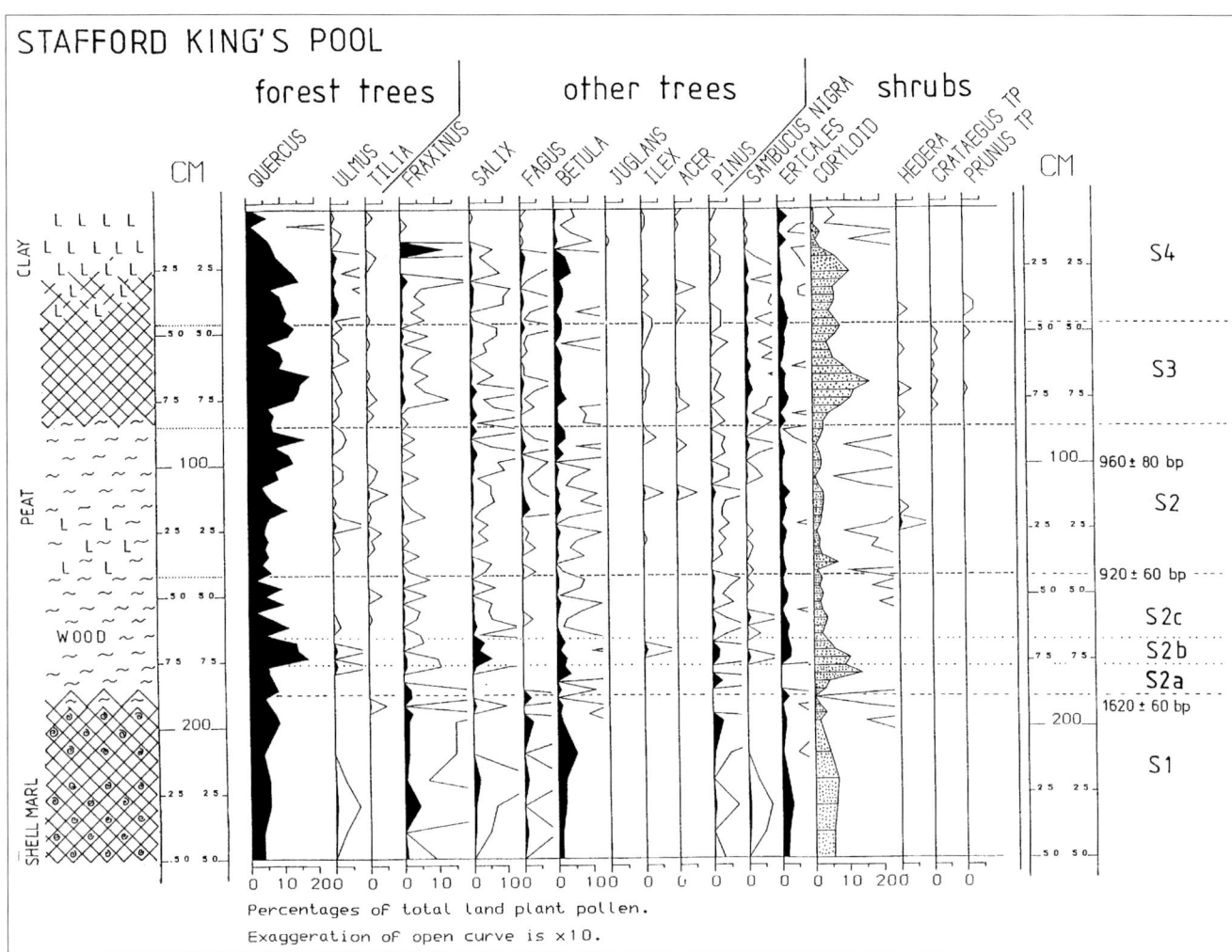

Fig. 3.38 King's Pool: pollen diagram, trees (Greig/Colledge).

Cattle bones were always the most numerous, followed by sheep and then pig, but there is some variety in the proportions between the tenth and thirteenth centuries. Taking the main episodes of dumping as the most representative waste, it can be observed that for a short time in the twelfth century sheep captured some of the popularity of cattle and presumably mutton replaced beef. The proportion of pig bones is always small and becomes relatively still smaller in the thirteenth century. Red deer and roe deer as meat-bearing animals are present in dumping layers until the marsh was sealed off (C1123) in the late twelfth or early thirteenth century. The marsh then began to receive an increased quantity of inedible animals including the bones of six dogs and a small bear (*ursus sp.*). The bear was probably a dancing bear or a bear used for baiting, and was found articulated in C1081 (Chapter 5, p. 122). The suggestion that this bear was indeed a dancing bear comes from observations of deformed hind limbs (Rackham, pers. comm.) resulting from being forced to adopt an unnatural position.

There was evidence for the working of antler from C1198 (Late Saxon) and goat horn from C1185 (twelfth–thirteenth centuries); a pig metacarpal from C1189 (twelfth–thirteenth centuries) had been drilled to produce a toggle, presumably to fasten clothing.

Pollen sequence from King's Pool[52] (7 on Fig. 3.1)

King's Pool is a now a large marsh through which the Pearl Brook flows, lying on the north-east side of Stafford, just outside the city walls (grid reference SJ 9254 2340) (Fig. 3.37a). It was formerly a lake, as shown by the deposits of lake marl, around 20 metres deep, which were found during borings made before the building of a bypass road across the area in the late 1970s. The marshland is now only flooded in wet seasons. When James Greig and Sue Colledge collected

---

52 Abridged from the report in archive by Sue Colledge and James Greig, University of Birmingham, FR10.2.

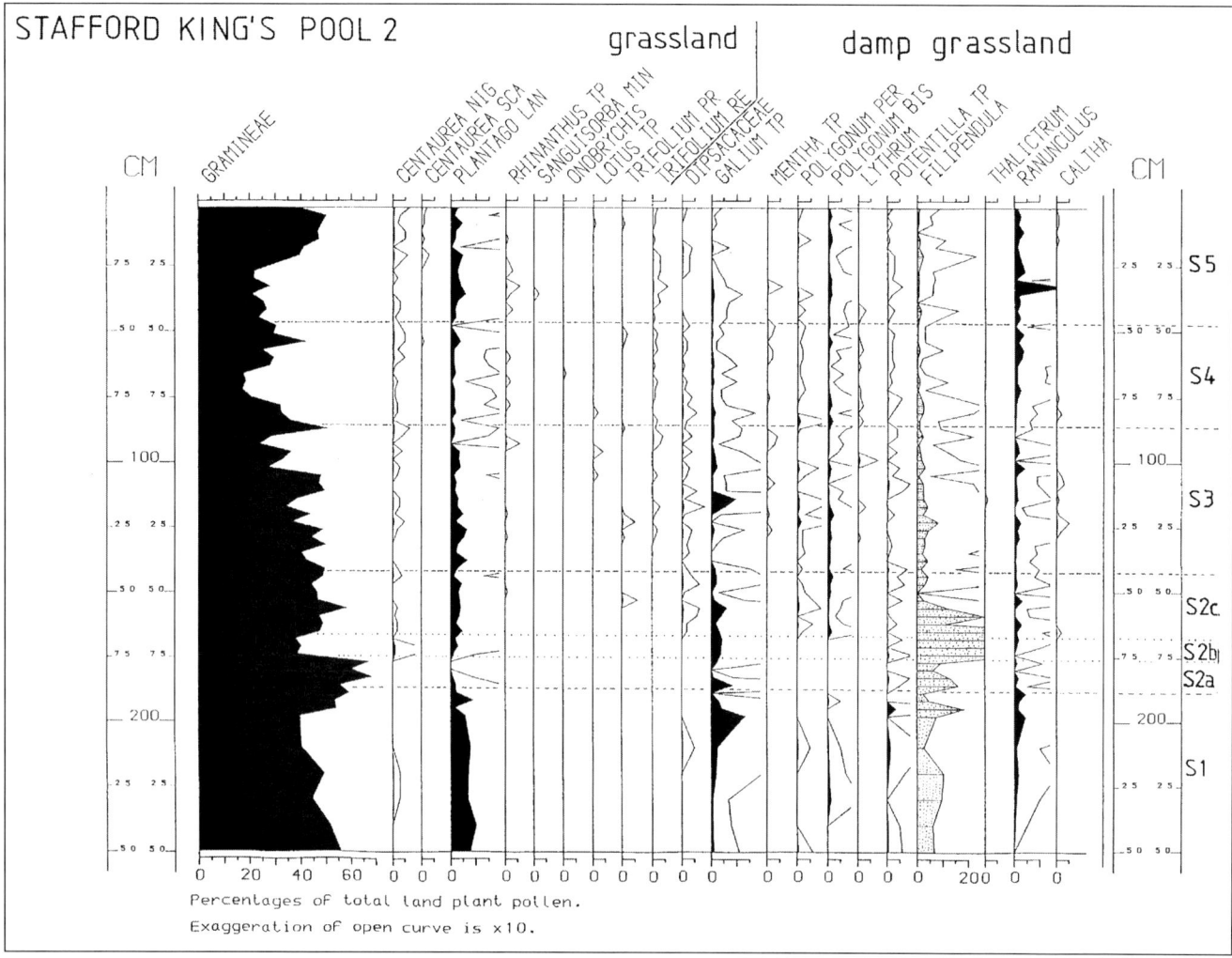

Fig. 3.39 King's Pool: pollen diagram, grasses (Greig/Colledge).

a pollen core in 1976 (Fig. 3.37), the marsh surface was covered with vegetation mainly of *Sparganium* (bur-reed) growing into a layer of clay. This had to be dug through to allow the Russian-type borer to penetrate through to the softer sediment underneath. The coring was done to a depth of 2.5 metres because the main interest was in the upper sediments which would cover fairly recent vegetational history. The samples taken were numbered by depth from the surface in centimetres (e.g. KP100).

After the first results had been obtained, a second series of borings was done in 1977 to provide dating material, nearly at the same spot as the first, although it was then under water. The radiocarbon samples consisted of five borings to the same depth in the peaty layers in order to provide sufficient organic material for dating. The stratigraphic relationship between this material and the pollen core was checked by pollen counts. In addition, many boreholes were made by the civil engineering firm Messrs Balfour Beatty – these were for the piles to support the road that now runs across the pool and these cores also yielded some stratigraphic data.

In a subsequent investigation, D. D. Bartley and A. V. Morgan examined the earlier part of the King's Pool sequence, taking a stratigraphic profile across the King's Pool, and recording the pollen from its base at about 19 metres to the surface, covering a date range from c. 13000 BP to AD 650.[53] They put the first major episode of forest clearance and the beginning of cereal cultivation in the Iron Age, at about 800–600 BC. Thereafter, there was no regeneration of the forest and cereal production remained strong, with peaks in the late Roman period and again in about AD 650.

The Greig and Colledge pollen diagram, covering the Roman and post-Roman period, was drawn up on the basis of the percentage of the pollen of dry land plants, omitting Coryloid (*Corylus* and *Myrica*). A selection of the pollen records are presented (Figs 3.38–3.41); the rest are listed in archive.

---

53 Bartley and Morgan 1990, esp. 184, 191, 193; see Digest A2 for the dates. See also Greig 1982a.

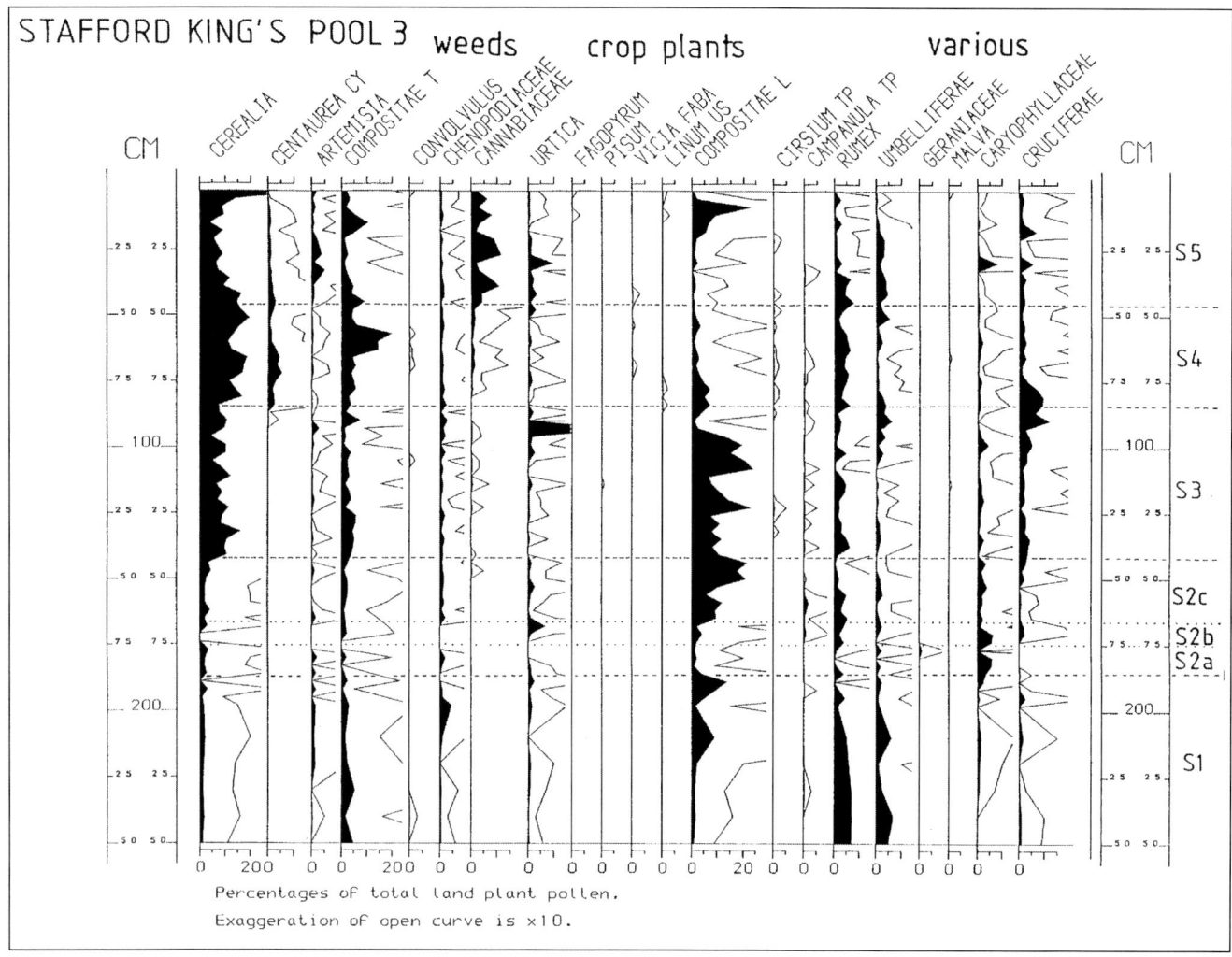

Fig. 3.40 King's Pool: pollen diagram, crops (Greig/Colledge).

Chronology

Dating samples were collected from the horizons where there was organic peaty sediment that could be recovered from the multiple borings. The wood noted in the stratigraphy would have been ideal material for radiocarbon assay, although not enough could be recovered from the borings to make this possible. The other sediments were less suitable for dating; the lake marl would have carried the risk of hard water error if plant remains resulted from photosynthesis involving inorganic carbon from limestone. Radiocarbon measurements were done by Harwell (Digest A2).

The pollen zones have been numbered S1–S5 (deepest first) to distinguish them from David Bartley's zones ST1–ST9. In the part of the Greig pollen diagram that may represent the Roman period (S1), radiocarbon dated between the third and fifth centuries, there are few signs of agriculture, and a possible interruption. In the post-Roman period (S2) there is increased pollen from grassland and trees (oak). In zone S3, with two radiocarbon dates in the tenth to eleventh centuries,

there are increased signs of cereals. Then, in S4, further increases in cereals together with Cannabaceae, probably from hemp, seem to represent medieval agriculture. There are also signs of peas, beans, flax and walnut having been grown or processed locally. There are also some signs of regeneration of natural vegetation which may represent later medieval events. Finally, there is agriculture with very marked growing or retting of Cannabaceae, and signs of buckwheat which show this to be probably post-medieval (S5).

There is thus a slight difference in interpretation between the Bartley and Morgan sequence, which reports continuous cereal production with a peak about AD 650, and the Colledge and Greig sequence, which suggests a hiatus in the third to fifth centuries and a peak in the tenth century.

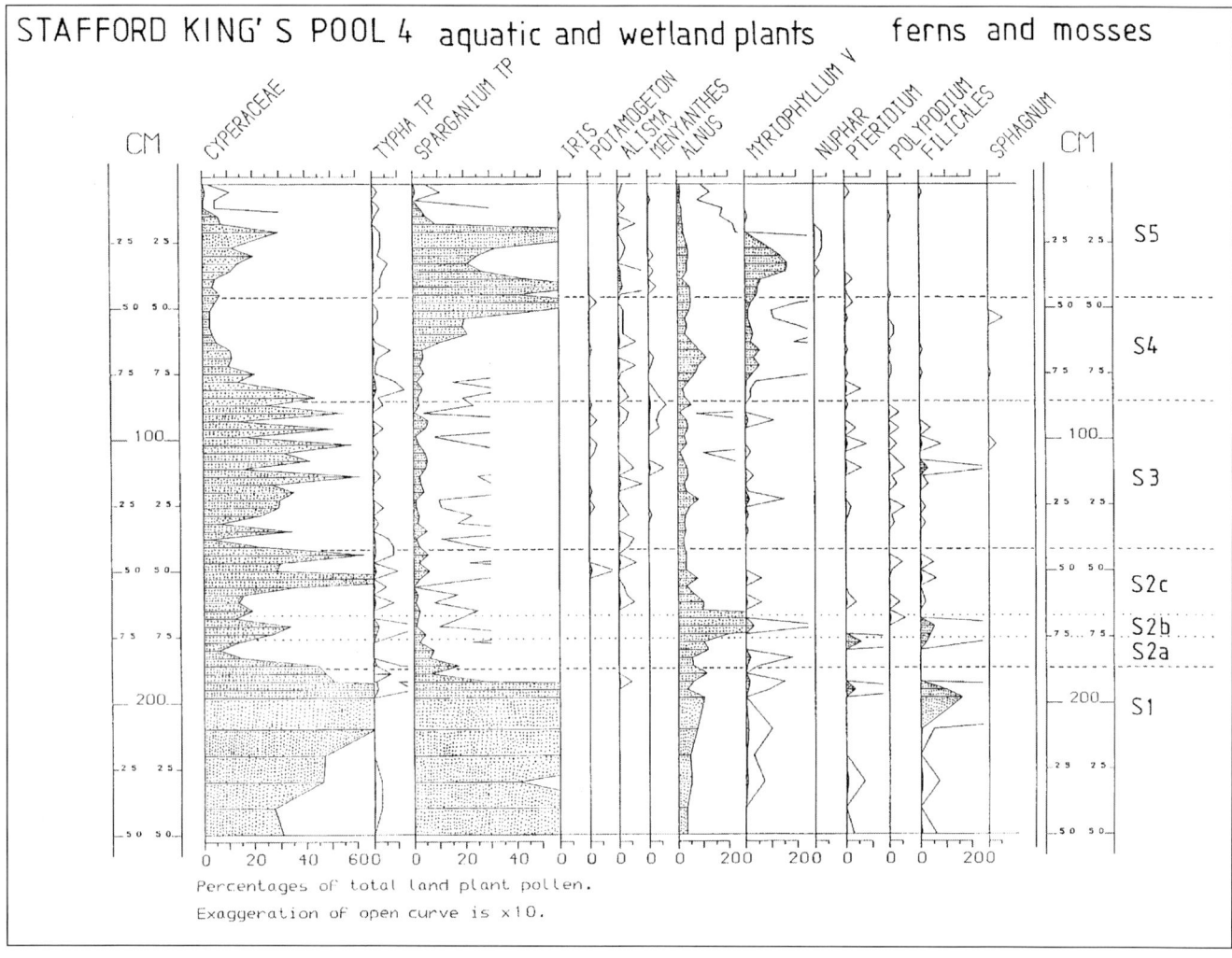

Fig. 3.41 King's Pool: pollen diagram, wetland plants (Greig/Colledge).

Synthesis (Table 3.1)

The story so far presents us with several consistent themes. There is a scatter of Iron Age activity, with grain-processing in the centre of the peninsula, in the form of four-posters implying storage and settlement, in a context of forest clearance and the onset of cereal cultivation in the vicinity. In the Roman period this central area comes under cultivation, as seen in the ploughsoil at St Mary's Grove, although this is unnoticed by the pollen record. In the post-Roman period there is little sign of life on the peninsula, and at Clarke Street the surrounding marsh, perhaps reclaimed in the Roman period, relapses into stagnation.

There is a slight hint from one of the pollen studies that cereal production continues into the post-Roman period and peaks in the mid seventh century, although this is not endorsed by the other. Apart from this equivocal result, there is no good evidence, either from artefacts, structures or radiocarbon dating, for occupation between the Roman period and the tenth century.

It may be that an Anglian establishment was present, but if so it had a very slight imprint or has yet to be found. The Iron Age, with a similarly slight imprint, was, however, detectable. This matter will be revisited in Chapters 4 and 6.

The impact of the Late Saxon development was sudden, planned and ubiquitous. In the central part of the peninsula there was a church and ordered space dedicated to grain delivery, bread-making and smithing. This area also contained pointers towards a defended enclosure. On the west side of the peninsula an area was set aside for making Stafford-ware pottery. A fenced enclosure defined a workshop area. Further to the east, on the edge of the marsh, pottery wasters and animal bone were dumped. The people were fed largely on beef. The nature of the Late Saxon settlement will be discussed in Chapter 4.

As documented in the seriation studies (Digest A3), every one of our windows suffered a hiatus of some kind at the end of the period in which Stafford ware was the sole pottery in use. This was marked by a layer

Table 3.1. Concordance over six interventions

Period	St Bertelin's	Bath Street	St Mary's Grove	Tipping Street	Clarke Street	Environment
Iron Age			Granaries		Marsh	
Roman			Cultivation		Meadow	
Sub Roman/ Middle Saxon					Marsh	
Late Saxon	Church	Smithy	Grain processing Baking *Cattle*	Potting *Cattle* *Pigs*	Dumping *Cattle* *Red Deer* *Roe Deer*	Cereal cultivation
Norman	Church	Abandon	Quarrying *Pigs*	Abandon	Abandon	
Late 12th c.	Church	Residence	Horn working *Cattle* *Cats*	Iron Forge *Sheep* *Cat* *Fowl*	Dumping	
Early 13th c.	Church	Residence	Malting *Cattle*	Residence Mortar mixing	Residence *Cattle* *Dogs* *Dancing bear*	Cereals, hemp
Mid 14th c.	Church	Residence	Malting *Cattle*	Cultivation	Fire and abandon	
14th–16th c.	Church	Residence	Malting *Cattle*	Abandon	Cultivation	

of abandon at Tipping Street and by radical changes of land use at St Mary's, Bath Street and Tipping Street. After a fire likely to have destroyed the timber church, St Bertelin's was rebuilt in stone. The bread ovens were abandoned at St Mary's Grove, although a well stayed in commission, and the site saw some low-level subsistence. The debris of the Late Saxon grain-processing episode was cleared away and dumped in massive quarry pits. At Tipping Street (north), the site reverted to cultivation and the pottery kilns were truncated by ploughing. At Clarke Street, the town tip continued in use in the eleventh/twelfth century with the clearance of Late Saxon debris.

All the sites took off again around the late twelfth century. The central area was largely residential, with

some craft (bone working), while at Tipping Street the site was redeveloped as a smithy with a forge. If the large assemblage in pit F234 is related to it, the forge's craftsmen were making and mending iron tools. The same site began to fill pits with lime mortar, perhaps an indication of the construction of St Chad's church on the adjacent plot. At Clarke Street, the old tip was sealed off and a tenement of dwellings constructed. This renewal was short lived. In the centre, life and brewing endured. But east of Greengate Street our sites had reverted to cultivation by the later fourteenth century, and were not to revive until the sixteenth. These signs and indications of a roller-coaster medieval boom and bust will be examined in Chapter 5.

4

Æthelflæd's Town

Before the burh

The sand and gravel peninsula, which was to provide the arena for Stafford town, formed part of a prehistoric landscape, although not one that is yet well known (Fig. 4.1). The King's Pool on Stafford's north-eastern shoulder is a deep channel which trapped up to 21 metres of organic deposits, commencing in 13000 BP at the end of the last ice age. The subsequent pollen record shows the expected sequence of afforestation and elm decline, but the major episode of tree clearance is here dated to the mid Iron Age between 800 and 600 BC. From then on, cereal cultivation appears to be active, with later peaks possible in the seventh century and marked in the tenth and eleventh (see Chapter 3, pp. 53–55).

Iron Age

Excavations in the town and casual finds outside it have produced a handful of flints, one Mesolithic, the remainder Neolithic in date, and an antler pick from the pool.[1] This may be seen as part of a general spread of prehistoric 'dark matter' without so far indicating a focus. But by the Iron Age the peninsula is largely surrounded by open water and there is a settlement at its centre. An Iron Age settlement is not easy to find under a modern town, but in this case we have enough evidence to identify one in the form of four-post granaries at the St Mary's Grove site (Fig. 4.2).[2] There were two four-posters and part of a third[3] (Fig. 4.3). The post-holes were defined against natural sand subsoil and contained charred matter. Samples examined proved to be 90% wood, but grains of emmer and spelt, with

small amounts of bread wheat, rye and barley were also present.[4] A radiocarbon date on wood from S19 came in at 520–190 cal. BC.[5] No artefacts were recovered from the post-hole fills, but the interface between 2240 (the natural subsoil) and the soil 2238/9, which sealed the four-posters, produced two fragments of possible Iron Age pottery. An area of subsoil 15 x 20 metres was cleaned at recovery level D but no other features were identified which could belong to this phase.

The grain assemblage is interpreted as deriving from the storage of cereals.[6] Emmer chaff fragments and grains, with spelt in slightly greater numbers occur mainly in the post-holes from the Iron Age four-post structures. Both also occur sporadically in later contexts all the way through the medieval period, but are considered to be residual after the Iron Age. Although Saxon cultivation of spelt has been suggested for other parts of England,[7] it is not suspected at Stafford. The few weed species present in the Iron Age granaries are all common species of arable and disturbed ground, such as knotgrass (*Polygonum aviculare agg.*), orache (*Atriplex sp.*), sheep's sorrel (*Rumex acetosella*) and two of the weedy grasses – broome (*Bromus secalinus/mollis* group) and wild oat (*Avena fatua/ludoviciana*). None of these species has strongly marked preferences for soil types, except for sheep's sorrel, which is generally found on acid soils. The percentage of grains and chaff fragments is roughly equal in the samples from one structure, with grains predominating more in the other. The relatively large numbers of unbroken spikelet forks suggests that the grain was stored whole, perhaps to inhibit decay.[8] Although the emmer and spelt crops probably were stored as whole spikelets, these seemed to have been well sorted before being put into storage, as there are few straw remains (just two culm bases) and few weed

---

1 FR2.3.3, a1–10; FR2.3.1, 32 and 56.

2 Note also two sherds of prehistoric pottery a few hundred metres further south; FR2.3.1, 54.

3 S19 (F596–F599), S20 (F238, F594, F600, F604) and S22 (F663–F664). S19 and S20 formed structures measuring 2.5 x 2.5 and 2.5 x 3.5m respectively, while the posts of S22 were 4m apart.

4 From three post-holes in S19 and one in S20.

5 2253/F596, Digest A2.

6 This paragraph is owed to research by Lisa Moffett, FR10.1 and Moffett 1994.

7 Murphy 1985.

8 Ethnographic data by Hillman 1981.

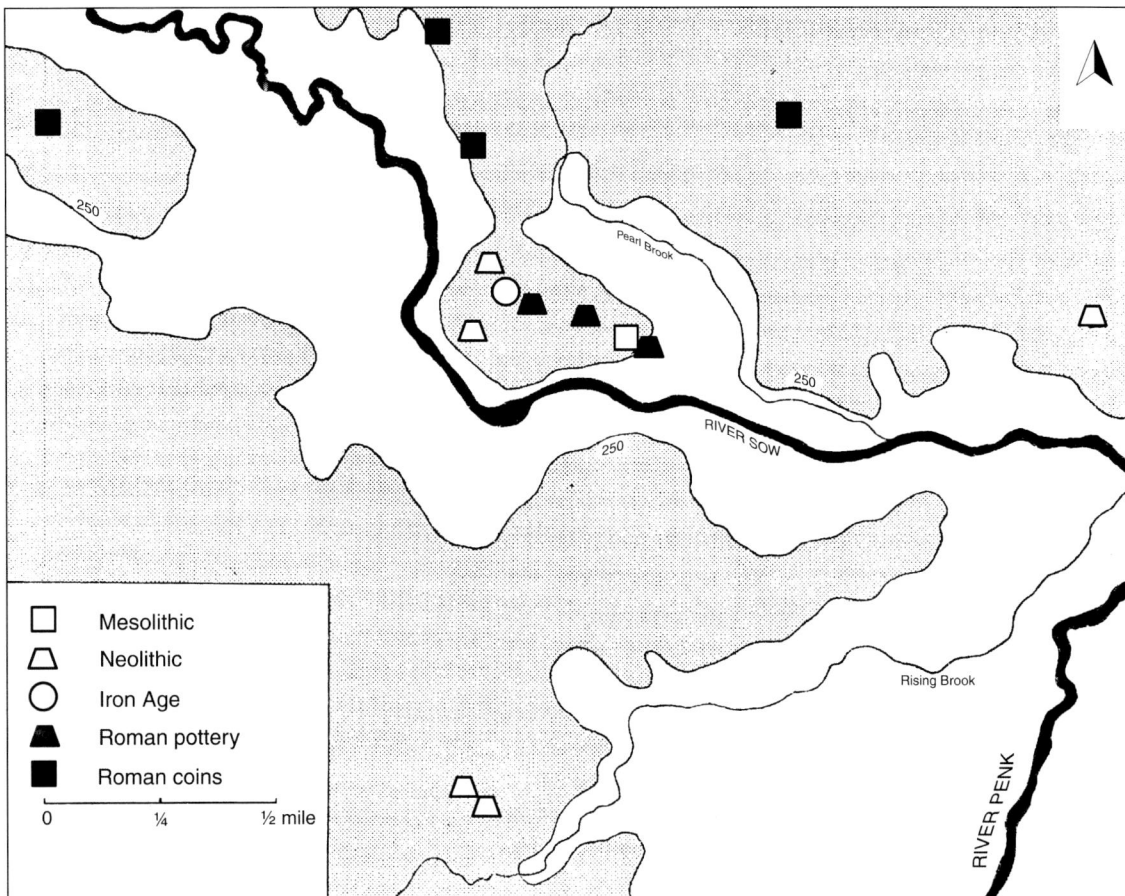

Fig. 4.1 Stafford in its prehistoric context (after Walker 1975). Some locations approximate.

seeds.[9] Some of the grains in the samples had slightly germinated, suggesting perhaps that they were harvested damp or were coming to the end of their storage life. The assemblage suggests the storage of spelt and emmer, probably still in the spikelet, with minor residuals of other crops. The crop species represented are similar to those found to the south in Warwickshire at Tiddington, a large settlement on the second terrace of the Avon,[10] and at Wasperton, a smaller settlement also on a terrace of the Avon.[11]

Roman Stafford

By the Roman period, the oak, lime and elm forests have been mainly cleared. Beech, ash and birch imply copses and hedgerows. There is cereal cultivation and open land under grass. The local pollen record is not unnaturally dominated by alder, reeds and sedges – forming the fringe of the King's Pool, which flanks

the peninsula on its north-east side and, together with the loop of the River Sow, makes it almost an island.[12] The Iron Age four-post features were sealed by two consecutive layers (2239 and 2238) together about 30 centimetres deep, but thinning out as the ground rose to the west. This well-mixed soil was probably the result of a long period of cultivation.[13] The pottery from this layer consisted of small, abraded sherds, almost all Romano-British but with some Stafford ware of the tenth century. It seems likely that a period of cultivation had continued until the construction of the Period 3 ovens and driers, and that the few sherds of Stafford ware are intrusive. The cultivation may thus be Roman, with sherds perhaps resulting from manuring, or it may have begun later, disturbing a pre-existing Roman settlement. In this case we may imagine that the land was under the plough when it was commandeered in the tenth century.

Evidence for a Roman presence of some kind on the Stafford peninsula is plentiful. There was a minimum of 27 sherds at St Mary's Grove, dated to between the second and fourth centuries, and two coins of

---

9   Weeds were present as no more than 3% of the number of items in a sample.
10 Moffett 1986c.
11 Bowker, 1982.

---

12 Environmental information from Colledge and Greig FR10.2; pollen zone S1.
13 S. Limbrey, pers. com.

Fig. 4.2 Iron Age four-post structure at St Mary's Grove, foreground (J. Cane).

Constantine I (early fourth century) from later contexts at the same site. An almost complete Severn Valley-ware jar was unearthed during construction work at 10 Market Square in 1961, at a depth of about 12 feet (3.6 metres) which implies it was in a well.[14] A minimum of 77 sherds was recovered during the excavations at Clarke Street from layers deposited at the edge of marshy ground. The stratified and residual pottery taken together comprise an assemblage dominated by Severn Valley ware with a few examples of Samian ware, mortaria, black burnished ware and grey ware (second–third centuries AD). Fabrics assigned to Severn Valley ware, black burnished ware and grey wares were also recorded in the Tipping Street excavations: a minimum

of 39 sherds was so identified, all contained residually in early medieval layers.

Overall, *Severn Valley ware* is the dominant fabric (66%) and is represented by jars (Fig. 4.4, nos. 1–8), tankards (nos 10 and 11) and possibly bowls (no. 9). Severn Valley ware was made in a fine orange fabric tempered with sand, and was produced initially in the lower Severn Valley with a distribution as far north as Chester. It was prevalent in the West Midlands from the first to the late fourth century AD. The *black burnished ware* from Stafford is BB1 and was probably supplied from Dorset. The fabric is a reduced coarse ware tempered with rounded sub-angular quartz, burnished on the exterior and the forms represented were jars (nos 12–14) and dog-dishes (Fig. 4.5, nos 15–18). This material can be dated to the second to fourth centuries AD. The five sherds of *mortaria* are of the hammer-head type produced at the Hartshill-Mancetter kilns in Warwickshire.[15] They date between the second and fourth centuries AD (Fig. 4.5, nos 19 and 20). The base and body sherd of Nene Valley ware found at St Mary's Grove probably belong to a globular colour-coated beaker decorated with white foliage patterns (Fig. 4.5, no. 21). This type of vessel was produced in the Nene Valley during the late second and throughout the third century AD.[16] The single rim sherd of *Oxford Parchment ware* (Fig. 4.5, no. 22) is in an off-white fabric with a pinkish core with a brown-painted exterior, and is probably late third- or fourth-century in date. The *Samian-ware* sherds are small and highly abraded which, together with their rarity in the Stafford assemblage, suggests that the exploitation of the peninsula happened after the apogee of the industry in Britain in the first to second centuries AD. The nature of these forms and fabrics, particularly Severn Valley ware, and their widespread occurrence on the peninsula (including at least one whole vessel) ensure that they would have been encountered by the Late Saxon potters, whose products arguably resemble them (see p. 93).

In the Iron Age, the Stafford peninsula lay in the territory of the Cornovii, seemingly beyond the frontier of coinage and decorated pottery (Fig. 4.6). There were hill forts within 25 kilometres at Wall, Bury Walls, Berth Hill and Bury Bank. Stafford lies north of the Roman line of advance from the south-east marked by

14 FR2.3, a12.

15 Hartley and Webster 1961.
16 Cf. Howe, Perrin and Mackreth 1980, no. 49.

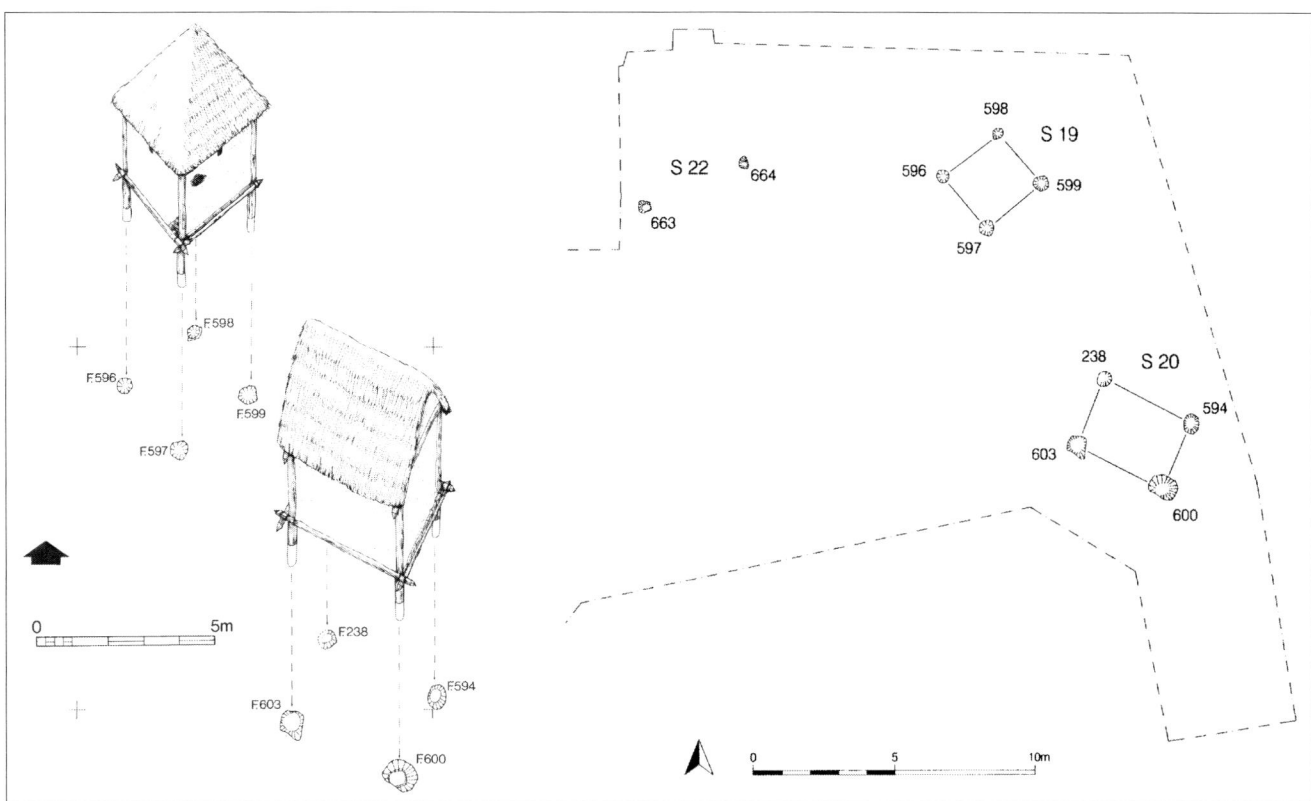

Fig. 4.3 Iron Age four-post structures: plan and reconstructions (J. Cane).

Watling Street, with its destination Wroxeter, via forts at Wall and Penkridge. This axis was effective from the first century, and the ease of Roman penetration into Cornovii territory has suggested that there was a treaty with the Romans, and a subsequent role as a buffer state against Wales.[17] During the second to fourth centuries, the Stafford peninsula might have been called to perform above the level of basic agriculture. Bowkett noticed that the roads setting out north from Penkridge (Pennocrucium) and south from Buxton (Aquae Arnemetiae; situated north of the road connecting Chesterton and Rocester) would most likely pass by the Stafford ford across the Sow and he found some endorsement for the route in a trickle of coins, which generally reflect the road system in these areas[18] (Fig. 4.7). Thus the Stafford site is a candidate for a stop-over point or way-station (*mansio*) to change horses and take refreshment, which could have developed into a Roman establishment of modest size. Some endorsement that the Stafford peninsula might have hosted a working Roman site is given by its contrast with the neighbourhood. Villas are few in this region, the majority of known midland villas being south and east of the Trent or in the lower Severn Valley. Even Roman pottery is relatively scarce

in the Cannock Chase area. Barry Cunliffe notes that Romanisation, as exemplified by towns and the villas dependent on them, did not extend much beyond the Fosse Way even after the Roman province of Britannia was three and half centuries old.[19]

The fifth to tenth centuries

The abiding archaeological theme of the Anglian or Middle Saxon period at Stafford is its persistent absence. Documentary historians have been more sanguine, promoting the likely presence of the British church, or noting the rise of Mercia in the seventh century and expressing a firm belief in a royal centre or monastery as the precursor of every Late Saxon burh.[20] We will return to these arguments in the last chapter. The purpose of this one is to marshal the archaeological evidence, equipping ourselves for the business of historical model-building by opening and testing as many archaeological doors as possible.

As we have already seen in Chapter 3, there are no finds or structures or radiocarbon dates from Stafford that can be placed with certainty in the period from the fifth to the tenth century. A sherd of pottery found

17 Cunliffe 1978, 130–1.

18 Bowkett FR11, 40, 52; for casual finds of Roman coins in the Stafford area, FR2.3.3, a13–16.

19 Cunliffe 1979, 363.

20 Blair 2005, see chapter 3, n. 23, and chapter 6.

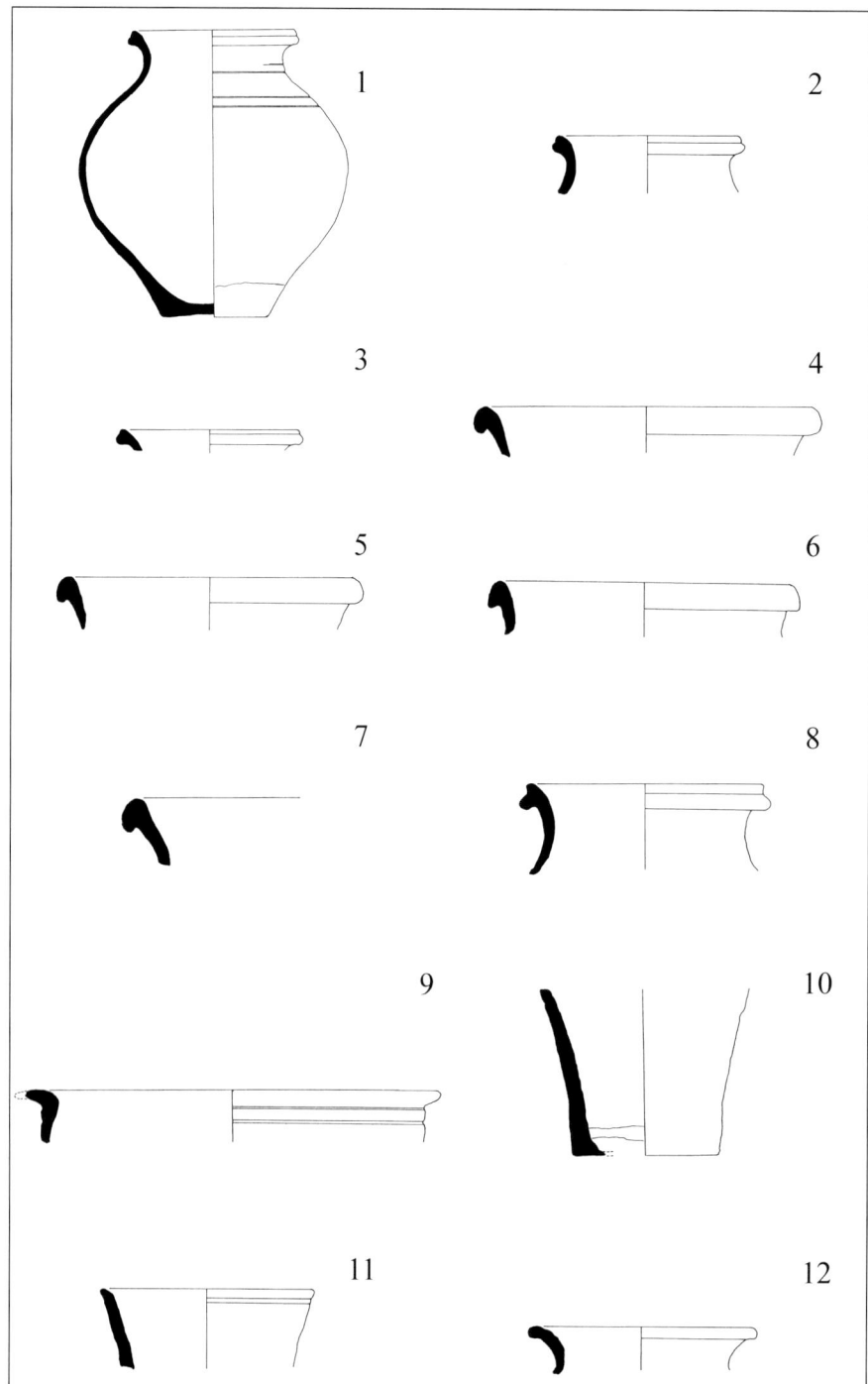

Fig. 4.4 Roman pottery from Stafford, nos 1–12 (for provenance see Digest A4).

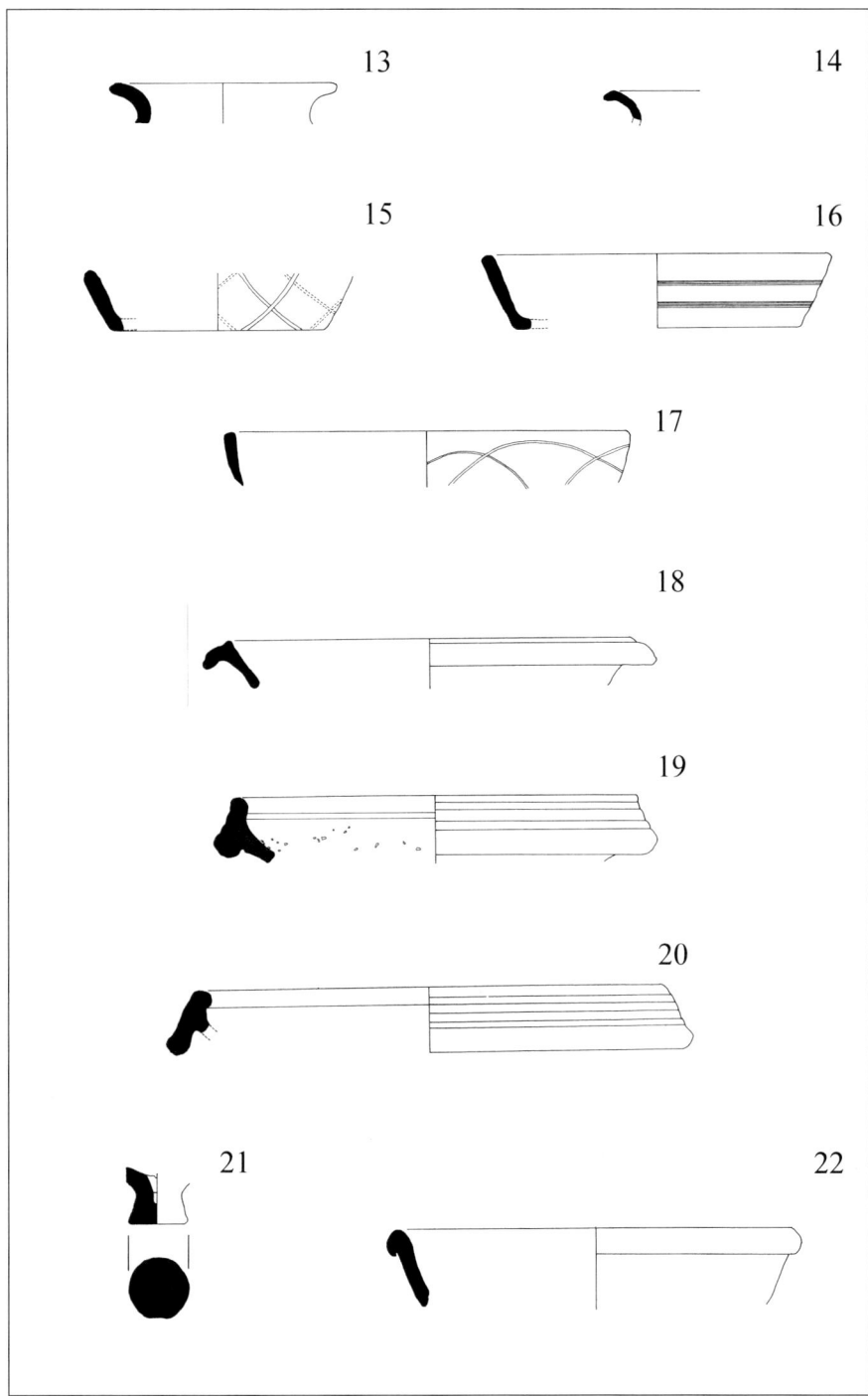

Fig. 4.5 Roman pottery from Stafford, nos 13–22 (for provenance see Digest A4).

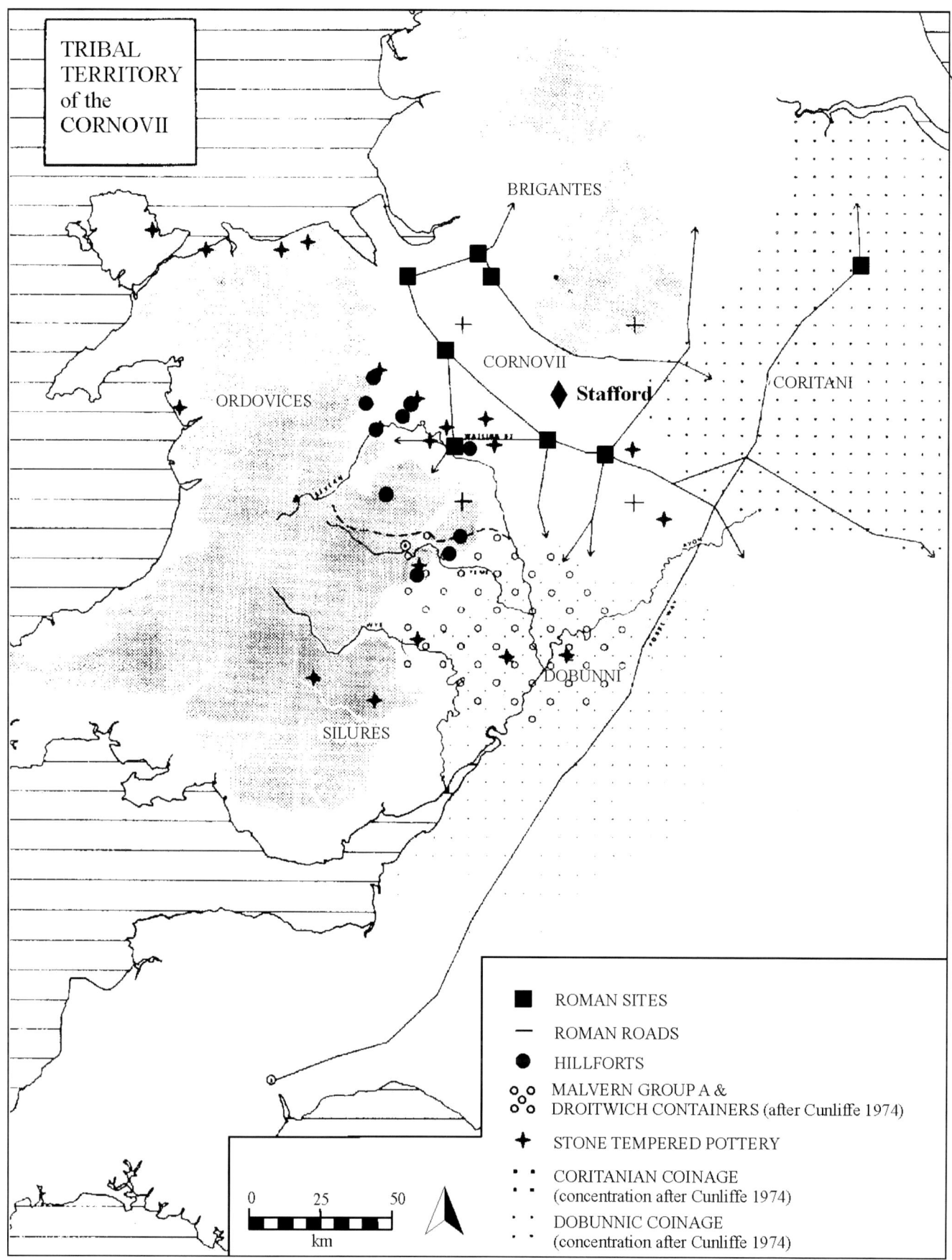

Fig. 4.6 The Iron Age and Roman hinterland (L. Bowkett).

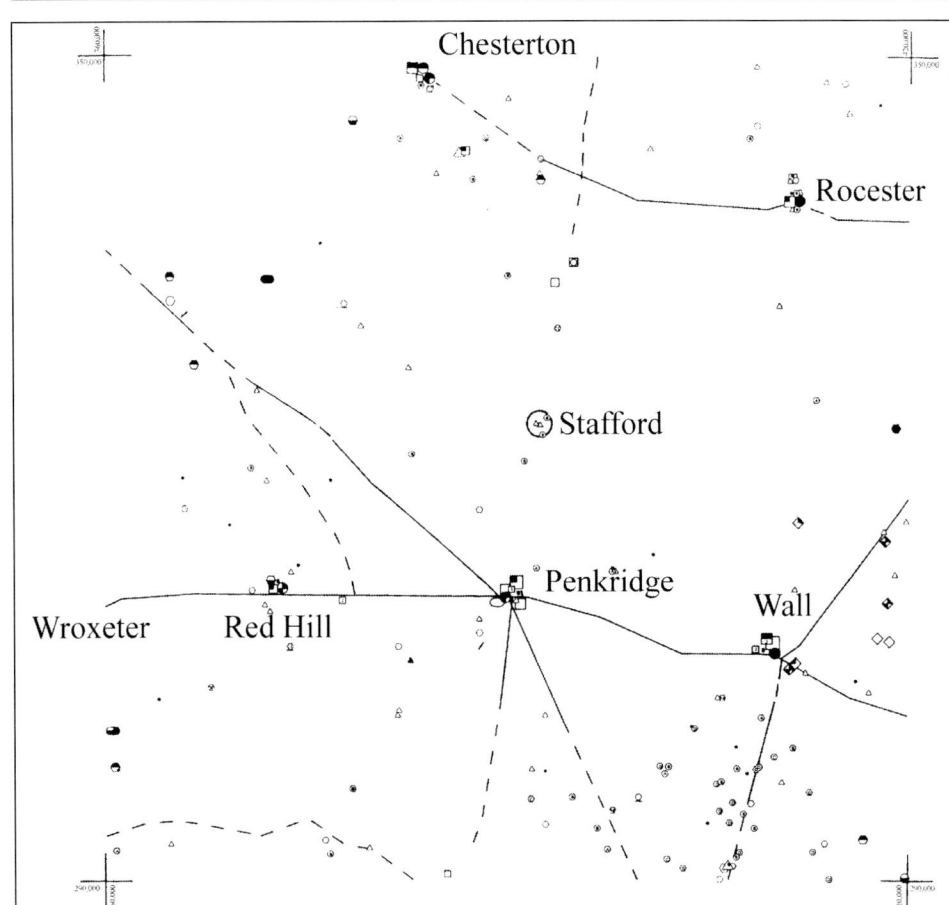

Fig. 4.7 Roman roads, known centres and casual finds in the Stafford area (for legend see FR11, figs 11–12) (L. Bowkett).

on Coton Hill in 1969 was pronounced '7th century AD' by Peter Gelling, but this has not been endorsed.[21] The pollen sequence at King's Pool shows a change in the deposit from marl to peat, suggesting that open water has become marsh with alders. There is an increase in grassland and tree cover and a reduction in crops. The date for this change lies between a fifth-century and a seventh-century radiocarbon date, a time when Colledge and Greig note 'a reduction of farming and of human influence on the landscape'.[22] At the same time the mid seventh-century date is identified by Bartley and Morgan, admittedly at the end of their pollen sequence, as the point at which they observe a peak in agriculture.[23] The experts are thus undecided, but it would be good to leave on the table that possible seventh-century peak in cereal production, with its implications of early Mercian investment.

Swings in intensity of land use are also reflected in the sequence of early deposits at the edge of the marsh at Clarke Street, although these were not precisely dated.

The earliest layer contacted was a sandy deposit (1243) with yellow flecks, probably an indication of reducing conditions caused by standing, perhaps stagnant water. These should represent pre-Roman marsh conditions. The stagnation horizon was overlaid by a layer of peaty material (1242), which became a dark silt as it rose up over the natural gravel which formed the marsh-edge (1181). This silt (1177c) contained substantial amounts of Romano-British pottery. The peat represents the stabilisation of the marsh conditions into water meadow and perhaps marks a reclamation of land under Roman administration. A subsequent layer (1222) has yellow flecking, and so represents a return to reducing conditions, with standing water. This might be seen as the result of declining land management during the post-Roman period.

These observations are consistent with a return to basic subsistence and herding between the fifth and seventh centuries. Of the seventh- to tenth-century period we currently have very little to show, apart from the one indicator mentioned above: a possible rise in cereal cultivation in the mid seventh century or thereabouts.

21 FR2.3.3, a20.
22 FR10.2.
23 Bartley and Morgan 1990, 184.

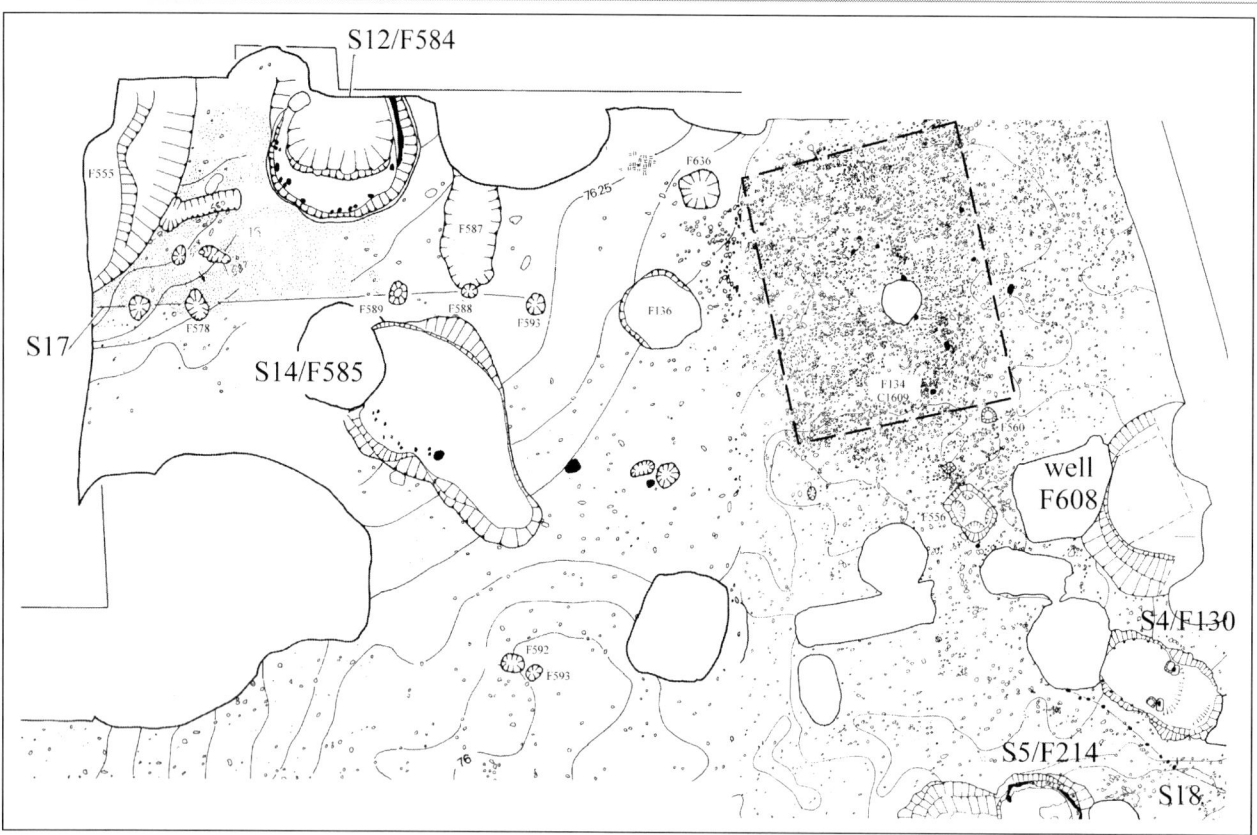

Fig. 4.8 Contour map showing pebble surface, Late Saxon platform, bread ovens and associated features (see Fig. 4.9) at St Mary's Grove (J. Cane).

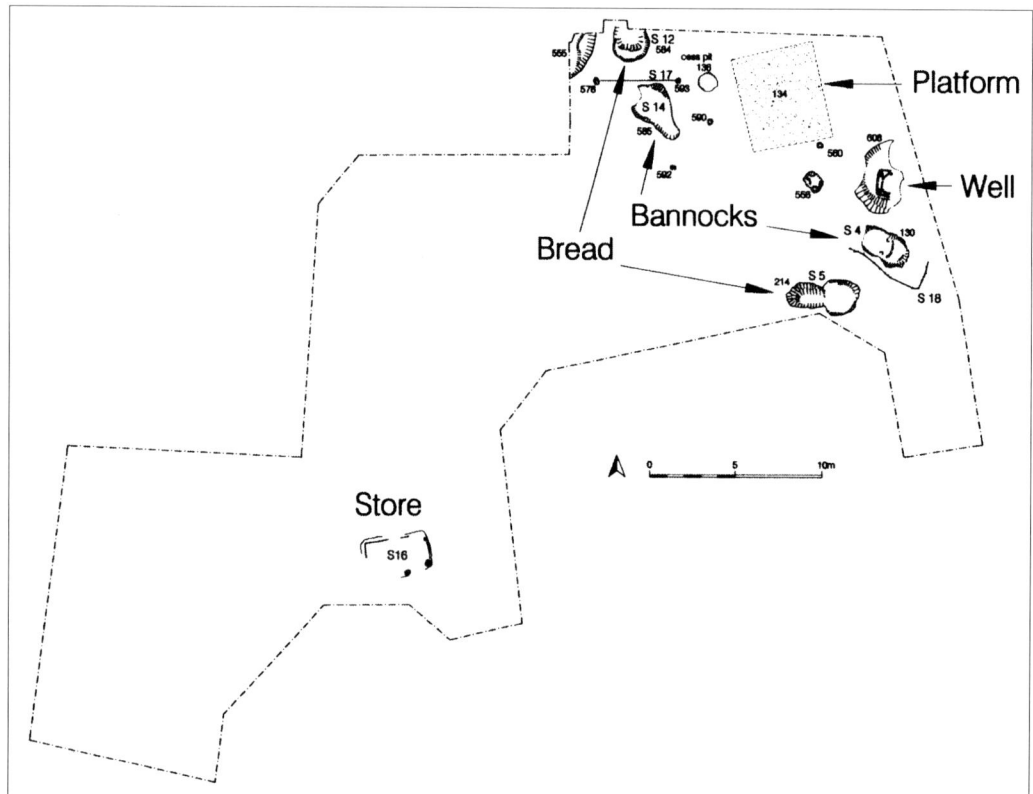

Fig. 4.9 Late Saxon grain processing at St Mary's Grove. Interpretation: platform for a building, ovens making bread from wheat and bannocks from oats, well and store.

Developments in the tenth century

Environment
The arrival of the tenth-century settlement is as clearly marked in the pollen record as it is in every other way.[24] Cereals leap to three times their previous level, which may imply either an increase in arable cultivation and harvesting near the King's Pool or an increase in the carriage of crops into Stafford – or, of course, both. Elder and holly indicate cleared ground, hedgerows or secondary growth. The start of the Cannabaceae pollen record at this point could represent either hemp (*Cannabis sativa*) or hops (*Humulus lupulus*), and its sudden appearance is thought by Colledge and Greig to be more suggestive of a crop plant than of something growing wild in damp woods and hedgerows. Evidence of grassland, perhaps pasture, is shown by pollen records of white clover (*Trifolium repens*) of which there is a more or less continuous pollen record from now on. The increased Compositae (L) pollen may also represent grassland.[25] The land appears to be thriving, with cereal cultivation and grazing.

Crop processing in central Stafford
This general environmental picture of the Stafford peninsula in Late Saxon times has been greatly enhanced by the assemblage of plant macrofossils from the St Mary's Grove excavations. These plant remains, preserved by waterlogging or burning, were found in an extensive settlement area in the north centre of the peninsula, with a pebbled platform, ovens within fenced enclosures and a timber-lined grain store (Figs 4.8, 4.9). The ovens produced copious quantities of burnt grain, as did the wooden store-house, which had itself been destroyed by fire. The development began on a soil that had been under cultivation and may have still been arable at the time of the initiation of Late Saxon exploitation (to explain the presence of intrusive sherds of Stafford ware).

The first action appeared to be the laying of the hard standing (F134), originally of closely set pebbles (Fig. 4.8). The platform was still intact on its west side, but more broken to the east. The densely set western half appeared to mark out a rectangular platform measuring 4.5 x 8.5 metres, suggestive of the floor of a building, entered from the east where the pebbles were scattered. Such a building would have had to be timber-framed and resting on the ground surface, since diligent searching produced no post-holes (S23). To the west of the platform were two ovens (S12 and S14) separated by a fence (S17) (Fig. 4.9). To the south was another pair, S4 and S5, with a fence S18 embracing S4.

Each of these pairs formed a complementary couple: one was lobed in plan, with a nearly circular wattle dome attached to a firing chamber (S12, S5; Fig. 4.10) and the other a more oval shape (S14, S4). Next to the southern pair was a well F608. Between the western pair and the platform was a latrine pit, F136. One other contemporary structure belonged to this workplace: the sunken-floored timber store S16, which was situated some 20 metres to the south-west (Fig. 4.11). Its distance away suggests that the whole workplace was much more extensive, as does the fact that burnt grain was found in later pits right up to the western and southern limits of the excavation. The plentiful presence of Stafford ware, together with radiocarbon and dendrochronology dates, places all these features in the tenth to eleventh centuries (see Chapter 3, p. 31).

Closer examination shows us something of the design and operation of this industrial site. The topography took the form of a re-entrant or shallow coombe leading from the north-east. The U-shaped terminus at the south-west rose to about 1 metre above the coombe floor, so that it suggested a hollow way leading from the neck of the peninsula that had here reached its destination. On the flat base of the combe stood the pebble platform (F134), which included a thin scatter of Stafford ware, decayed bone and iron slag. The slag derived from smithing but there was no hammerscale, and its presence can probably be explained as hard core. Smithing slag was also spread over the west of the peninsula (see Bath Street below), suggesting the presence of some iron-working before the grain processing was established.

The principal features of the workplace
On the shoulders of the combe on each side was a pair of ovens, with associated stake- and post-holes. Each pair consisted of two kinds of oven, separated in each case by a fence. The *lobed ovens* (Fig. 4.10) were distinguished by having a nearly circular wattle and clay chamber, containing an internal flat clay shelf, crescentic in plan. The detail provided by S12 showed that there was at least one large post setting between the stoke hole and the chamber, implying an oven door. The fire was made in the stoke hole and the embers pushed into the chamber to heat the oven behind an oven door. The chambers of the lobed baking ovens were not baked hard (as in a pottery kiln), and contained cereal grains and spikelets. Jon Cane's experimental studies showed that these structures would have functioned satisfactorily as ovens for baking bread, baking fifteen to twenty loaves at 300°C every forty-five minutes with continuous stoking.[26] The *oval ovens* had a semi-circular chamber with a wattle-work frame, and a pair of posts separating it from the fire pit. Jon Cane's experiments showed that if the above-ground wattle wall was jacketed by an earth bank, such a

---

24 Pollen Zone S3, see Chapter 3 above. The ascription to the Late Saxon period is supported by two radiocarbon dates with a calibrated range AD 860–1213.

25 College and Greig, FR10.2.

26 FR5.2; Moffett 1994, 61.

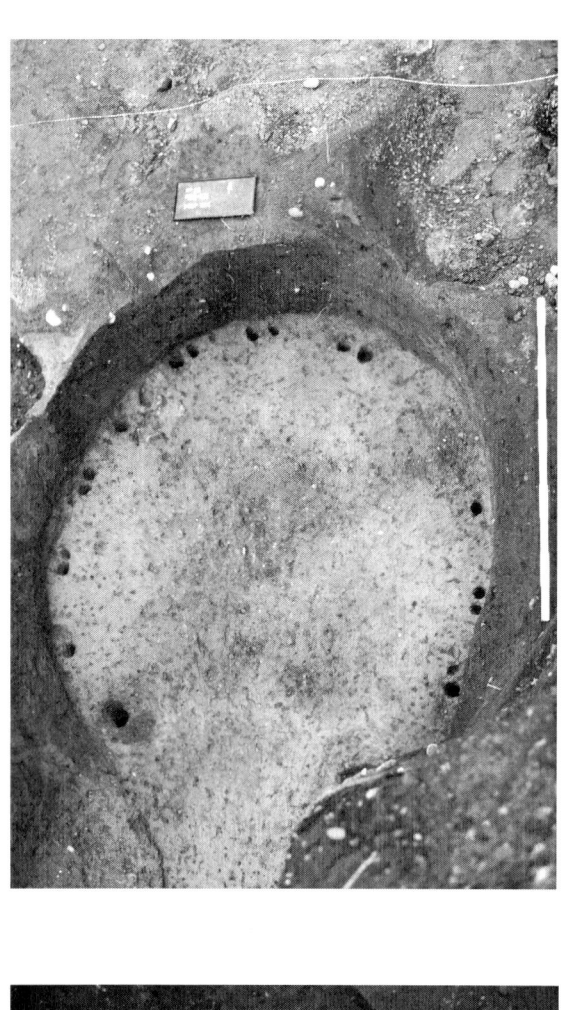

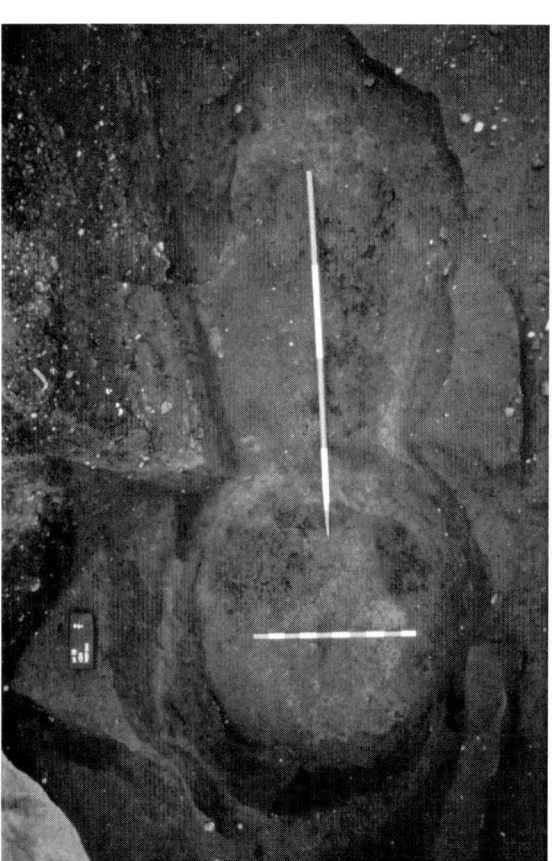
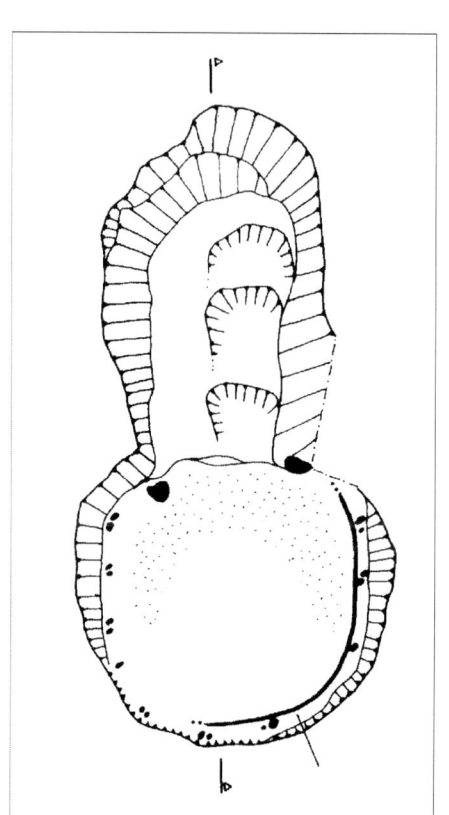

Fig. 4.10 Late Saxon lobed ovens at St Mary's Grove.

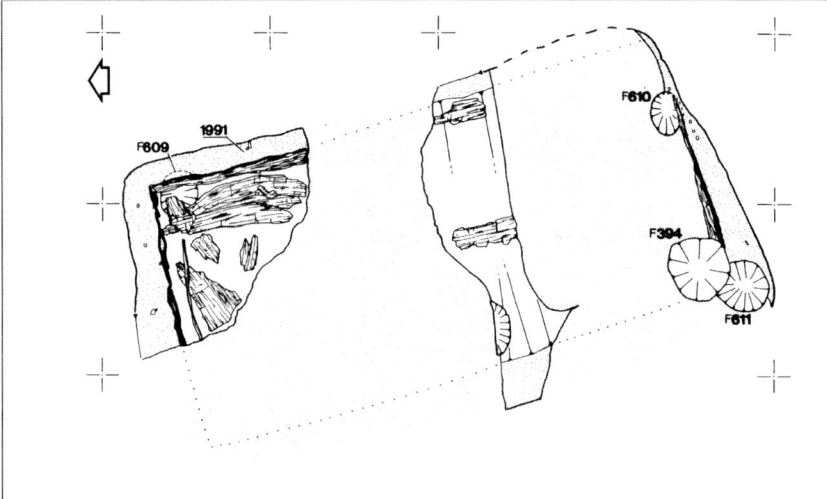

Fig. 4.11 Late Saxon timbered cellar store (S16) at St Mary's Grove, plan and photograph (J. Cane).

from these that gave a felling date in the summer of AD 1007. This implies some use of the planked well in the tenth century. F608 is recorded as cutting layer 1607, but an important aspect of this layer, recorded by the excavator, is that it was homogeneous and that it was continually being developed during the life of the ovens. Thus it is not improbable that F608 was contemporary with its neighbouring ovens. Its final fill contained a single EVE (equivalent of one vessel) of type 17A cooking pot, suggesting that it lay open until after the conquest.

The sunken floored, plank-lined pit F517 (S16; Fig. 4.11) in the central part of the site floats stratigraphically between the subsoil and the quarry pits F426 etc. of Period 4 (see Fig. 3.12). The pit was lined with oak planks which had extra peg holes, suggesting that the planks had been recycled from elsewhere. The plank frame was supported by at least two sturdy posts at the corners (F609, F611). The planks and posts had been carbonised in situ by a fire. Planks lying at the base of the building were collapsed from the sides: there was no sign of a floor-lining. Evidence from later phases implied that the features in this area had been truncated by up to 0.3 metres by later cultivation. This would mean that S16 could have been about 0.6 metres deep when built. Burnt grains were found in the pit, and were especially well sorted (see below). There were also traces of cloth, a shrub implying building materials or bedding and a flax seed. The least complicated interpretation is that a secure, sunken-floored, plank-lined cellar had been burnt down, at which point it had contained cleaned wheat, rye and oats, possibly in sacks.

The plant assemblage
Understanding the purpose and function of this workplace owes much to Lisa Moffett's study of the burnt grain in the ovens and waterlogged plant remains in the well.[28] The oven assemblage as a whole was dominated by three cereals: rye, oats and wheat, with some barley and plants associated with cereal cultivation and grassland.[29]

structure could have functioned as a grain dryer, drying batches of 15 kilograms of damp grain on a hurdle to acceptable humidity (10%) in an hour. The post and wattles were unaffected by the fire.[27] Alternative reasons for the differences between the two types of oven will be discussed presently.

The features assigned to the Late Saxon period (Period 3) were in general those sealed by the layer 1607, but two exceptions to this rule have been admitted: Well F608 and plank-lined cellar F517.

Well F608 was defined in the eastern edge of the site (Fig. 4.12). The original construction had had a plank lining supported by four sturdy posts. Following the decay of the lower planks this had been repaired with a ring of close-set timber posts, and it was a sample taken

---

27 FR5.2; Moffett 1994, 61.

28 FR10.1.

29 Weeds: cornflower (*Centaurea cyanus*), corncockle (*Agrostemma githago*), darnel (*Lolium temulentum*), stinking mayweed (*Anthemis cotula*) and ryebrome or chess (*Bromus secalinus*);

Fig. 4.12 Late Saxon well at St Mary's Grove (F608) (J. Cane).

Grains emanating from the Period 3 industry were also recovered residually in large quantities from features of Period 4 (F426, F435). These showed again that wheat, oats and rye were all received in quantity with barley less in evidence. The massive grain deposits in the later quarry pits suggested the fired and ejected contents of barns that had stored uncleaned rye and bread wheat. These secondary deposits imply that the grain processing area continued at least 10 metres to the south-west.

The sunken floored-building (S16) might be an appropriate place to start our inspection of the crops, since its content was nearly clean grain with few chaff or weed contaminants. The main plants present are bread wheat, rye and oats with very little barley. Most of the weeds in the samples probably came in with the crops. A fragment of charred cloth, a flax seed and a fragment of plum stone suggest a minor element of possible household debris. The plant material is consistent with

the use of this building for storage, containing cereals ready to be prepared for consumption or grinding, and should be representative of the principal commodities being processed.

Assemblages in the ovens
Determining the use of the ovens depends partly on what was found in them and partly on what it was doing there. The ovens contained grains and chaff of rye, wheat and oats and weeds. The type of cereal and the relative proportions of chaff, weeds and grains reinforce the division between the two types of oven already noted. *Lobed ovens* S12 and S5 contain more than 50% chaff fragments, though still with large amounts of grain, and relatively low percentages of weeds. The cereals represented by the grains were mixed. In S5, which contained a relatively small amount of material, grains were more abundant than chaff remains and bread wheat was the most common cereal, at 48% of identifiable grains. *Oval ovens* S4 and S14 are dominated by grains, though S14 also has a high percentage of weed seeds. The cereal grains represented were mainly oats (at around 87%). Oat grains are abundant at Stafford in both the Saxon and the medieval periods. Oats were often grown for fodder, but the consistent association of oats with the other cereals at Stafford suggests that at least part of the oat crop was probably intended for human consumption.

The chief cereal present in the chaff is rye – rye grains are relatively abundant but the main component of the assemblages is rye rachises. As a winter-sown cereal, tolerant of climatic extremes, rye may well have provided an important food source, and was well represented at the Anglo-Saxon village at West Stow, possibly because of its relatively greater suitability for the local sandy Breckland soils. It seems probable that rye would have been a suitable and successful crop on the local soils of the gravel terraces.[30] However, Lisa Moffett notes that the proportion of rachises to grains is still considerably greater than would be expected for whole unthreshed ears, and she suggests that this implies the primary use of rye chaff for fuel. The main concentration of charred material from S5/581 came from the flue/stoke hole area of the oven (2242) where it was considered to be in situ, whereas the main concentration from S12/584 was in situ on the chamber floor (2247). Experiments suggest that chaff is more likely to be destroyed than grains, so the original charge of chaff is likely to have been much greater, endorsing its identity as fuel. By the same token, the grains that are found may also constitute the better surviving component of a fuel. This would account for the mixture of cereals present. Thus the identified burnt grain need not be directly diagnostic of the use of the

---

grassland clover (*Trifolium spp.*), the tares (*Vicia hirsuta* and *V. tetrasperma*), vetch (*Vicia sativa*), crested dog's tail (*Cynosurus cristatus*) and timothy (*Phleum pratense*).

30 Moffett in FR10.1, citing Murphy 1983a and 1985. Tusser says that 'gravell and sand is for rie and not wheat' (Tusser 1580).

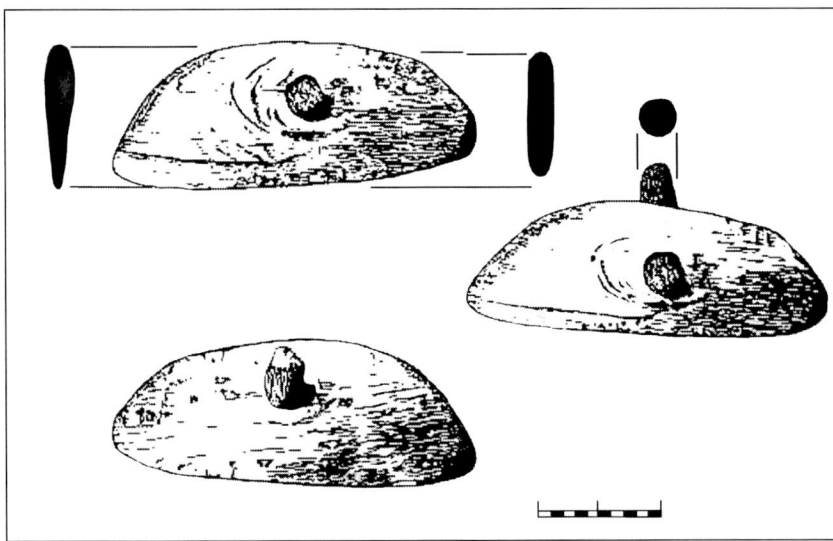

Fig. 4.13 Late Saxon cereal rake from St Mary's Grove (F404); width of blade 20cm (for provenance see FR8.3.1)

oven. It may have come in with the fuel; it may have remained from drying, it may have been used to prevent loaves sticking to the baking surface, and last (and least) it may indicate what was actually baked in the oven.[31]

Cereal processing

Most cereal crops of wheat, barley, oats and rye are processed by similar methods.[32] The cut and stacked sheaves are threshed by beating or trampling, loosening the grains and chaff. Grains and chaff are separated by winnowing (throwing them up in the air) which blows the lighter chaff to one side and leaves behind the grains and heavy chaff and weed components such as straw nodes, some rachises, and all but the lightest weed seeds. The grain component is sieved once or more and finally hand sorted. All the by-products can be used as animal feed, fuel or temper for pottery.

Wheat grain is ground into flour, mixed with water, kneaded into dough and baked in an oven to produce a loaf of bread. The process needs a quern or mill to produce the flour. Oats may follow a slightly different trajectory. The oat grain may be burnt off its stalks, without the need for threshing (*graddanning*). The oat grains would be ground into oatmeal using a quern or flaked with a wooden mallet and mortar. Mixed with water the oatmeal is rapidly baked to make an oatcake or *bannock*. Examples of oat bannocks recorded in twentieth-century Scotland were 2–3 centimetres thick and up to a metre in diameter and could be baked over or next to an open fire. Oats were also eaten mixed with hot water, as *brose*, or boiled and mixed with ale, *pottage*, or the hull boiled into a paste, *sowens*.[33]

Use of ovens

There are a number of well-documented uses of ovens in connection with cereal-processing. *Drying* ovens are used to dry a crop that comes in wet and to inhibit fungus. The capacity of the Stafford ovens appears to be roughly similar to a Romano-British 'corn-drier' and would perhaps be impractical for drying a whole harvest's worth of grain. Drying ovens may be used to dry oats as fodder for horses. *Parching* grain hardens it for better milling.[34] Damp grain is inefficient to mill as it tends to crush and smear between the millstones rather than grind to a flour. Experiments using a restored Romano-British rotary quern found that a pound of parched grain ground to a flour in a few minutes, and needed to be put through the quern twice, but a pound of unparched grain took three quarters of an hour and needed to be put through the quern eight or nine times.[35] Partially germinated grain may be roasted as part of the *malting* process. But in this case the charred grain showed little sign of germination. The use of ovens for *baking* is naturally a likely circumstance, reinforced in this case by the shelf seen in S12. The lobed ovens have a dome-like structure, suggesting a long bake with a slow all round heat, while the oval ovens, with their more open U-shaped chamber, suggest a quicker hot bake, as with a flat bread. The find of a wooden rake (Fig. 4.13) adds to the impression of a reusable oven like a pizzeria.[36]

The production system

The provision of two pairs of ovens either side of a platform of hard standing, and the quantity of grain redeposited in later features suggests grain-processing

31 FR10.1; Moffett 1994, 57.

32 This paragraph after Moffett, FR10.1, citing Hillman 1981, Jones 1984. See also Greig 1982b.

33 Fenton 1999, 98–9, 104–6, 168, 176.

34 Fenton 1978; Evans 1957.

35 Curwen in Curwen and Hatt 1953, 125-6.

36 From 2141, in the Period 4 cess pit, F404, situated between the oven pairs.

on an industrial scale. The oven pairs were originally distinguished by the excavator as being one for baking (lobed) and one for drying (oval),[37] but the juxta-positioning of a dryer and an oven is odd, since drying would normally be followed by grinding and there were no querns. Since the 'dryers' were mainly treating oats, one output from these ovens could have been some sort of oatcake (bannock), for which the oats would require flaking and mixing with water. The contrast between the 'oven' and 'dryer' drawn by the excavator might actually refer to the use for baking bread on the one hand, and making bannocks on the other.

However, the presence in later phases of large quantities of residual burnt grain shows that whole grain was being processed dried and stored; this is not a place that has to do solely with flour. If we eliminate malting, and thus beer, the most likely products of the Stafford cereal station are dried grain and a variety of provender, perhaps especially wheat loaves and oat bannocks. Grain drying alone seems an inadequate explanation in the light of the shelves in the lobed ovens, and the contemporary well. Given the sample we have, from a putatively much larger site, we must assume that it was dedicated to both the drying of grain and the baking of bread and bannocks, and these functions were grouped together because they were hot and dangerous.

Local environment

The St Mary's Grove well (F608) produced a range of wet ground plants and ruderals, with some arable weeds and cereal remains that were mainly charred. Fruitstones were present and included bullace or damson (*Prunus domestica* ssp. *insititia*), morello or sour cherry (*Prunus cf. cerasus*), and apple (*Malus* sp.), as well as a possible raspberry (*Rubus ? idaeus*) and a single sloe (*Prunus spinosa*). Many of the bullace/damson and cherry stones appear to have been gnawed by rodents, and two of the bullaces/damsons still had the fleshy mesocarp adhering and had obviously not been eaten. Dill (*Anethum graveolens*) was found in the well and a probable dill seed also came from one of the ovens (S4). Dill is a pot-herb with a long history of use. The species represented by the largest number of seeds was stinging nettle (*Urtica dioica*), which may have grown near the top of the well after it was abandoned. Stinging nettle produces prolific numbers of seeds and is often the main component in well assemblages. There was no trace of the hemp that was found in the pollen record and apparently heralded a new crop. However, it was the fibre that was used, and it would have been in the wet places (such as King's Pool), where the pollen fell, that the stems were retted so that the fibre could be obtained.[38]

The use of the workplace

The crops will probably have arrived from the north or east, since these were the routes into the centre of the peninsula over solid ground. They were threshed and winnowed in the vicinity since both grain and chaff were to be put to use. Clean grain was oven-dried, using chaff (particularly from rye) as fuel, and stored in a timber-lined shed. It was milled and ground, perhaps in a water-mill on the Sow, as in the later Middle Ages. The meal was then carried back to the delivery point where it was mixed with water from the well and baked into bread, bannocks or oatcakes, or fed to horses. The large amount and great variety of Stafford ware, predominately jars but including bowls and thick-stemmed lamps (could these have been used for grinding?), implies a connection with grain: carrying it, measuring it, crushing it, mixing it with water – and eating porridge, pottage, sowens and brose.

The varied production implied by these findings implied in turn a varied clientele: upper classes (wheat), lower classes (oats) and horses (straw, chaff, rye). This at least would be the spectrum deduced by analogy with later Scotland.[39] The daily allowance for servants in the Carse of Gowrie in 1794 was 1 pint of milk and 36 ounces of oatmeal – one large bannock. The purpose, or at least one purpose, of the burh on this reasoning was to turn tribute from estates into rations for troops. In this case the pebbled yard might have provided hard standing, or a barn, for outgoing rather than incoming deliveries. The output would have been about 200 bannocks a day – enough to feed an army.[40]

The large amounts of burnt grain turned over in all parts of the site in the Norman phase could mean that the workplace was surrounded by large hills of waste products, accidently burnt in ovens or perhaps infested by rats. A more violent and sudden ending might seem equally probable – the firing of a grain supply depot during a war.

Defence and smithing

The Bath Street site to the west of St Mary's Grove was a relatively small and shallow site, consisting of pits and post-holes cut into natural sand. It was argued in Chapter 3 (p. 39) that it was occupied during the Late Saxon period and indeed this is probable seeing that it is the highest point on the peninsula. Apart from Stafford ware, the main component of the assemblage was slag from smithing.

The earliest structural elements, all attributable to the Late Saxon period, but no earlier, consist of a linear slope running north-south, parallel with the later Earl Street, with a row or two rows of post pits on its inner (eastern) flank (S1 on Fig. 4.14). The slope running downwards

---

37 FR5.2.
38 FR10.2; Murphy 1983b for fruitstones.

39 Fenton 1999, 168–70.
40 Cf. Moffett 1994, 62.

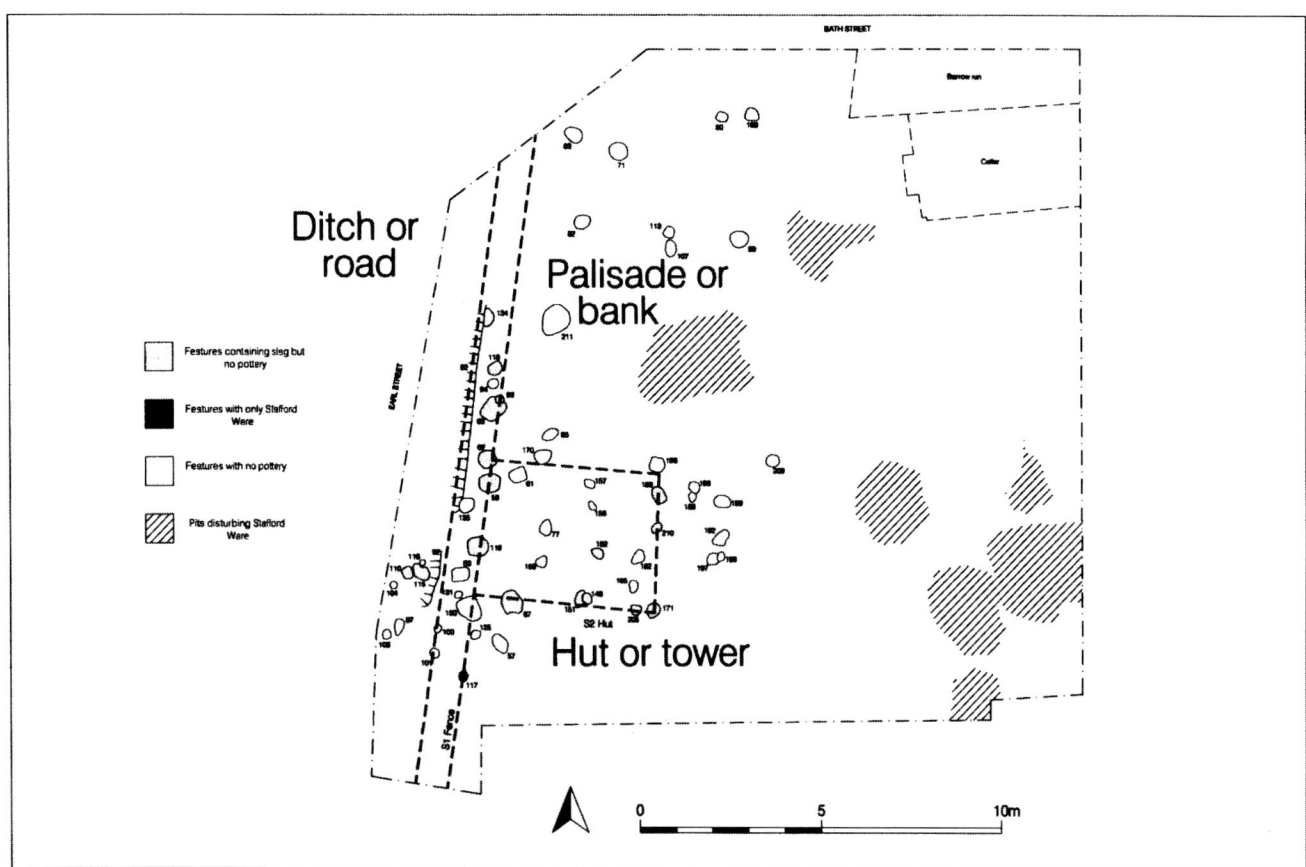

Fig. 4.14 Locations of Late Saxon boundary ditch, palisade and possible tower at Bath Street.

to the west is assumed to represent the shoulder of a ditch now under the road. Alternatively it is itself the hollow formed in the sand by an earlier road or track, contemporary with a palisade. At a certain point the family of eligible post-holes broadens into a rectangular structure (S2 on Fig. 4.14). This was designated as a shed in one of its interpretations and a stable in another, led on by the presence of a horseshoe amongst the smithing debris.[41]

If the smithing phase, and even its association with horses, is accepted, it preceded some of the principal post-holes, as happened in the platform at St Mary's Grove – and thus could represent the debris from a camp site. The structures therefore might be a secondary development and, if all of a piece, suggest a defensive work with tower. The elements of such a work are certainly equivocal, as we have seen (p. 39), but a ditch, road, timber palisade, bank and timber tower are economical explanations of its linearity. We will return to the possible significance of this defensive work when considering the overall plan of Late Saxon Stafford (below).

41 FR5.3, FR8.6, Fe 64–7.

St Bertelin's church

We remain in the central area to consider the implications of the sequence at St Bertelin's that was worked out in Chapter 3 (p. 26). The minimum early presence consists of a timber structure aligned east-west, contrived from a group of eight post-holes of different sizes and a narrow beam slot (Fig. 4.15, F17–F19). This structure was erected on a cultivated soil, resembling that at St Mary's Grove. While its assembly of features is not very coherent, we must accept that the area was badly turned over by later graves, and, given the early stratigraphic position of the majority of the post-holes, a timber predecessor of the stone church is not improbable. Roughly in the centre of the building, as we have it, is the pit (F13) containing a thick deposit of carbonised wood, seen by the excavator as a cross, and in the present analysis as a tree-trunk coffin. Its location with respect to the building is consistent with a special role of some kind, of which a dedicatory burial seems the least unlikely. Of the three objects found that could date to the Late Saxon period (Fig. 4.16), the farthing and the stocking hook are not especially clerical, but the

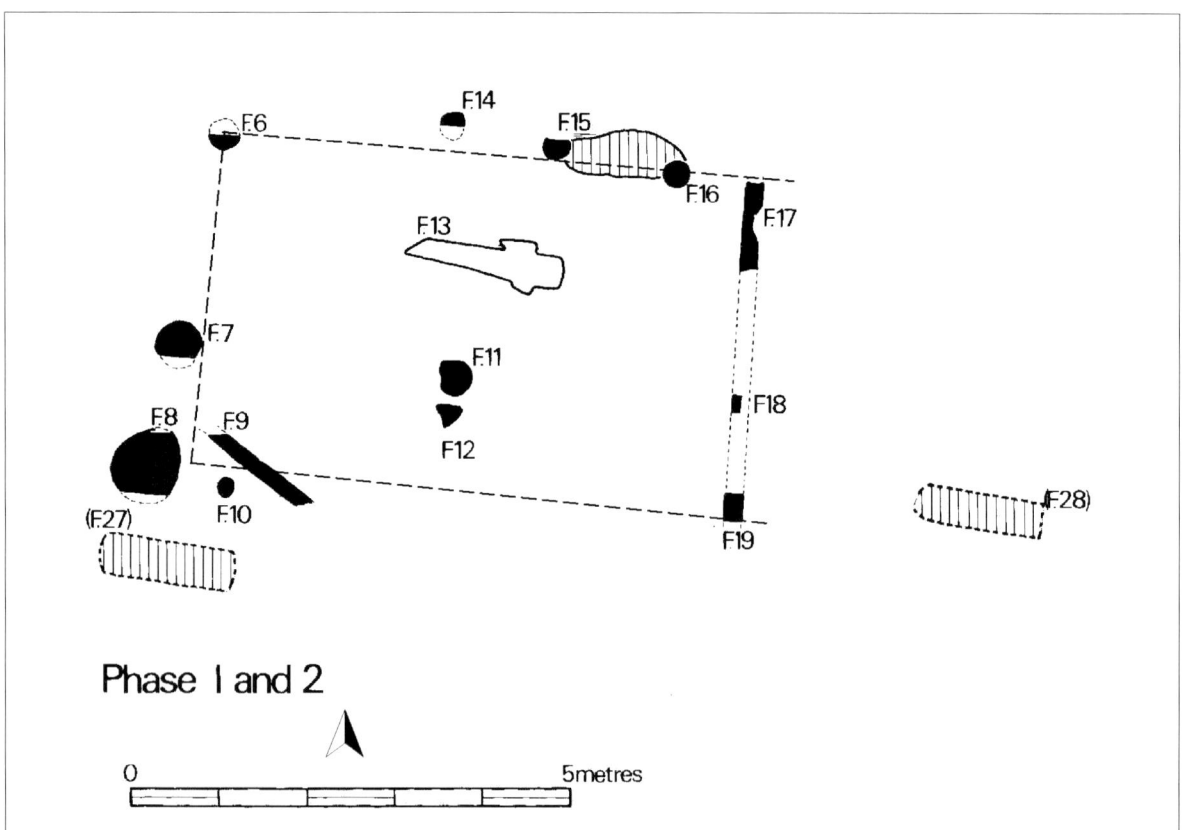

Fig. 4.15 St Bertelin's Church. Features likely to be Late Saxon.

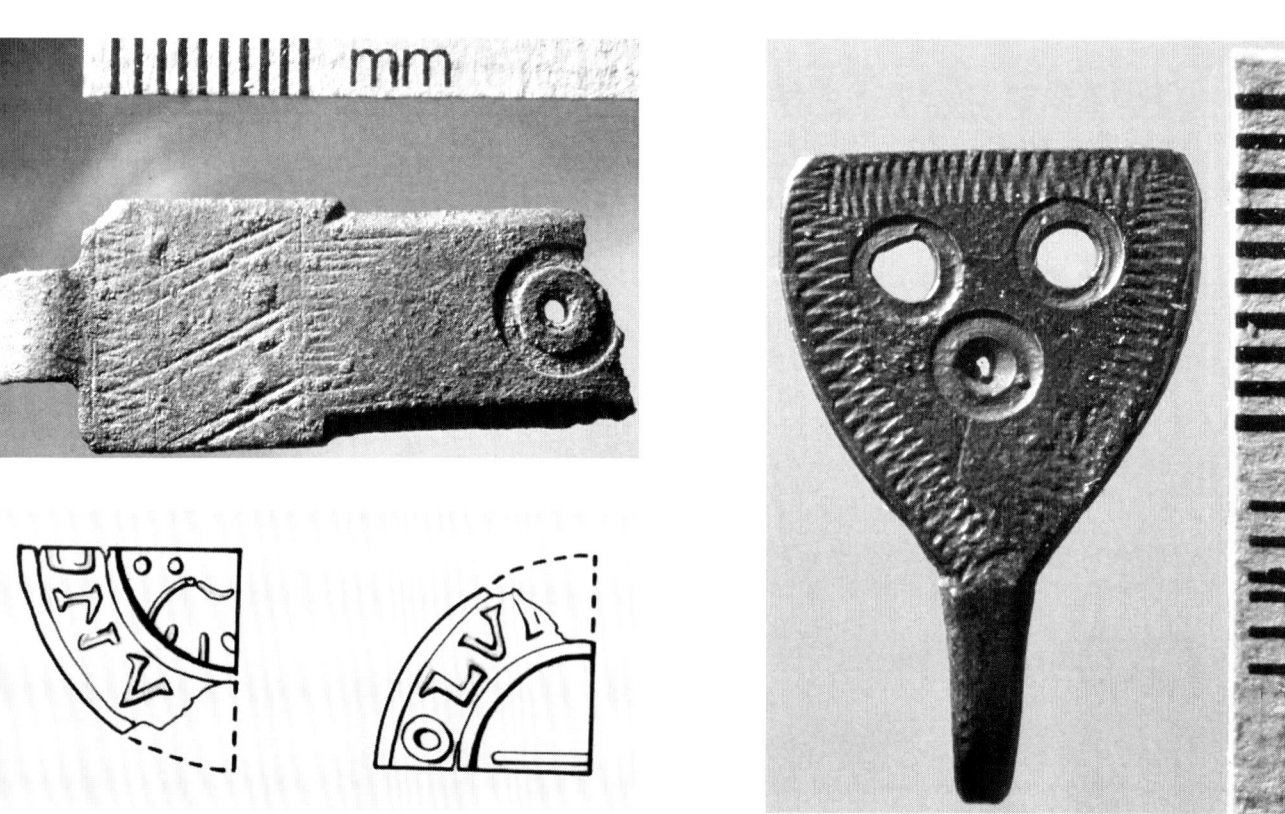

Fig. 4.16 Late Saxon finds from St Bertelin's: book clasp, stocking hook and farthing.

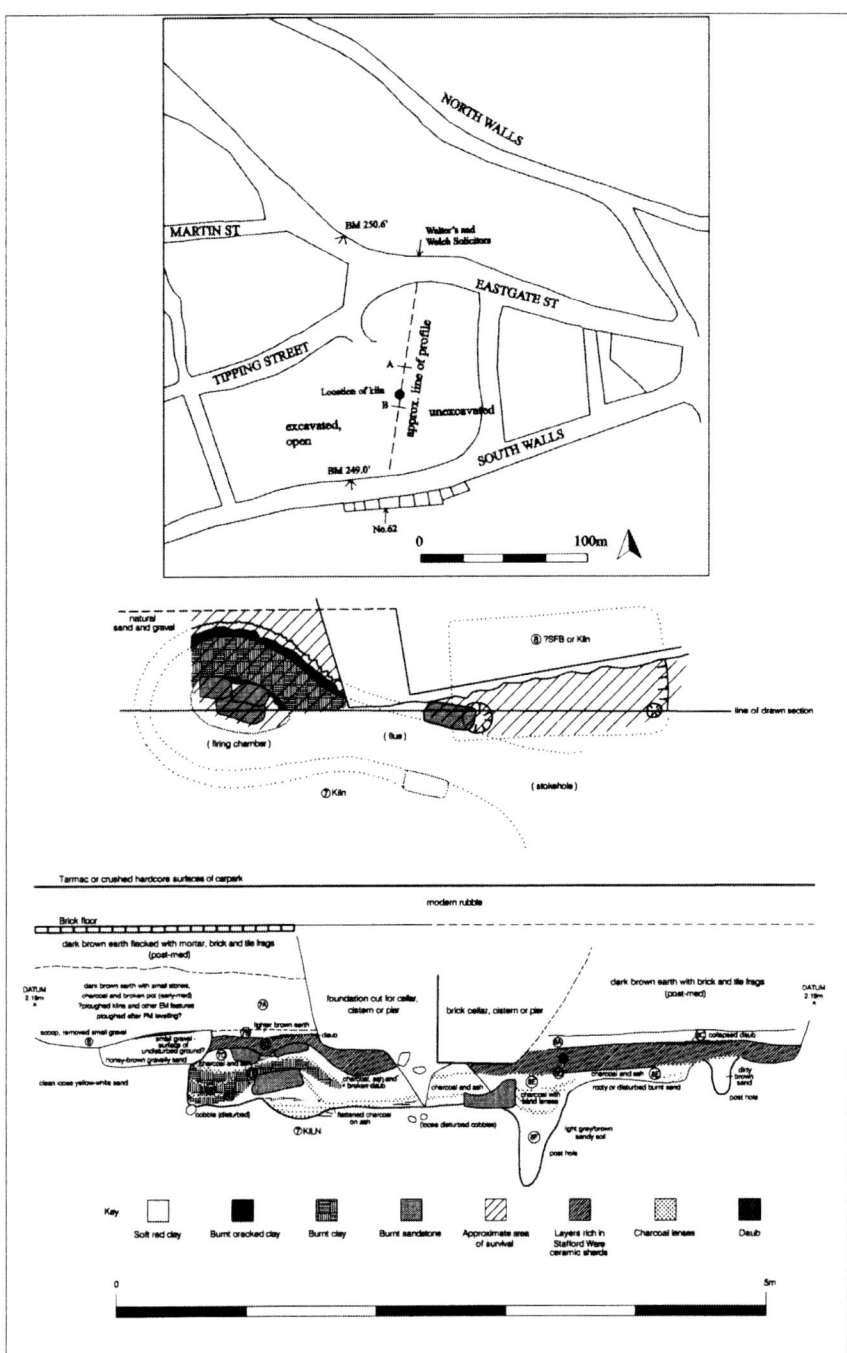

Fig. 4.17 Stafford-ware pottery kiln at Tipping Street (south), 1977: location, plan and section (FR2.3, fig. 2.8).

small bronze ornamented plaque may be identified as a book clasp.[42] There were at least two other burials likely to belong to this phase (F27 and F28). Both contained wooden coffins and F27 was also a 'head support burial' with stones each side of the head. Elsewhere this kind of burial rite has been seen as indicating a British context,[43] while the tree-trunk burial is known from sites in East Anglia.[44]

The east wall is suggestive of an internal division, and the structure must surely be incomplete and might be expected to continue to the east. It would be reasonable to surmise that further and more complex ecclesiastical developments would lie further east still, where St Mary's church now stands. But of this we currently know nothing.

There is no archaeological justification for placing any of these features, the earliest found on the site, into a period before the tenth century, and there is some support for this late date from the dedication to Bertelin, which refers generally to holy men of

---

42 Cf. Cramp 2005, II, 248.

43 See discussions in Carver 2008, 81 and Carver et al. 2009, 131.

44 Carver 2005, 292–8.

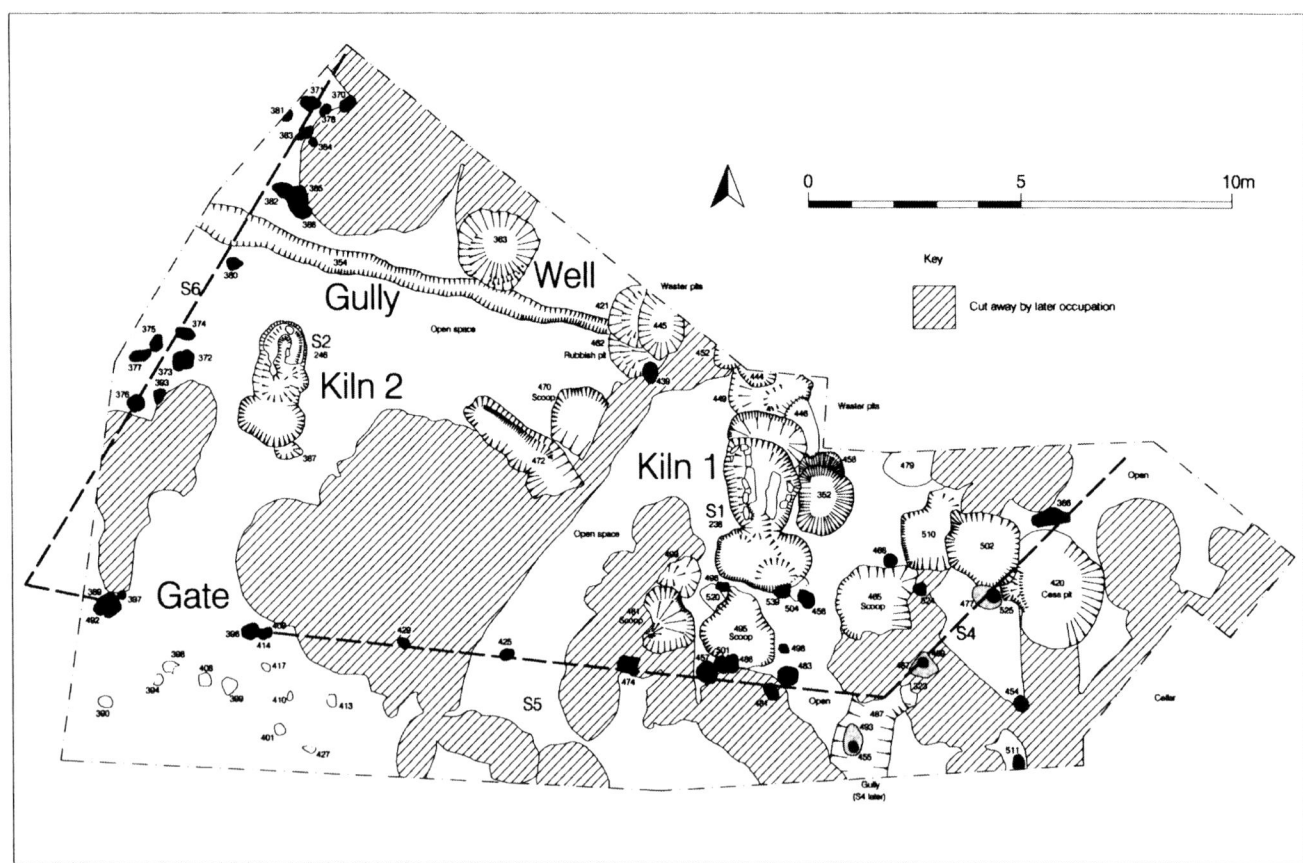

Fig. 4.18 The potter's workshop at Tipping Street (north).

the eighth century or later.[45] The original dedication appears to have been to Beorhthelm, a Mercian ancestor, a choice likely to be due to Æthelflæd, who had a fondness for sanctified Anglo-Saxons.[46] She also commemorated Beorhthelm at Runcorn, Alkmund at Derby, Shrewsbury and Whitchurch, and Werburgh at Derby and Chester. She transferred some relics of King Oswald of Northumbria to Gloucester in 909 and founded a chapel dedicated to him at Chester.[47] St Bertelin later accrued a hagiographic dossier compounded of persons with similar names, legendary or otherwise. *Beccelinus* was an associate of Guthlac, the seventh-century hermit remembered by Felix in a hagiography written between 730 and 740 and dedicated to Æthlwulf, king of the Angles who died c. 749. According to a fourteenth-century life written by Ingulf, *Bettelinus* was a hermit at Crowland and died there. In a list of tombs of the saints, Hugh Candidus

(died c. 1175) mentions a *sanctus Bethelmus martyr* in *Stetford*. Writing in 1516, Wynkyn de Worde constructs a life of St Bertelin from various unknown sources, which may have included these. *Bertelinus*, the son of the king of the people of Stafford, turns his back on his sinful father and emigrates to Ireland where he abducts and impregnates the daughter of an Irish king. He returns to England where his wife and child are unfortunately eaten by wolves. He retreats to the solitary life, becoming an associate of St Guthlac, and eventually asking his royal father to grant him a place of hermitage, whereupon he is given the island of Betheney, otherwise the site of Stafford. It is not impossible that Wynkyn obtained and confected elements of his story from the clergy of St Bertelin's who themselves relied on legend to supply them. This presumably happened long after the original Beorhthelm, and the dedicatory coffin buried in the time of Æthelflæd, had been forgotten. The current debate on the likelihood of a pre-tenth-century religious centre will be visited in Chapter 6.

The Stafford-ware potteries

St Mary's Grove, Bath Street and St Bertelin's have given us three glimpses of what was going on in the centre of

---

45 Edwards 2004 presses the idea of an Anglian monastery for Stafford on the basis of the importance of St Mary's in later medieval documentation; see Chapter 6 below for discussion on Stafford's elusive pre-Æthflæden history.

46 Thacker 1985; Walker 2000, 39: a 'late and very confused tradition records the commemoration by c.900 of a St Beorhthelm at Stafford and subsequently at Runcorn'.

47 Butler 1986, 47; see Chapter 6 below for discussion.

Fig. 4.19 Stafford-ware kilns at Tipping Street (north): (left) S1 (F238); (above) S2 (F246).

the peninsula, west of the axial routeway. It is now time to look at three more, this time on the east side. Here is where the evidence for potting was concentrated, each side of Tipping Street, at Salter Street and at Clarke Street, where wasters and animal bone from centralised processing were dumped.

The first Stafford-ware kiln was found south of Tipping Street (Fig. 4.17) and exposed in section during a one-day rescue expedition. It had an hour-glass shape in plan, one chamber for pots and the other for stoking. It seemed to have experienced a number of firings as indicated by the layers of burnt clay on its floor. The area around the kiln was littered with pottery and pottery wasters of which 1,200 were recovered at the time. Charcoal from the final firing gave a radiocarbon date between AD 670 and 1020.[48]

By contrast, the opportunity five years later at Tipping Street (north) presented us with a whole potters' workshop (Fig. 4.18). Apart from a small group of flints in the south part of the site, there was no evidence for any activity before the Late Saxon period. And apart from one small pit (F387) cut by kiln S2, but also containing Stafford ware, there is little convincing evidence for any pre-industrial occupation here.[49]

The site was laid out in a logical way with little encroachment or overlap. A row of posts suggests a fence (S5) running east-west on the south side, parallel to the course of Tipping Street, a version of which is likely to have come into existence at this time, leading from the centre of the peninsula to the causeway over the marsh to the east. At the south-west end, two post clusters 3.5 metres apart on this line (F389, F396) look like a gateway into the potter's enclosure. Outside (south of) this gate are some post-sockets (F399, F427 etc.) which may have belonged to a hut of some kind, but they coincide with the later posts of the medieval structure S7 too well, and the area was devoid of Stafford ware – so these probably belong to Period 2. On the east side was a row of posts running south-west to north-east (S4; F455, F467, F477 and F366). They may have been associated with contemporary posts immediately to the west (i.e. near Kiln S1). Since there was little suggestion of Late Saxon activity in Int 33, these factors suggest that S4 was a fence marking the eastern edge of the workplace. On

---

48 FR2.3.3, ST17; Digest A2.

49 The three radiocarbon dates are (when calibrated) perfectly compatible with an occupation after AD 913 and before

AD 1066, see Chapter 3, p. 45 above. The excavators were misled, perhaps by uncalibrated dates, into thinking that there were ninth-century features at Tipping Street (FR6.3). They also assumed that features with no wasters must belong to an earlier phase than the kilns. But the wasters are clearly disposed of in dedicated pits in a particular location. The distinction (waster/no waster) is more likely to be functional than chronological.

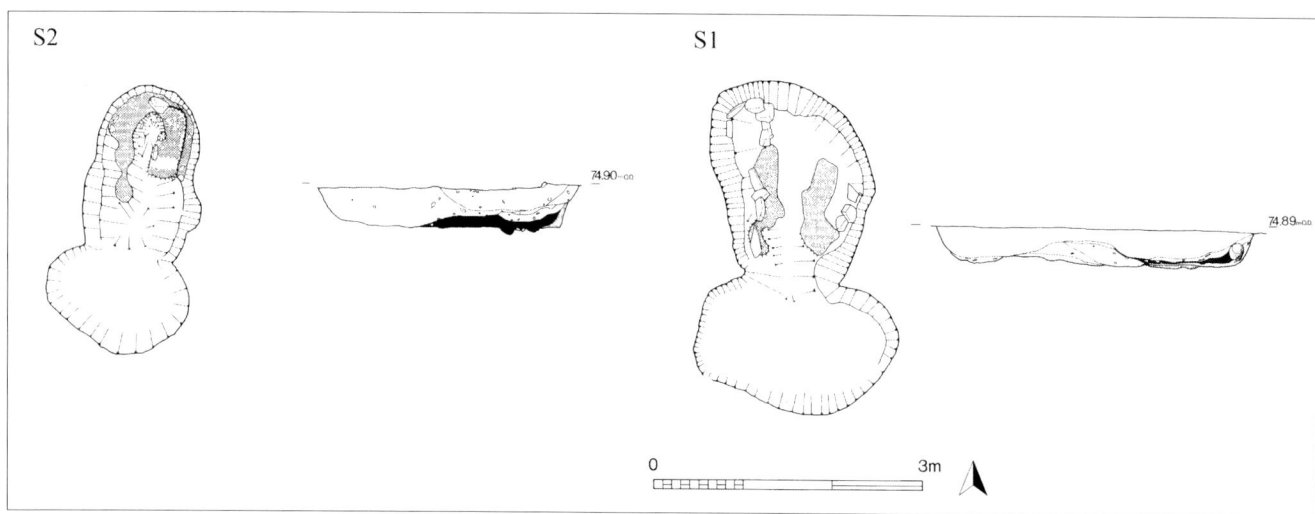

Fig. 4.20 Pottery kilns S1 and S2.

Fig. 4.21 Skull in a waster pit at Tipping Street (north).

the north-west side, eighteen post-holes outline another structure about 8 metres long (S6). The relatively intact surface here was sufficient to suggest that this pattern represents the whole line of a structure. It may have been the east wall of a rectangular dwelling, otherwise outside the excavation; or it might have been another fence, making an enclosure with S5 and S4. The interpretation as a fence is perhaps supported by the gap either side of the post 380/192 and the emergence through the post-line of gulley F354. It is also parallel to S4 and orthogonal to S5. The Late Saxon tenement was thus enclosed by fences, presumably post and rail, on at least two, possibly three sides. The potting area continued north to include

the kiln at Salter Street, and there was a sister site south of Tipping Street (ST17).

Inside the enclosure formed by S4, S5 and S6 were two pottery kilns and a well. The busiest of the two kilns was S1 (F238; Figs 4.19, 4.20), which had been rebuilt at least once and was surrounded by a penumbra of hollows or scoops to the west and south (F470, F499, F461, F495, F490, F465) and a dense cluster of pits used to dispose of wasters to the north (F352, F452, F444, F446, F458). Kiln S2 (F246; Figs 4.19, 4.20) to the west stood on its own without scoops or pits and probably represented a singular venture (new or old) that did not persist. It was making large storage vessels. The kilns conformed to

Musty's type 1b.[50] Examining kiln fragments in Stoke-on-Trent museum, Deborah Ford found signs of the shaping of the clay superstructure: part of a clay firebar formed around wattles 22 millimetres in diameter, impressions of wattles, stones, numerous finger marks and a possible sleeve.[51] Charlotte Cane suggested that the form of the kiln would have been a clay dome sufficient to stack about forty cooking pots, joined to a stoke hole with a clay arch.[52] The pots would have been fired at 950°C. and oxidised by removing the top and letting in air in the latter stages. The kiln excavated by John Darlington at Salter Street was 1.94 metres long internally and 1.2 metres across with a central pedestal of stone held together and daubed with clay from which firebars radiated. One surviving radial firebar 600 x 100 millimetres in diameter and several similar firebars were found collapsed in the kiln.[53] These kilns were fired with wood or charcoal.[54]

This vigorous but short-lived industry naturally generated a great deal of material — mostly Stafford ware, which was present in Period 1 (17,000 sherds in S1 alone) as well as in all subsequent features. A human skull was recovered from F505, a Period 1 scoop, and parts of another human skull were recovered from a pit F342. The Tipping Street skulls were highly fragmented (Fig. 4.21) but identified as human, one from an adult, possibly male, and the other from an adult of indeterminate sex.[55] No other human bone was recovered on the excavation, and the skulls are isolated finds in features otherwise associated with the potting industry.[56]

The contemporary well F363 was made of vertical planks forming a circular cylinder and may have been a re-used barrel (Fig. 4.22). It contained mainly plants of disturbed and wet ground and dominated by species of the *Polygonaceae* family, especially *Polygonum hydropiper*. Stinking mayweed, fat hen and chickweed are also well represented. Many of these may have been growing in the immediate vicinity of the well. Possible household debris is rather sparsely indicated by a fragment of

hazel shell, a dill seed, a sloe stone, and a small amount of cereal remains including some uncharred rye and barley rachises. The well may have been intended as a replacement for the gulley (F354). There were some signs of facilities: stake-lined (originally wattle-lined) pits (F502, F507) may be latrines; other pits (F495, F445) may be for rubbish.

The scene was set for a demarcated workplace, in which there were scoops for puddling clay, mixing it with water, shaping it and firing it, with (inevitably) the occasional disaster generating numerous wasters. The wasters were most likely recycled to provide props for new firings, although stones were also used for this purpose as well as for lining the flue. The water was supplied by a well, which may have replaced an earlier gulley. The sandy clay was presumably quarried from the river system — perhaps in connection with water management schemes, and presumably brought onto the site by cart. This industry, which sprung up in an area where no pottery had been made since the Roman period, 600 years earlier, was dedicated to the manufacture of Stafford ware.

The Stafford-ware industry

Stafford ware is made from sandy clay, fired in general to an orange or pink colour, and occurs in the form of jars, cooking pots, bowls, lamps, cups, skillets and pitchers. The fabric and the form of the jar resemble to some degree the whole pot found at Castle Esplanade, Chester, in 1950, which contained a hoard of Late Saxon pennies deposited about AD 970 (Fig. 4.23).[57] Chester has yet to produce any waster tips, and wasters are rare in any of the other places in the West Midlands that have produced similar pottery (see below). Thus since 1980, the pottery briefly known as Chester ware or West Midlands early medieval ware has been known as Stafford ware or Stafford-type ware, with Stafford to date the only known production centre. Stafford has so far produced about 75,000 sherds of Stafford ware, as compared with fewer than 1,000 from all other known sites.[58]

Fabric
The clay from which this pottery is made is common in the region, without so far indicating any distinctive provenance.[59] The clay was tempered with sand, sometimes too much as in the case of the waster dump at Clarke Street (see below). Vessels were hand-formed using coils of clay and then wheel-finished

---

50 Musty 1974, 44.

51 Ford 1999.

52 FR8.2.3.

53 Ford 1999; FR2.3.3, 56. Dated AD 1000–1080 by archaeomagnetism.

54 C. Cane in FR8.2.3.

55 The heads had clearly parted company with their owners but 'no pathology was noted'. Examination by Alison Cameron, University of Bradford.

56 Although both features are securely stratified in Period 1, neither was located on the plans. F505 (seen in Fig. 4.21) is associated with three other scoops (F461, F499 and F540), two of which are located immediately south of kiln S1 (Fig. 4.18). A manuscript sketch by M. Taylor shows F342 (interpreted as a 'grave') as the corner of a pit otherwise cut away by the north-western wall of the nineteenth-century cellar bordering the south-eastern edge of Int 32. The pit also contained a sherd of Stafford ware.

57 Webster et al. 1953.

58 The figure was 781 in 1986 when Table 4.1 was compiled.

59 Initial study by David Williams, University of Southampton. Williams 1985.

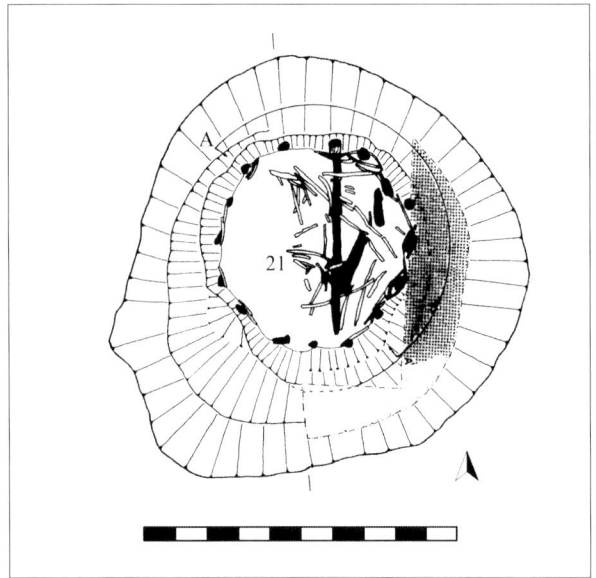

Fig. 4.22 Late Saxon well (F363) at Tipping Street (north).

Fig. 4.23 Late Saxon Stafford-type ware pot found with a hoard of silver pennies in Chester in 1950.

with particular attention paid to the rims. The bases and rims were made separately and then joined.[60] The fabric occurs in a range of hues from bright orange to dark grey, representing, respectively, firing in oxidising and reducing conditions. However, the grey was in a minority on all sites (Table 4.1) and orange colours dominate the finished products. Five sherds with spots of green glaze were noted at Bath Street, but this is considered to be unintentional.[61] Some body sherds carry parallel swathes of a light clay on the surface, as through the application of slip using a fast wheel. Examples from Tipping Street (south) were burnished to a rich dark red.[62] 98% of Stafford-ware sherds are undecorated; the 2% that are show rouletting on the shoulder or stamps on handles.

Table 4.1. Summary of Stafford-ware finds

Sites	No. of sherds	% grey	% decorated	Types of decoration	Min. no. vessels	Ratio of cooking pots to bowls
Stafford						
Tipping Street (N)						
(kilns)	49,000	20%	2%	All	400	2:1
(non-kiln)	758	13%	1%	11,6,1	–	3:1
Tipping Street (S)	1,200 (salvage)					
St Mary's Grove	1,254	7%	3%	6	57	2:1
Clarke Street	c.20,000 fragments					
Bath Street	fragments					
Hereford	395	0	10%	6	2	No bowls
Shrewsbury	192	6%	3%	6	14	6:1
Chester: Lower Bridge Street	156	8%	8%	6,11	–	one bowl
Lichfield	19	21%	1 sh	6	2	no bowls
Dublin	8–12	–	–	–	–	no bowls
Worcester	several	0	–	6	2	no bowls
Rocester	5	–	2 sh	6	3	1:2
Barton Blount	2	–	–	–	–	no bowls

61 Ford 1995, 29; 1999, 28.

62 Ford 1999, 21. At ST17 the burnishing runs in a continuous band round the jar body from shoulder to base angle, a feature not noted elsewhere.

60 Ford 1999, 19–20.

Fig. 4.24 Stafford ware pots, skillets and lamps.

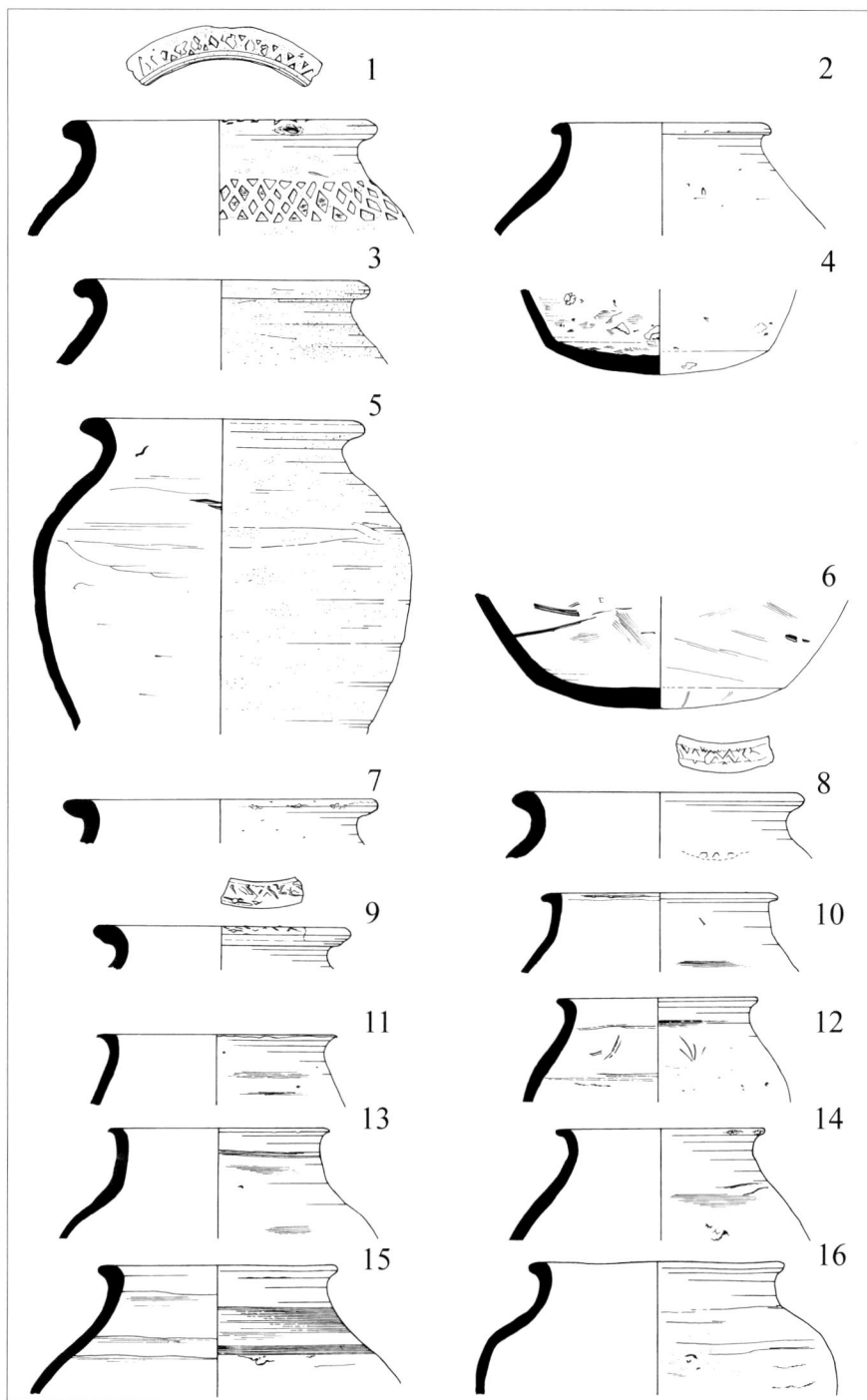

Fig. 4.25 Stafford ware pots 1–16 (for provenance see Digest A4). Scale 1:4.

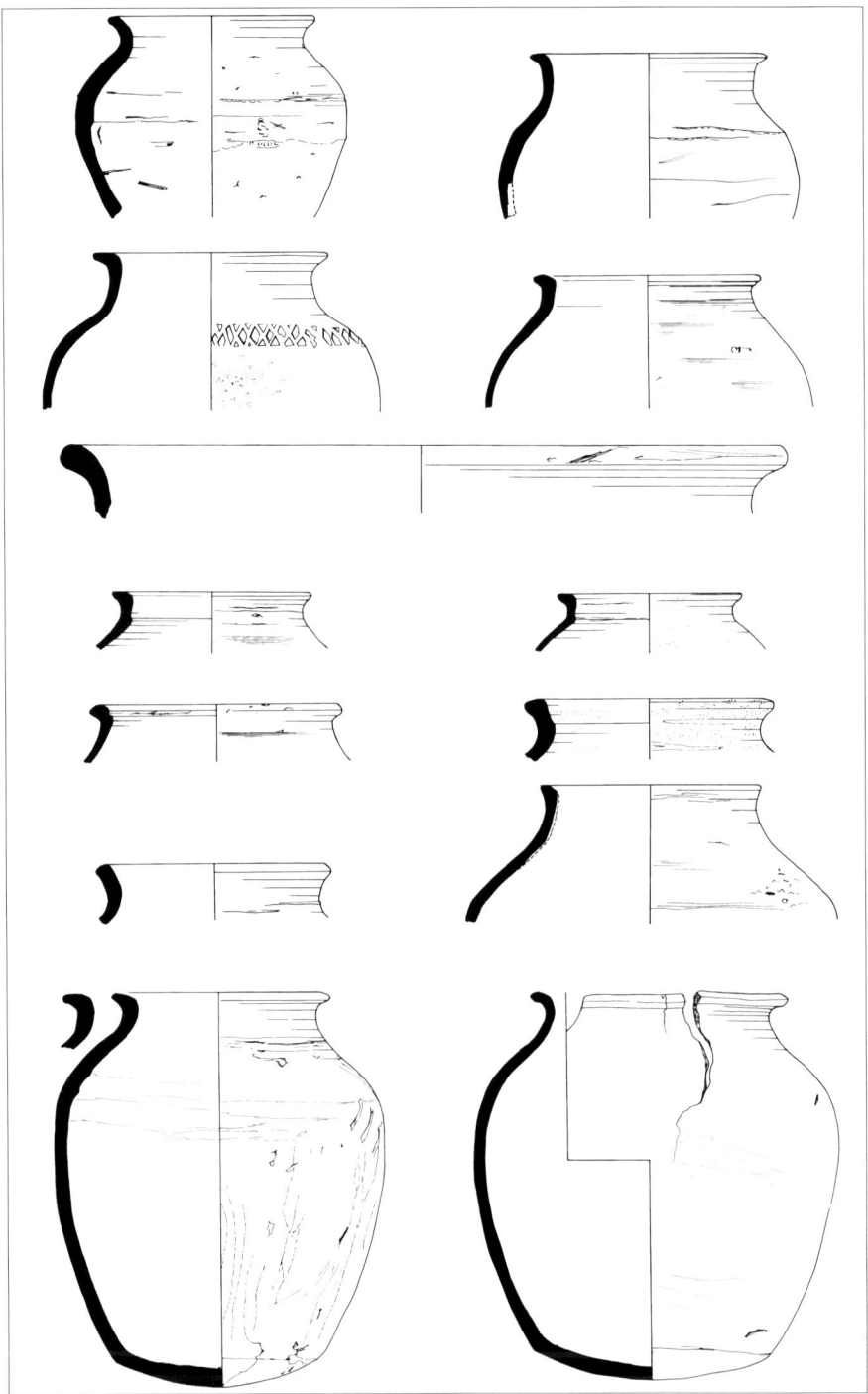

Fig. 4.26 Stafford ware pots 17–29 (for provenance see Digest A4). Scale 1:4.

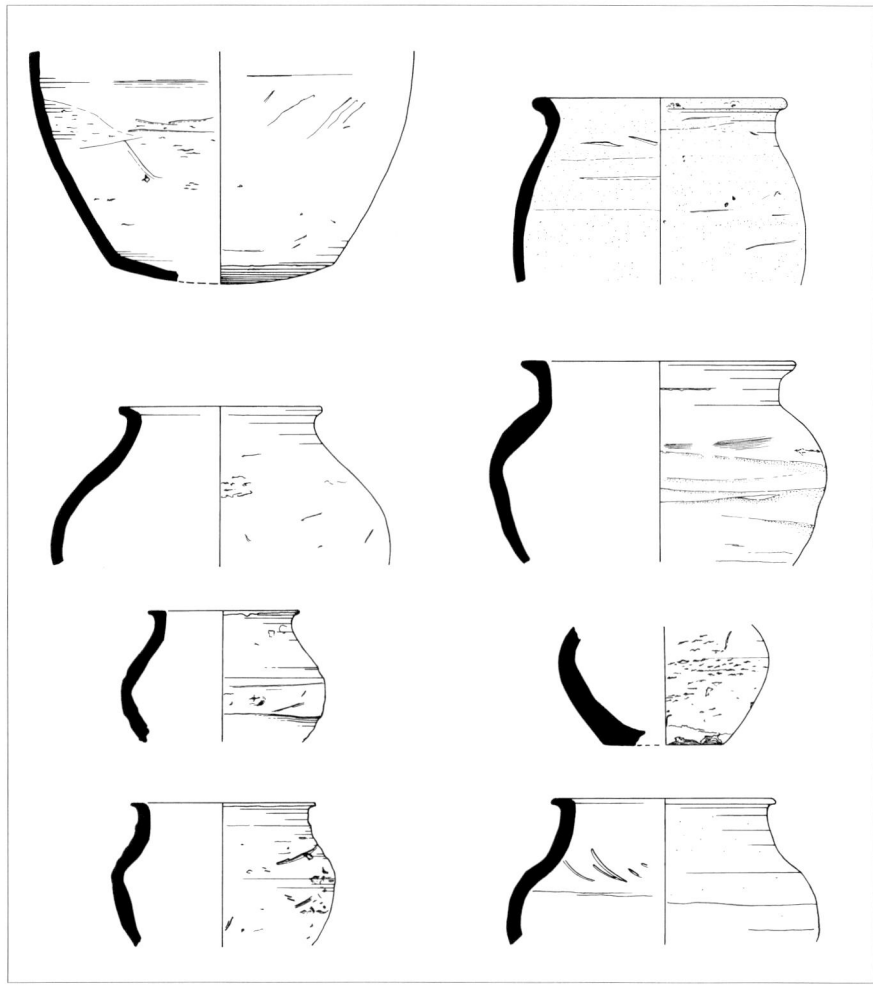

Fig. 4.27 Stafford ware pots 30–37 (for provenance see Digest A4). Scale 1:4.

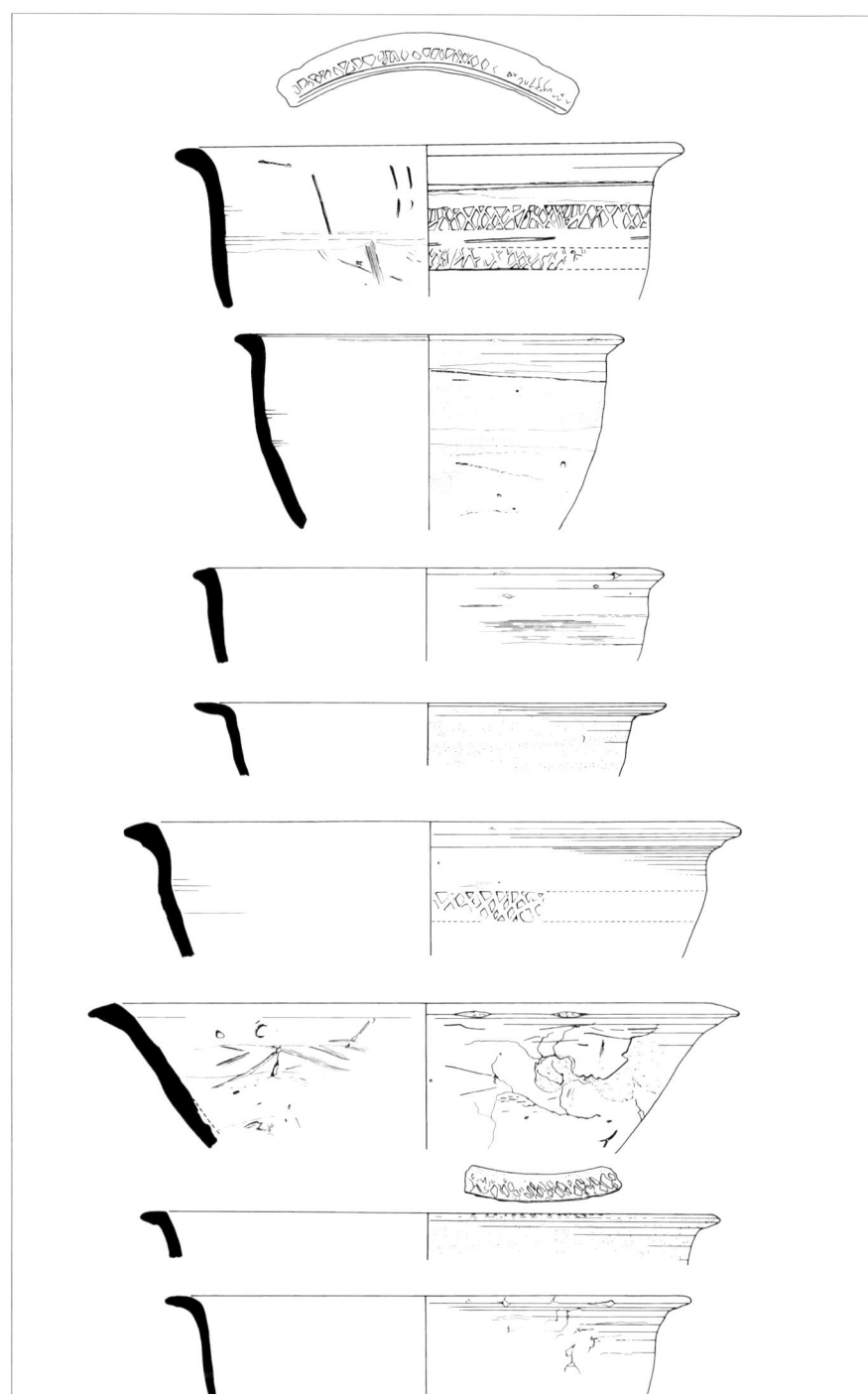

Fig. 4.28 Stafford ware bowls 38–46 (for provenance see Digest A4). Scale 1:4.

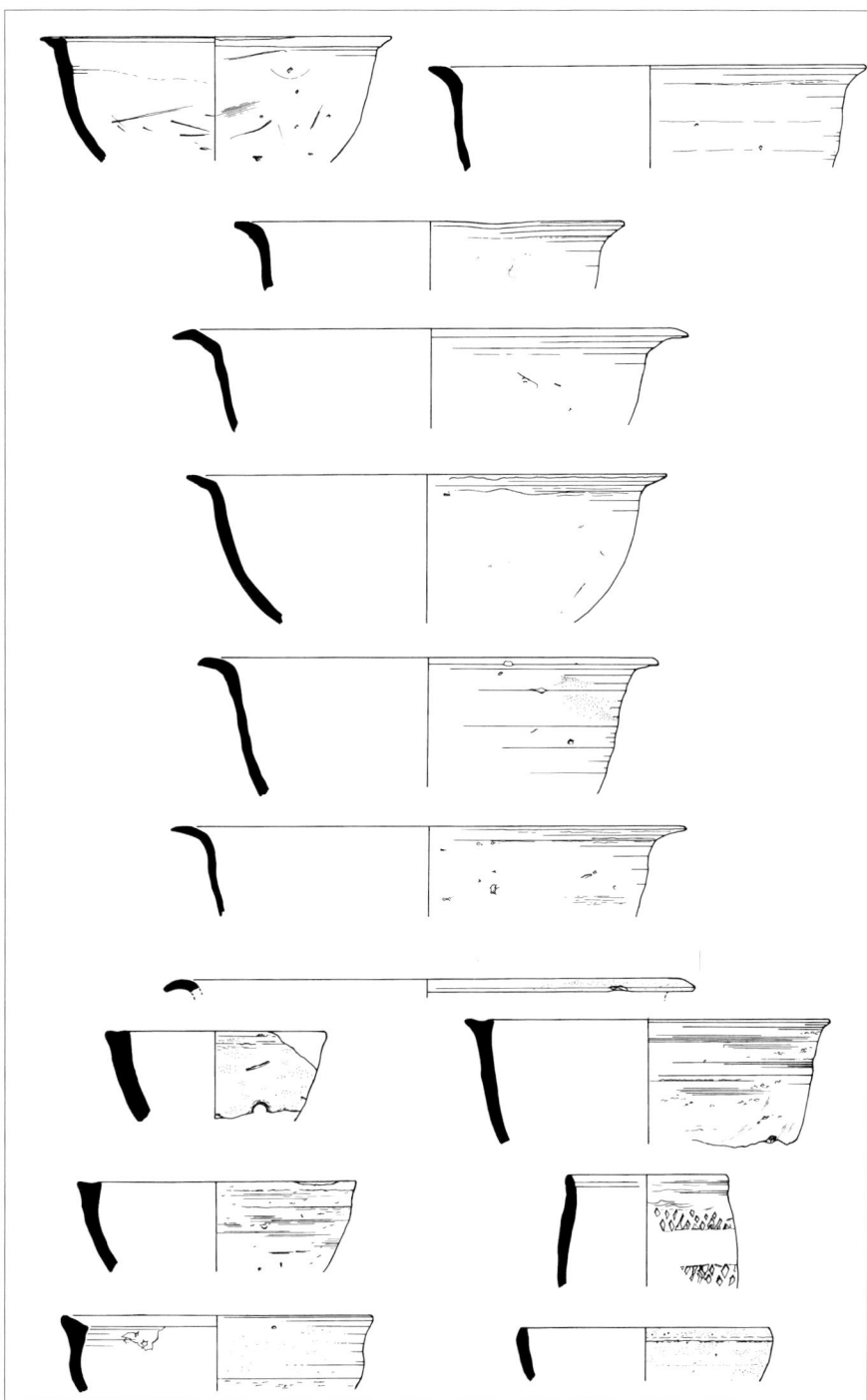

Fig. 4.29 Stafford ware bowls 47–60 (for provenance see Digest A4. Scale 1:4.)

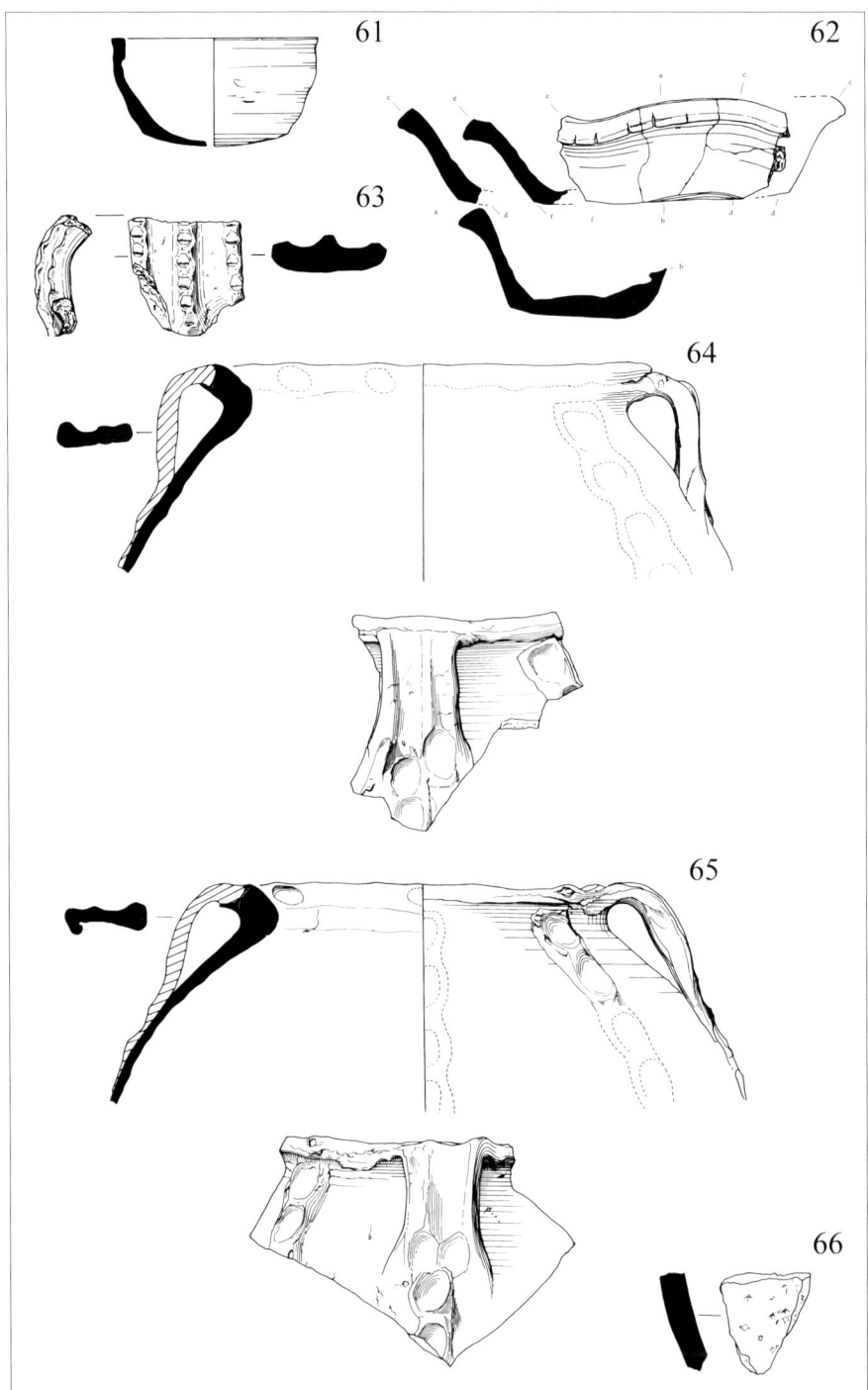

Fig. 4.30 Stafford ware bowls 61–62 and pitchers 63–66 (for provenance see Digest A4). Scale 1:4.

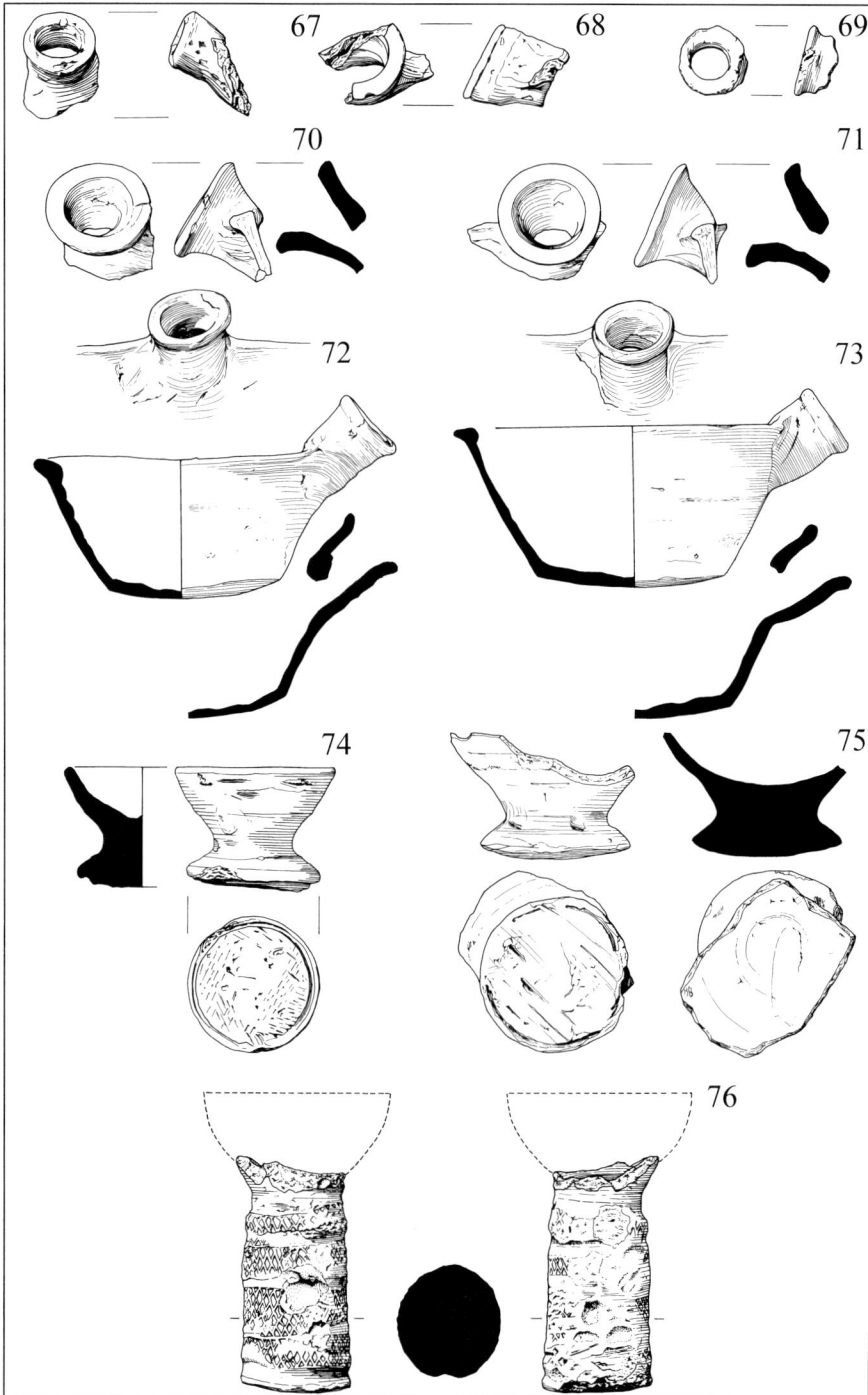

Fig. 4.31 Stafford ware spouted bowls 67–73 and lamps 74–76 (for provenance see Digest A4). Scale 1:4.

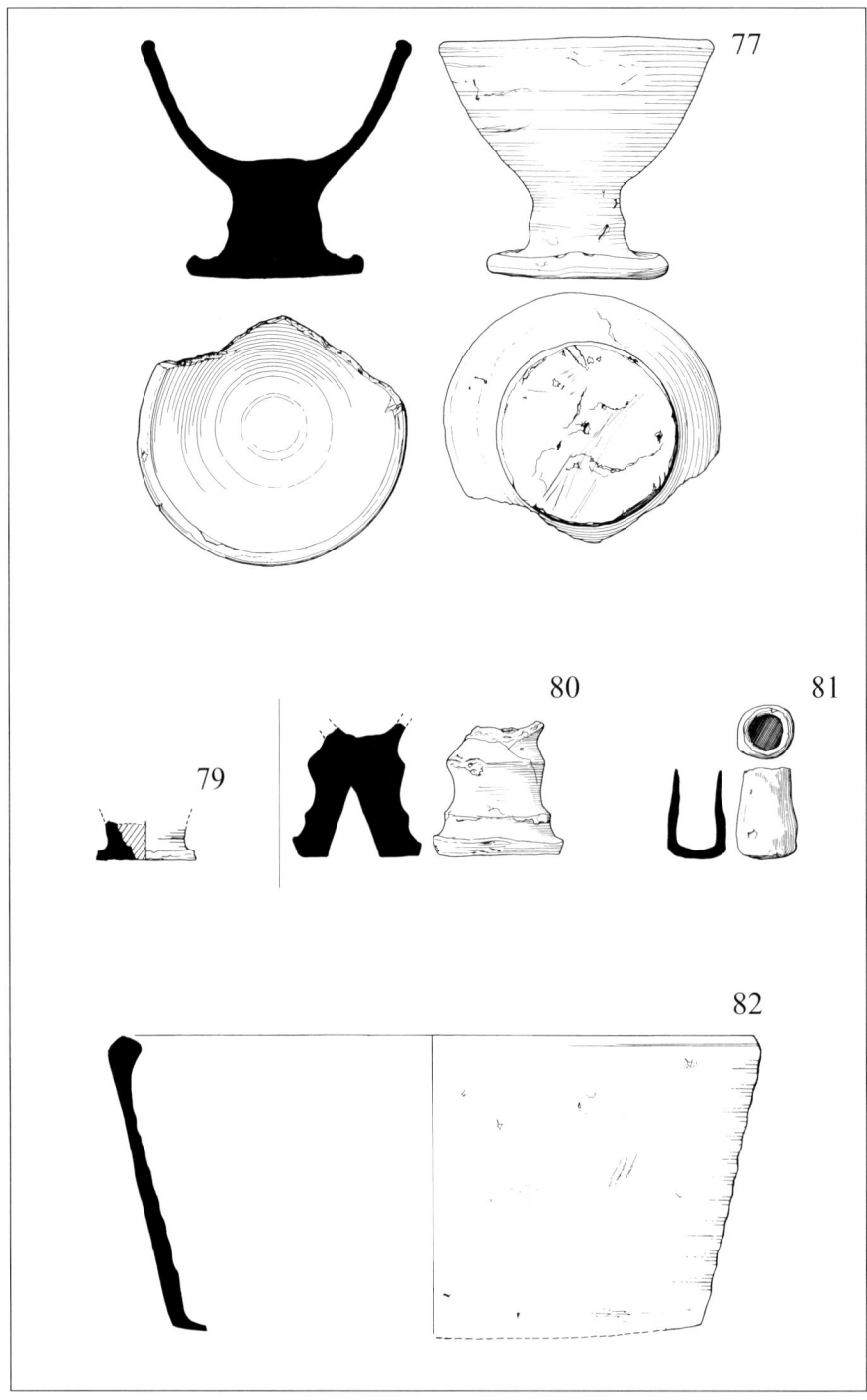

Fig. 4.32 Stafford ware cup 77, pedestals 79–80, thimble 81 and bowl 82 (for provenance see Digest A4). Scale 1:4.

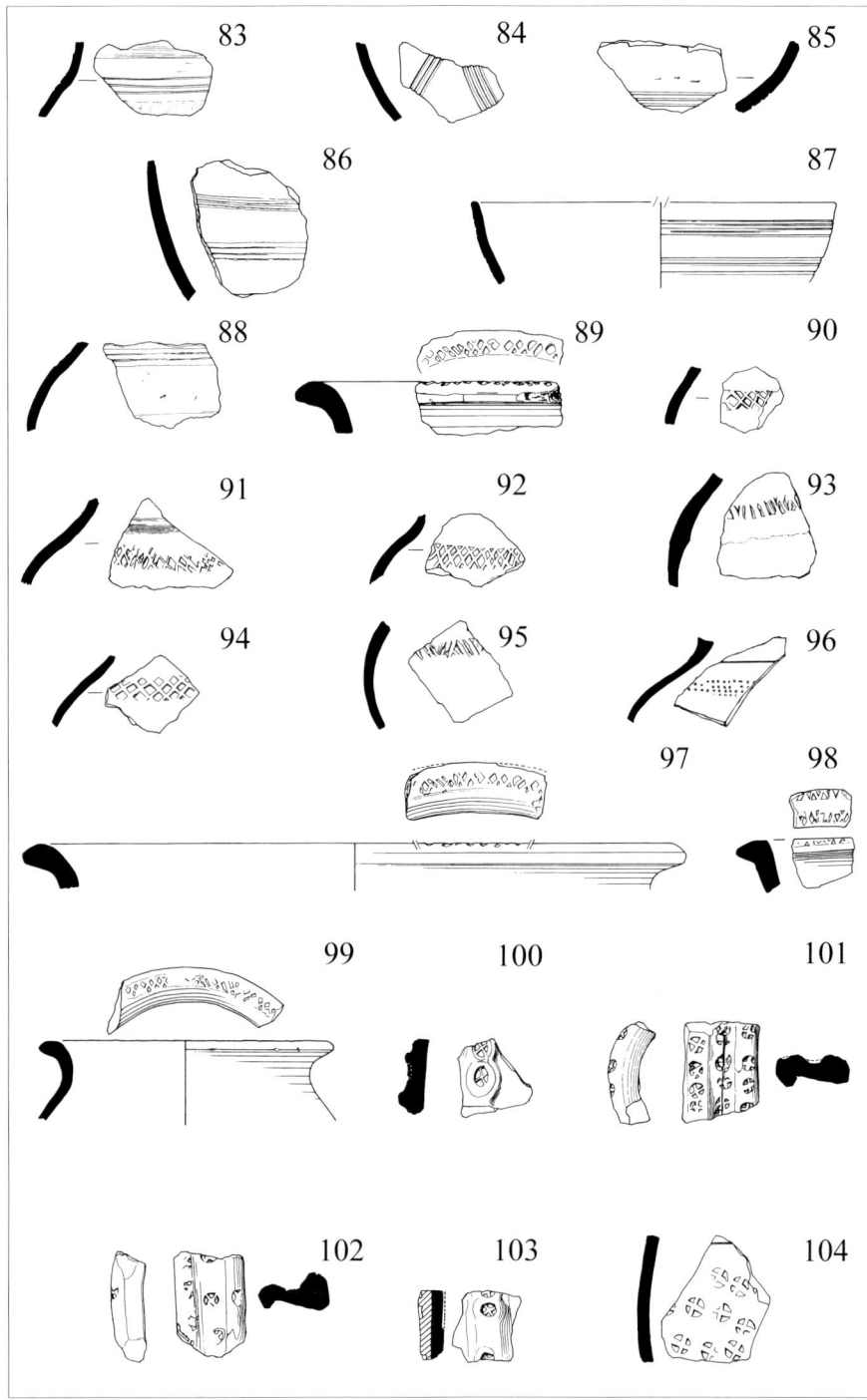

Fig. 4.33 Stafford ware decoration 83–104 (for provenance see Digest A4). Scale 1:4.

The types of decoration are listed in order of frequency for each group. Key: 1 – thumbed strips with punched circles, usually quadranted; 3 – thumbed strips; 6 – lozenges; 9 – incised lines; 11 – small squares.

Forms and functions

The repertoire of Stafford-ware forms is illustrated in Figs 4.24–4.33.[63] The most common form is the plain pot or jar (nos 1–37). The bases are always sagging. Some rims have an internal groove suggesting a seating for a lid, others have a roll or everted rim, very occasionally decorated on top with rouletting (nos 1, 8, 9). Just as rarely, a band of rouletting is carried around the shoulder (nos 1, 19). The complete examples are taller than they are wide, and thus resemble *jars* rather than *cooking pots*. However, sooting on some base sherds shows that some were used for cooking.

The Stafford sites have produced an astonishing range of *bowls* (nos 38–61). These vary from broad and shallow with a sharp lip (no. 44), to small and upright (no. 61). They would serve to eat food and present it and deserve the name of tableware. Large *storage jars* or handled pitchers (nos 63–66) are noted for their thumbed strips and thumbing on the handle. They were usually fired grey, had a soapy feel and occurred only on Tipping Street where they were the subject of the last firing of kiln S2.[64] Ford reported conjoining sherds from 'very large jars' at Tipping Street.[65] Some of the *spouts* (nos 67–73) may have belonged to pitchers, but they can be seen adjoined to bowls or *skillets* (nos 72, 73) where they may serve as spouts for pouring or separating liquids, or possibly sockets for wooden handles. A number of pedestalled vessels suggest special uses. Nos 76, 79 and 80 resemble *lamps*, and nos 74 and 75 may have been lamps too. The form of no. 77 is more like a *goblet*, and was notable for its high quality finish. No. 82 is a large deep dish, such as might be used to separate cheese. Fig. 4.33 shows a range of *decorated sherds*: grooves, rouletting and stamps. Decoration is carried on jars and bowls, with thumbing on storage jars or pitchers

(Table 4.2). Decorative schemes are not common at Stafford, but sufficient to indicate its allegiance to the broader family of Late Saxon pottery industries.

Distribution and date

Within Stafford, the distribution is naturally skewed by the production sites, and there is no special 'signature' to the 1,000 sherds at the non-production sites examined, namely St Mary's Grove and Bath Street (Table 4.1, p. 81). All sites have cooking pots/jars and bowls, in the ratio 2:1, which represents the Stafford 'kit'. Apart from one highly decorated lamp from St Mary's Grove (no. 76), all the distinctive forms were from the kiln sites or dumps.

Stafford ware has been found all over the West Midlands region but in a very narrow range of locations. To those listed in Table 4.1 (a list which dates to 1986) can be added a single sherd from Gloucester and one or two possible sherds from Tamworth, Cold Norton, Grange Cow Worth, Tatton Park, Leintwardine and Wroxeter church.[66] It is absent from Wales. It can be noted that the sites where this pottery is present in any quantity (Hereford, Shrewsbury and Chester) are all burhs. Apart from the handful of sherds for Dublin, the distribution would appear to indicate or define the region of tenth-century Mercia.

Radiocarbon dates suggest that production in Stafford was confined to the tenth and eleventh centuries, proposals for earlier dates now being discounted.[67] Stafford-type ware excavated outside Stafford has not yet been attributed to contexts earlier than the tenth century. Evidence from Hereford suggests that it continued in use into the eleventh century but examples from the late eleventh century may well be residual. Large-scale excavations at Stafford Castle, a late eleventh-century foundation with an associated village, have not recovered any Stafford ware.[68] Thus Stafford ware appears to have a lifetime of just over a hundred years, from the early tenth century to the mid eleventh century.

Table 4.2. Contents of Kilns

Intervention no.	No. of sherds	% decorated	Decoration types	Form types
ST17	1,200 [salvage]	4%	Lozenge	Mainly cooking pots, some bowls, few show lid seatings
ST 32 S1, F238	17,000	2%	70% squares, some lozenge, incised lines, 4 sherds thumbed strips containing punched circles	Mainly cooking pots, some bowls, many show lid seatings
S2, F246	1,400	2%	99% thumbed strips containing punched circles usually quadranted, 1 sherd incised lines	The decorated sherds seem to come from large jars and strap handled pitchers

---

63 See Digest A4 for provenance of the illustrated pottery.
64 C. Cane, FR8.3.2.
65 Ford 1999, 21; ST32 contexts 1294, 1390, 1511, 1514, 1515.

66 Ford 1995, 31; 1999, 18.
67 See Chapter 3, p. 45. The earlier dates were drawn from uncalibrated radiocarbon dating or unsatisfactory stratigraphy.
68 'Not a single sherd', Darlington 2001, 28.

Inspiration

It is of the greatest interest that such an industry should spring up fully formed in an area with no post-Roman pottery tradition. No pottery had been made in south Staffordshire since the Roman period, but this is clearly significant. The local Roman pottery was Severn Valley ware – made in a hard sandy fabric in 'flower-pot orange', and coming predominately in jars, with flanged dishes and storage vessels (Figs 4.4). The forms, colour, rouletting, burnishing and slip observed on Stafford ware strongly suggest that its model is local Roman pottery. There was a wealth of exemplars at Wroxeter, Wall and elsewhere, and the find of a complete Severn Valley-ware jar at 10 Market Street means that models were not lacking even in Stafford itself.[69] There is little doubt that Late Saxon people could recognise Roman artefacts, and they must frequently have encountered examples of whole pots.[70]

Stafford may have been founded within a tradition that began at Gloucester (see Chapter 6), so it is interesting to see that the Late Saxon wares excavated there share many forms with Stafford, and that the Gloucester variant occurs with Stafford-type wares in Hereford and in Worcester.[71] The Gloucester pottery does not occur in strata earlier than the ninth century so that, even if it represents the earliest experimentation, it still belongs to the time and the context of the West Saxon initiative in Mercia.[72]

Alan Vince found that Late Saxon London was supplied by potters in the Oxford area, who had a virtual monopoly in the city and presumably used the Thames for transport. The Shelly wares included cooking pots, spouted pitchers, socketed bowls and lamps, as in Stafford, and presented a sharp contrast to the fabrics and forms of the Middle Saxon period. None of the Late Saxon wares occurs earlier than the end of the ninth century and the supply stopped abruptly in the early eleventh.[73]

The idea that the Late Saxon aristocracy was consciously modelling its campaign of conquest and control on Roman ways is a principal theme of this book, to be discussed further in Chapter 6. Meanwhile it can be noted that their inspiration was not only obtained from books, but from material culture. Æthelflæd and her colleagues were archaeologists too.

The town tip

At the south-east corner of the peninsula was a confluence between the River Sow and the Pearl Brook which ran beneath the King's Pool. It is a boggy place that was briefly reclaimed in the Roman period but had reverted to marsh by the tenth century. Some Stafford ware had been thrown into the marsh before the first post-Roman development, which took the form of an embankment of redeposited gravel embedded along the marsh edge, presumably to provide hard standing for carts. A wattle fence, interrupted in places, provided access to, and separation from, the marsh area (Fig. 3.34, C1223, S1). There is little doubt what the purpose was: into the marsh were thrown large quantities of waste pottery and animal bones. Both were excavated in the form of heaps – as of a cartload deposited or thrown out with a shovel. The pottery (about 20,000 sherds) was extremely fragmented, and had been over-tempered and under-cooked, suggestive of an unsuccessful firing. The sherds left a little heap of sand when placed on a table. A human skull was found in one of the earlier consignments.[74] The gravel ramp continued in use during the eleventh century, developing a layer of tread (1184) and showing hoof prints where cattle had been led to drink.

Animal consumption

If the pottery was relatively uninformative, other than as the herald of the Stafford-ware industry, the Clarke Street sequence offered the best assemblages of animal bone from the campaign of excavations that was otherwise on mainly industrial sites where the animal bone had been largely residual or in short supply. At Clarke Street, bone was plentiful and deposited in stratified dumps, each of which gave a sample of the town's animal use during successive periods (Fig. 3.33).

From this we learn that the tenth-century community was largely dependent on a supply of adult cattle, processed centrally. The assemblage for meat-bearing animals was dominated by maxillae, mandibles and skulls, representing waste from animals butchered elsewhere. Sheep and pig are sparsely represented but the Clarke Street assemblage does not imply that pork was being distributed differently to beef and mutton. There are no young animals and limb bones show the same bias towards the numerical dominance of head and foot bones, as in the case of cattle.[75] Red deer and roe deer were also butchered for their meat throughout

69 The resemblance is general, not exact. The fabric is certainly similar: Severn Valley ware is sandy, predominately orange sometimes with a grey core. It comes as tankards, but also as jars and bowls with a roll rim (Tyers 1996, 198–9, nos 9, 22).

70 For example two whole Roman pots found in tenth- to eleventh-century strata under York Minster (Phillips and Heywood 1995, 194).

71 Heighway et al. 1979, 172–5.

72 Hurst 1986, 129; see Chapter 6 below.

73 Vince 1985, 30–4.

74 ST15, C1231. As at Tipping Street (above), this was an isolated skull, without other human bone. It was located in a stratified dump consisting largely of Stafford-ware wasters (Fig. 4.34, Dump 1 and Digest A3).

75 Hummler in FR9.2, table 4.

the Late Saxon period. Clarke Street showed that fowls were also consumed. Elsewhere, there were horse bones at St Mary's Grove, and the bones of a piglet at Tipping Street (north), but no Late Saxon dogs or cats. The assemblage as a whole suggests a 'command economy' where a supply of meat, mainly beef, was acquired and redistributed.[76] This endorses the authoritarian or military feel of the settlement (see Chapter 6).

The Stafford mint
Nicholas Thomas[77]

From their mint-signature, coins are known to have been struck at Stafford over a period spanning 230 years, from the reign of Athelstan (c. 930) to that of Henry II (c. 1165).[78] Due to the under-representation of Stafford coins in both Scandinavian and British hoards, however, many types are very rare, even unique, while for some periods there are no Stafford coins recorded, namely 975–991, 1040–1050, 1070–1083, 1100–1116, 1123–1135, and for much of the reign of Stephen, through to the commencement of the Tealby issue of Henry II in 1158. While no coins are known for the brief reign of Harold II, the dies of Edward the Confessor's Pyramid type were probably still in use during this period. A list of moneyers known to have struck coins at Stafford is shown in Table 4.2.

In 928, during the reign of Athelstan, laws were established for the governance of the royal mints at the Synod of Grateley (Hampshire). There should be one kind of money within the realm, and no moneyer (*myniere*) should mint other than in a town.[79] The coins were to bear both the moneyer's and mint name, although this practice soon fell into decline and a number of issues were produced with only the moneyer's name.

The actual process of making a coin in Anglo-Saxon times involved placing a silver disc between two dies and hitting the top die with three firm strikes. The design thus pressed into the disc might include on one side the name and 'portrait' of the reigning monarch, while the reverse side featured a cross with the name of the moneyer and mint around the edge. Stafford was then known as *Staethford*, the contraction of which might be *STÆTH* or *STÆ* or other variations. The coins of Edward the Elder, Athelstan through to Edgar also have the word 'Moneta' or 'M-O' for moneyer, while later coins may have 'ON', which stands for 'in'. The runic letter 'wynn' Þ was used for W and 'eth' Ð used for th.

There is little early evidence of the social status of a moneyer, but there is an indication from the time of Æthelred II, when a moneyer had workers for whom he was responsible, and from Domesday Book, which appears to show that one Stafford moneyer owned an estate (see below). It is not clear how much profit the moneyers were allowed, although a margin of 8% is generally accepted. With the change of the design of the coinage, initially every six or seven years but later every two or three years, new dies had to be purchased and safely escorted from London – a great expense which could hardly have been recovered by production in the case of Stafford. For instance, the accounts for 1158–1159 contain an entry relating to the payment made by the Stafford moneyer called Colbrand.

Moneyers were subject to rigid controls. Both Æthelred II and his successor, Cnut, passed laws pronouncing that the punishment for false coining was for the moneyer to have his hand cut off and nailed over the mint, and the reeve who controlled his work could also be liable. Henry I reacted with summary violence to the debasement of the coinage in 1124:

> In this year King Henry sent to England from Normandy before Christmas, and ordered that all the moneyers who were in England should be mutilated – i.e. each should lose their right hand and be castrated. That was because the man who had a pound could not get a pennyworth at a market. And Bishop Roger of Salisbury sent over all England and ordered them to come to Winchester … When they got there, they were taken one by one and each deprived of the right hand and castrated. All this was done before Twelfth Night, and it was done very justly because they had ruined all the country with their great false dealing, which they all paid for.[80]

It is not known if Stafford moneyers Edric(us) or Raulf(us) were among those summoned to Winchester, nor if they suffered the same fate as all but four of the realm's moneyers (the lucky four were all from Winchester).

The sequence of moneyers at Stafford
The earliest moneyers whose names may be associated with Stafford with any degree of certainty are Eardulf (read by Dr Robinson as a contraction of Eardwulf), Wigmund (or Wihgmund), and Wihtemund, all of whom struck the Circumscription (Cross) type BMC v, of Athelstan (924–939). Wigmund also struck coins under Athelstan but without a mint signature. Wihtemund also struck a BMC v variety found only

---

76 As noted in the Middle Saxon sites of Hamwih, Lundenwic and Eoforwic: Bourdillon 1994; Rackham 1994, 131; O'Connor 1994, 139.

77 High House Museum, Stafford.

78 This contribution draws on and revises the pioneering study of the Stafford moneyers by Paul Robinson (1968–70).

79 ii Athelstan 14; Stenton 1971, 535–6.

80 Whitelock (ed.), *Anglo-Saxon Chronicle*, E-text, s.a. 1125.

Table 4.2. Moneyers or families of moneyers active at Stafford

Moneyer's name	Striking at Stafford	Monarchs served
Eardulf (Eardwulf)		Edward the Elder 899–924/5 (unproven)
Eardulf (Eardwulf)		Athelstan 924–939, Eadmund 939–946, Eadred 946–955
Wihgmund, Wihtemund		Athelstan 924–939
Wihgmund, Wihtemund		Edmund 939–946
Amund(es)		Edmund 939–946, Eadred 946–955, Eadwig 955–959
Amund(es)		Edgar 959–973
Ælfsie (Ælfsige)	959–975	Edgar 959–973
Siulf (Sigewulf)	959–975	Edgar 959–973
LAPSED?	975–991	
Ælfwold	991–1017	Æthelred II 978–1016
Godric I	991–1009	Æthelred II 978–1016
Ægenulf (Ægenwulf)	997–1003	Æthelred II 978–1016
Ælfric	1017–1035/6	Cnut 1016–1035
Scandinavian copy	1016–1035	Cnut 1016–1035
Ælfric	1038–1040	Harold I (joint king with Harthacnut 1035–1037, sole king 1037–1040)
LAPSED?	1040–1050	
Ælfric	1050–1053	Edward the Confessor 1042–1066
Ovmund (Godmund)	1053–56	Edward the Confessor 1042–1066
Culling (Cullinc)	1059–1062	Edward the Confessor 1042–1066
Godwine	1065–1066	Edward the Confessor 1042–1066
Godwine	1066–1070	William I 1066–1087
LAPSED?	1070–1083	
Wulfnoth	1083–1087	William I 1066–1087
Ælfnoth	1083–1100	William I 1066–1087
Godric II	1083–1086	William I 1066–1087
Ælfnoth		William II 1087–1100
Godric II	1087–1100	William II 1087–1100
LAPSED?	1100–1116	
Eadricus	1117–1119	Henry I (1100–1135)
Raulfus	1121–1123	Henry I (1100–1135)
LAPSED?	1123–1135	
Godric III	1135–1140?	Stephen 1135–1154
LAPSED?	1140?–1158	
Colbrand	1158–1161	Henry II 1154–1189
Willem	1161–1165	Henry II 1154–1189

at Stafford, Chester, and Shrewsbury, while a moneyer by the name of Eardulf also minted under Edward the Elder, but his coins cannot be attributed to Stafford for the lack of a mint signature.

During the reigns of Edmund (939–946) and Edwig (955–959), coins from only two moneyers may be associated with Stafford: Eardulf (Eardwulf) from his coins of Athelstan and Amund, from a coin of Edgar. Dr Robinson also notes coins of Wihtemund in the reign of Edmund (probably Two Line type BMC i). By the beginning of Edgar's reign in 959, and up until his reform in 973, it still not commonplace to carry the mint name on the coin, but after that date the mint name almost always appears, giving a clearer picture of the operation of both mints and moneyers. Under Edgar

(959–973) the life of each issue appears to have been six to seven years, but this gradually gave way to a two-to-three-year cycle after 1035.

The coins of Edward the Martyr (975–978) are very rare and Stafford might not have issued any at all, nor for the first issues of Æthelred II. The 'CRUX' issue of c. 991–997, therefore was the first for over fifteen years with two moneyers, Ælfwold and Godric I being recorded. Two moneyers struck the next two issues: Long Cross (997–1003) of Ægenulf and Godric I; Helmet type (1003–1009) of Ælfwold and Godric I. The number of moneyers had been reduced by Æthelred II who decreed there should be: 'For every chief town three'; and 'For every other town one'. Stafford, as the county town, was presumably entitled to its full complement of moneyers, although there never seems to have been more than two in office at the same time.

Stafford was also one of the ten mints to have struck the 'Agnus Dei' issue (the others being Derby, Hereford, Leicester, Malmesbury, Northampton, Nottingham, Salisbury, Stamford and Wilton). Of the sixteen examples thus far recorded, only two have English find-spots, the remainder coming from Scandinavian or Baltic hoards. Half of the known examples have been pierced for wear as ornaments, while the issue must have been familiar to the Danes who struck their own imitations. While surviving Agnus Dei coins are exceedingly rare from England, tenth-century brooches bearing either the Agnus Dei or the Holy Dove are more common and may have their influence in this coinage and the circumstances surrounding its issue. The most likely occasion for issuing the Agnus Dei coins would be the year 1000, but the moneyers concerned only begin coining during the Helmet Type (1003–1009). Æthelred II's Last Small Cross type (1009–1017) is only known from a single moneyer, Ælfwold, and represented his last issue.

Stafford coins of Cnut are known from the Quatrefoil type (1017–1023) through to his Short Cross type (1029–1035/6), all struck by a single moneyer, Ælfric. The majority of these coins, and those of Edgar and Æthelred II, are to be found in Scandinavian museum collections – a reflection of the many large hoards of Anglo-Saxon coin that have been recognised there during the last 180 years. These largely consist of coins brought back as booty from raids or as part of the Danegeld, which was not finally abolished until 1051. One coin of King Cnut's Pointed Helmet type (1024–1030) was evidently so familiar to the Vikings that they struck their own pennies based on the Stafford coin. It may be noted that despite the tens of thousands of coins of Æthelred and Cnut recovered from Viking hoards, fewer than twenty-five examples of all the Stafford issues may be found in the Stockholm cabinets.

No coins have, as of yet, been recorded as having been minted at Stafford during the reign of Harthacnut, which is probably due to the fact that he only reigned for two years (1040–1042). The small numbers of Stafford coins of this era in the major British museums is perhaps surprising, given that a large hoard was discovered in the town in late 1800, said to have contained coins of 'Ethelred, Canute and Hardicnute' and to have been deposited 1016–1040.[81]

While no coins are recorded for the first eight years of the reign of Edward the Confessor, a unique penny of King Edward the Confessor's Expanding Cross type (1050–1053) survives. It was struck by Ælfric (II), who was presumably the descendant of the earlier Stafford

moneyer of the same name. It is evident that the family could not provide a successor to the position, as in 1059 a moneyer called Culling (Cullinc) had to be brought in from nearby Tamworth (the ancient capital of Mercia), his name appearing there well into the reign of William I. The last issue of Edward the Confessor is recorded from Stafford. The mint was apparently closed during the brief reign of Harold II, although it is likely the moneyer Godwine would still have possession of his Pyramid dies which could be used while he waited for a new issue to be made.

Following the Norman Conquest many Saxons were stripped of their power and wealth, the control of the land and the Church passing to William's followers. The Saxon coinage was of a sufficiently high standard, however, as to be left alone. Godwine continued as moneyer through the Conquest, the rebellions of 1069 (battle of Stafford) and 1070, and the assassination of Earl Edwin. Three moneyers, Ælfnoth, Godric II and Wulfnoth, occur in the first William's reign. Ælfnoth continues minting into the next reign along with Godric, who later became the sole moneyer at Stafford.

The majority of surviving Stafford pennies from Edward the Confessor's Pyramid type through to the Bonnet type of William I are thought to have originated in a single find known as the Oulton hoard.[82] Among the estimated 4,000 coins, ten different types were represented including many from Stafford, the latest being the Bonnet type of William I, suggesting the hoard was deposited around the time of the Staffordshire rebellions. Dr Robinson has suggested that the hoard, which included silver bullion as well as coinage, represents the stock of one of the Stafford moneyers (presumably Wulfnoth, as Godwine continued to mint after 1083 and there would have been later issues present). The hoard could equally have belonged to one of those caught up in the fighting or the Norman retribution. Domesday Book makes no mention of payments from Godwine in respect of the royal mint, but this is not unusual as there are only a dozen or so references to the office of moneyer within Domesday Book. On the other hand, there is a tantilising reference to a now lost parcel of land, which appears under the holdings of Robert de Stafford in Pirehill Hundred:

> In MONETVILE 1 hide. Walter and Ansgar holds from him. Earl Edwin held it. Land for 2 ploughs. They

---

81 *Staffordshire Advertiser*, 13 December 1800; see Archive 2.3.5.2.

82 'As the gardener of Mr Shelley of Oulton, near third place, was digging in his master's orchard, he found a gold ring, and upward of a thousand small pieces of silver coin, most of which were perfect; and on examination proved to be the coin of St Edward the Confessor, one of our Saxon kings, who reigned upwards of 700 years ago – It could not be discovered in what they had been kept, as the covering, whatever it might have been, had mouldered into dust.' *Staffordshire Advertiser*, 7 March 1795.

are there, in lordship, with 8 smallholders. Meadow, 2 acres. Value 10 shillings.

The name Monetvile has been linked with the town's mint, while the ending 'vile' suggests a Norman influence. The name is not without precedence: the Domesday Book records that at York 'Nigellus de Monneville has one mansion of the moneyer.'

Two coins are known from the reign of Henry I (1100–1135): one struck by Edric(us) is of the Cross Fleury type (1117–1119); and the other by Raulf(us) is the Full Face type (1121–1123). The turbulent times of Stephen (1135–1154) produced many irregular coins minted in the names of the warlords who had rebelled against the king. Stafford, however, struck only the official issue, known as the Watford type after the large hoard discovered there in 1818.

With the succession of Henry II (1154) the coinage might be expected to have improved. However, although more uniform in type, the general standard declined further. In the Pipe Roll for year five of the reign of Henry II (1158–9), the sheriff of Staffordshire renders an account for one mark of silver under the heading of Nova Placita which is for 'de moneţ de Staff', or the moneyer(s) of Stafford. The Staffordshire entry for year six of the reign of Henry II (1159–60) records the moneyer Colbrand (a name with origins in the Norse Kolbrandr) rendering an account of 2 marks which he pays in full. The amount of a mark of silver (13s 4d) might have included privileges attached to the position, such as the rents from the smithy or of tenements such as the lost parcel of land called Monetvile which could have been 'the village of the moneyer'. Monetvile appears in the Domesday Book but soon disappears, possibly dying along with the office of the Stafford moneyer.

The Stafford Mint closed around 1165 as part of a reduction in the number of provincial mints. The last of the Stafford moneyers was a man called Willem, once again a Norman-French name. However, following the introduction of the so called 'short-cross' issue in 1180 there appears an entry in the sheriff's accounts of 1184 which reads: 'Et in Custamento ducendi vij falsonarios de Stafford ad Gloecestriam x.s. per breve Regis'. It is not certain as to whether the seven accused of forgery were from Stafford but the apparent closure of the 'new smithy' in the town and the deportations for trial may not have been just coincidental. A hoard of forgeries may one day reveal the truth of the matter.

Concluding thoughts

This sequence relies on finds of coins, and thus can be radically overturned by the discovery of a new hoard. Discontinuities in minting may therefore be more illusory than real. With that caveat, it can be said that the Stafford mint began in the reign of Athelstan,

perhaps using a moneyer (Eadwulf) who had already struck under Edward the Elder. The personal names suggest Anglo-Saxon or later Scandinavian origin, rather than British Celtic. The same moneyers, or families of moneyers, might have served several kings in succession. Amund (939–973) was one of the longest serving and struck coins for four monarchs. The periods without known coins, if real, may imply periods of unrest (975–991) or payment of the Danegeld (1040–1050). The gap in minting between 1070 and 1083 would equate with the harrowing of the region by William I.

No Late Saxon coins were found in the 1975–1985 campaign. There is a farthing of c. 1000 from St Bertelin's (above), an eleventh-century coin of Edward the Confessor from Greyfriars[83] and a coin-hoard found 'in a small jug in Mr Kingstone's tan-yard … about one yard from the surface' in Eastgate Street in about 1800. It contained 200 to 300 silver pieces of Æthelred, Canute, Harthacnute or later. But it is now lost.[84] Coinage in Stafford had very limited use and circulation. The coins were being minted by means of dies and silver supplied by the crown, so presumably the crown was receiving something in exchange. It is suggested in Chapter 6 that Late Saxon towns went through three phases, in the second of which they functioned as places to turn tax into coin, and in the third as long distance trading places. The absence of archaeologically recognisable overseas imports at Stafford suggests that this town never reached phase 3: the Stafford coins simply represent the commutation of tribute into treasure, with a consequent limited supply and circulation.

★

Other industries

Late Saxon Stafford was a producer (of bread, meat, pottery and coins). The only recognised imports are a few vessel equivalents from Stamford and St Neots.[85] There was some sparse evidence for subsidiary industries: worked antler at Clarke Street (1198), a bone needle from 1222 on the same site, a wooden baker's rake from St Mary's Grove (Fig. 4.13), planks used horizontally for a well lining at St Mary's Grove, and vertically at Tipping Street (north) (Fig. 4.22). There were ten spindle whorls, implying spinning, six of clay, three of stone and one of bone (Fig. 4.34). They averaged 35mm in diameter by 25mm in thickness, and weigh 15–25g. Of these, five were in Late Saxon contexts, all in the potteries, of which four were of clay, one certainly in

83 FR2.3.1, 12.
84 FR2.3.3, a25.
85 See Digest A3.

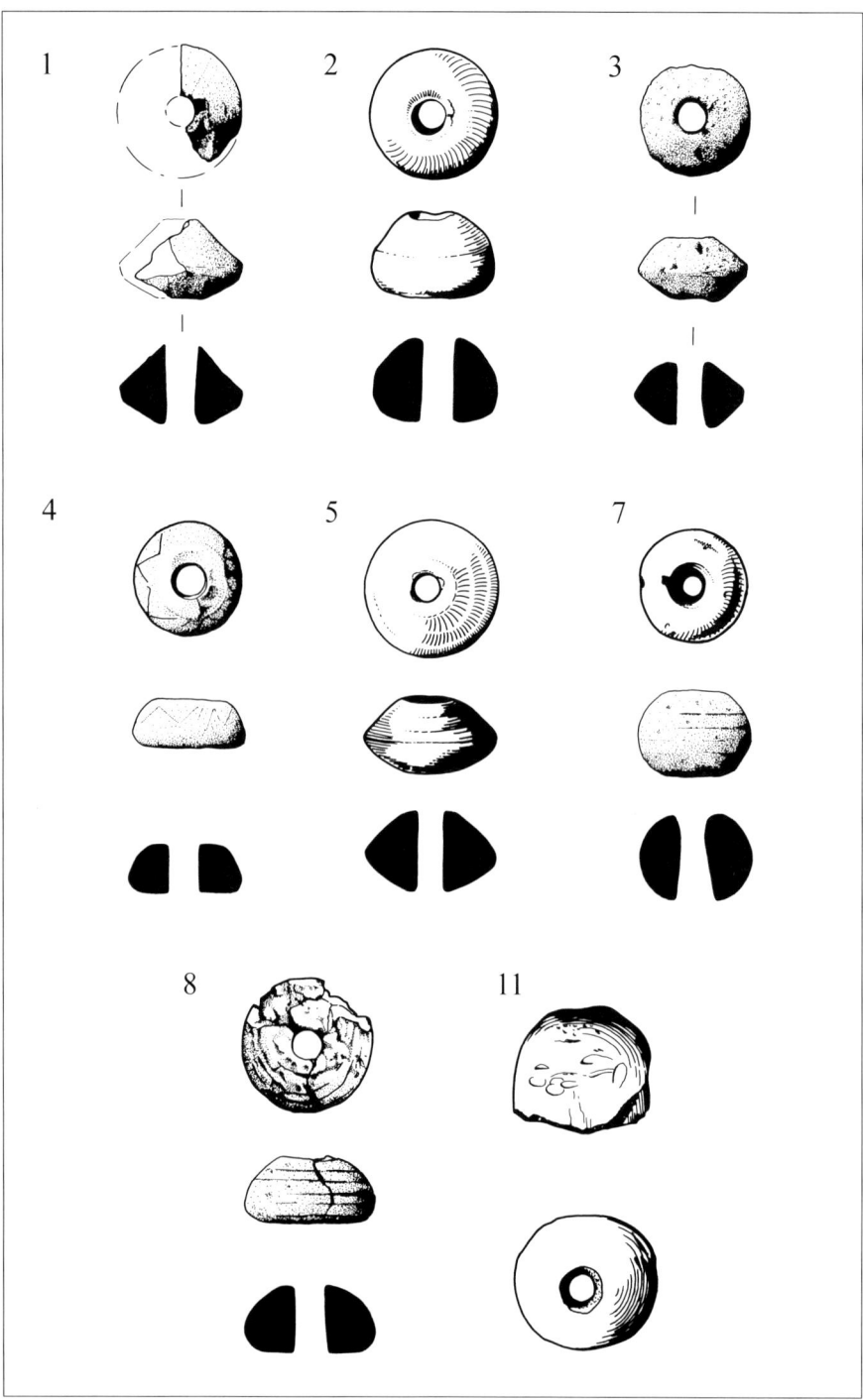

Fig. 4.34 Late Saxon spindle whorls from Stafford. Scale 1:2 (for catalogue see FR 8.4).

Stafford ware, implying they were being made there. The fifth, made of soapstone, was probably a model.[86]

There were two fragments of iron in the S2 kiln on Tipping Street, but it is not excluded that later iron pieces were residual from the Late Saxon period. Among the candidates advanced are the many fragments of iron and slag from Bath Street, which include horseshoes, for which a Late Saxon origin has been argued (p. 73 above).

The fort (Fig. 1.3)

Stafford enters documentary history in AD 913 when, according to the Anglo-Saxon Chronicle, Æthelflæd, Lady of the Mercians, built a burh at *Stæthford* before Lammastide.[87] Given this well documented fact and the research of the last thirty years in southern and midland England, there is a not unreasonable expectation that there will be at Stafford a set of defences sufficient to earn the title of burh. But it is fair to admit that the evidence here is elusive and circumstantial.

We must first dispose of the William Salt map, a document which claims to show the location of an Anglo-Saxon castle at Broadeye. This map (Frontispiece II) originated in the early seventeenth century and exists as a 'facsimile' dated 20 January 1885. It says of its original (now lost) that it was 'made apparently after the fall of St Mary's [steeple] 1593 but before the building of the stone bridge over the Sowe at the Broadeye ante 1611'. This copy glosses the area of Broadeye in the following words: 'the old castle built by Etherbert and in memorie fortified with reel [real] walls'. Etherbert has been reproduced as Edward the Elder in the Staffordshire County Council education pack.[88] According to the Victoria County History, the William Salt map says that Edward the Elder built a castle on the mound at Mount Street, a supposition that it finds

'highly improbable'.[89] The confusion about the site of Broadeye has been unravelled by Young and Morgan, who showed that it was the site of a Norman motte and bailey castle built about 1070.[90] Cuttler et al. found good archaeological evidence for the motte ditch in 2003–2006, but their argument for a co-located defence of the Late Saxon period carries less conviction (see Chapter 3, p. 39).[91]

With this Norman intrusion out of the way, we may examine the case for the likely location of the burh using the sparse materials at our disposal: archaeological observations, the medieval street plan and later documentation. These all generate different kinds of hypothesis, but they can be presented as convergent. Archaeological excavations provide no endorsement for a Saxon defence at the edge of the marsh. At Clarke Street, the Late Saxon activity at the edge of the marsh is known and did not include a palisade. The wooden palisade shown in the William Salt map defines the limit of the medieval town and also of the inhabited peninsula. There is little doubt that this same area was the zone of occupation for Late Saxon Stafford too, as indicated by the spread of Stafford ware.[92] But such a palisade cannot have stood from the Saxon period. Excavations at Broadeye in 1984 appear to have contacted medieval timber defences, and at North Walls located possible medieval defences in stone[93] without in either case claiming a coincident Late Saxon structure.

Of the five excavations that set out to test possible lines of the Late Saxon burh, none has succeeded.[94] This leaves the possible contact made by Paul Robinson at Water Street in 1971, which was in advance of the general recognition of Stafford ware.[95] Lastly there is the highly tentative suggestion made above, that the Bath Street excavations encountered a ditch or road, palisade and possible tower of Late Saxon date along the line of Earl Street.

One of the few factors that might offer support to the Earl Street boundary is the nature of the medieval street plan, as captured by Speed's map (Fig. 2.10) and largely conserved until recently. Four elements are enduring: Greengate Street forms the main axial street that bisects the peninsula and leads from its neck down to a crossing of the River Sow in the south. We do not know how old this crossing point might be, but this axis follows that of the putative Roman road proposed by Lawrence Bowkett (above). Thus this street suggests,

---

86 FR8.4. The whorls from Late Saxon contexts are sw1, 2, 3 (in Stafford ware), 7 (soapstone) and 12.

87 1 August.

88 Staffordshire Schools History Service's 'Stafford Maps', which includes a copy of a map from the collection (66/92). I am indebted to Julie Jackson of the William Salt Library for the following note: 'the correct reference for the map supplied is 55/2/74, a copy map of Stafford borough and suburbs, c. 1600. This map was given to the Library in 1974 by one of our former Trustees, Mr J. S. Horne, who has since died, and so we are unable to investigate further as to where Mr Horne acquired it from. The map resembles that of Speed's map of Staffordshire. The marginalia are extracted from borough minutes, etc., and are probably derived from an original now lost, possibly from Lord Stafford's Estate Office or the Borough Archives. As one of the marginalia refers to the William Salt Library, this copy cannot be pre-1872. The information on the map is representational and not the result of a detailed survey.'

---

89 *VCH*, VI (1979), 200.

90 Young and Morgan 2001, 33.

91 Cuttler et al. 2009.

92 See FR2.3 for occurrences of Stafford ware.

93 FR2.3.2, ST44 and ST37.

94 FR2.3.2, 38 (1982), 39 (1983), 43 (1984), 45 (1984), 54 (1988); *BUFAU* 7, map on p. 12. And see Chapter 2, p. 17 above.

95 FR2.3.2, ST 08, at SJ 9209 2304.

prima facie, a likely early through-route and crossing point by bridge or ford.

On the west side of Greengate Street is a rectangle formed by Earl Street on the west, Stafford and Broad Streets in the north and Mill Street to the south. At the centre of this rectangle is St Mary's (and St Bertelin's) church, and to the north is the grain-processing area unearthed at St Mary's Grove. The ditch shoulder and boundary proposed at the Bath Street excavations follow the inner line of Earl Street. This hypothetical fort, which may be marked by a ditch and bank and towers, measures about 400 x 200m on the ground, a 1200m perimeter equivalent to about 952 hides. The Burghal Hidage calculator reminds us that for the maintenance of 6 furlongs of wall 960 hides are required;[96] thus the Stafford fort, if it existed as implied by the street plan, and if it followed this rule, could have been laid out as a rectangle measuring 1 x 2 furlongs with a designated garrison of 960 men.

The County Hidage has 500 hides for Stafford implying a circuit half as long, around 630 metres, or 2066 feet. If this measured 1 x 0.5 furlongs it would be too narrow to stretch from Greengate Street to St Bertelin's. But a small square fort with a side about 150 metres long (a 600-metre circuit) could be accommodated between Crabbery Street, Earl Street, Greengate Street and St Mary's Grove. While neither of these models is underpinned with strong evidence, they do serve to make the point that a rectilinear fort is more compatible both with the Hidage and the surviving street plan, than with a hypothesis involving the neck or the edge of the peninsula.[97]

Setting out eastwards from the axial road of Greengate Street are four streets, now Salter Street, Market Street, Martin Street and Tipping Street. All four converge into Eastgate Street, leading eastwards to the edge of the marsh and a causeway across it. The northern and southern streets (Salter and Tipping) have given evidence for pottery kilns, and thus may have been active in the Late Saxon period. This street pattern gives some encouragement that the larger of the two hypothetical forts did at least represent the central enclave of the burh in its final form. The four streets show a pattern characteristic of four routes setting out from different parts of an enclosure towards a common destination or exit point, in this case leading to the east across the marsh. The secondary character of this part of the town is endorsed by its becoming St Chad's parish in the twelfth-century redevelopment. By the same token, the area west of Greengate Street is

broadly coincident with the later college estate.[98] These tenuous arguments form the basis for my suggestion that the focus of the Late Saxon town at Stafford was a rectangular fort west of Greengate Street (Fig. 1.3, p. 6).

Conclusion: Character of the Anglo-Saxon burh

While accepting that the suggested size and location for Æthelflæd's fort amounts to little more than a convergence of inferences, it plays a logical role in the broader geography of Late Saxon Stafford, archaeologically considered (Fig. 1.3). We should first recall that there is no archaeological evidence for a settlement before the tenth century, even though this remained a constant quest throughout the campaign and after.[99] The hiatus will itself be sufficient to keep alive expectations of a Mercian *villa regalis* or a minster. In the case of Stafford, it can be argued that neither of these putative predecessors is unlikely or indeed especially significant (see Chapter 6). The Late Saxon development is of very high impact compared with anything that has gone before: it is extensive, organised and materially energetic.

Since every innovation we have noted smacks of Rome, we can extend the connection to the initial layout: a Roman-type fort laid out on one side of a previous Roman road, with a Roman-type industrial *vicus* on the other. Unlocated, but contained within this area, ought to be the headquarters of the upper military class with its horses and smithies, and we would expect to find a home for the mint there too. There is certainly a church, and a workplace to the north of it dedicated to receiving, processing and storing grain, and making bread and bannocks in sufficient quantities to feed an army. This community also fed on beef, centrally processed.

The *vicus* by contrast was largely dedicated to the making of pottery, which apparently formed an essential part of the overall project. The pots were designed to transport and serve food, and are made in the Roman image. They should therefore be designed both to give out rations and to embellish the lifestyle. They were not actually necessary to do either, since the people of north

---

96 Hill 1969, 91; but this use of the Hidage has been challenged, see Chapter 6, pp. 133–4 below.

97 Hill 2001, 151 suggests a defence across the neck of the peninsula 1000 feet long (rated at 242 hides).

98 Lambert 1923, 1925, 1939; *VCH*, VI (1979), 206.

99 As stated at the campaign's conclusion: 'placing the origins of the early medieval settlement will depend entirely on the laboratory dating of charcoal, pottery and kilns. If the manufacture of Stafford ware turns out to be as early as we think, then origins may be sought in a 8/9th century royal manor or 'villa regalis'. If not, then the origins can be assigned to the traditional construction of a burh by Æthelflæd in 913 AD. In either case, the structure of the settlement is the same. A central area around St Mary's church … is a reserved enclave, possibly the burh itself, later to be fossilised as the College Quarter' (Cane et al. 1983, 51).

Mercia, who had always required food and transport, had done without pottery for several centuries. This encourages us to emphasise its special roles, symbolic and official, in the Late Saxon project of occupation. Beside the road leading out of the *vicus* is the town tip, where the waste products of potting and butchery are dumped in an organised manner.

It goes without saying that the interpretation I have given to these findings and the way I have presented them are powered by a belief, first sensed on site and increasing ever since, that Stafford was a fort founded in the Roman image and run on Roman lines by a determined and educated leader. This ideal appears to have been mobilised in the service of a conquest of territory by the house of Wessex which was increasingly portrayed as a reconquest by the heirs of Rome. These matters will be reviewed in Chapter 6.

5

Aftermath: Norman and Medieval Stafford

What happened at the Norman Conquest?

Eadric the Wild (*Silvaticus*) with men of Cheshire and Wales rebelled against William I and besieged Shrewsbury in 1069. William met them at Stafford and destroyed the uprising, returning the following year to crush the remnants and redistribute the Mercian lands among his own followers. This was a traumatic event that reached deep into everyday life: areas ravaged at the time were still derelict at Domesday, seventeen years later. Stenton comments 'the operations of 1069–70 were distinguished from ordinary warfare by a deliberate attempt to ruin the population of the affected districts'.[1] We may anticipate that the residents of Æthelflæd's burh would not have been unaffected by the momentous events of the mid eleventh century. Here the intention is to focus on their fate as demonstrated by the archaeology. The first question, What happened at the Norman Conquest?', will be followed by others: When did redevelopment start? Did Æthelflæd's vision endure? Was there a second hiatus? How far did Stafford continue to embrace the urban idea? In each case I shall refer only to events on or under the ground (Fig. 5.1). Once we have got these right there will be opportunities to paint in broader medieval landscapes, using more expert hands than mine. As was observed in Chapter 3, Stafford town survived, but not at a consistently urban level. This has some implications for both the archaeology and the more general history of the town in Britain, and these will be briefly aired before returning, in Chapter 6, to our main theme: the Late Saxon burh and its context.

In order to construct a narrative archaeologically, and give it some useful historical precision, we draw on three kinds of evidence: stratification, which shows where Late Saxon features, already identified, were succeeded by something new; dendrochronology of timbers where we have them, which gives the first use of a piece of wood to the nearest year; and pottery. Although pottery is hard to date within twenty-five years, it is ubiquitous and therefore labels nearly every event. In Stafford we are fortunate in having a strongly defined sequence.[2] Stafford ware is distinctive in both form and fabric, consisting mainly of orange-coloured jars, pots, bowls, lamps and pitchers (Chapter 4, pp. 76–93). The first *medieval* fabrics are dark, iron-rich and coarse; they come in the form of broad, squat cooking pots (Fig. 5.2), soon joined by bowls, dishes and skillets. A new horizon is marked by the arrival of another distinctive Stafford product, green-glazed pitchers. Then the jugs arrive in white fabrics with green glaze (Fig. 5.3), while the later jugs are purple (Fig. 5.4; see Digest A3). This sequence of types is well represented stratigraphically at Stafford, and is compatible with their occurrence elsewhere. As a rule of thumb, Stafford-ware assemblages and medieval assemblages are mutually exclusive (see seriation tables in Digest A3). A few sherds of the iron-rich cooking pots are found in the few Late Saxon features that lie open, but this occurs when Stafford ware is no longer in use, by the later eleventh century. The green-glazed pitchers arrive in the late twelfth century and the white-ware jugs in the early thirteenth. The assemblage changes in the later fourteenth century with the dominance of Midlands purple ware. These cultural markers can be used to construct a broad narrative with pivotal points in the later eleventh century (end of Stafford ware, arrival of iron-rich cooking pots), late twelfth century (arrival of green-glazed pitchers), early thirteenth century (arrival of white-ware jugs) and mid fourteenth century (end of white ware, advent of Midlands purple ware). These cultural changes and their dates, proposed from comparative study, are well represented by the Stafford sequences, particularly those from St Mary's Grove and Clarke Street.

---

1 Stenton 1971, 605. The devastation in Staffordshire, though less complete than in Yorkshire, was 'on the same general scale'. For a useful summary of documented events relating to the Stafford castles see the contribution by Deborah Young and Philip Morgan to Darlington 2001, 32–33.

---

2 See Digest A3; the typology and dating is owed to Debbie Ford (Ford 1995; 1999).

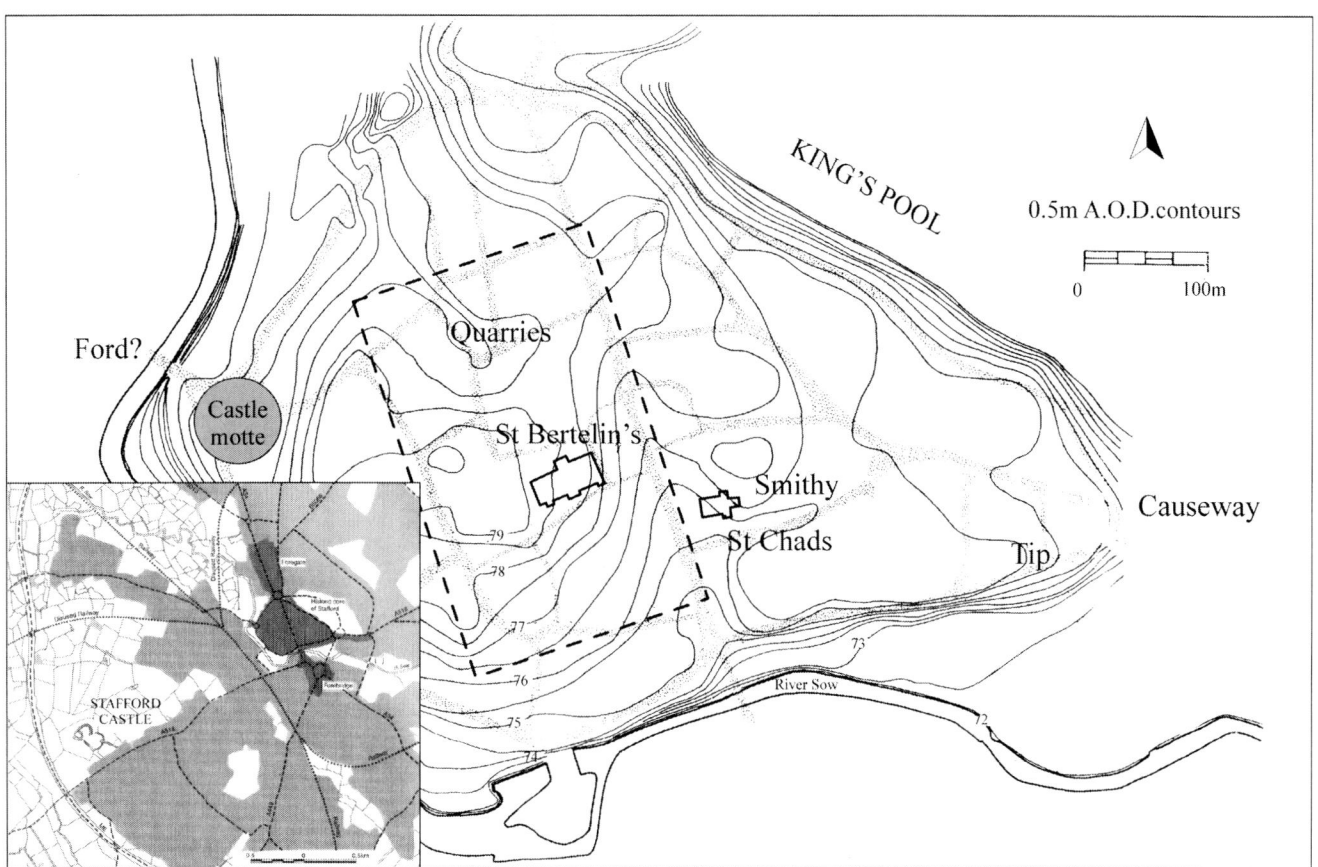

Fig. 5.1 Archaeological events in Norman Stafford, with the sites of the Stafford castles.

The consequence of the Norman Conquest was abandonment on the east side of the peninsula, and a new regime on the west (Fig. 5.1). St Bertelin's timber church was burnt down, an event followed by a period of disuse.[3] Further north the ovens were extinguished. The cereal store S16 was burnt down. Over these remains of the grain station, a layer of tread developed, which was subsequently cultivated (1607). It contained only five sherds of St Neots ware, and should represent a period of eleventh-century downturn, in which the new cultural marker (medieval iron-rich coarse-ware cooking pots) had yet to arrive (Digest A3, seriation of ST29). Cut into this layer are latrine pits accompanied by a small cluster of unresolved post-holes. One latrine pit (F404) was lined with timber between 1173 and 1183 as measured by dendrochronology (Digest A2). The well, F608, which was refurbished in AD 1007, stayed open and was perhaps still functioning until the first sherds of coarse-ware cooking pot were dropped in it.

Apart from these forlorn survivors, the main Norman activity at St Mary's Grove was the digging of ten giant quarry pits, up to 10 metres across and 2 metres deep

(Fig. 3.15). Quarrying for sand seems the most likely purpose of these pits, which are large, deep, ragged and contain copious amounts of burnt grain deriving from the Late Saxon industry.[4] The quantity and heaping of this grain implies one large-scale fire rather than a hundred mistakes, the grain being carted and tipped into the pits in a single clearing operation.

The Late Saxon bakers' establishment was thus destroyed by fire, and quarried for sand and then cleared up and levelled. We have no date for the fire, but the clearing up operation took place at a time when medieval coarse ware was plentiful, and the latest quarry pit (F290) also received a few sherds of white-ware jug. If this backfilling and restart was a single episode, it should belong to the later twelfth or early thirteenth century.

At Bath Street the site mutates from its surmised Late Saxon defence into a medieval tenement off Earl Street, with a house platform at the front and pits in the backyard. This has happened by the time medieval cooking pots and green-glazed pitchers have arrived on site together, which they do in F73, a probable cess pit

---

3   See Chapter 3, p. 29 above. C1005, C1004.

4   See Moffett in FR10.1.

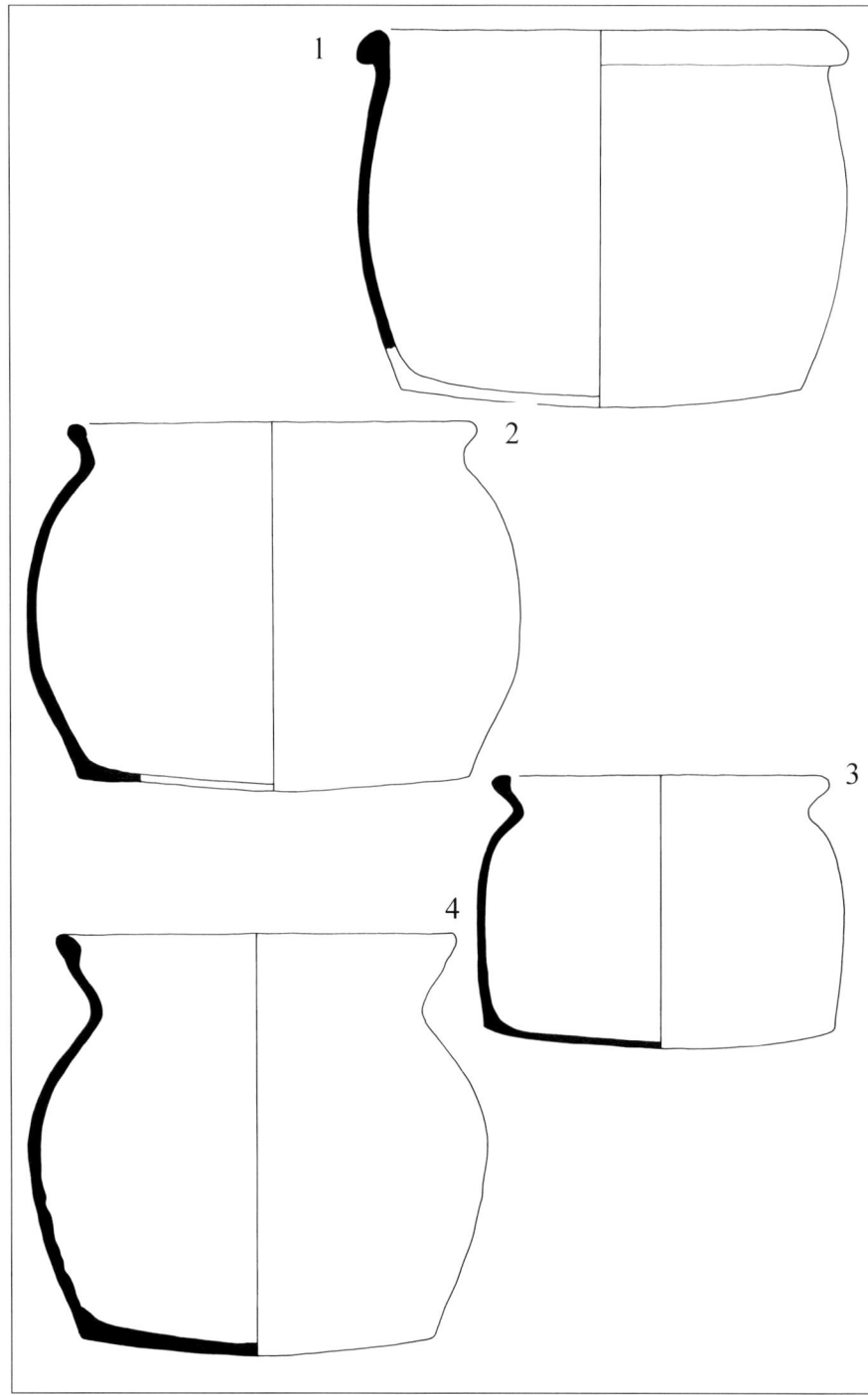

Fig. 5.2 Medieval twelfth/thirteenth century cooking pots 1–4 from Stafford (for provenance see Digest A4). Scale 1:4.

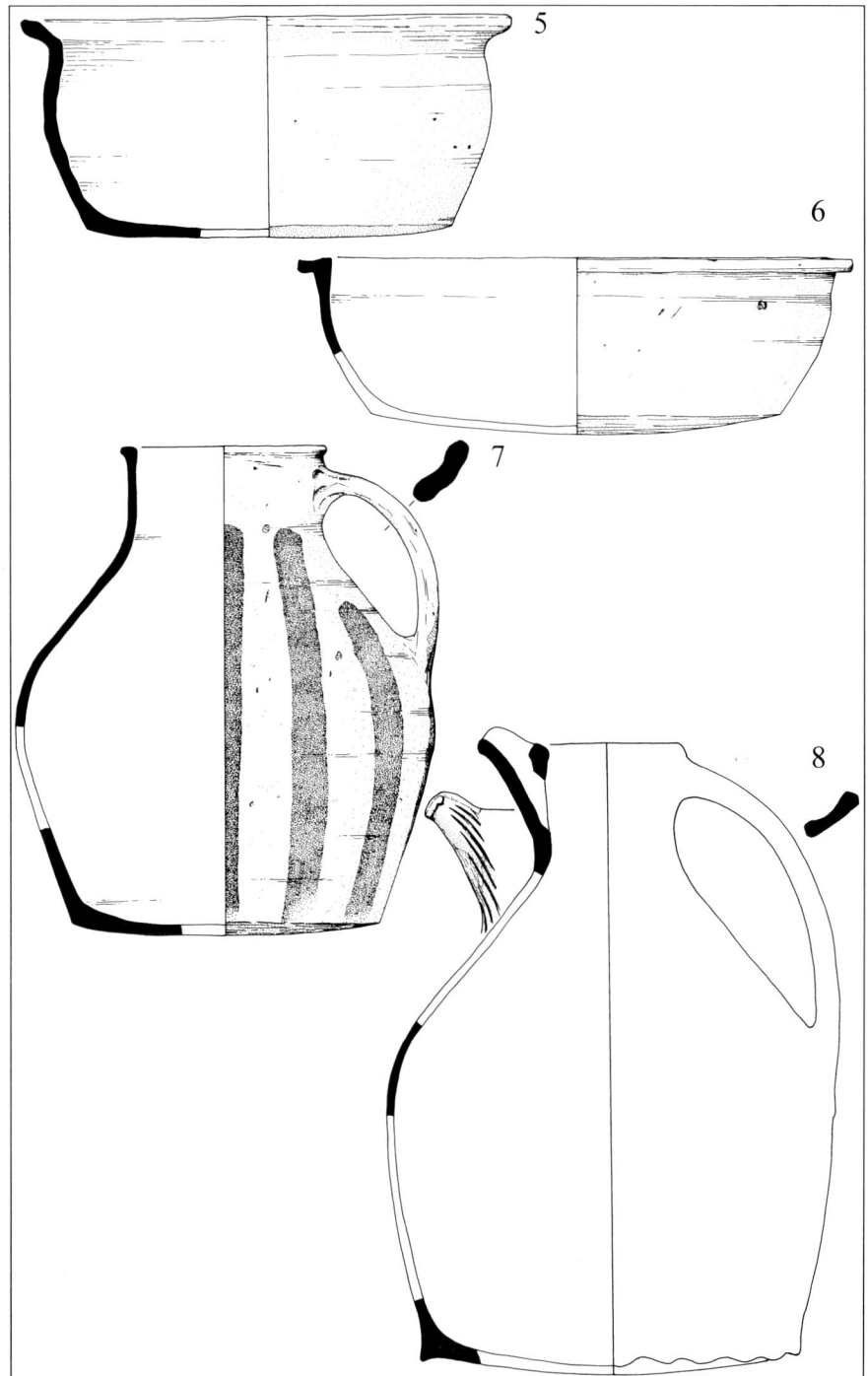

Fig. 5.3 Medieval thirteenth century bowls 5–6 and jugs 7–8 from Stafford (for provenance see Digest A4). Scale 1:4.

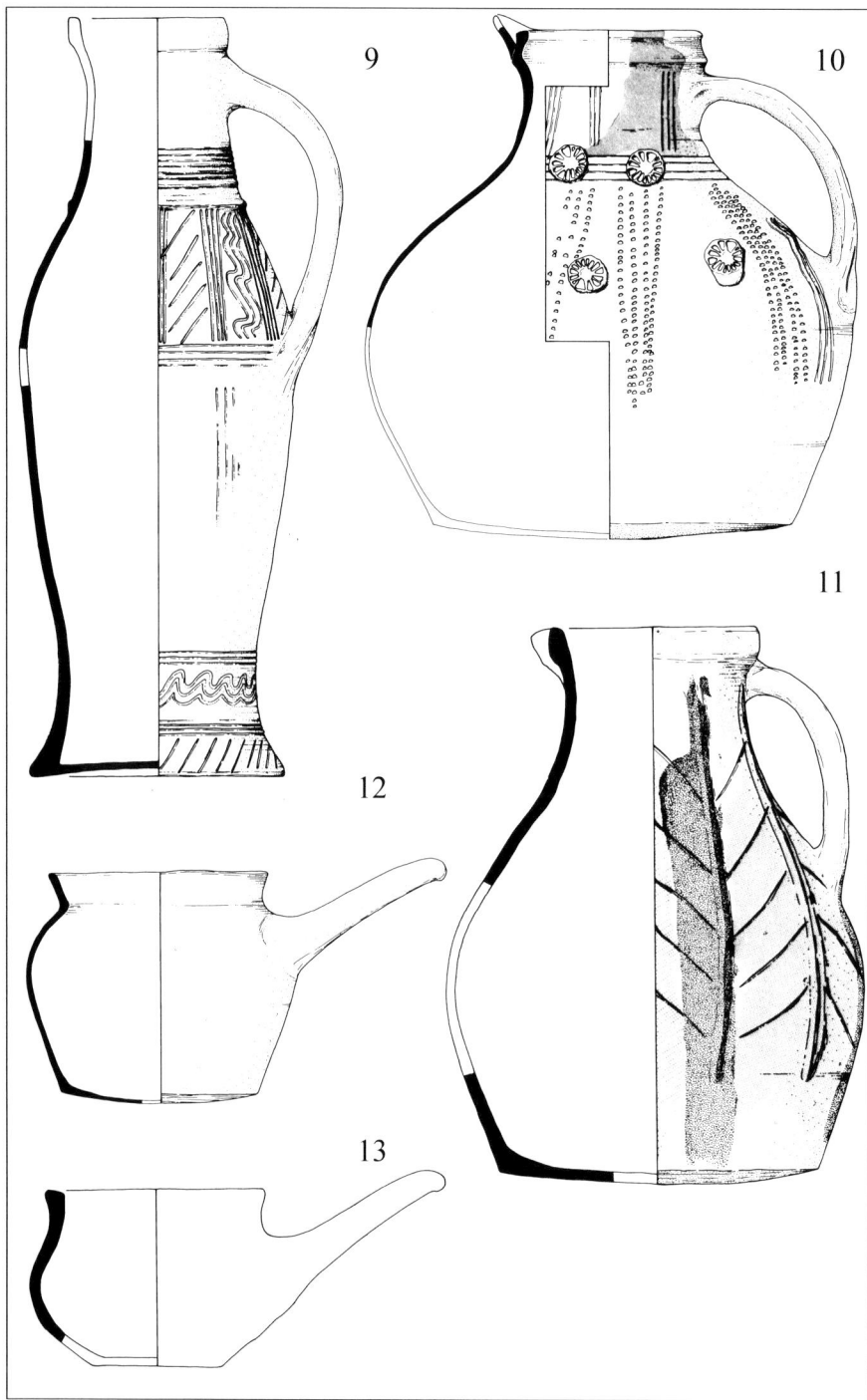

Fig. 5.4 Medieval jugs 9–11 and skillets 12–13 from Stafford (for provenance see Digest A4). Scale 1:4.

or urinal.[5] The ditch proposed as part of a Late Saxon defensive scheme remained a feature in the landscape (F92) and received coarse-ware cooking pot sherds with its first backfill (1090). It thus began to be backfilled at the same time as the quarry pits on St Mary's Grove.

Relevant to the fate of Stafford's heartland on the west side of the peninsula is the site of the Norman castle, a subject of traditional confusion (Fig. 5.1).[6] The present 'Stafford Castle', situated to the west of the town (at Castle Church) was built between 1071 and 1088 as a honorial castle by Robert I of Stafford, a Norman member of the Tosny family. His elder brother, Ralph of Conches, had fought at Hastings. He had received the lands held by Earl Edwin in Staffordshire (after the latter's fall in 1071).[7] The motte and bailey of this castle is still visible at Castle Church, and it has been the subject of detailed archaeological and documentary study in recent years.[8]

Documentary references also have a castle in the town built in 1070 and destroyed by 1086,[9] but although only briefly active, it was long remembered. *Prima facie*, the two most likely locations for the town castle are at Mount Street (at the neck of the peninsula, a classic defensive location, as at Shrewsbury) and at Castle Street (on the west side of the peninsula, where it presumably overlooked a ford or bridge). The second of the two is the more convincing and was almost certainly a motte of Norman type located at Broadeye, as demonstrated from documentary research by Deborah Youngs and Philip Morgan[10] and by means of excavation by Richard Cuttler and colleagues (Fig. 3.23).[11] The entry in Domesday Book for Henry of Ferrers' estate at Chebsey has a note to the effect that 'to this manor belonged Stafford land on which the King ordered a castle to be made; it has now been destroyed'. In the account of the borough itself, Henry of Ferrers' dwelling is given as 'unoccupied', *wastae*.[12] In a charter of c. 1200, Hervey Bagot and his wife Millicent, the daughter and heir of Robert II of Stafford, confirmed a grant of Robert III of Stafford mill to William son of Wimar. Stafford mill and its pools included land from the great bridge, later Green Bridge, 'with covert and fishponds from the old castle' as far as the mill. In a charter of Ranton Priory a tenement in Mill Street is said to lie next to the lane which led to the old castle. In 1397 the borough court

established a public tip in Castle Hill. In 1429 a grant referred to a garden on the walls of Stafford adjacent to the old castle mound ('unum gardinum super muros Stafford iuxta le Oldcastellhull'), and in 1438 the same piece of ground was described as lying in the town of Stafford against the motte (*montem*) called Old castle hill, extending from the motte to the end of the town ditch.[13] Young and Morgan thus make a strong case that the castle stood where it was marked as Castle Hill in Broadeye (no. 12 on John Speed's map) and where 'Castle Street' is now.[14] It seems highly probable that the excavations of Richard Cuttler and his team located and defined the motte ditch of this castle[15] (Chapter 3, pp. 39–41).

In the old *vicus* east of the axial street, the potteries at Tipping Street (north) were abandoned and the site was ploughed, truncating the kilns.[16] The restart, when it came, acknowledged little of what had gone before apart from the line of the street. At the town tip at Clarke Street the principal disposal of Stafford ware is in Dump 1 (1216), which is followed by a period of trample (1120/1) in which cattle are brought to drink (1173). When dumping starts again (Dump 2), it includes a notable consignment of medieval coarse-ware cooking pot and green-glazed pitchers.[17] These types of pot also occur in the latrine pits on the marsh edge. It is not clear how long an interval might separate the Late Saxon dumpers of Dump 1, from Dump 2 and its neighbouring latrine pits. If the area was frequented (e.g. to water cattle) it was not yet developed. This was to come and the argument will be, on this site as elsewhere, that this did not happen until the later twelfth century.

Stafford in the Norman period appears from its archaeology as a bleak place. There was a major burning event on the west side, on the site of St Bertelin's, and the crop-processing station within the putative burh. The Late Saxon grain and pottery industries ceased. Waste land was sparsely occupied as indicated by the occasional latrine pit. Cattle were watered and land was eventually tilled even in the town centre. The fury of William I had left its mark. It was no doubt the motte that was built at Broadeye in 1070 that was largely responsible for the initial paralysis of everything around it. By 1086, life in Stafford had become too miserable even for the Normans, and the headquarters had shifted definitively to the castle in the countryside to the west, henceforward Stafford Castle.

And yet the town must have remained active to some degree. Domesday Book records 128 occupied houses

---

5   This was noted in records as a 'sawpit'. It also contained animal bone and tile.

6   *VCH*, VI (1979), 200.

7   Darlington 2001, 9.

8   Darlington 2001.

9   *VCH*, VI (1979), 200.

10 See Chapter 3 above, pp. 39–41; Young and Morgan in Darlington 2001, 32.

11 Cuttler et al. 2009.

12 Darlington 2001, 32.

13 Summarised from Young and Morgan 2001, especially p. 33.

14 See also Chapter 4, p. 99, for the discounting of the castle 'built by Edward the Elder'.

15 Cuttler et al. 2009.

16 C1790, C1573.

17 Digest A3. These are types 5 and 7 at Clarke Street.

(with perhaps another 18) and only 51 or 52 houses which were waste.[18] The minting of coinage continued, albeit intermittently (Chapter 4, p. 96). Although one moneyer works for Edward the Confessor and for William I (Godwine), he does so only until 1070, and there is a gap with no known issues between 1070 and 1083. These slight indications of life can probably be assigned to the workings of the castle and its garrison. We see nothing as yet to indicate any surviving elements of culture from the Late Saxon town or its people.

A late twelfth-century revival

The notion that the revival of the town came on all four sites at the same time, and that that time was the late twelfth century, depends on a convergence of the dating evidence. The first certain cultural marker of the post-Saxon period, to appear on all sites, is the iron-rich coarse-ware cooking pot, and closely allied to it is the Stafford green-glazed pitcher (above).[19] Stafford ware occurs residually throughout the town, but there are no contexts of which it could be said that Stafford ware and medieval pottery might have been in use together. At St Mary's Grove, the well F608 which had served the bakers and was refurbished in AD 1007, stayed open long enough to receive the first sherds of coarse cooking pot in its upper fill. Latrine pits were dug after the baking industry had gone. F449 (containing only Stafford ware) cuts bread oven S14; F443 (containing only medieval coarse-ware cooking pot) cuts the pebble platform. Latrine pit F404, which contains coarse ware and the first load of Stafford green-glazed pitchers, used stakes supporting its timber lining that were felled in 1187. At Bath Street the stratification is not strong, but the first Stafford pitchers occur with coarse-ware cooking pots in a urinal (F73). At Tipping Street the first coarse ware and pitchers occur together in the earliest rubbish pit to be dug into the cultivated soil that buried the Late Saxon kilns. The first absolute dates that follow are c. 1170 (archaeomagnetic) for a forge and 1189 (dendrochronological) for a well. At Clarke Street, the coarse-ware cooking pot and the Stafford pitchers dominate the post-Stafford-ware use of the marsh edge until it is sealed off with clay.

The concordance here seems good. The iron-rich cooking pot may have come into existence in any decade in the aftermath of the Norman invasion, but at Stafford at least it makes its appearance in the late twelfth century, and does so in the companionship of a local high quality type – the green-glazed pitcher.

The latter at least is a sign that some kind of civilised domesticity is now possible.

The revival is not a gradual, organic re-awakening but another jump start with a central investment and a controlling design. The Stafford experience appears to endorse the pattern described in a recent historical survey of urbanism in Britain: 'from the late twelfth (from about 1180) to the mid thirteenth century there is a remarkable concurrence of evidence to demonstrate a period of rapid urban growth'.[20]

The old town centre, twelfth to thirteenth century
By the late twelfth century, St Bertelin's church had been reconstructed with stone foundations on its remembered site (Fig. 3.8). In 1186, King Stephen gave the Bishop and Chapter of Lichfield and Coventry an 'ancient free royal chapel and small college', the chapel presumably being that alluded to in the Domesday Survey and identified as St Bertelin's. St Mary's church is also thought to have been built at about this time, eventually incorporating St Bertelin's church in its fabric.[21] The medieval cemetery was to spread as far north as St Mary's Grove, where eleven individuals of pre-sixteenth-century date were examined.[22] The waste ground of St Mary's Grove was quarried and the pits backfilled with the Late Saxon burnt debris. It is not known to what kind of use such large quantities of sand were destined, but making mortar for stone buildings is clearly a possibility.

While the north end of the St Mary's Grove site remained waste until the sixteenth century, its south end began to experience development in the early thirteenth century, in the form of a small group of pits. One of the earliest pits (F342) contained a coin of King John (1203–1218). One of the latest (F471) contained horn-working debris. The horn working may have begun quite early as a small-scale survival strategy, and then held on over the following centuries: F608, a Saxo-Norman well (Periods 3–4), F471 (Period 5, twelfth–thirteenth centuries) and F320, a stone-lined pit (Period 6, thirteenth–fourteenth centuries) all showed evidence for stripped horn-cores associated with supplies for horn working. The thirteenth-century pits also contained a high proportion of identically chopped cattle shoulder blades, suggesting joints prepared for the larder or sold on.

At Bath Street, a putative timber-frame building (S1) was erected on the lip of the old Saxon bank. It had a latrine to the north and rubbish pits out at the back. The orientation of the layout was on an axis east-north-

---

18 *VCH*, VI, 186
19 See Digest A4 Table 2, and Ford 1995, figs 10 and 11.

20 Astill 2000, 46. Astill 2006, 247 proposes a period of de-urbanisation that lasted much of the twelfth century.
21 FR 2.4, 1
22 By Alison Cameron, see FR 9.1; the burials are in Period 6 (Chapter 3, Fig. 13).

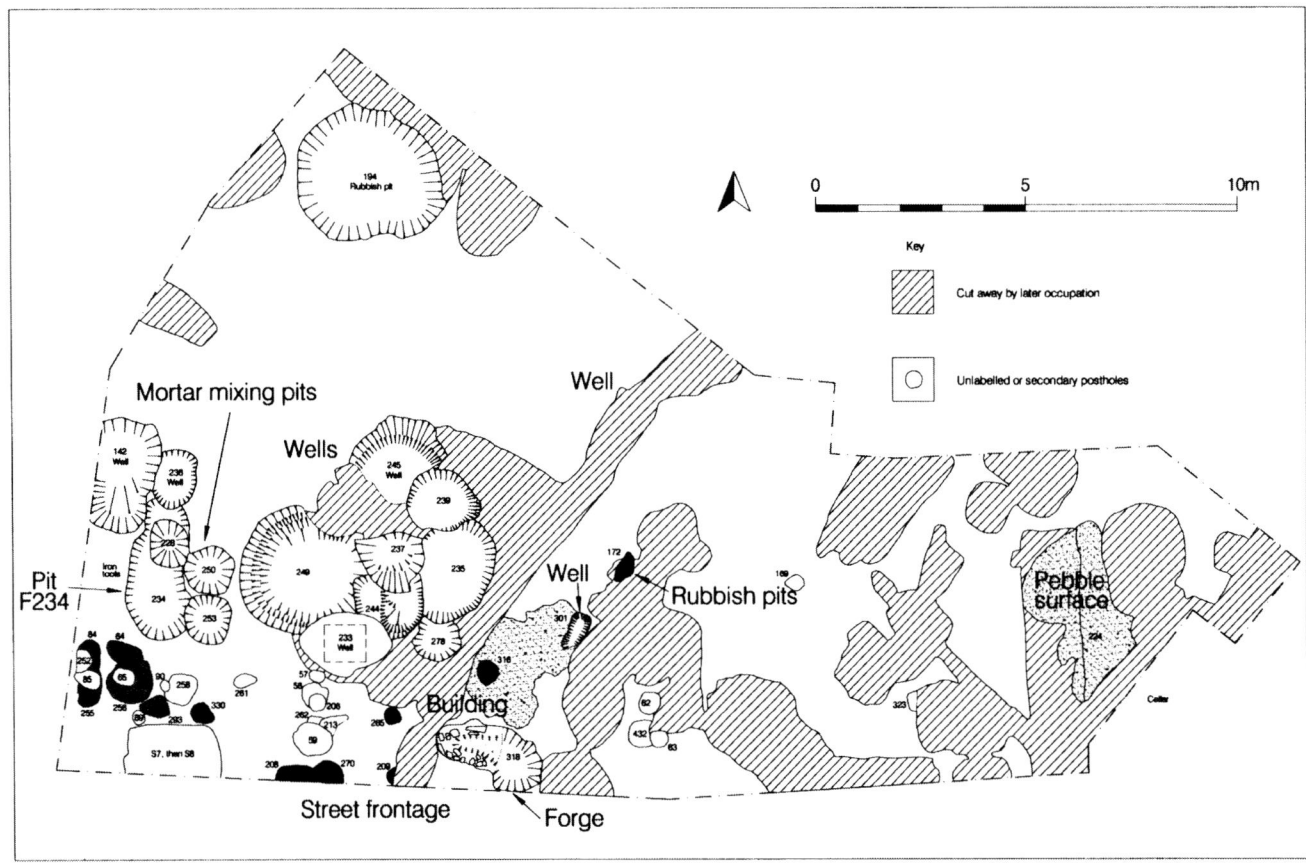

Fig. 5.5 The smithy and associated features at Tipping Street (north), c.1180–1350.

east to west-south-west, roughly 15 degrees off east to west, and represents a slight change in alignment. Rows of post-holes and stake-holes along the south edge suggest a property boundary (Fig. 3.21).

Street pattern

As assumed in Chapter 4, the medieval street pattern was that of the Late Saxon town, and the distinction between the administrative west and the artisanal area east of the axial street was now reinforced. The eastern quarter became the parish of St Chad, mentioned in a deed probably of the later twelfth century,[23] while the church building itself appears to date slightly earlier, from the mid twelfth century.[24] To the south, Forebridge was a suburb by 1170.[25]

On the east side, a smithy sprang into action at Tipping Street (Fig. 5.5). This took the form of a U-shaped forge (S3) with a pebbled apron, surrounded by numerous rubbish pits and a sequence of timber-

lined wells. The forge gave an archaeomagnetic date of c. 1170, which would be its first firing, and the earliest of the wells was dated by dendrochronology to AD 1189. There was a possible residential structure or workshop on the street frontage (S7, Chapter 3, pp. 45–6). One of the pits (F234) contained a famous assemblage, to be described presently. Other pits showed evidence of mortar mixing, perhaps to be linked to the nearest stone building, St Chad's church.[26]

The area adjacent to the east was interpreted as a residential tenement.[27] Other residences presumably began to front the streets, spreading east until they reached the town tip. The old tip itself was sealed off with clay and there was a local development of a post-built house with hearth and hut at the back, laid out end on to Eastgate Street (S1–S3). There was no evidence for craft, and the whole is interpreted as a residential house, shack and garden (Fig. 3.35).

---

23 *VCH*, VI (1979), 245.

24 *VCH*, VI (1979), 246. The extant architecture of St Chad's suggests a twelfth-century date of construction; an inscription citing Orm as the maker perhaps refers to the 'Orm of Eastgate' appearing in twelfth-century documentary references.

25 *VCH*, VI (1979), 186.

26 'mortar-mixing pits', ST32/F227, F228, F253, F322 and F213.

27 According the excavator, ST33 comprised a fence of small posts at right angles to Pitcher Bank (S9: F44, F81, F82, F84, F71, F72); a building of large posts parallel to Pitcher Bank (S10: F62, FF73, F79); two cess pits beside the building (F74, F57); later rubbish pits beside the building (F9, F16, F28); and later rubbish pits on the south-west side of the fence (F70, F36). FR6.2.

A town defence was built, encircling the whole peninsula with gates at north, south, east and west. Piles were used where it crossed marshy ground, and a timber revetment was contacted at Broadeye.[28] This renewed town was to thrive through the thirteenth century. To its well-documented streets and buildings we may now provide further illumination by bringing some selected aspects of its material culture into focus, beginning with the Tipping Street craftsmen.

The Tipping Street forge

The Tipping Street forge contained a high concentration of slag, most of it relating to smithing.[29] At a given moment, datable before the mid fourteenth century, the occupants deposited in a nearby pit (F234) an unusual collection of iron tools and a complete bone comb, objects that have been studied by John Darlington, Cecily Spall and Steve Ashby, and are here described in summary.[30]

The pit contained six layers, with the finds in the top two (representing disuse of the pit). Layer 1503 included animal bone, worked bone and horn, two spindle whorls and sixty-one parts of metal objects, mainly iron tools. Context 1474, the final fill, contained the comb. Animal bone, smashed into small fragments, was present in large quantities, 800g in 1474 and 3kg in 1503; some horn was also found – suggesting handles.[31] This implies that the metalworkers were involved in production in the round, so that the comb, with its metal rivets could equally be part of their output, rather than a sign of vanity. The pit also contained 20kg of discarded twelfth- to thirteenth-century ceramics, adding to the impression of a major clearing-out operation. The tools as a whole constitute an assemblage sufficiently large and rare to merit its presentation here. They evoke the activities of a blacksmith serving a community of tailors, carpenters, gardeners and farmers in a thriving town and hinterland, mending or making scissors, shears, spades and axes and with a side-line in jewellery.

The metal-workers' assemblage
Cecily Spall[32]

The assemblage of iron objects included a variety of bladed tools, horse furniture and structural ironwork. The non-ferrous assemblage included a decorative clasp, a buckle and an offcut of lead. The admixture of items appears primarily to represent a cache of used and broken tools and structural ironwork for recycling (Figs 5.6–5.9).

Shears

The complete shears (Fe 51) take the form of Ward Perkins Type 1b (eleventh–thirteenth centuries)[33] and were deposited into pit F234 in a useable, though possibly blunt condition.[34] Similar examples have been found at London,[35] Pevensey,[36] Thetford,[37] Northampton[38] and Beverley.[39] Notably though, the Stafford pair has copper-alloy wire banding around the arms and compares most closely with a pair found at Trondheim (albeit probably residual within a sixteenth-century context).[40] A complete pair with silvered decoration on the blades from a building at Weoley Castle, Birmingham, was dated to the thirteenth century (AD 1200–1260),[41] and two elaborately decorated pairs with inlaid silver decoration on the blades from London was dated to the late thirteenth century.[42] Another pair of shears from the assemblage is represented by a small length of arm and part bow (Fe 52b).

Scissors

The pair of scissors (Fe 52a) is represented by two blades attached by a rivet at the pivot and a fragmentary length of arm and handle. Though sporadic examples of scissors are known from the early medieval period, Ward Perkins asserts that scissors 'make a convincing reappearance in everyday life' in the thirteenth and fourteenth centuries, and cites a pair found with the remains of a man thought to have been killed by a falling megalith at Avebury, who also carried two silver pennies of Edward I (dated 1307).[43] Examples recovered and published subsequently support a strengthening trend from the late

---

28 FR2.3.3, a30, a41–a4; FR2.3.2, ST44.

29 Darlington 1985.

30 The pit is F234 stratified below well F142, which was lined in AD 1256 according to dendrochronology, but some evidence for re-use of timbers was observed by Jon Cane who suggests a disuse in the early fourteenth century (as implied by pottery, FR6.3). The reports will be found in Darlington 1985, FR8.6.2 (Spall) and FR8.4 (Ashby).

31 The bone specialist was not so sure (FR9.2). 'Horncores of sheep and cattle form an insignificant proportion of the assemblage. Altogether, a combination of refuse from meat consumption and butchering is put forward as an interpretation of the F234 assemblage.' Much the same effect would be produced by the butchering of a carcass to extract bone.

32 FAS Heritage Ltd, York.

33 Ward Perkins 1940, 154, fig. 47.

34 Darlington 1985.

35 Cowgill et al. 2000, 106, fig. 70, 311.

36 Dulley 1967, 228.

37 Dallas 1993, 102–3, fig. 120; Rogerson and Dallas 1984, 87, fig. 126.

38 Williams 1979, 271, fig. 118.

39 Armstrong et al. 1991, 136, fig. 105.

40 Long 1975, 28, fig. 10v.

41 Oswald 1962–3, 129, fig. 51, 4.

42 Cowgill et al. 2000, 106, fig. 70, 316–17.

43 Ward Perkins 1940, 151.

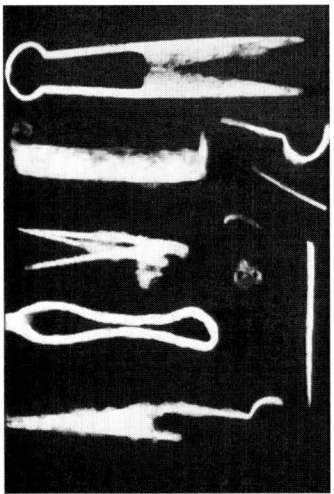

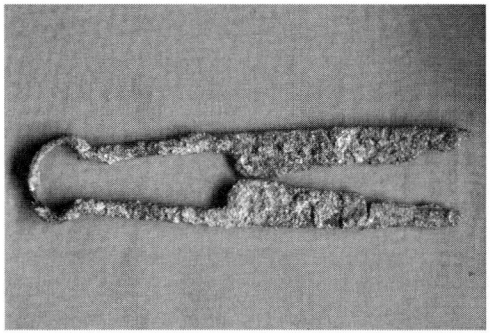

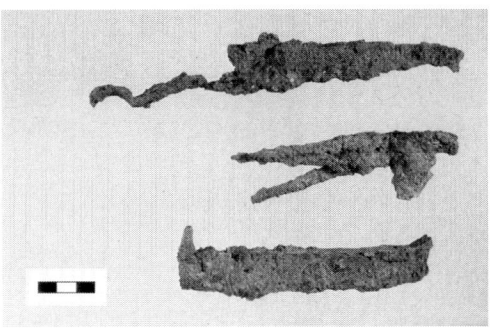

Fig. 5.6 Assemblage of tools from pit F234 at Tipping Street (north): clockwise from top left: X-ray image, shears, dividers, axes, draw knife and scissors. For a catalogue of all objects from F234 see FR8.6.2.

twelfth century. A fragment of scissors is known from a late twelfth-century (AD 1188) deposit at Lurk Lane in Beverley[44] and another complete pair was found in Thetford, also dated to the late twelfth century.[45] Two examples from early to late fourteenth-century deposits were recovered during riverside excavations in London,[46] three pairs have been recovered in York, one pair in an early fourteenth-century context at the Bedern[47] and two from mid fourteenth- to early sixteenth-century

contexts at Fishergate, one pair of which was recovered from an assemblage of seventy items of metalwork thought to represent a cache of scrap metal.[48]

Drawknife
A drawknife (Fe 72) was included among the tools and is complete but for a small section of tang. The tool is similar to examples recovered at King's Lynn dated 1250–1350[49] and an example from York recovered from a thirteenth-century deposit at 16–22 Coppergate.[50]

44 Armstrong et al. 1991, 136.
45 Dallas 1993, 102–3, fig. 120, 46.
46 Cowgill et al. 2000, 114, fig. 75.
47 Ottaway and Rogers 2002, 2741, fig. 1347.

48 Spall and Toop 2005.
49 Clarke and Carter 1977.
50 Ottaway and Rogers 2002, 2728, figs 1336–7.

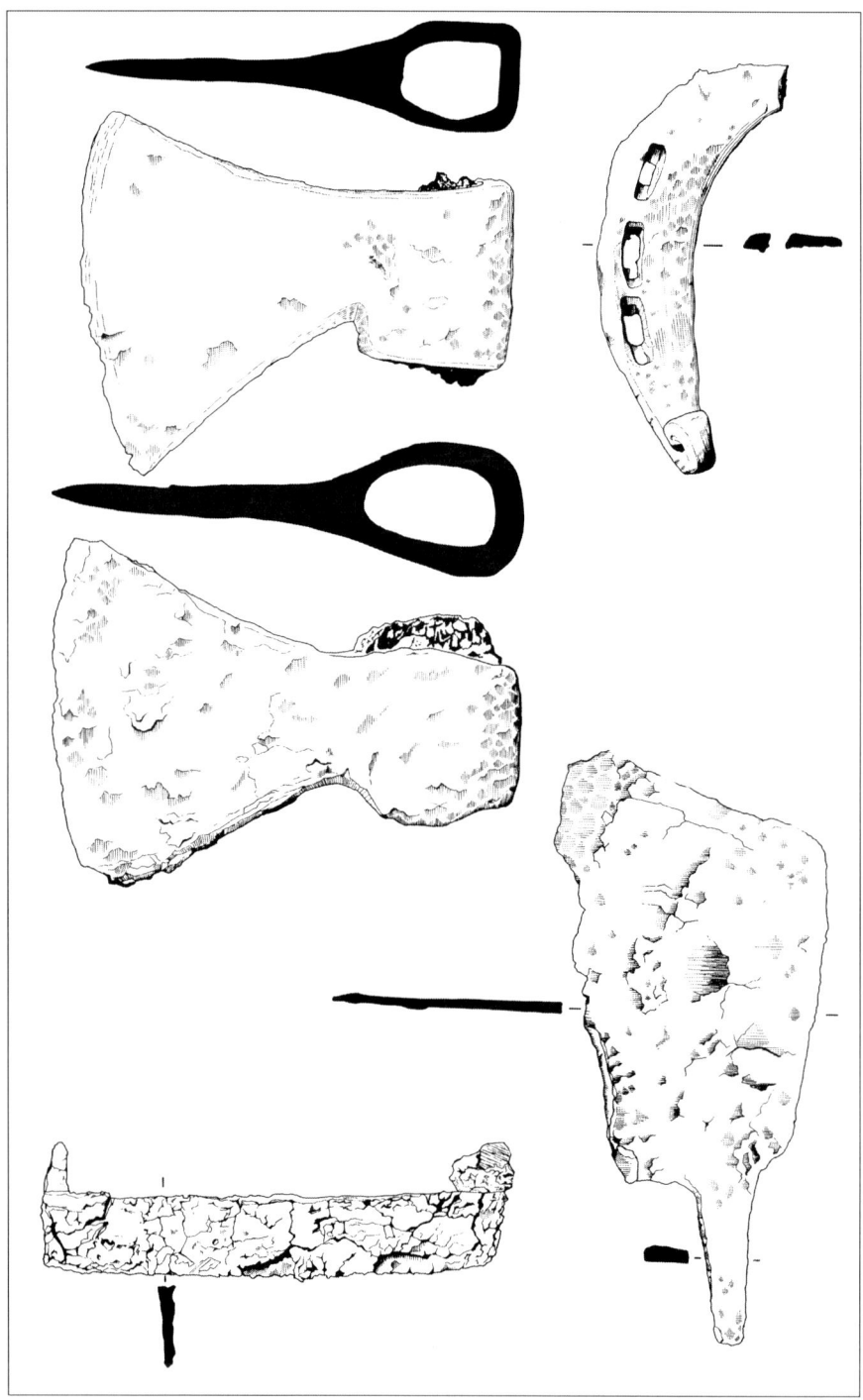

Fig. 5.7 Iron objects from F234: axes (Fe 73, 74), cleaver (Fe 41), draw knife (Fe 72) and horse shoe (Fe 63). For a catalogue of all objects from F234 see FR8.6.2; for a list of all iron objects see FR8.6.3

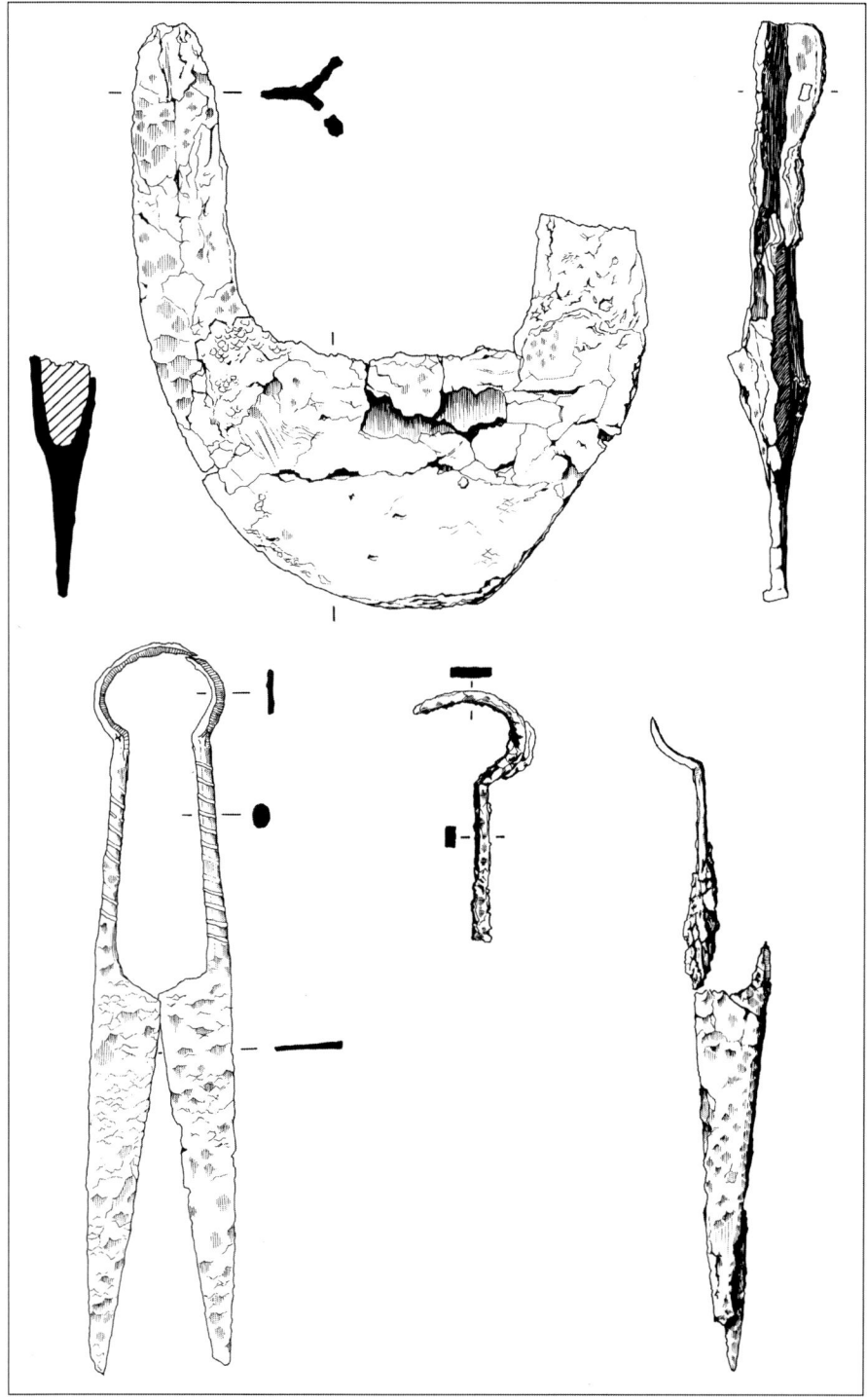

Fig. 5.8 Iron objects from F234: (top) spade shoe (Fe 4), shears (Fe 51, 52b), scissors (with detached handle) (Fe 52a). For a catalogue of all objects from F234 see FR8.6.2; for a list of all iron objects see FR8.6.3.

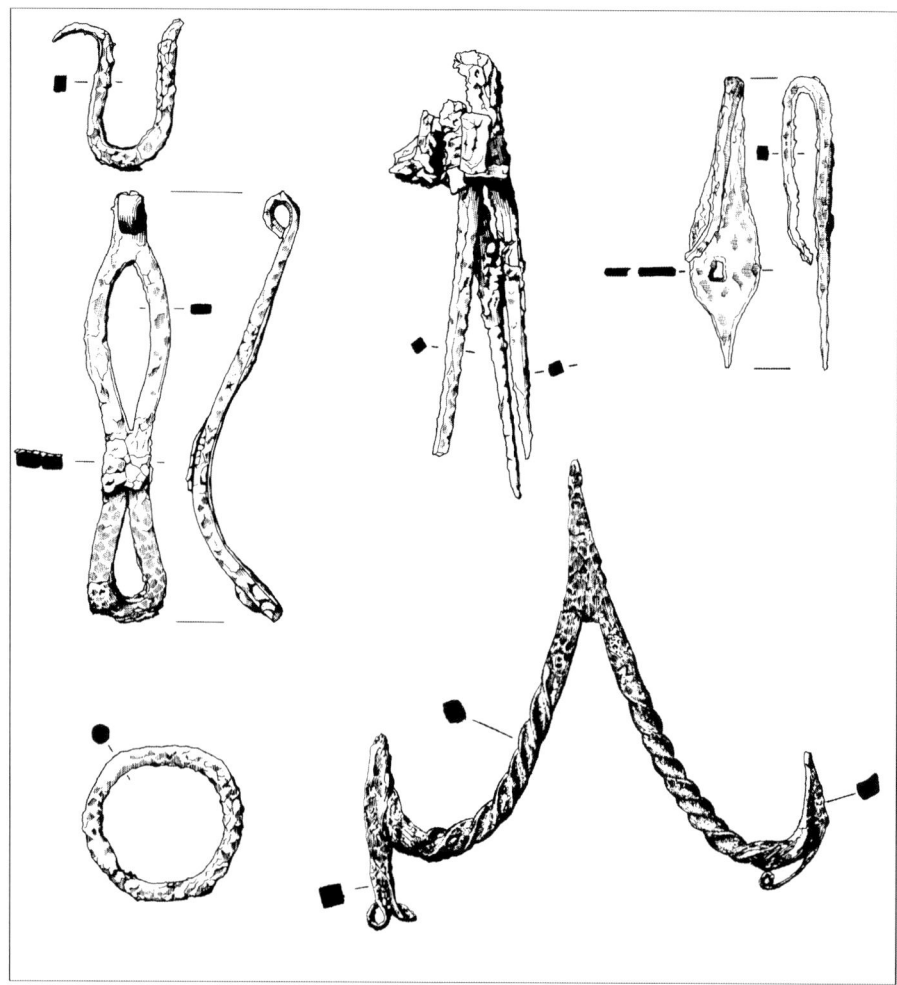

Fig. 5.9 Iron objects from F234: hasp (Fe 115), figure of eight latch (Fe 114), dividers or cluster of nails (Fe 130), hinge (Fe 97), hook (Fe 123), ring, perhaps from harness (Fe 129). For a catalogue of all objects from F234 see FR8.6.2; for a list of all iron objects see FR8.6.3.

Axes

Two bearded axe heads (Fe 73 and Fe 74) were included in the assemblage in a complete condition, apparently hafted, judging by the mineral-preserved wood remains and iron peg. Axe head Fe 73 was the subject of metallographic examination which established the axe had been manufactured by welding a ferrite/pearlite back onto a tempered bayanite tip to ensure a sharp, hard cutting edge able to absorb cutting blows.[51]

Cleaver

A fragmentary blade has been tentatively identified as a cleaver (Fe 41) and consists of a tanged blade over 70mm broad. Metallurgical analysis suggested either a low quality blade with no hardening to the cutting

edge or a blade so well-used that the cutting edge had been worn away.[52] Cleavers are often identified by a solid iron handle such as the example recovered from a fifteenth-century context at Sandal Castle,[53] although a similar tanged, 70mm-broad blade recovered in London is published simply as a possible blade dated to the late fourteenth century.[54]

Spade iron

The round-ended spade iron or shoe (Fe 4) is similar to early examples of similar dimensions from tenth- to eleventh-century contexts at Thetford,[55] and 16–22

51 Darlington 1985.

52 Darlington 1985.
53 Mayes and Butler 1983, 246, fig. 6.
54 Cowgill et al. 2000, 93, fig. 62.
55 Rogerson and Dallas 1984, 81, fig. 121.

Coppergate, York,[56] and to spades illustrated on the Bayeux Tapestry, although in the latter the form of the iron and its attachment cannot be determined.[57] Whether rectangular, round or point-ended, Ward Perkins states that there 'does not appear to be any chronological distinction' in spade iron form during the medieval period,[58] and these early examples may be misleading as parallels for Stafford. Another close parallel comes from excavations at Norwich Castle though is not dated more precisely than late eleventh century to 1600.[59] Notably, four spade irons were recovered from a forge context at Sandal Castle including a small round-ended example very close to the Stafford iron; though dated to the mid seventeenth century, the context of possible recycling is noteworthy.[60]

Horse furniture

The part horseshoe (Fe 63) can be identified as Clark Type 3 dated in London to 1200–1350, but predominant between 1270–1350.[61] The presence of a calkin, in this instance double-folded, might strengthen a thirteenth-century date for the Stafford shoe.[62] In addition, at Winchester and Waltham Abbey fiddle-key nails are largely identified with thirteenth-century contexts.[63] A Ward Perkins Type A cheek bit (Fe 129) was also within the assemblage, but is not diagnostic of date.[64]

Buckle

A small copper-alloy buckle (Cu 8) was recovered from the assemblage and consists of an oval buckle frame with offset buckle bar (Fig. 5.11). The buckle pin remains in place, although the plate is missing. In London, buckles of this form are not catalogued before 1350,[65] but two examples similar to the Stafford buckle from Winchester date to the early and mid to late thirteenth century respectively.[66]

Decorative Plaque

A decorative copper-alloy mount (Cu 24) was among the assemblage and stands out as an elaborately decorated item among the ironwork (Fig. 5.11). A frame carrying four settings, some containing decayed ?glass, is clench-riveted to a sheet with a further central quadrilobate decorative mount, the settings of which

conceal two attaching rivets, while a central rivet-hole may indicate the position of a lost mount.

Dating the assemblage

Some items within the assemblage remain long in general use, such as figure-of-eight hasps, staples and nails. Nonetheless, the form of a number of tools and the horseshoe represent objects with more precise stylistic indicators and together the latest dated objects within the assemblage suggest deposition during the late thirteenth to early fourteenth century. Other items within the Stafford assemblage have a longer currency, from the eleventh to thirteenth and fourteenth century, and some may be genuinely old items within the group, since hoards of scrap metal, presumably used extensively by the medieval smith, may include items a generation or more older than the date of deposition.[67]

Deposition of the assemblage

The deposition of the group is entirely consistent with the abandonment of a forge. The condition of the items when deposited appears from metallographic analysis, and in some instances the incompleteness, to indicate material intended as stock scrap for recycling, particularly the spade iron, shears and scissors, which were deposited in a broken condition. Indeed, the group of three contorted nails appears to represent the early stages of binding the items together to form a billet for re-working. The axe heads were apparently hafted and functional when deposited and might appear hoarded, although (more significantly) are rare finds on archaeological sites since they are expected to be the subject of 'assiduous' recycling for their steel content.[68]

Few of the items hold obvious craft-specialisation associations. The shears are for light use and could have been employed in a domestic context, and the same is true of the possible cleaver and scissors, notwithstanding their comparatively unusual appearance. The bearded axes are of a type described by Ward Perkins as a 'general-utility tool for civil use'[69] and more generally the use of axes was by no means restricted to specialist use.[70] The drawknife suggests a level of wood-working specialism but stands out as such among a more quotidian assemblage.

★

56 Ottaway 1992, 555, fig. 224; Morris 2000, 2315–16, fig. 1137.
57 Ottaway and Rogers 2002, 2747.
58 Ward Perkins 1940, 126.
59 Ayers 1985, 32, fig. 28.4.
60 Butler 1991, 70; Goodhall 1983, 242, fig. 5.
61 Clark 2004, 96.
62 Clark 2004, 82.
63 Goodhall 1990, 1059; 1973, 174, fig. 13b.
64 Ward Perkins 1940, 80, fig. 19a.
65 Egan and Pritchard 2002, 22, fig. 11.
66 Hinton 1990, 512, fig. 129; 516, fig. 130.

67 Clark 2004, 93.
68 Ottaway and Rogers 2002, 2724.
69 Ward Perkins 1940, 61.
70 Morris 2000, 104.

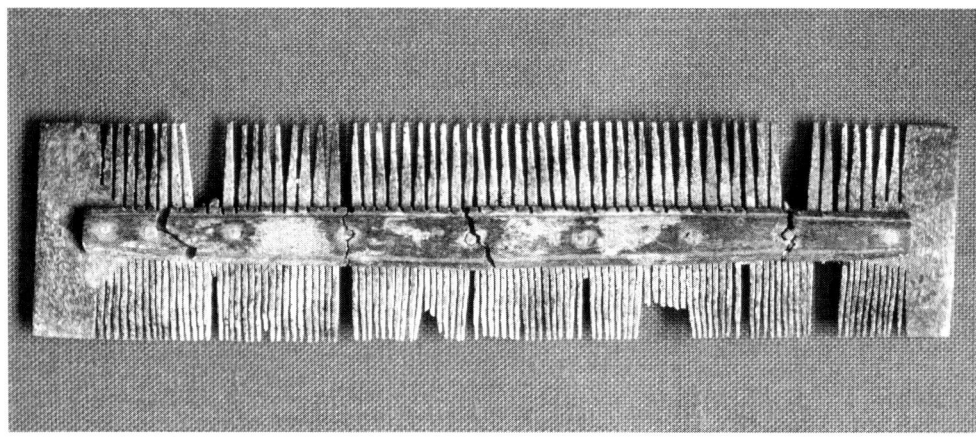

Fig. 5.10 The comb from F234. For the full report see FR8.4

The comb[71] (Fig. 5.10)

The comb was double-sided and composite, made of
bone riveted with bronze, and it measured 18.5 x 4.0cm
with a weight of 30.16g, as found. It was made from
a flat piece of bone, sandwiched between two thicker
pieces of bone held together by nine bronze rivets, 1mm
square, at intervals of 20–25mm. The teeth had been cut
after this 'sandwich' had been assembled, as was evident
from cuts made in the cladding bone. The bone had lain
in waterlogged conditions and had shrunk.[72]

Comment on the comb
Steven P. Ashby[73]

Double-sided composite combs with differentiated
teeth and copper-alloy rivets fit into Ashby's type 13.[74]
Such combs have their origins in the workshops of the
Scandinavian medieval towns, and date broadly to the
period between the late twelfth and fifteenth centuries.[75]
They reached northern Scotland and the islands of the
North Atlantic as products of North Sea trade, and they
were also traded to the south and east of the Baltic,
whereupon they were actually manufactured in some
of the important trading towns of eastern Europe and
European Russia.[76] However, such finds are scarce in
England and Ireland.[77] A fragmentary example from

Lurk Lane, Beverley, features openwork decoration, and
is more finely ornamented than the Stafford example.[78]

The internal chronology of type 13 combs is not
yet well understood. There is no overarching sequence,
although a number of local typologies have been
developed.[79] There is confusion as to which elements of
morphology relate to chronology, and which represent
spatial variation,[80] but some basic patterns are apparent.
The long, straight-ended form, with functionally-
arranged rivets (as represented by the Stafford comb)
does seem to predate smaller, more ornate models,
which may feature offset teeth, ornately profiled ends,
ring-and-dot decoration, decoratively positioned rivets,
zoomorphism, or any combination of the above.[81]

The deposition of a double-sided composite
comb in midland England sometime after the late
thirteenth century is consistent with this chronology,
but nonetheless demands explanation. The form never
became popular in England, and it is notable that this
example, at least, fits into the 'simple, undecorated' group
that may represent the earlier end of type 13's range. Its
Scandinavian contemporary, the type 9 comb, is a rare
find. By contrast, single-sided composite combs were
being made in England in the eleventh century, and
local forms such as types 7 and 8, which date broadly
to the period between the tenth and twelfth centuries,
are frequent finds in English urban excavations.[82] All
indications point to the use of Scandinavian combs
declining in England after the eleventh century, and
perhaps plummeting fairly rapidly after this point.

In this context, the Stafford comb represents one of
the last gasps of the Scandinavian-type comb and would
have stood out in late thirteenth- or fourteenth-century

71 Find no. 32/F234/1474/1.
72 Information from Joanna Williams, Conservator, Birmingham
    City Museum.
73 Department of Archaeology, University of York.
74 Ashby 2006, 2007, 2009.
75 For example Flodin 1989; Hansen 2005; Persson 1976; Rytter
    1991; Ulbricht 1980; Wiberg 1977, 1979, 1987.
76 Ashby 2006, ch. 8; Batey 1987, 208–12. E.g. Amorosi 1992,
    121; Luik 1998, 68–128; Smirnova 2005, 305.
77 Ashby 2006, table 7.2; MacGregor 1985, 94–5. See Dunlevy
    1988; Hurley and Scully 1997, figs 17.1 and 17.2.

78 Foreman 1991, 185, 191, fig. 128, no. 1120.
79 Flodin 1989; Wiberg 1987. Cf. Hansen 2005, 180–6.
80 Cf. Clarke and Heald 2002; Wiberg 1987.
81 Cf. Wiberg 1987, type D3; Clarke and Heald 2002.
82 Galloway 1990; MacGregor et al. 1999.

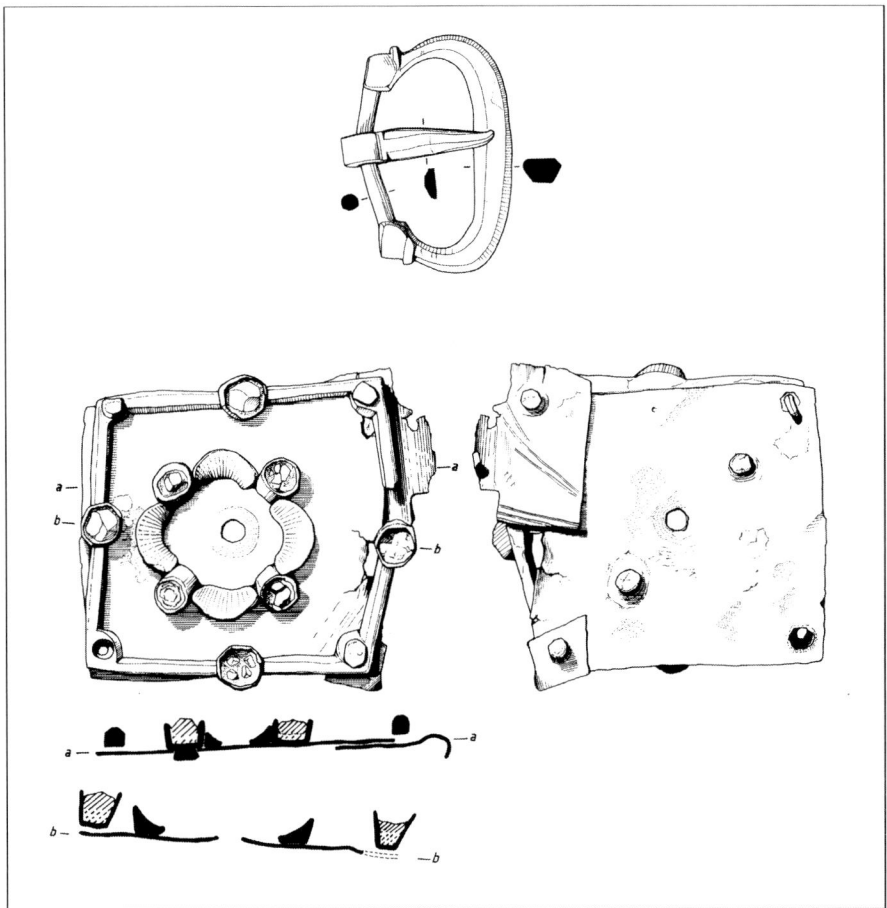

Fig. 5.11 Copper-alloy objects from F234: buckle (Cu 8), decorative plaque (Cu 24). Scale 1:1. For a list of all copper alloy objects see FR8.5.

England. The use of composite bone/antler combs in general was close to its end at this date, and it seems most likely that the grooming accessory of choice was made in perishable materials such as horn or boxwood. In such surroundings, the owner of the Stafford comb must have been conscious of its associations. Perhaps the comb represented a piece of exotica obtained through travel, or through contact with travellers and traders from overseas, or perhaps it was a piece of home for a Scandinavian settler in central England. Maybe it was an heirloom, long curated before being lost in a general clear-out.

★

Other medieval industry

All the other sites also produced varying quantities of ironwork; some categories are common to all major excavations, for example, knives and household and building fittings.[83] The St Mary's Grove site in the town

centre produced horseshoes and horse furniture,[84] and from the same site came three iron arrowheads and two spurs.

Bronze objects were more evenly divided[85] (Figs 5.11–5.13). St Mary's Grove produced ten buckles, four keys (all of the keys found in this campaign) and a heraldic pendant, probably used on a horse bridle (Cu 18). Tipping Street produced eleven bronze buckles, including one with raised decoration in the form of an animal (Cu 13) and a square plaque, perhaps a buckle plate with four stone settings (Cu 24). If we want to maintain the primacy of the central area, it is not excluded that the Tipping Street finds represent material in for repair. Medieval coin loss also divides evenly between St Mary's Grove (8) and Tipping Street (5). The kings represented are William I, Henry II, John, Henry III, Edward I and Edward II.[86]

St Mary's Grove produced all the examples of architectural stone, none especially specific but including

---

83 There are 176 items; see FR8.6.3.

84 FR8.6.3; nos 53–61, 68–70.

85 FR8.5.

86 FR8.5.1.

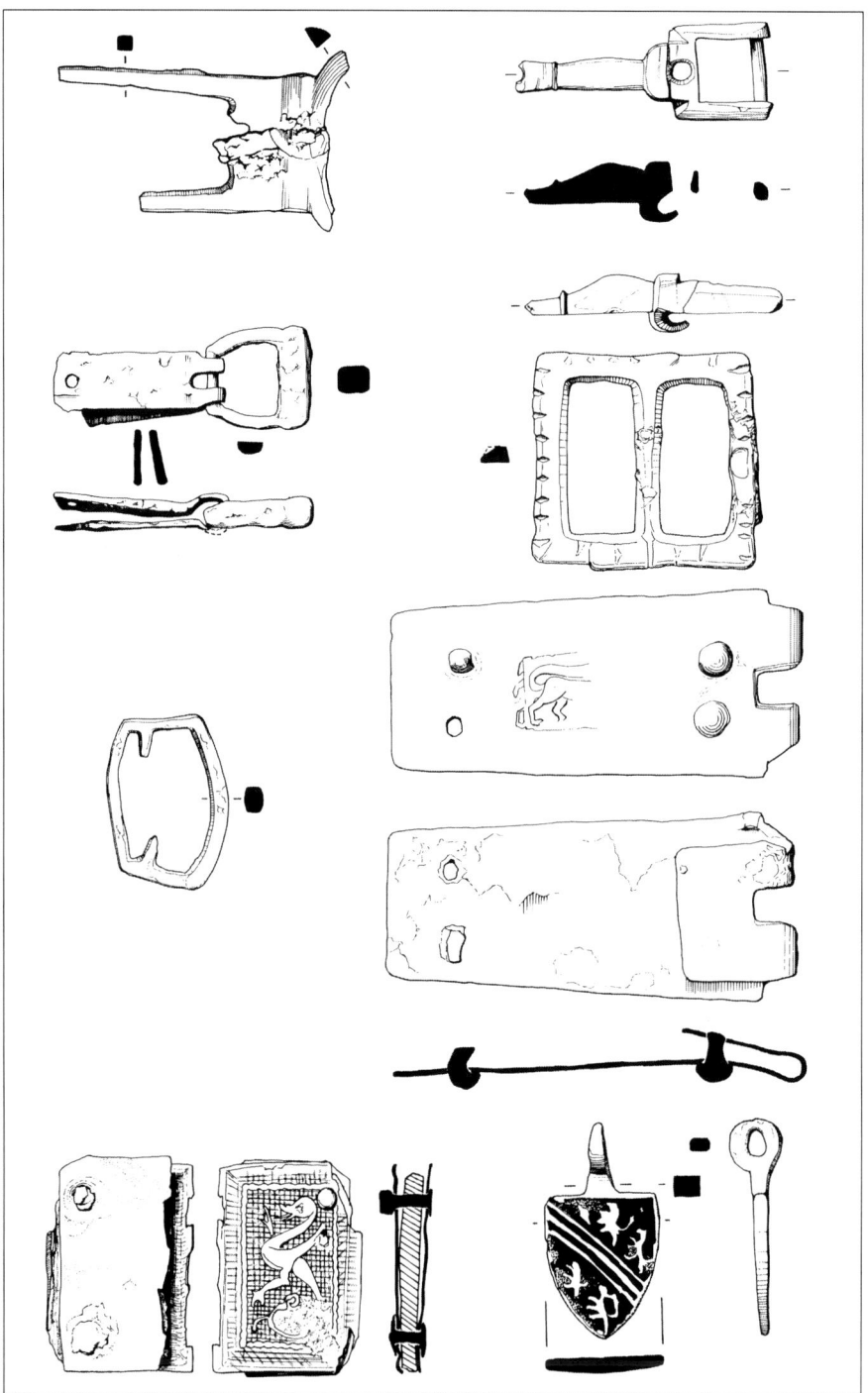

Fig. 5.12 Copper-alloy objects from medieval Stafford: fragment of buckle (Cu 1 from ST29), small buckle with two iron rivets (Cu 3 from ST29), stirrup-shaped buckle (Cu 4 from ST32), square buckle with incised decoration (Cu 7 from ST32), small buckle (Cu 9 from ST32), rectangular buckle-plate with four rivets (Cu 10 from ST29), rectangular buckle-plate with animal ornament (Cu 13 from ST32), heraldic pendant, copper-alloy with enamelled inlay, probably from horse harness, possibly of de Bohun family, earls of Hereford (Cu 18 from ST29). Scale 1:1. For a list of all copper-alloy objects see FR8.5.

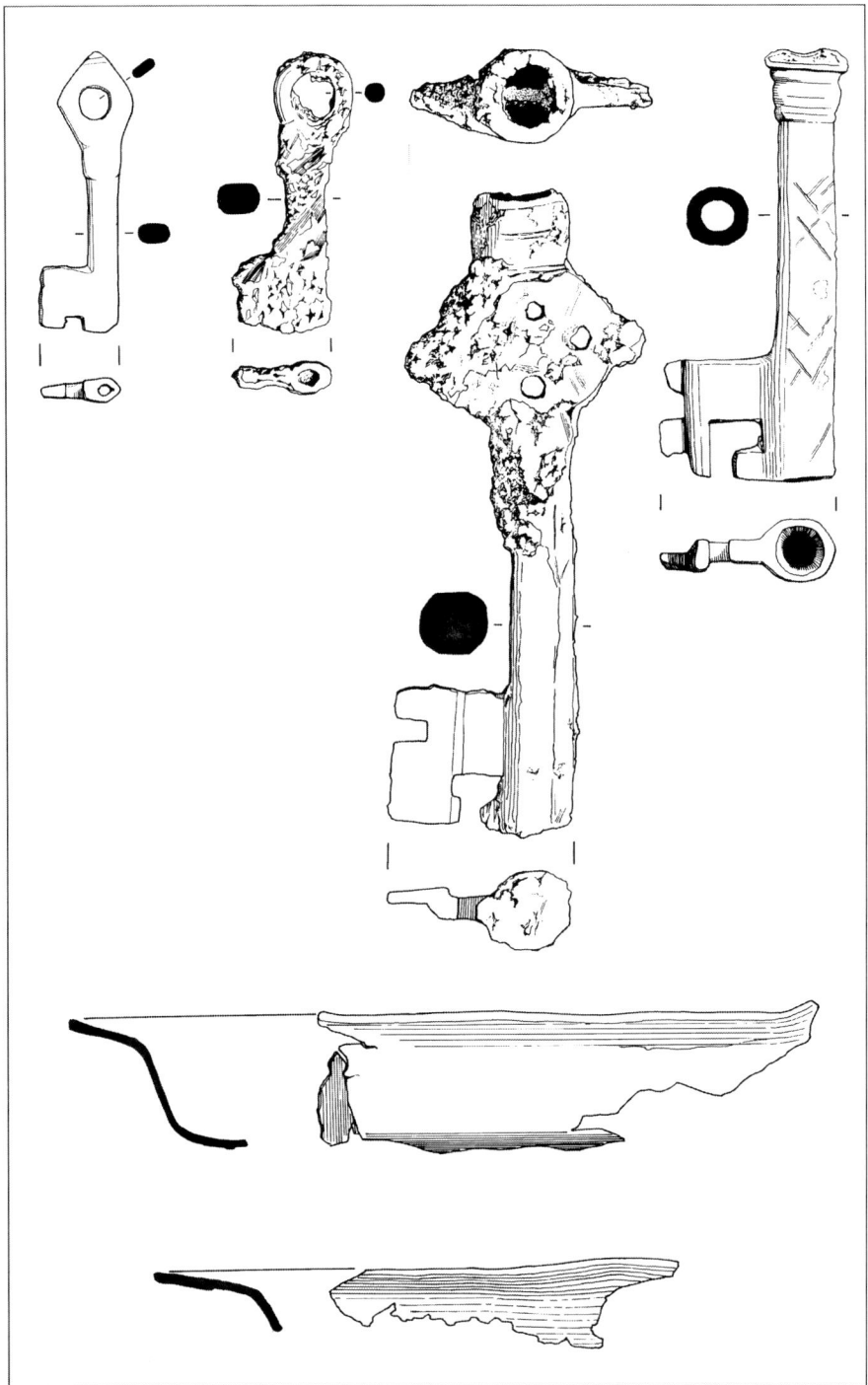

Fig. 5.13 Copper-alloy objects from medieval Stafford: keys (Cu 25–28, all from ST29) and two fragments of bronze vessels (Cu 29 from ST29 and Cu 30 from ST32). Scale 1:1. For a list of all copper-alloy objects see FR8.5.

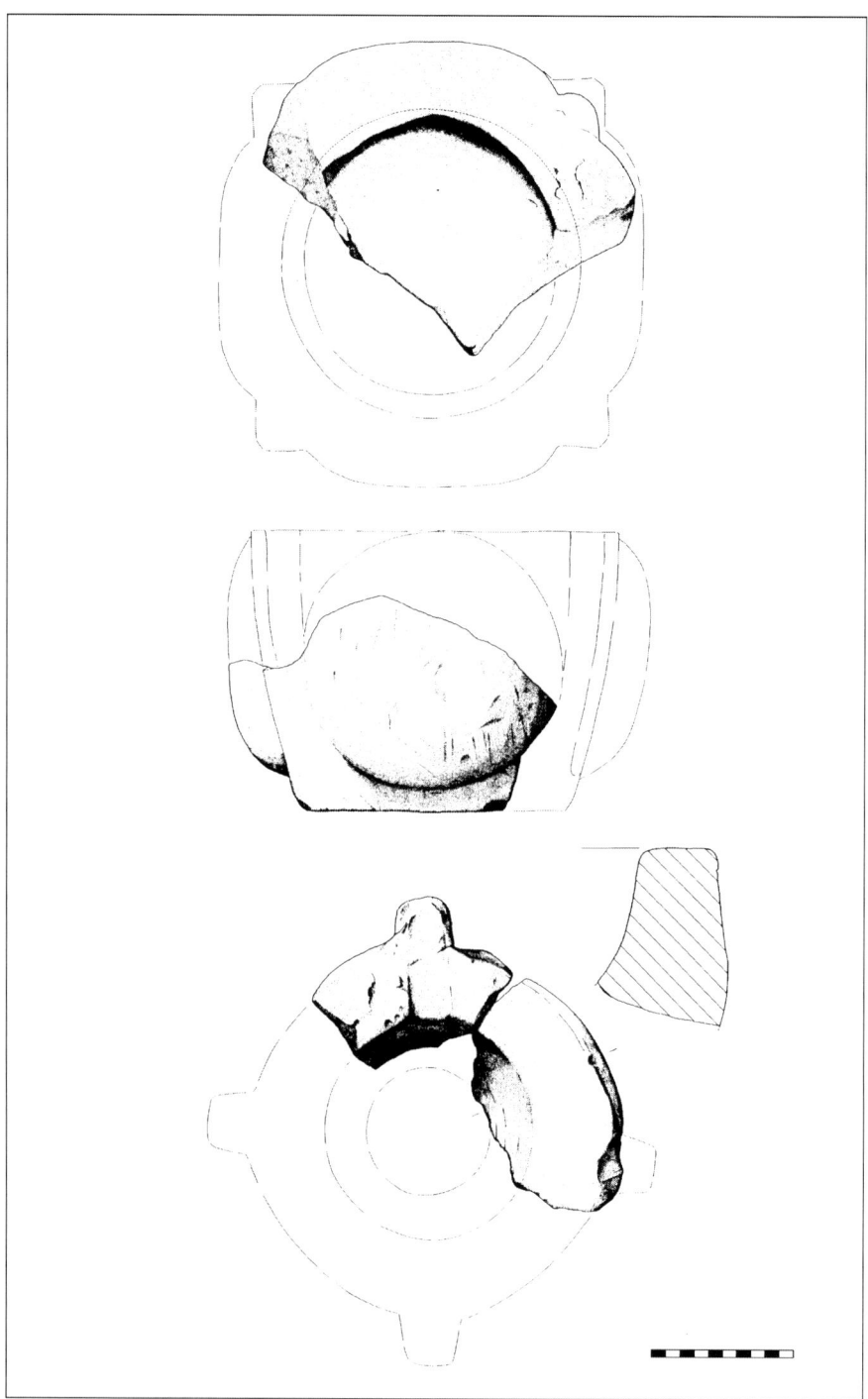

Fig. 5.14 Mortars from St Mary's Grove (WS 3 and WS 4/5). For the list of all stone objects see FR8.4.

two hollowed-out sandstone vessels that may be mortars or holy-water stoups (Fig. 5.14). This exiguous material perhaps reflects the proximity of Stafford's central church.[87]

Plants[88]

As in the Late Saxon period, the medieval plant assemblages proved a powerful indicator of the environment and economy. Two new crops made their appearance: vetch (*Vicia sativa*) and rivet/macaroni wheat (*Triticum turgidum/durum*). Vetch appears in pit F227 from Bath Street, in a late twelfth- or early thirteenth-century context, and is otherwise known from documentary records to have been grown from at least the early thirteenth century.[89] Rivet/macaroni wheat was found from the twelfth century at St Mary's Grove, roughly contemporary with its arrival elsewhere in Britain.[90] A Period 5 pit at St Mary's Grove (F471) produced an abundance of rachises of *Triticum turgidum/durum*; otherwise the only primary feature which contained any of this wheat was the stone-built kiln (S8) which is dated to Period 6. Unfortunately the assemblage from the kiln S8 was not diagnostic. The cereals present are the familiar mix of club/bread wheat, rye, barley and oats, with a trace of rivet/macaroni wheat. One pea and one bean were found, both substantially smaller than normal and possibly having come from the tail ends of the pods and representing a waste fraction. The proportion of chaff fragments was low, with rye rachises again accounting for most of the chaff. It seems likely that the kiln had been cleaned out and its contents disposed of.

A medieval pit at Bath Street (F227) contained several spreads and lenses of charred material, including a moderate number of wheat rachises, but other chaff material was sparse except for rye rachises. Weed seeds were abundant and the range of species present was large. The assemblages are in fact rather similar to the Late Saxon oven assemblages. This pit is of uncertain date but cuts the line of the putative bank; the material it captured may be a part of the Late Saxon burnt grain assemblage.

Two waterlogged medieval wells and a waterlogged pit were examined, all from Tipping Street. One of the wells (F233) produced an assemblage primarily of plants of waste ground. Some, such as *Ranunculus subgenus Batrachium*, and perhaps *R. Lingua* and *Scirpus maritimus/tabernaemontanii*, could possibly have grown in the well after it had started to fill in. The flora

indicated disturbed ground in the vicinity of the well, but probably not heavy trampling, and this too could be indicating the disuse of the well. There were no food plant remains apart from a single seed of fennel, which could have been growing as part of the waste ground assemblage rather than under cultivation.

The other well (F245) contained charred cereal grains and seeds of arable weeds, and a flax seed, a sloe stone and a dill seed provide some indication of household rubbish. Substantial numbers of sedge, wood-rush (*Scirpus sylvaticus*), a couple of *Juncus* sp. seeds and some heather flowers (*Calluna vulgaris*) suggest these plants may have been collected for flooring, bedding or thatch and dumped in the well with other rubbish. Cannock Chase, a few miles to the south-east, or the southern end of the Pennine ridge, would have been a plentiful source of heather although it is possible that other sources may have existed nearer to the town.[91]

In the King's Pool pollen sequence, the second and greater peak of cultural indicators should represent part of the medieval period.[92] Cereal pollen is at its highest. This may represent more cereal growing, especially near the King's Pool, or more transport, processing or disposal of cereal products in the town beside the pool. *Linum* (flax) appears in very scattered pollen records from 84cm upwards. Flax pollen is very poorly represented in pollen diagrams, so this horizon may therefore not represent the beginning of flax growing at Stafford, but could represent an increase. The King's Pool may have been used for the retting of bundles of flax.

The Cannabaceae pollen record, probably representing *Cannabis* (hemp), increases from 3% to about 10% and the weeds *Artemisia* and *Urtica* also increase. As with flax, the stems were retted for the fibre, which is the probable cause of this strong representation. Hemp was used for sacking, sailcloth and rope, such as that used for animal harnesses, and was therefore part of the everyday needs of people at this time.

The wetland and aquatic vegetation has large amounts of *Sparganium* and a peak of *Myriophyllum verticillatum* tp. as well, signs apparently of standing water rather than marshland in the King's Pool at this stage.

Animal use[93]

At the town tip from the twelfth century there is an increase in the relative proportions of sheep and pig and an increase in the quantity of discarded joints, which is read as indicating more local consumption of pork and mutton and more local discard. However, old habits die hard and the marsh continued to receive the

---

87 FR8.4
88 Abridged from Moffett in FR10.1.
89 Currie, 1988.
90 Greig 1983; Moffett 1986a; 1986b; 1987.

91 Edees 1972, 221.
92 FR10.2; Fig. 3.40 above, zone S4 81–46cm.
93 FR9.2.

waste products of the animal economy throughout the thirteenth century – overall an economy that remained heavily dependent on mature cattle. By the end of the thirteenth century the marsh had become a general town midden receiving the carcasses of dogs and, unusually, a dancing bear – a reminder of the many roles that animals were called upon to perform in medieval society, roles not often captured by an archaeological record dominated by food waste.

In Period 2, on Tipping Street, of the 240 bones identified in the metalworkers' pit (F234) 89% belong to the three main domesticates, the remainder being fish (3 bones), domestic fowl (16 bones), goose (4 bones) and unidentified smaller birds (4 bones). Sheep/goat is dominant (54% of domesticates). This may be due to the high number of metatarsal and metacarpal fragments (37, giving a MNI of 7, mature and immature). Tarsals and phalanges account for another 35 bones. This assemblage is closely associated with a manufacturer's waste but is not obviously at variance with animals somewhat vigorously butchered for food (above). A cat ended up in well F233.

In the thirteenth century there were tanners, shoemakers and glovers at work in Stafford, and wool was sold there by the fleece.[94] It should be expected that part or most of the cattle and sheep were being exploited for leather and wool production at near industrial levels.

A mid fourteenth-century decline

This busy and productive community was not destined to endure. At Tipping Street the latest well was constructed in AD 1256, and the date of the objects in the metalworkers' assemblage suggests that the smithy ceased business in the late thirteenth or early fourteenth century (above). The site was abandoned altogether and put to cultivation at a time reckoned from the pottery sequence to be before 1400.[95] There was a kiln producing pottery at Salter Street thought to have been operating about AD 1360.[96] At Clarke Street, the timbers of S2, S3 and the fence were destroyed by fire, resulting in a layer of charcoal extending along most of the western half of the site (1080, 1089). The pottery suggests this had happened before the arrival of late fourteenth-century types. The central site of Bath Street was levelled and under cultivation perhaps before the end of the thirteenth century, although gentrification

in the form of a garden is not excluded. An urban downturn is documented widely in England during this century, the century of the Black Death, even if these two misfortunes are not necessarily consequent on each other.[97]

However, at Stafford the impact was uneven: the western quarter, still the centre of kudos, was less affected and development appears to have continued without major interruption. After a period of disuse (1002) a new stone floor was laid in St Bertelin's church. This rebuilt chapel was offset to the south, so a refoundation from scratch seems possible. The new floor was associated with decorated tiles which were dated to the later fourteenth century.[98] At Broadeye, the site of the old castle was seemingly unoccupied,[99] but St Mary's Grove prospered (Fig. 3.16). The western part of the site saw the construction of a stone-built grain-drying kiln (S8) (Fig. 5.15) and a substantial stone-founded building (S7), with a privy (F320) (Fig. 5.16). Numerous rubbish pits suggest a residential workplace. S7 is likely to have been a substantial timber-frame building, in this case on a stone footing. Throughout the Middle Ages, archaeologists seeking to define house plans and to draw elements of social space from them are routinely defeated by the ingenuity of medieval carpenters, who construct colossal buildings with a very slight imprint on the ground (Fig. 5.17). The pottery seriation suggests that medieval residence here continued without a break up to the fifteenth or sixteenth century.

A sixteenth-century revival

It is also at the ever-resilient St Mary's Grove that the sixteenth-century bounce-back is most evident (Fig. 3.17). Features assigned to this phase cut an extensive levelling layer (1341/1710) which contained post-medieval pottery, and a sister layer in the south-west (1746) also contained post-medieval pottery, as did the graveyard boundary ditch in its final phase. This levelling seems to indicate a notice of intended redevelopment which subsequently arrives in the form of numerous pits, two houses and a malting kiln (S15), implying a brewery. The kiln contained an appreciable quantity of germinated grain (at least 30%), chiefly rye and

94 *VCH*, VI (1979), 216.

95 FR6.3; J. Cane says that the area reverted to cultivation in the fourteenth century until the sixteenth. In spite of poor records, it can be said the site was only spasmodically occupied until its redevelopment in the early modern period.

96 Archaeomagnetic date; FR2.3.3, 56.

97 Palliser 2000; Dobson 2000, 274: the 'decades before and after 1300 witnessed a considerably less buoyant phase'. Ibid., 276: English towns lost a third of their population between 1347 and 1377.

98 Church 3 (20/1001). See FR3.3.

99 Cuttler et al. 2009: 'There was no pottery which with any certainty could be said to come from the 15th or 16th c. Overall the paucity of Midlands purple ware and the absence of late medieval orange wares and Cistercian ware really does tend to suggest an absence of domestic occupation in the late medieval and early post-medieval periods.'

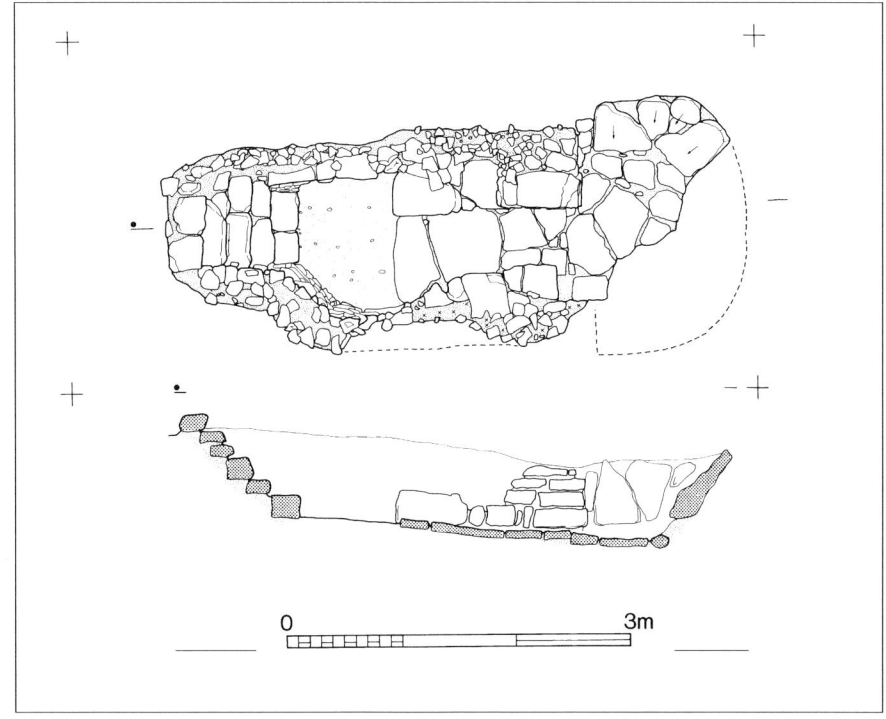

Fig. 5.15 Medieval grain-dryer (S8) at St Mary's Grove.

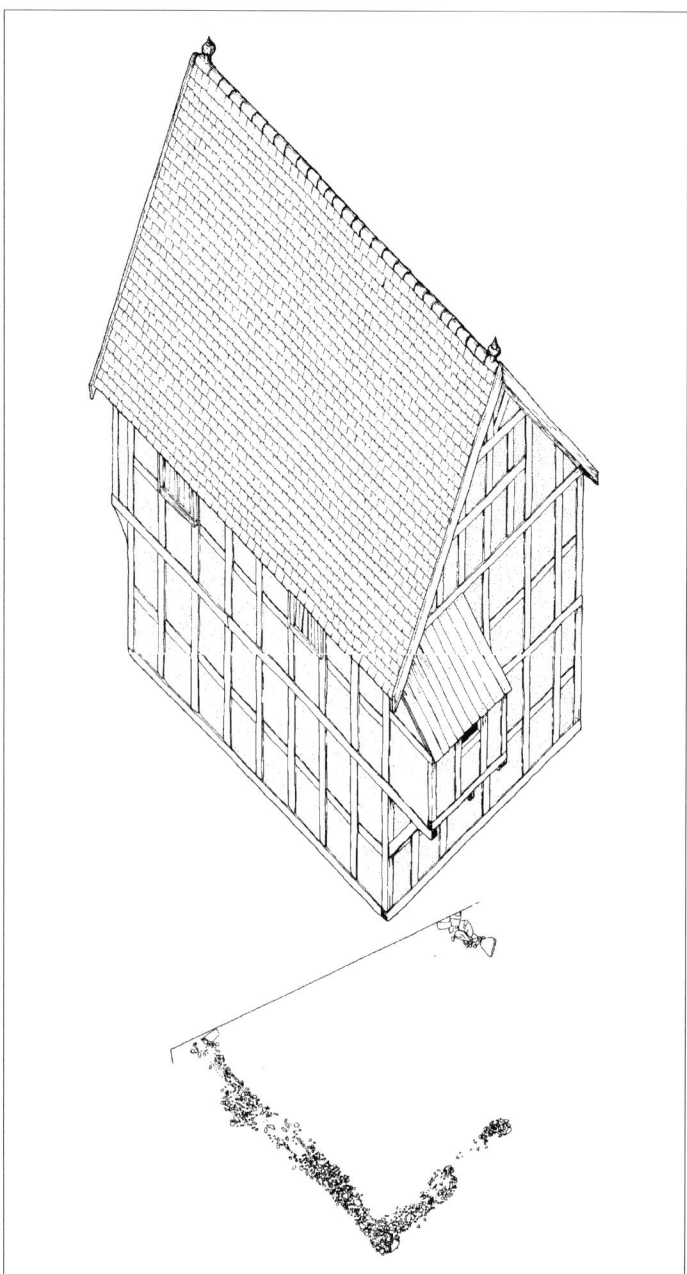

Fig. 5.16 Medieval house or barn (S7) at St Mary's Grove (reconstruction by J. Cane).

oats, and also a fair number of detached coleoptiles (evidence of sprouting) in one of the samples, implying the roasting of germinated grain as used in the process of malting, presumably to make oatmeal stout. The circular oven had no flue, and the fire was directly under the germinated grains, which would account for the charring. The oven contained large amounts of weeds which may have derived from fine sieving. S3 was a rectangular post-built structure immediately adjacent to the kiln and presumably connected with it.

Further south, in the centre of the St Mary's Grove site, lines of close-set posts were interpreted as a building, S10. There were numerous other post-holes in

the same area, most not well stratified but probably post-medieval. The excavator made several attempts to resolve the complex into buildings and fences (S11, S21, S23, S24), but these have not been pursued here. However, there seems to be some likelihood of a tenement division between east, centre and west to which some of the post-holes no doubt relate. If this division originated in the Norman period, different ownership might explain the very different histories of each part.

This new phase of investment may have been prompted by the visit of Queen Elizabeth I, which took place in 1575. The town council explained to her that one reason for the town's decay was that they no longer

Fig. 5.17 The High House, Stafford.

hosted the assizes and had thus lost valuable income, and another was that people had stopped wearing the woollen caps they made there.[100] The recovery also affected some areas in the east quarter. At Clarke Street, there was some development of the Eastgate Street frontage in the period, showing as a road, two barrel-lined pits, a scatter of post-holes and some rubbish pits. This probably represents no more than the first green shoots of economic recovery. When John Speed made his map in about 1610 most of the peninsula was built-up, with rows of dwellings along the majority of street frontages of the centre and east, including Tipping Street and Clarke Street. Only the western tenements lie open and undeveloped (Fig. 2.10). Evidence for the geography of the medieval town is summarised in Fig. 1.4.

Envoi

It is a striking characteristic of Stafford that, although undoubtedly a town, it never seems to have remained resolutely urban for long. Æthelflæd's outstanding concept and its realisation were extinguished at the Norman Conquest. This happened before it had really

got going and entered the later Saxon economic phases that characterised some other towns in Wessex and Mercia. These are matters that require further reflection in Chapter 6.

The Norman impact was severe, as severe and vengeful in fact as it was reported to be following the defeat of Eadric Silvaticus and his rebellious insurgents by William in 1069. This 'easy victory' took place at Stafford, and was followed up the next year with the crushing of the remnants of the Mercian army. William is said to have set out with 'sustained ferocity' to destroy the means of life in western Mercia and Northumbria.[101] Which indeed is what we found. The old town, including the fort and the church, and their tributary and production systems, were destroyed and Stafford was overawed by the hulk of a Norman motte. While the place remained a centre of authority, new attempts at civilised life on the street did not return, it seems, for a hundred years. Even the striking of money was not continuous, which probably reflects the inability of the people to deliver a surplus.[102] But there were, of course, long-term practices and subterranean memories at work – not just in the siting of subsequent churches, but in the activities of people. How else should we view

---

100 *VCH*, VI (1979), 201, 216. Woolly caps had been a Stafford speciality since at least 1498 (*VCH*, VI (1979), 216.

101 Stenton 1971, 605.
102 P.H. Robinson 1968–70, 10–22; see Chapter 4, pp. 94–7.

the maintenance of the street plan and the *longue durée* of cereal processing at St Mary's Grove – in its Late Saxon, thirteenth-, fifteenth- and seventeenth-century manifestations?

The late twelfth-century rebirth brought an urbanism rather different to Ætheflæd's. The ecclesiastical organisation was comprehensive. St Bertelin's was revived in stone, with St Mary's constructed by 1203. St Bertelin's was the senior establishment, as implied by its association with out-of-town parishes and rights of burial.[103] Attempts to push back its antiquity into the Anglian period by these means have been unconvincing (if not improbable).[104] St Mary's was associated with a secular college with its own estate, and in the sixteenth century King John (1199–1216) was regarded as founder of both.[105] The construction of St Chad's and the creation of its parish should belong to this same period (above). Perhaps the church was founded by the bishop for tenants of his estate within the borough.[106] Meanwhile, the horn workers at St Mary's and the smiths at Tipping Street represent the commercial servants of the new order, more especially in the development of frontages and the laying out of tenement divisions on each of our four sites.

---

103 In the early fifteenth century these included the parishes of Ingestre, Tixall and Cresswell, whilst the townships of Marston, Salt, Coton and Whitgreave by old custom buried their dead in the church and graveyard of St Bertelin.

104 Edwards 2004.

105 See above. The likely correlation of the college estate with Æthelflæd's burh has received no endorsement from archaeological research.

106 *VCH*, VI (1979), 245.

The decline of this flourishing town in the fourteenth century raises inevitable thoughts of the Black Death and its resulting depopulation. However, those who were left would naturally take advantage of unoccupied land to grow their own food: it is cultivation rather than waste that seems to be signalled. The development at St Mary's Grove is noted for its large grain dryer, indicating surplus, as well as its grand house, a cousin of the extant High House. The pollen diagram also suggests that farming life always won through; when the town failed, the countryside recolonised it. However, the town was to get further boosts of reinvestment in the manufacturing sector in the sixteenth and nineteenth centuries.

Archaeology is sometimes better at generalities than specifics, so our picture is painted with a broad brush. The samples offered by our 'windows' are more effective for the earlier periods where information is otherwise thinner, than the later in which they can seem to blur the subtleties. Nevertheless, the stratigraphic sequences seem to allow us to experience the switchback ride that is Stafford urbanism. We can of course look upon it as simply a chapter of accidents, in which the people of Stafford were caught in the cross-fire of the aristocracy's relentless quest for ever more centralised power. Or we can view it as the consequence of natural catastrophes of disease and climate. Or we may take a longer view and note that, whatever the inspiration of successive leaders, the people of the upper Trent, from the Romans onwards, never really aspired to urban life as the continent might define it.

6

Anglo-Saxon Stafford in Context

Introduction: The origin of the burh idea

The archaeological campaign examined the sequences at each of our chosen 'windows', following the story in each case from its beginning, in Iron Age or Roman times, to its end, usually in the sixteenth century (Chapter 3). From this inquiry emerged the information that the Late Saxon period at Stafford was a prominent one – as indeed had been predicted by the evaluation and targeted by the research design. Summarising the contacts we made with Æthelflæd's burh (Chapter 4) and its spasmodic aftermath (Chapter 5) has only taken us so far in understanding why it was as we believed it to be. Explanation of the model and endorsement or critique of its interpretation must now be sought from its contemporary context. What was the likely genesis of the burh, the rationale for the selection of its site, the inspiration for its design, the purpose of its industries? Does it belong to a series of initiatives special to Mercia, or can we see it as a standard instrument of the Wessex mission? Do its idiosyncrasies betray the solution to a local problem or an underlying trait of early English urbanism more generally? In this chapter I will attempt to start addressing this daunting agenda.

As summarised in Chapter 1, the Anglo-Saxon Chronicle and the Mercian Register offer a broad historical context to the early events and activities that have been elucidated by archaeological research at Stafford. In his wars with the Danes of the later ninth century, Alfred of Wessex introduced a defensive system based on a network of forts, or burhs, with dedicated garrisons designed to confront raiders and protect local people. The strategy was successful, and in the early years of the tenth century the war was carried into midland and northern England under the direction of Alfred's son Edward the Elder, his daughter Æthelflæd and her husband Ethelred, who between them built twenty-eight or more burhs. Stafford was one of these.

Historians have raised expectations that the choice and development of a burh site should depend on what was there before and we shall examine two of the most prominent theories: that the burh was an adaptation of a pre-existing tribute centre – which I call the *royal hypothesis* – or that it was a development of an ecclesiastical centre – the *minster hypothesis*. These are not as mutually exclusive as some of their protagonists desire, but it will be important to discover, if we can, whether these prior institutions are in some sense determinant, or just coincidental or irrelevant.

The role of archaeology in defining the character of the newly constructed burh has naturally been influenced by these historical ideas although, as we shall see, it gives little direct support to either. Even more influential have been the descriptions of the developed burhs in the Chronicle and their listing in the Burghal Hidage. While accepting that this latter document indicates a broad location for the sites, it is less clear that it is a reliable guide to their size or form. Archaeologists and geographers have been able to use the signals of street planning, which has led in turn to the thesis that burhs were not only planned, but planned from the beginning to function as towns. In using archaeological arguments it will be necessary to acknowledge that even the best investigation of an English town (at Winchester), so illuminating about its form and design, has failed to produce a clear picture of the nature of the link between the burh and its possible predecessors. We shall need to look hard at the supposed proto-burhs in Mercia, to see whether the Stafford ideas were generated locally or swept in from Wessex with the Æthelflædan campaign. I shall hope to show that archaeological reasoning does allow us to extend the likely sources of burh design, and to suggest another strong idea for their principal intellectual origin. This third hypothesis, prompted by the findings at Stafford, will be presented at the end of the chapter.[1]

---

1   This chapter proceeds from Martin Biddle's discussion of the archaeology of the Anglo-Saxon town in 1974 (Biddle 1976), the best review then and still illuminating today. For the most recent well-balanced reviews I chose Astill 2000 and 2006.

The royal hypothesis

The commonsense speculation that places chosen to become burhs were royal initiatives, applied to royal property, was developed with characteristic depth of learning by H. M. Chadwick: 'In earlier times most of the places mentioned in the Burghal Hidage must have been merely royal estates or villages.'[2] As part of a royal estate, the places were administered on behalf of the ruler by a reeve or *praepositus*, following a procedure in being at least from the eighth century in Kent, Wessex and Northumbria.[3] Chadwick considered that the burghal system itself was probably inspired by Danish influence, pointing out that 'most of the boroughs of the east midlands – Lincoln, Stamford, Nottingham, Derby, Leicester, Northampton, Huntingdon, Bedford, Cambridge and Colchester, perhaps also Norwich, Thetford and Ipswich – acquired their burghal character during the period they were under Danish government'. Originally the majority of the chosen places in the south had no great primacy of themselves, but only acquired it later when developed under Edward the Elder as the administrative centres of districts.[4] By this time, the burh was a town with allocated residential provision, in the form of *hagae*, for the aristocracy and senior ecclesiastical authorities.[5] The implication is that there had existed some system for the collection of tribute at royal estate centres, which was extended later to apply to larger districts administered from burhs, to be superseded in turn by hundreds and then by shires.

Royalty is concerned with the defence of its realm, so that a defended royal property should have a military as well as an administrative function. Nicholas Brooks showed that in England, as on the continent, the obligation to provide fighting men went with the ownership of land, and was being applied from at least the later seventh century. One man from every hide of land was required to serve the repair and defence of the west Saxon boroughs, and the same levy is implied for the maintenance of bridges.[6] The obligation to maintain forts and bridges and to serve in the army was so fundamental a component of a kingdom that it may not

have needed routine mention in charters. The Church was included in this duty. The grant of King Æthelbald of privileges to the churches of Mercia in 749 does not exempt them from paying for the building of bridges and the necessary defence of fortresses against enemies, but Brooks does not take this to indicate that monks were expected to serve in the army.[7] In a charter of 792, granting immunities from tax to the churches of Kent, Offa's secretariat points out that not relaxing their obligation to contribute to defence 'against the maritime pagans' ensures the long-term security of the other privileges. It seems that tenants on church land remained liable for call-up and the church must be prepared to lay out its own assets for the purpose of keeping forts and bridges in good order.

While the obligation to support a leader in battle is likely to have had a great antiquity, there are no records that bridges and forts demanded attention in England before the eighth century, at which point the initiative for their construction lay with the king. The residence of an eighth-century king could be fortified in some degree and constructed through conscription; thus theory and practice already had a tradition on which to draw. A story assigned by the Chronicle to 757 shows Cynewulf and Cyneheard fighting to the death at Meretun, described as a stronghold with gates. In the year 900, when Edward succeeded his father Alfred, his dissenting cousin Æthelwold seized royal residences at Wimborne and Christchurch and barricaded himself into the former.[8] By Alfred's day, if not earlier, the aristocracy was familiar with the concept and reality of the protected residence with government functions, of which the burh was to be a larger version.[9] Land would need to be found for such projects. The burh at Wallingford may have been built on 8 yardlands taken from the royal manor of Benson, and that at Oxford on 8 yardlands taken from the royal manor of Headington.[10] These examples support the idea that a burh was initiated and enabled by the crown.[11]

The minster hypothesis

The king's land at Oxford was later distinguished from that of St Frideswide's.[12] This probably implies a

---

2 Chadwick 1905, 255 citing charters of Aethelwulf 'in villa regali quae nominatur Vuiltun'. Rather than William Page, as Blair 2005, 266n.

3 Chadwick 1905, 260–1.

4 Chadwick 1905, 226: 'very few of the southern towns were of any importance before the 10th century ... we shall hardly go wrong in tracing their growth to the centralisation in them of authority over districts introduced under Edward the Elder'.

5 Ibid., 341–2: 'since most of the boroughs of the tenth and eleventh centuries were at some time the dwelling-places of kings or other important personages, including ecclesiastics, it is likely enough that *haga* was originally the term applied to the dwelling-places set apart for members of their retinues'.

6 Brooks 1971, 71 and note 1.

7 Ibid., 76–9.

8 Ibid., 83.

9 Astill 2000, 29: In Mercia, an increase in royal surplus resulted in power exercised from 'particular places' which could have economic and ecclesiastical functions but were 'primarily indicators of political development'.

10 Dodd 2003, 29.

11 'Every borough which had arisen in southern or western England since the beginning of the Danish wars had been created by an act of state' (Stenton 1971, 534).

12 The word used is *ara* (altar?).

pre-existing monastic establishment in its own precinct, founded on land originally granted from the same royal estate two hundred years previously. Middle Saxon monasteries are key political and spiritual players in the seventh and eighth centuries, as we know from Bede's history. In what sense were they the precursors of the burhs?

The idea that the church underpinned the burh system, among its many other contributions to Anglo-Saxon life, has been championed by John Blair, who also challenges the primacy of royal centres in this process.[13] Blair's argument identifies the minster as the principal driver of Anglo-Saxon society and its politics from the seventh century onwards. 'Minster' in this thesis conflates three types of institution: the monastery of devotees as pictured by Bede, the secular minsters associated with royalty of the seventh to ninth centuries and the more familiar post-Viking secular minsters that were to be reformed in the tenth century.[14] Minster is the Old English elided Latin term for monastery, so they are etymologically equivalent. But to use the term for the pre-Viking monasteries is unduly prescriptive, perhaps especially for archaeologists, since currently the best excavated examples of the type of monastery discussed by Bede lie outside England.[15] The early monasteries of the seventh to ninth centuries certainly differ from one part of Britain to another, so it might be better not to prejudge the issue by applying too narrow a terminology.

The minster, as the flag carrier of Christianity, should provide the axial continuity in England from the seventh century onwards, and thus potentially presents a key factor in the location and development of towns. Likewise, Blair doubts the initiative or role accorded to royal centres. He can find no good evidence that there were many centres of secular administration in the seventh and eighth centuries, and feels that the hypothesis which places a royal estate as primary for burh foundation has been fuelled by an anachronistic application of the eleventh-century palace.[16] He doubts that there was an administrative secular continuity, as on the continent, from the Roman period to the early Middle Ages, as advocated by Carl Brühl and promoted

by Martin Biddle.[17] Instead it is the minster that provides continuity, and as a corollary, any continuity should be credited to the minster.[18] Such continuity endures through Viking raids[19] and may be reasoned from early sculpture at later minsters (even if it occurs there relatively rarely),[20] or sometimes the presence of a tenth-century minster is itself a sufficient pointer.[21] Continuation of burial or buildings across the ninth to eleventh centuries (as at Flixborough and Eynsham) is held to imply an ecclesiastical rather than domestic continuity.[22] The royal administration on the other hand is a later arrival on the minster's coat-tails. It only finally achieved its territorial stability by 'battening onto minsters'.[23] The hall at Northampton belongs to an ecclesiastical, not a secular authority.[24] Cheddar was no palace but a minster, with a hunting lodge as 'the cuckoo in the nest'.[25] Blair's countryside is almost bereft of the traces of secular lordship. Thus the notion of royal institutional continuity espoused by Brühl and Biddle is replaced by another, equally prescriptive, which imagines an ecclesiastical rather than a secular power-base for the emergent kingdom.

Blair's thesis is appropriately evangelical, but also contradictory. 'We are not in a position', he says, 'to deny the archaeological existence of developed and stable high-status secular sites, but if they do exist they have not been found yet.'[26] This is a wise disclaimer, since the same is true of most of the bridges and roads of early England and all the ships of Alfred's navy. And to a great extent it is also true of monasteries under towns. We now know quite a lot about what a seventh-to ninth-century monastery looked like — and it is archaeologically very noisy, with copious amounts of crucibles, moulds, stone carving and animal bone. Not finding such things under towns begins to have some significance.[27]

---

13 Most recently in Blair 2005.

14 Thacker 1985.

15 Hoddom, Dumfriesshire (Lowe 2006), Inchmarnock (Lowe 2008), Whithorn (Hill 1997), Isle of May, Fife (James and Yeoman 2008), Portmahomack, Easter Ross (Carver 2008), Inishmurray, Ireland (O'Sullivan and Carragain 2008). It might also be a little contrived to refer to those sites in England excavated on a comparable expertise and scale, namely Monkwearmouth and Jarrow, as 'twin minsters', and its excavator, Rosemary Cramp, does not do so (Cramp 2005).

16 Blair 2005, 266.

17 Ibid., 267; Brühl 1977; Biddle 1976, 110–12. Biddle argues for the transfer of authority and territorial lordship from Romano-British into Germanic hands as conditioning the survival of some power centres. He also accepts the much rarer role of cult centres in encouraging continuous use.

18 Ibid., 268: 'Against this background the economic centrality of minsters should make more sense.'

19 Ibid., 299.

20 Ibid., 311–15.

21 Ibid., 302, 306.

22 Ibid., 321.

23 Ibid., 326.

24 Ibid., 285.

25 Ibid., 327.

26 Ibid., 281, 167n. Although, of course, such centres did exist in the seventh century, for example Yeavering, mentioned as such by Bede and found by archaeologists (Hope-Taylor 1977).

27 Examples cited in note 15. Cf. Astill 2000, 31–2, who points out that most of the evidence cited in support of minster origins is 'considerably later and topographic in nature'.

Blair admits that the existence of a monastery was owed to the secular power in the first place,[28] and that the burhs functioned as collecting points for food rents and for assembly.[29] And since, from the mid eighth century, 'the English kings began to be more successful at marshalling resources for capital investment in their power centres', he presumably agrees they had them.[30] While kings encapsulated minsters within their forts and harnessed their functions, 'in no case does the church have primacy in date or status'.[31] Blair also agrees that it is hard to tell re-use from continuity, but believes that the force of argument lies with the latter: 'While individual cases could be seen as re-use rather than continuity, it is the broad base of this correlation between the pre-Viking and post-Viking patterns which makes re-use implausible as a general and exclusive explanation.'[32] Even accepting this rather arcane reasoning, the surviving minsters did not seem to be very effective: 'from Alfred onwards … the kings of Wessex were developing an agenda which involved bending ecclesiastical institutions to their service'.[33] Both minster estates and the minster sites themselves are being appropriated for fortresses and towns.[34] The ecclesiastical establishments thus appear to be losing their autonomy at the very moment when they are supposed to be exerting it. He states with evident satisfaction that two thirds of the sites mentioned in the Burghal Hidage either contained or adjoined minsters. This seems surprisingly few for a Christian nation, and it rarely helps us with the question of whether they were there before. Some at least of the Mercian churches are accepted as minsters belonging to the time of burh foundation: 'The minsters founded by Edward the Elder and Æthelflæd at Winchester and Gloucester were built and embellished on a princely scale. Admittedly these were prestige court projects; but Æthelflæd's minsters in other west Mercian towns could be part of a broader programme of investment possibly connected with the development of the hundredal system.'[35]

Although forcefully argued with a wealth of detail, the net result of the quest to place the early monastery at the heart of burh development is 'maybe' and 'sometimes'. The sites chosen to build burhs may well have contained a minster, a monastery, or a royal centre already. In some ways it would be surprising if they did not. It is much less certain that either of such

establishments, if they existed, gave the choice of site its rationale.

Mercian fortifications before Wessex

How far was the concept of the Late Saxon fortified centre dependent on earlier, Middle Saxon, prototypes? Nicholas Brooks points out that where the defences of a Wessex burh are reasonably certain, as at Wareham, Wallingford or Cricklade, no pre-ninth-century predecessor has been found. But in Mercia he is more optimistic, reminding us of the early records of obligations to fortify (above) and citing the supposed pre-burh defence lines at Hereford and Tamworth.[36] Jeremy Haslam saw markets operating from fortified sites in the reign of Offa, which added enthusiasm for Mercian proto-urbanism.[37]

We shall visit Wessex in a moment, but must first examine the idea that there was a pre-echo of the defended planned enclosure in eighth-century Mercia since, if it existed, it may have provided a potential model not only for Alfred's Wessex, but for Æthelflæd's Stafford. Hereford was the prime candidate and it was possible in 1976 to speak of a fortified manned settlement including the cathedral site, astride an important route across the River Wye, and apparently dating to the eighth century.[38] However, studies of fifteen years of excavation on or close to the defences have been unable to show firm evidence for a stronghold predating defences that date satisfactorily to the mid ninth century, by which time Welsh affairs had become the responsibility of the West Saxons.[39] At Victoria Street, a corn dryer that gave an uncalibrated radiocarbon date of 640–810 was superseded by a timber building, a gravel rampart, a turf bank and then a stone revetment in that order. This sequence raised expectations of an early circuit.[40] But the separation of the elements of fortification into two phases with an interval between them remains uncertain and does not lead easily to the identification of a Middle Saxon fort (see below). Similarly, the single uncalibrated radiocarbon date of one burial to the eighth century is not really enough to claim a 'date range from the 6th to the end of the 8th century' near the later cathedral.[41] The authors of the most recent review of Hereford's archaeology conclude that in the eighth century there was a ford and

28 Ibid., 284–5 and examples above.
29 Ibid., 276, 278.
30 Ibid., 287.
31 Ibid., 289.
32 Ibid., 320.
33 Ibid., 323.
34 Ibid., 324.
35 Ibid., 342.

36 Brooks 1971, 81–2, then citing Gould 1968, 18–23 for Tamworth and P.A. Rahtz in *Current Archaeology* 19 (1968), 262–3 for Hereford.
37 Haslam 1987.
38 Biddle 1976, 120–2.
39 Shoesmith 1982; Whitehead in Shoesmith 1982, 14.
40 Shoesmith 1982, 71.
41 Shoesmith 1980, 25.

a cross roads, but the first bank and ditch enclosure at Hereford was mid ninth-century, extended in the later ninth century to the east to enclose St Guthlac's Priory. Its upkeep seems to have lapsed in the eleventh and twelfth centuries.[42]

At Tamworth a ditch 2 metres wide was found beneath the northern run of the supposed burh circuit, and also beneath the west gate, similarly attributed to the burh.[43] Gould decided that this ditch marked out the defensive boundary of Offa's palace, but Robert Meeson's later contour survey found a more modest 'palace enclosure' around St Editha's church.[44] More convincing of status is the water mill, situated outside all these defence lines, but again dated to the mid ninth century.[45] Reviewing the evidence for Hereford and Tamworth in 1977, Philip Rahtz remarked 'it is indeed difficult to demonstrate that any features and finds are pre-urban', where urban signifies the arrival of the documented burh.[46]

In a recent meticulous search for the early defences that he felt were implied by the historical references, Steven Bassett revisited Hereford, Tamworth, Winchcombe and Worcester, demonstrating how elusive was the evidence for well-dated defences of either the Middle *or* the Late Saxon period. Nevertheless, he felt able to conclude that while the principal defensive features at each place were datable to the campaigns of Ethelred and Æthelflæd, there were also traces of 'first stage defences' at least at Hereford, Tamworth and Winchcombe.[47] These consisted of the gravel rampart at Hereford, and ditches and post-holes at Tamworth and Winchcombe.[48] While there is no doubt that these features existed, it is a big leap to claim they belong to an earlier or separate defensive system. Of Winchcombe, Bassett asserts: 'The stratigraphical evidence which the excavators recorded leaves no room for doubt that there were two distinct stages/periods of defences.'[49] Actually all that can usually be said about horizons and discontinuities seen in section in a trench is that there are two (or more) phases of construction, which is not the same thing. In fact we know little as yet about how Late Saxon defences were designed, laid out and built, and it seems rash to assume that there were no temporary camps, no marking-out ditches and no labour division, as with Roman or indeed Iron Age ramparts. The historical evidence may well encourage

us to believe there were Middle Saxon fortified sites in Mercia (and in Wessex), but there is no good reason for assuming they were in exactly the same places as the later burhs.

These examples are brought out at this stage because they have been claimed to provide the best indications of a precursor to the burh in Mercia, where the defensive tendency is supposed to start.[50] There are of course other prominent sites north of the Thames where the early fortifying tendency, if there is to be any, should appear. At York, where the scale of excavation has been outstanding, there is Anglian activity south-west of the Ouse, and on the east bank south of the town.[51] The Vikings probably fortified the area of the confluence of the Ouse and the Fosse. The Late Saxon burh was implanted in the Roman legionary fortress, where the fifth to ninth centuries have largely failed to materialise, even under York Minster.[52] The focus of Middle and Late Saxon York lay in different zones.

In their investigations at London Bridge, Watson et al. found little evidence for a precursor to the Late Saxon bridge and burh. The Middle Saxon settlement was at Lundenwic on the Strand, where the Thames was fordable. But at the old Roman city, the 'tidal foreshore was used as a landing place in the late 9th c for the first time since the building of the riverside wall in late 3rd c'. In the early tenth century, the Late Saxon builders re-established London Bridge, probably re-using some of the Roman piers, and fortified or refortified both ends of it. This looks like the work of the Wessex/ Mercia alliance (see below).[53]

The authors of a recent study of Roman and medieval Lincoln note that, while settlement of the fifth to ninth centuries is archaeologically recognisable, and has been recorded in the countryside, there is virtually none of it in the old Roman city. In spite of expectations of a Middle Saxon church and a wic, there is no evidence for either (especially not at Wigford as proposed in 'an elaborate theory' by Bassett).[54] The nearest seventh- to ninth-century presence is located outside the west gate. Settlement activity returns to the city only in the late ninth century, when it was refounded, probably re-using the Roman walls (which survived into the Middle Ages). Within two hundred years the population had filled out the city and was expanding into suburbs.[55]

42 Thomas and Boucher 2002, 1–12.

43 Gould 1968, 1969.

44 Rahtz and Meeson 1992, 4; Blair accepts Tamworth as royal, 2005, 289.

45 Rahtz and Meeson 1992, 14.

46 Rahtz 1977, 111.

47 Bassett 2008, 180; for Worcester, see below.

48 Bassett 2008, 191, 213, 214.

49 Bassett 2008, 214.

50 Perhaps best summarised in Astill 2000, 35: 'some centres of authority apparently fortified in the 8th–9th century, but this is as far as the evidence will take us'.

51 Tweddle et al. 1999; Kemp 1996; Spall and Toop 2008.

52 Carver 1995, 177–205.

53 Watson et al. 2001, 52–5.

54 Jones et al. 2003, 145.

55 Jones et al. 2003, 143–59.

That these high profile examples from Roman and non-Roman places north of the Thames have failed to produce any convincing precursor to Late Saxon renewal must perhaps loosen the grip that antecedent Middle Saxon palaces and monasteries seem to have on the imagination. We do have power centres and minsters, or at least their implied sites, in the eighth century, but they have not been found in direct relationship to the later burhs. It is accepted that the wandering of settlements of different periods around a particular focus could imply continuity of a kind.[56] But the fact that new sites are chosen for the burh, and that the development takes new forms, is a sign that a new agenda was being set. The Midlands has yet to produce the wic-type sites associated with incipient urbanism, and the fact that there may have been Middle Saxon strongholds (that we have yet to see) does not oblige us to accept them as models for the Late Saxon town.[57] Rather than assuming continuity, it is the innovation and the reasons for it that should command attention.

Of course we must acknowledge a technical problem here. Urban investigations between 1970 and 2000 have been largely opportunist and perfunctory, with research design playing a minor (or non-existent) role. A high status multi-functional settlement like Yeavering or Jarrow consists largely of shallow foundations or the post-holes of timber buildings which are exceedingly grand but can only be seen in a large scale excavation, and only then with ingenuity, caution and plenty of time. Nevertheless, if we remind ourselves of the presumed status that drives the expectations of a palace or a minster, they ought to have a fairly obtrusive materiality. One only has to look at the fourth- to ninth-century complex under Geneva cathedral to appreciate what urban or ecclesiastical continuity actually looks like.[58] It may be worth repeating that, even in Britain, the real monastic establishments that have been excavated have produced many thousands of metal objects, moulds, crucibles, slag, carved stone and animal bones.[59] These would certainly be found, even if residually, in a place like Lincoln or Wallingford. Even if the secular or monastic ghosts of Middle Saxon Mercia and Wessex do lurk in some evanescent form in the fissures of urban deposits, there has to come a point when one doubts the significance of an establishment that is so difficult to see. If a 'minster' consists only of a building made of five or six timber posts and no crafts or animal bones it is a fair assumption that, even if it really exists, it is of very little consequence. The same is true of supposed defence lines. We know what previous

examples of defences looked like because they have survived from the Iron Age at Maiden Castle and from the Roman period at Portchester; thus, since people had got no smaller in the interim, it is a fair assumption that Late Saxon commanders knew what an effective defence looked like too, made use of them and, when they built from scratch, produced something equally impressive. Thus a ditch 2 metres wide, easily leapt by a reasonably fit Viking, fully laden, should not be allowed to enter the literature as a 'possible defence' simply because it is found in a suggestive location.

In brief, it is now permissible to entertain the possibility that burhs, rather than developing from pre-existing centres, were created *de novo* in pursuance of a particular ideal. Before considering what that was, we should briefly review the evidence for the burhs we have, first in Wessex and then in Mercia.

The Wessex burhs

Martin Biddle's pioneering work at Winchester, which began in 1964 and ended in 1972, set the agenda and archaeological standard for the investigation of British towns, although it is still only appreciated largely through a series of interim reports, albeit unusually fine ones. Here the question of continuity has been prominent, and excavations have provided evidence for small-scale occupation in the seventh and eighth centuries, attributed to a royal residence, an episcopal community, some enclosed private dwellings and some service population along High Street, with wide open spaces in between.[60] It is not claimed that this settlement was urban or defended, although the Roman walls still stood. Because the church founded in 648 did not become a bishop's seat until the 660s, and because the later tenth-century palace lay immediately west of it, the likely rationale for the early re-use of Roman Winchester is argued to be the siting of a palace with its church. This church survived to be called the 'Old Minster' when a New Minster was built to the north of it.[61] In a famous passage, Biddle compared this putative royal centre at Winchester with the trading place at Hamwih, 'two complementary settlements, the one royal ecclesiastical, ceremonial, heir of an ancient and still lively dignity; the other bustling, crowded, commercial, outward-looking, from which the shire was named'.[62]

Urban rebirth came in the ninth century (probably 880–886) when the old Roman town of Venta Belgarum was refurbished. The Roman south gate was blocked, and the Late Saxon defences otherwise followed those of the Romans. A new planned town was laid out

56 Biddle 1976, 111, n. 100.

57 Cf. Dyer and Slater 2000, 613–14.

58 Bonnet 1993.

59 E.g. Whitby (Cramp 1976, 223–9); Jarrow (Cramp 2005); Portmahomack (Carver 2008); and see above.

60 Barlow et al. 1976, 450.

61 Biddle 1975, 125.

62 Biddle 1976, 114.

in the form of a street grid and water-courses, not coincident with the Roman ones except for the main east-west axial street. The 8.6 kilometres of streets were made from about 8,000 tons of flint cobbles and imply a single operation. The original purpose was defence and the provision of refuge for 20 miles around. But by the tenth century the town was commercially active with crafts and trades already confined to particular localities.[63] These results introduced three important and enduring ideas to the study of the Late Saxon town: that it was planned, intended as a town and, archaeologically, represented a radical change from what had gone before (in this case a royal and/or ecclesiastical estate). The Winchester model of a Late Saxon planned town was subsequently picked out in a number of Wessex burhs, or inferred from their modern street plans.[64]

The argument that Late Saxon Winchester was intended as a town from the first was based on the massive investment in the streets and the assumption that such a place would not be defensible without a settled population.[65] The street grid included the wall street, implying that the defences and the grid were conceived together; and the streets ran not only beneath the Norman castle of 1067 but the New Minster of 901. Even if the original impetus was military, people would need some inducement to stay and develop tenements. Some documentary references even imply that trade was hosted from the beginning; but the majority of archaeological sightings tended to suggest a second more commercial phase of development in the tenth century.[66]

However, it is worth noting the possibility that this sequence would also fit perfectly well with the layout of a grid that was intended to provide the initiating framework for a military camp. Biddle's study suggests that the original grid was parcelled out to lay and ecclesiastical lords;[67] but these would also need somewhere to billet the militia they had provided. A parallel might be drawn with the armies of early Islam, which consolidated the separate allegiances of warbands by allocating them 'quarters' on a family basis, within the enclosure and separated from the sites reserved for the palace and mosque. Originally these quarters were places to pitch tents, but as the territory came under control they became built-up and began to trade. In this way,

the allegiance of a rural people became urban.[68] Thus it should not be taken as axiomatic that a Late Saxon fort had no grid or that a place founded as a fort could not become a town. It is not impossible that the occupation of tenements ultimately derived from rewards for military service, in the Roman manner.

The conception of the Wessex burhs was taken to a new level of interpretation by David Hill, who examined the Burghal Hidage[69] and deduced that it could be used to predict the size of a town by the number of hides given.[70] For Hill, the size also implied the function. Armed with the supposed size of all the burghal places, he announces: 'In the central period (870–930), when the bulk of the burhs were founded, it should be clearly understood that the King founded forts or he founded towns – towns did not grow out of forts, nor did they appear spontaneously. As this is an important fact I should explain briefly how we can be sure, and as the map makes the distinction between fort and town that distinction should be justified.'[71] He attempts to do this by noting that documented foundations that did not become towns were generally smaller than those that did. He deduces that the smaller foundations, which did not become towns, were founded as forts. A fort is smaller than a town, so that all the places with areas larger than about 20 acres were founded as towns.[72]

In addition to the circularity of this argument, the basic premise, that the size of a place is given by its hidage, has proved to be flawed. This can easily be seen from two places where the Late Saxon circuit is actually known: Winchester at 58.2 hectares and Wallingford at 41 hectares are different in size but both assessed at 2,400 hides. This shows that the hidation, while it may assess the manpower needed to defend a place, repair a place, garrison a place or operate from a place, does not need to reflect the length of the extant outer perimeter wall, although it may. At many of the sites where the circuit is unknown there is a clear disparity between the hidage and the most suggestive defence lines on the ground. Some peninsula sites have a neck too narrow to accommodate the hidage (Christchurch, 591 metres for an approximately 400-metre neck; Bridport, 956 metres for an approximately 500-metre neck) and others too

---

63 Barlow et al. 1976, 448–69. The lowest stratified post-Roman street had a silver penny of 925, so out of use within a few years of this (demonetarisation). The street above had a Kufic silver dirham of c. 898. The third street had eleventh-century finds. This leads to the interpretation that the first street was laid down in the late ninth century.

64 Biddle and Hill 1971.

65 Brooks 1996, 137; 144–5; Reynolds 1999, 84–92.

66 Biddle and Hill 1971: the towns of Wessex were placed on a more commercial footing during the reign of Athelstan. See also Vince 1994.

67 Biddle 1976, 133.

68 Carver 1996.

69 Hill 1969.

70 Hill 1981, 85–6, Hill and Rumble 1996, 92–7. The calculation given in Version A of the Hidage (Hill 1969, 90) states that one hide supplied one man and 4 men can defend one pole of wall; thus the number of hides can be used to calculate the length of the defended perimeter. One pole can be reckoned at 5½ yards, or 16½ feet, or 5.03 metres. One hide is thus equivalent to 1.26 metres of wall.

71 Hill 1981, 143.

72 Biddle uses the division of town and fort but expresses caution, 1976, 126, n. 208.

wide (Lyng, 126 metres for a 219-metre neck; Lydford, 176 metres for a 311-metre neck). For the 'long' hidages, the mismatch can be massaged by supposing an extra length of wall along a flank of the peninsula, but Hill offers no convincing resolution of the 'short' hidages.[73]

Nicholas Brooks noted that many of the hidage assessments require 'much interpretation and many favourable assumptions' to achieve even a 5% margin of accuracy. He concludes that 'it is not possible to devise a scenario to explain away all these inconsistencies' and 'it is therefore unsafe to use the hidage figures to deduce the length or location of any borough's defences'.[74] It would be curious if the calculation had no basis in fact, but if it were based only on the length of the defensive circuit it would hardly need writing down. Brooks assumes that the burghal places, even the smallest, already had some role in government at the time of their selection, having 'features that made them appropriate as administrative centres'. The hidage indicates the resources required by a burh as a proportion of the shire levy as a whole.[75] This implies a readjustment of existing dues to suit a new strategic role. Another possibility is that the burghal ratings are in fact accurate measures of wall length, but the fort has not yet been found. One implication here is that the short lengths may all apply to rectilinear forts set on the promontory, ranging from about 30 x 30 metres (Lyng) to about 240 x 240 metres (Bridport). In this case, the model for all the burhs would be the same: a Roman fort.

In Wessex, as in Mercia, archaeological evidence for Middle Saxon forerunners remains piecemeal and indirect and its uncertainties are exemplified by Jeremy Haslam's recent discussion of the origins of Cricklade.[76] The topography, the results of excavation and the known settlement of the hinterland have suggested two components provoking the choice of the site and its early development. 'The first alternative would suggest that the Roman centre, sited at a crossing of the river by a major Roman road, became a high-status middle Saxon settlement with special royal connections, performing significant central-place functions at the boundary of two kingdoms – the Hwicce (later the Mercians) and the West Saxons.' The second assumes that the church at Cricklade was an early minster, so that 'the main elements of this royal settlement would on this interpretation have been a minster church, an open market area and a royal palace enclosure, forming a close-knit complex on a topographically distinctive site

and approached by early routeways'. However Haslam is obliged to turn aside from this attractive vision. 'Against this hypothesis is the fact that there is no evidence of post-Roman settlement at Cricklade dateable to before the layout of the late Saxon defences (apart from a very few middle Saxon pottery sherds), and no evidence that the church at Cricklade was a minster of the conversion period. The middle Saxon pottery found at various times at Cricklade is insufficient to allow the certain inference that there was a settlement at Cricklade of any significance in the middle Saxon period.'

The Late Saxon settlement is by contrast rectilinear, planned and defended. The template was provided by the internal walkway, which was laid out as a perfect square with a side 96 poles long, apart from a slight bowing on the east to follow the 80-metre contour.[77] A Late Saxon minster was founded in the south-west quadrant, and the north-west quadrant, which yielded no evidence for Saxon or later occupation, has probably always been open. Haslam concludes that the Cricklade fort was laid out as part of the 'crash programme of fortress-building by King Alfred in the years 878–9', for the defence of Wessex. The rationale of its location is strategic: this is the point where Ermine Street crosses the Thames. If there is a pre-existing royal and/ or ecclesiastical centre in the vicinity, it probably lies further south at Purton.[78]

In most cases, there is little doubt about the rough location of the cited burhs (Fig. 1.1), and these offer a convincing picture of a deliberately networked defensive system which has a credible context in the Danish wars. This implies in turn that the sites were selected in the first place for their strategic location. Within this specification, the Wessex burh builders of the ninth century chose old Roman forts (Winchester, Portchester, Bath, Exeter and Chichester), where they adopted part or all of the old Roman wall lines and in some of these places, and perhaps in all, laid out a new grid of streets. Sites not known to be Roman, but with a known circuit, are seen to have been constructed on a Roman model, with proven rectilinear defences and a street grid (mainly read from the medieval street plan), as at Wareham, Wallingford, Cricklade, perhaps Avebury.[79]

73 Hill and Rumble 1996, app IV, 208–210.

74 Brooks 1996, 130–2; and see Haslam 2009, 111–14, who suggests that the Hidage 'can best be interpreted as a "top-down" set of summary prescriptions from the originators of the system to those responsible for setting it up in the field'.

75 Brooks 1996, 134.

76 Haslam 2003.

77 Haslam 2003; a pole of 16½ feet is used. The new perimeter is calculated at 2,235 yards (as opposed to 2,046 in the Hidage).

78 Haslam 2003, conclusion. Likewise Middle Saxon evidence recently found in the region of Southampton: numerous post-holes and pits, animal bones and plant remains, and a well-furnished seventh- to eighth-century cemetery (Birbeck 2005). If these are elements diagnostic of a royal (or an ecclesiastical) centre, their connection with the Late Saxon settlement is characteristically indirect.

79 Reynolds (2001) defines an English rectangular fort constructed at the west entrance to Avebury ring, dated by two radiocarbon readings to the ninth century, and an extant stone church of c. 1000. The perimeter is proposed as 1,040 metres in length. He supposes it to be comparable in size to

Other sites are suggestively rectilinear (Eashing, Rye) and others may be former hill-forts (Chisbury). Most of the remainder are peninsula or confluence sites (Bridport, Buckingham, Burpham, Christchurch, Newenden, Langport, Lydford, Lyng, Malmesbury, Shaftesbury, Wilton). This kind of site, especially if ringed by marsh, provides good protection against both horse- and boat-borne enemies. But it should not be excluded that a rectilinear fort was also constructed on the promontory, which would allow a chance of reconciliation with the burghal ratings (see p. 134 opposite).

The Roman places were repaired and gaps blocked with drystone walls of rubble or recycled ashlar (Winchester). Types of fortification used on new sites resemble those of the Iron Age: clay and turf fronted by a turf wall, later revetted with stone, and fronted by a double ditch (Cricklade); layers of turf, with possible palisade and later stone revetment, fronted by three ditches (Lydford); turf, later faced with stone (Christchurch); at Wareham a bank 16.8 metres wide and surviving at 5 metres high, fronted by a ditch. This bank too was later faced with a stone wall.[80]

In the broadest sense, then, the Wessex rulers appear to have inherited a network of earlier aristocratic residences, some of which were fortified and most of which would have had churches. These were the points where dues were delivered. This system of dues would be put to work to support the set of new defended places, not necessarily coincident with the old, that was created in the ninth century. These burh sites were chosen for their strategic location and defensible properties. Pre-existing defence works were repaired and new ones constructed using a dump rampart. Burh-builders were attracted to Roman towns or to other positions where good communications by road, river and ford were combined with good defensive assets, for example as provided by a surrounding marsh. Some or all of the requisitioned sites may already have contained administrative centres, churches or monasteries – the latter especially having a predilection for peninsula, promontory and island sites. But in the absence of evidence for any convincing continuity of function, it seems likely that the pre-existing institutions, if they survived, would have been subordinated to the new strategic project of the crown.

The Mercian campaign

Did the Mercians apply the Wessex approach or modify it? If there are additions or differences we might wish to attribute them to Mercian initiative or, if the campaign in its execution was 'pure Wessex', it may help to discover aspects that have yet to be seen further south. Mercia, the marchland, ran between Wales and England, and a strong influence is expected from the British Iron Age tradition, the British church and British upper class.[81] These much desired signals are notoriously elusive. The Trent, Tame and Sow are pre-English names, and many of Mercia's documented demographic sub-groups – the Pencersæte, centred on the River Penk, the Tomsæte on the Tame, Pecsæte around the Peaks and the Wreocensæte around the Wrekin – are labelled by natural features with British names.[82] Much of western Mercia has no burial grounds which are culturally Anglo-Saxon. Even the River Sow, which is a tributary of the Trent, has no sign of Anglo-Saxon influence until the seventh century.[83] Stafford and Stone, both of which are Roman sites on the Roman road discovered by Lawrence Bowkett, have *Walton* settlements close by, implying British communities that endured until the seventh century at least.[84]

In the seventh and eighth centuries most commentators imagine the arrival of an Anglian upperclass with 'many royal residences and monasteries'.[85] In the late eighth and early ninth centuries, with the rise to fame of Æthelbald and Offa, Mercian leaders are thought to have fortified Hereford, Tamworth and Winchcombe, although, as we have seen, the archaeological evidence for this is so far exiguous. The death of Offa in 796 was followed by a period of unrest in which the Mercian court lost control over its tributary states and by 829 it was itself tributary to Wessex.[86] In a recent study, Ian Walker charts the subsequent rise of Wiglaf and the ascendency of the 'B' (Beorhtwulf) and 'C/W' (Ceolwulf/ Wigstan) dynasties of Mercian earls and their confrontation with others and the Vikings. The Great Army entered Mercia in 868 and seized Repton

---

smaller forts mentioned in the Burghal Hidage (e.g. Twineham and Wilton), although Hill (1996) actually gives 591 metres for Twineham=Christchurch and 1,760 metres for Wilton.

80 Hill and Rumble 1996, gaz.; Jarvis 1983, 25–31; RCHM(E) 1959, 126. Biddle 1976, 128 says the stone facing was invariably added later.

81 The march of Mercia may refer to the belt of high ground connecting the Forest of Arden to the hills of Cannock Chase (Stenton 1971, 40).

82 Stenton 1971, 291–2; Chadwick (1905, 265n) suspected Welsh influence but did not discuss it further.

83 Viz. seventh-century furnished graves at Wyaston, Barlaston, and perhaps Tissington and Rushall (FR11, 86–7). The south Staffordshire hoard found near Wall in 2009, with its links with Sutton Hoo, might suggest a wealthy Anglian upper class in Mercia, but its actual origin and its context of discovery are currently obscure.

84 FR11, 74.

85 Dyer and Slater 2000, 613–14; and above.

86 Walker 2000, 22, 35. I owe the paragraph that follows to Walker's useful synthesis.

in 874. In 877 King Burgred capitulated and left the country for Rome, where he died. Mercia was divided between the Vikings and the C dynasty's successor King Ceolwulf II. Explaining the remarkable turnaround that followed, from the misery of Mercia in 877 to its prominence by 911, Walker makes an attractive case for the importance of a Mercian/Wessex alliance, with considerable diplomatic and martial credit accorded to the shadowy figure of Ealdorman Ethelred.[87] Possibly a native of Gloucester, Ethelred was a successful general who by 883 had regained the Hwiccan territory, perhaps in the same way that Alfred had regained Wessex, and as a result was the effective leader of Mercia. His alliance with like-minded Wessex was cemented by his marriage to Alfred's daughter, Æthelflæd. When Alfred regained London in 886, he handed it to Ethelred as Mercia's *de facto* regent. Ethelred subsequently beat the Danes at Benfleet, Buttington and Chester, and was responsible for the decisive victory at Tettenhall in 910. He died in 911, probably of wounds sustained in this battle. He was buried in Gloucester in the church built for the relic of St Oswald that he had previously acquired from Bardney in Lincolnshire.[88]

Æthelflæd was herself a partner in the war effort long before she was a widow. As Alfred's daughter she could hardly have been unaware of the chronic crisis, and she was present at the London meeting of 898 convened to discuss its new defence and street plan.[89] She was present at the planning meeting for the burh at Worcester in 899, visited Shrewsbury with Ethelred in 901, restored Chester in 907, and in late 910, when Ethelred was incapacitated, built a burh at *Bremesbyrig*, probably in Gloucestershire.[90] Thus by the time she began the reconquest of England in partnership with her brother Edward, she was well educated in military matters.

In his admiring portrait, F. T. Wainwright emphasises Æthelflæd's military and political skills; she was effectively conducting simultaneous military operations on three fronts.[91] She opposed the settlement of an Irish-Norwegian host north of the Wirral by restoring Chester in 907 and building forts at Eddisbury in 914 and Runcorn in 915. She confronted the old enemy, namely the Welsh, through forts constructed at Chirbury (915) and probably Weardburh (also 915), and by mounting a punitive expedition into Welsh territory to avenge the death of Abbot Egbert and his companions (916). Meanwhile she linked up with Edward in 913–914 to close Mercia's north-eastern gap with forts at Stafford, Tamworth and Warwick – each of which had a Danish headquarters in its sights less than 30 miles

away: Derby, Leicester and Northampton respectively. In 917, as Edward handled a Danish breakout around Bedford and Cambridge, his sister moved to take Derby. In 918 she took the submission of the Danish armies at Leicester and York, and beat Ragnald at the second battle of Corbridge, striking alliances with the Scots and Irish.

Dying in June 918 after an exhausting three months, she just missed seeing the collapse of the last independent Danish armies in the Midlands. As she had probably anticipated, Edward was quick to take ownership of the political assets of his elder sister. These assets included secure borders with the Welsh, Scots, Norse and Danes – no mean achievement. Æthelflæd, Lady of the Mercians, was recognised in the west and north as leader of the coalition and 'her fame spread abroad in every direction'. After her death, Edward diminished this fame, with its Mercian loyalties, in favour of the creation of an integrated kingdom with a West Saxon inheritance, and Æthelflæd's daughter Ælfwyn was deprived of power, perhaps in the understandable expectation that she would know how to use it.

Did Æthelflæd's burhs have an ecclesiastical origin? Alan Thacker clarifies the issues by first distinguishing the pre-Viking monastery, which contained monks, from secular minsters, which had parochial duties. He reminds us that the royal house was intimately associated with both, but perhaps especially with the minsters, and in particular the documented minsters of Staffordshire, Derbyshire and Shropshire which survived from the pre-Viking period in the form of royal free chapels with large parishes. The midland minster 'parish' may actually be co-terminous with the area under the control of a royal centre. Thus in these cases the minster is synergetic with the royal centre.[92]

This connection is especially marked in the Mercian burhs with which we have to deal, by the dedications to murdered members of rival dynasties and the enshrinement of their relics. Of these, Thacker names Werburg at Hanbury and Mildburg at Wenlock as examples of saints possibly established in their shrines by the seventh century. Æthelbald may have introduced Guthlac's cult into Hereford after 716. Otherwise the murdered saints are themselves late eighth- or ninth-century: Kenelm at Winchcombe, Wigstan at Repton, Ealhmund (Alkmund) at Derby and Shrewsbury, Æthelbert at Hereford. These dedications must be of the ninth century, and can be brought into the purview of burh-founding, just as Ethelred and Æthelflæd's celebration of Oswald at Gloucester (909) and Werburg at Chester (907) belonged to this later post-Viking revival. Æthelflæd's promotion of these cults was possibly intended to mollify Mercian resentment of West Saxon dominance, as Thacker suggests. At the same time there

---

87 Walker 2000, 69; see also Keynes 2001.

88 Ibid., 92–5.

89 Brooks 1996, 143. See Chapter 1.

90 Walker 2000, 94.

91 Wainwright 1959.

92 This and the following paragraph draw on Thacker 1985.

may have been memories that required veneration in her adopted family and among her own Mercian followers.

Thus a dedication on its own at a place can mean either that there was a pre-Viking minster or the enshrinement of a relic at a new post-Viking site. As we have seen in the case of St Bertelin (Chapter 4, pp. 73–76) the archaeology has been unhelpful in distinguishing between the two, in Stafford as elsewhere. The case for direct continuity is vanishingly small. However, if we accept the close association of the minster with the crown and the granting of royal land as axiomatic, then the royal hypothesis prevails. The burh sites, in the west Mercian examples at least, were driven by the crown.[93]

Archaeology and the Mercian burh

Edward and Æthelflæd's twin campaign is itemised in Table 1.1. On the eastern flank, Edward built thirteen forts of which one was a re-used Roman place (Colchester) and three had been Viking forts (Bedford, Nottingham and Stamford). Here he added a second fort on the opposite side of the river to the Danes while at Buckingham a fort on each side of the river seems to have been part of the original design. On the western flank, six of the burhs were Roman places: Gloucester, fortified by Ethelred, Worcester (Ethelred and Æthelflæd together), Chester and Leicester (Æthelflæd), Manchester and Towcester (Edward). Two of Æthelflæd's other burhs were hillforts (Chirbury and Eddisbury) where the enemy were inhabitants of hilly country, and the remainder were riverside and often peninsula sites (Stafford, Tamworth, Warwick, Shrewsbury), where the enemy were likely to arrive by boat. Leicester and York, and probably Bridgnorth, had already been fortified by the Vikings. London and Oxford can also be classed as Mercian burhs, the one a Roman fortress, the other a confluence site.

Assuming Ethelred's earliest experiments were in Gloucester, they seem to have been applied to the extant Roman fortress, which in the late ninth century was a 'ruinous walled town whose once great buildings were used as quarries and whose spaces were given over to agriculture'.[94] Seven out of nine pre-Conquest churches are within these walls, where the street plan also implies an 'organised recolonisation' of the interior, as at Winchester. At the Westgate and Southgate, modifications to defences and streets occur no earlier than the ninth century and follow a period of post-Roman disuse.[95] St Oswald's was later included in the

circuit, and the intra-mural land of St Peter expanded northwards to join it – although archaeologically it is unclear whether this happened after the acquisition St Oswald's relics in 909, or after the Norman Conquest.[96]

As we have seen, the earliest fortifications known so far in Mercia, that is in Gloucester, Hereford and Tamworth, seem to begin no earlier than the mid ninth century, and the others were founded in the late ninth and early tenth centuries. This means that they were being built no earlier than the reign of the Mercian king Burgred (852–874) who was married to Æthelswith, daughter of Æthelwulf, king of Wessex, or the supremacy of Ealdorman Ethelred, friend of Wessex (from 881) and husband to Æthelflæd, Alfred's daughter (from 910). Thus Wessex thinking would be familiar to the Mercian court (and vice versa) throughout the decades that the burhs appeared. Ethelred, Æthelflæd and Edward had a common point of departure, the two latter as very young people, coming to prominence after the Wessex burhs had been put in place. They were all present at the London meeting in 898. It was presumably Ethelred who fortified Gloucester using the Roman walls (above) and it was Æthelflæd who restored Chester, also using the Roman walls.[97] Roman towns are targeted in the west, presumably where the enclosure could readily be made safe. The Danes provided exemplars in the east. The actual size of the fortified areas is not usually known for the Mercian burhs, and we do not have a Burghal Hidage, except for Warwick and Worcester. As in Wessex, the evidence for pre-existing royal residences and monasteries, and their influence, has been assumed more than it has been demonstrated.

The case of Worcester illustrates how uncertain the picture really remains. The description of the initiation of the burh by Ethelred, Æthelflæd and Bishop Werferth acting together is very promising. A defence is created for the protection of 'all the people'; taxes are divided between the church and the crown, the bishop getting enough to keep the walls in repair, plus a bit of profit, and the crown getting the real benefits.[98] The seat of a bishop from the seventh century is an intimation of a pre-existing ecclesiastical authority. Unfortunately this cosy picture of burh creation gets little additional focus from archaeological discovery. Worcester seems to have had its origins in an oval Iron Age hilltop fort beside the river, but the Roman and Late Saxon

---

93 Thacker 1985.
94 Heighway 2001, 102.
95 Hurst 1986, 129–32.

96 Hurst 1986, 131–2; Baker and Holt 2004, 20 suggest that the burh at Gloucester was constructed in the context of rebuilding after the defeat of the Danes in 878. A new minster (St Peter's) was built at the same time.
97 Biddle 1976, 135. As in Gloucester, the re-occupation of Chester appears to start in the later ninth century (Griffiths 2001, 213) and mainly redevelop walls and streets within the extant legionary fortress (map in Ward 2001, 163).
98 Brooks 1996, 143.

circuits remain unknown.[99] In a highly speculative article Baker et al. treated the oval fort as Roman and proposed an exploitation of the site by the British church, which filled the gap between Roman and Late Saxon periods.[100] A British origin for churches on the highest ground, while not improbable, has not been demonstrated archaeologically. Although there are good historical reasons for placing an Anglo-Saxon church at Worcester from 680, there is no substantial evidence for archaeological occupation of the site, Anglo-Saxon or otherwise, between the fifth and ninth centuries. Following their excavations at Deansway, Dalwood and Edwards again reviewed the options, deciding that the Roman circuit was still unknown and the evidence for post-Roman occupation very slight. Their own sequence at Deansway was largely blank between the fourth century and the late ninth.[101]

Deansway has, however, provided a good sighting of an original ninth-/ tenth-century northern defence. Built around this date, perfectly compatible with Werferth's foundation, was a defensive work consisting of a turf and clay bank 13 metres wide, with a stone revetment (which may be secondary) fronted by a berm 3 metres wide with a ditch beyond. The ditch was filled in by the later eleventh century. There was a bread oven just inside the defended boundary, with an archaeomagnetic date of c. 577–810.[102] Bassett's study reaffirmed a later phase of stone revetment, but decided that a Mercian defence, if there was one, would have to lie elsewhere.[103] The definition of the Roman town and the Late Saxon burh, and of any occupation between the two, thus remains elusive. But there is no reason to doubt they will eventually come to light. Worcester was a Roman site, probably by a river crossing with a hypothetical Roman bridge and harbour,[104] and it may have been occupied by a Christian community in the fifth to ninth centuries. The one part of the burh we know of did not coincide with a Roman defence, and the ninth-century church appears to be Anglo-Saxon and relevant as a collector and beneficiary of dues. The least contrived explanation is that, whatever may have been there before, Worcester was chosen as the site of a burh primarily to suit the strategic demands of the Wessex-Mercian royal alliance.

At Oxford the first-phase burh, with a rectilinear plan, was implanted on royal land north of and adjacent to the riverside monastery of St Frideswide, rather than including it (above). The northern defences have been seen at 24A St Michael's Street: a bank of turf interleaved with clay or soil, with a timber face tied to horizontal timbers and a stone facing added later.[105] The excavation at Lincoln College in the north-east quadrant of the first circuit suggested that 'there might have been quite a substantial building or complex in this area that was associated with large scale storage of grain and possibly with baking or malting'. The authors comment that, given the potentially early dating, 'it could represent a more formal arrangement associated with the defence of the burh; perhaps there were granaries here for the storage of food for the burh's defenders during times of trouble'.[106] Edward the Elder is regarded as the founder of the burh between 911 and 914–919, but a coin of Alfred might imply that it was being planned or in operation in his time.

Thus, as in Wessex, the Mercian burhs make use of Roman forts and Roman roads, promontory sites and rivers. They are under construction from the mid ninth to the early tenth century. Where Roman enclosures are usable, they are repaired. New sites are protected with dump ramparts. These earth/timber/turf defences are later refurbished with outer stone revetments, most probably in the reign of Ethelred II (995–1016) in connection with his own Danish wars.[107] Fig. 6.1 offers a diagrammatic summary of the links that would have played between the principal actors involved in the military engineering of the day. It is proposed as a trajectory of evolving design, fed by prehistoric, Danish, Middle Saxon and Roman ideas, transmitted through those who exercised the power.

Economic development

We can now add to this basic design model some characteristics of a burh's subsequent performance as a town. At Stafford itself are three major industries which began when the burh began: the processing of cereals, the provision of beef and the manufacture of Stafford ware. The burh itself is argued to be a rectilinear fort in the centre of the peninsula, containing the grain supply and a new minster church, while over to the east is a suburb in which pots are made and butchers' waste is dumped.

Ovens for drying or baking bread just before or after the erection of defence lines have also been found at Worcester and Hereford, and there was a centralised

99   Barker 1970. The hypothetical circuits were reviewed and re-assessed in Carver 1980b, 1–5; Dalwood and Edwards 2004, 13.

100 Baker et al. 1992, repeated in Baker and Holt 2004, 145–7 even though here the more likely origin of the oval enclosure as an Iron Age hill fort rather than a Roman fort is acknowledged.

101 Dalwood and Edwards 2004.

102 Dalwood and Edwards 2004, at pp. 13, 19, 219, 61 and 52.

103 Bassett 2008, 227–30: 'If Worcester had serviceable defences in the Middle Anglo-Saxon period they must have been based on its Romano-British ones.'

104 Carver 1980b, 20–1.

105 Dodd 2003, 149–51.

106 Dodd 2003, 31, gaz. 123.

107 Astill 2000, 42; Bassett 2008, 232.

baking facility at Oxford, as noted above, which was seen as crown supply rather than trade.[108] Such a provision, denoting an authority feeding its servants, was a widespread feature of the first millennium. Circular bread ovens with a single chamber up to 3 metres across are found in commercial and military contexts throughout the Roman world; these tend to use a stone base and a brick vault. These ovens are assumed to have distributed bread under the direction of the state. Monasteries too had to cater for subservient groups: the ninth-century St Gall Plan features circular bread ovens in the kitchens of the guest house, in the almonry and in the bakery, which has contiguous rooms for brewing and the storage of grain and flour.[109]

It has been harder to assess the scale at which meat was supplied at Stafford, since we have only one large dump of butchered bone, but the heaps at Clarke Street suggest that we are dealing with a centralised supply, and the supply was of beef. Provisioning a royal foundation with beef was not an innovation of the burh – Middle Saxon Hamwih and Eoforwic were supplied in a similar way, and bread too might have been provided for any subservient population (Chapter 4, p. 67). What is new is the pottery industry, which therefore should be connected to the overall mission. The standard form of the pots and their distribution – which favours other known burhs – point to a role of distributing food. Of what kind of food, we know little but might guess much: honey, dripping, malt.

The Stafford picture is that of a military depot where tribute was collected in the form of farm produce and turned into transportable commodities for redistribution in pots. If land owners were obliged to provide fighting men and camp labour, their ultimate reward for providing food was probably silver from the royal exchequer issued in the form of coin; stamped with the mint mark, it could function as a receipt as well as treasure (see below). If this is correct then the years at which the mint was active signify the years in which food (the people's only resource) was being supplied in response to royal command. This works quite well at Stafford, since the hiatus in minting coincides with the town's virtual desertion (Chapter 4, p. 96).

Anglo-Saxon Stafford showed very few signs of production beyond bread, beef, pottery and coinage – which, as just suggested, could constitute a closed military system. Was it then only a fort, or a town that suffered from some basic deficiency? If so, it might not have been so unusual. Recent studies have emphasised

that the commercial aspects of urban life, already present in the Middle Saxon period (seventh to ninth centuries) were slow to reappear archaeologically: in virtually every Late Saxon town so far examined whether in Mercia or Wessex, the material clutter of town life is a feature of the late tenth and eleventh centuries.[110]

Writing in 1994, the late Alan Vince was one of the first to propose the new model for the urban sequence in Anglo-Saxon England. He saw the *wics*, active mainly in the east, as serving aristocratic initiatives in international trade between the seventh and ninth centuries, but he found that, so far, archaeology had failed to provide evidence for places supporting large populations in the seventh to ninth centuries, although they may have been important as ecclesiastical or administrative centres.[111] The new urbanism that began in the mid ninth century was generally discontinuous with the old. The new towns begin as forts and serve in their *first phase* as garrisons provisioned by the countryside and centres for the conversion of tribute into coin. In a *second phase*, around the mid tenth century, the forts begin to become urban, functioning as local markets.[112] In Wessex, pottery is made in the traditional rural centres, while north of the Thames it is being made in the towns. The first Late Saxon wares are reaching London supplied from Oxfordshire from about 930, and Vince associates the appearance of pottery in Mercia with Edward's (and Æthelflæd's) campaign of reconquest. In a *third phase*, from about 1000, these towns become international. The first London waterfront is dated by dendrochronology to the late tenth century, but before c. 1000 the numbers of imported sherds 'could be counted on the fingers of one hand'. Vince decides that London could not have been active in international trade between 886 and 1000, although it had been before, and would be again. He sums up: 'I would suggest as a hypothesis that the inland towns of southern England mainly came into existence as forts in the 9th century, developed local marketing roles in the 10th and early 11th centuries and only later became part of the network for distributing goods to the coast in one direction and circulating imports inland in the other.'[113]

One indication of the role of a Late Saxon town should be the distribution of its coinage; but here we have a conundrum. The documentary record encourages us to find a working exchange economy, using coins: from the time of Athelstan every burh was to have a

108 Ovens, possibly for cereal drying or baking, have also been noted at Nottingham (Webster and Cherry 1972, 190; 1973, 170), Chester (Webster and Cherry 1980, 219) and Chichester (Youngs et al. 1985, 202).

109 Curtis 2001, 366–7; 2008, 378–9; Horn and Born 1979, I, 77–125; II, 215–64. I am most grateful to Caroline Goodson for this information and the references.

110 Astill 2000, 35–41; 2006, 234.

111 Vince 1994, 118.

112 Ibid., 112: 'There then follows a period in which a number of places originally founded as forts, with or without the intention of supplying them with a permanent garrison, became towns.'

113 Ibid., 114.

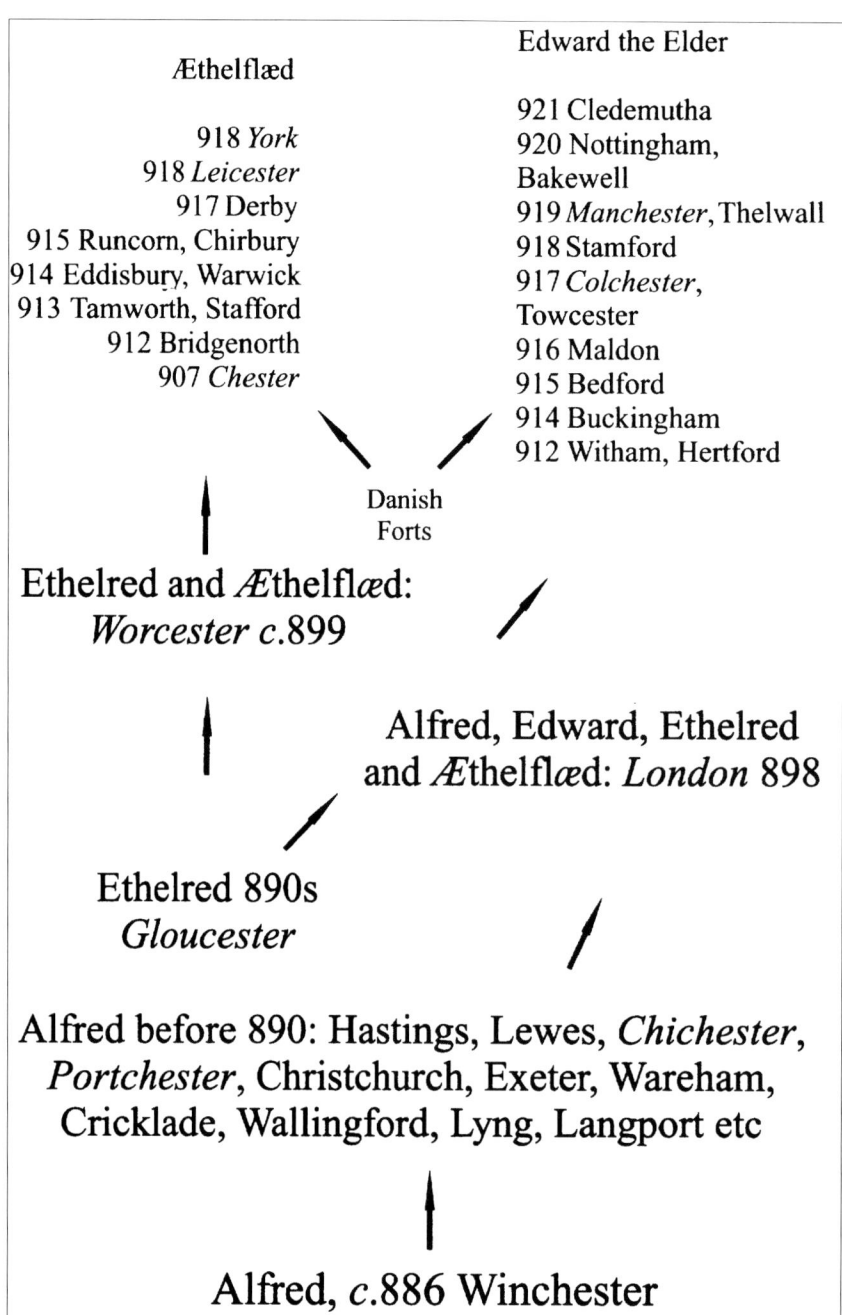

Fig. 6.1 Trajectory of burh design.

mint, and the moneyer and mint marked on the coin (Chapter 4, p. 94). But this is not what the archaeology sees. *Sceattas* were presumably used in trade,[114] but the use of the Late Saxon penny is not so clear. The king, having supplied the silver and dies in the first place, released it through his reeve, presumably in exchange for services such as supplying the army with food, purchasing weapons, and taking responsibility for fortifications. The coin should then pass down the line and disperse into a town's hinterland. However, this would be reflected in the distribution of coins, with the home mint predominant, and the distribution should include coins dropped in the town itself. But at Stafford four area excavations produced no Late Saxon coins at all, and the economic hinterland of a town, as indicated by single-coin finds, is not evident, although this may change.[115]

In practice, Staffordshire had managed without freshly minted coins for five centuries, and a system such as that implied by the St Mary's Grove bakery could work without them: grain could be brought into the burh by farmers as tribute or tax, and there made into bannocks issued to men giving military service. Grenville Astill reasons that since the rate of coin loss in early burhs is so slight, barely different from that of rural estate centres, there was little difference between the two in terms of economic role.[116] In the south of England, the contrast between Middle Saxon and later coin distributions is marked: the eighth-century level of coin loss was not regained until the last quarter of the tenth century at the earliest, perhaps not until the twelfth century.[117] Thus the main purpose of the Late Saxon coins appears to be to record receipts of commodities and then return it as tax, not to circulate them among the population to facilitate purchase.[118] We can note also the central control of silver and dies, and the necessity of stamping the coin with the name of the moneyer, the person who is to be held to account (severely) in the event of any depreciation of the bullion value (Chapter 4, p. 94). The Late Saxon coin is clearly based on Roman exemplars, collected and recycled for generations. But it appears to operate as treasure, rather than currency, and to pass up the line, from the burh to the crown (or via the crown to the Danes), rather than down it to the producer.

Astill observes that if burhs were intended as towns from the outset, they would have had to be integrated into the existing economic networks.[119] But the material evidence of manufacture, internal exchange and external

import and export, and the dense residential occupation that goes with it, reappears in the southern burhs only at the end of the tenth and into the eleventh century.[120] For earlier, ninth- and tenth-century, signs of commercial town life, we must look to the north-east and the Danelaw.[121]

These thoughts draw a contrast between what was required of a town by the two warring factions: the English desired a protected facility for collecting tribute from the land, under the strict control of the crown and its agents, the Danes, a mechanism for generating wealth through long-distance trade; and the two only converged in the eleventh century. If the declared intention of the English crown was to concentrate markets in the place chosen for military defence and the collection of dues, then it was still a work in progress at the Conquest.[122] On this reading, Stafford, although relatively undeveloped, was not too far behind Wessex and the rest. But we have done little to illuminate the question of where long-distance trade and commodity exchange were happening in otherwise wealthy tenth-century England.

Given the size of its peninsula, over all of which the Anglo-Saxons were active, Stafford had every chance of developing into a more diversified urban centre, but apparently failed to attain much of Vince's phase 2 and nothing of his phase 3. But this is clearly not unusual. We can accept that England in the eighth century had both royal centres and monastic (i.e. minster) sites, and that these belonged to a fiscal system that could be manipulated to support a new military and urban initiative. Even if England was not yet urban in the eighth century, collecting the resources required and the duties owed for royal use must have operated from somewhere.[123] The wics were an obvious source of revenue, but there may have been many others, perhaps now indicated by those concentrations of rich finds coming to light through the Portable Antiquities Scheme. A recent study of King's Lynn linked the location of these so-called 'productive sites' – that is, sites where metal detectorists have found a wealth of metalwork – with the formation of burhs. The author concluded that these sites were centres for the collection of taxes, rather than 'markets', and were places where tribute and service was turned into coin. These rural spots are likely to have been the origin of those beef rations that were used to provender wics.[124] Given the existence of numerous and dispersed redistribution and management centres, 'urbanisation seems to have consisted of trends towards the centralization of

114 E.g. Dyer and Slater 2000, 613.

115 E.g. Lyon 2001, 78; it may change by virtue of the Portable Antiquities Scheme.

116 Astill 2006, 246.

117 Astill 2006, 242.

118 Astill 2000, 37.

119 Astill 2006, 241.

120 Astill 2000, 41; 2006, 234, 242.

121 Astill 2000, 38.

122 Astill 2000, 42.

123 Astill 2000, 29.

124 Carver 1993, 60.

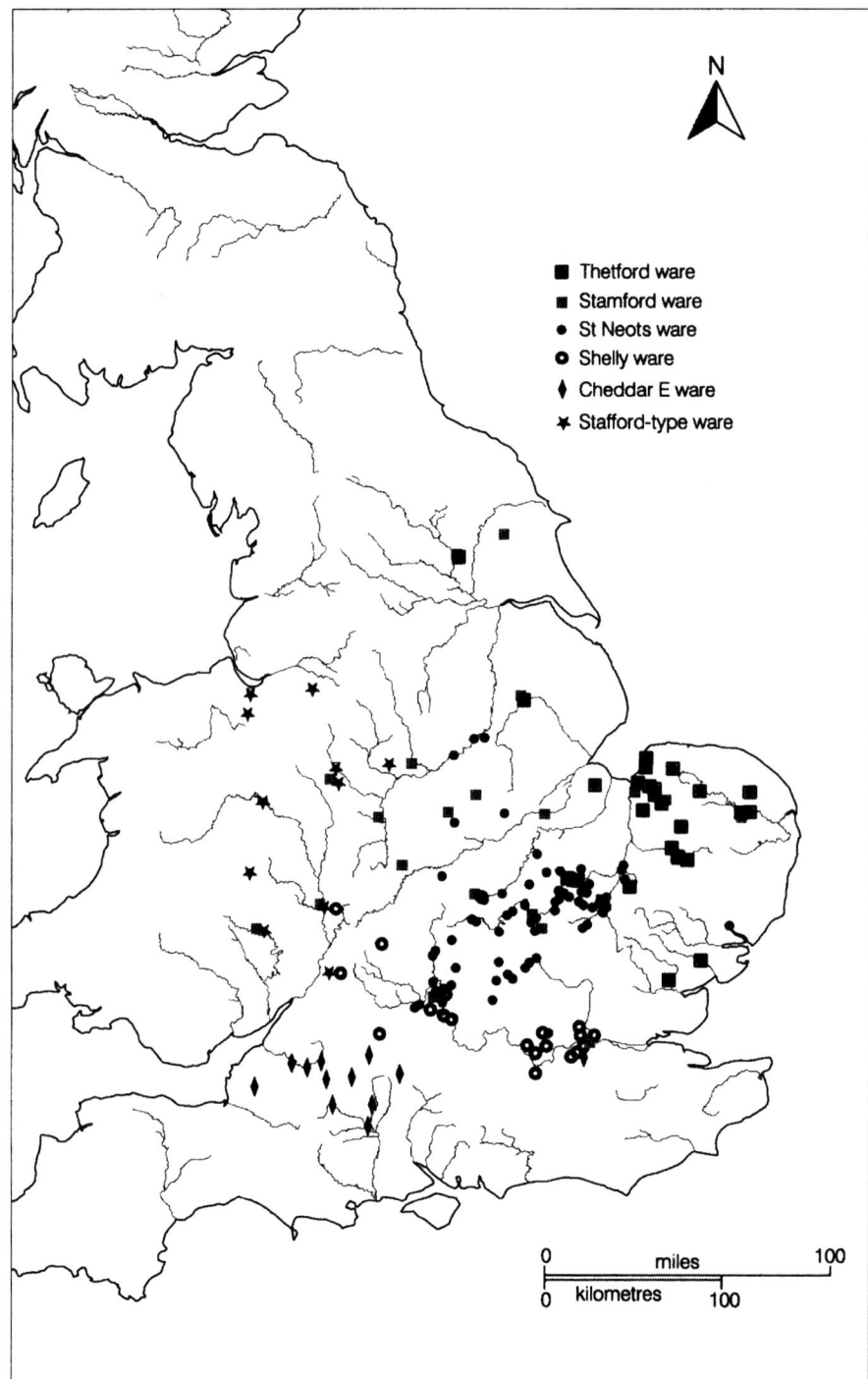

Fig. 6.2 Map showing the approximate outreach of the Late Saxon pottery industries.

government roles, which had previously been distributed throughout a number of foci'.[125] Whether such roles will prove to be endorsed by new excavations and the Portable Antiquities Scheme itself, they at least broaden the range of likely instruments that burh-builders could draw on.

The Roman hypothesis

While some of the minsters, royal residences and taxation points were co-located under burhs, on the whole they have not appeared there and we cannot reasonably argue that the burh concept simply grew out of such places. The hope that a prototype defended place may have been tested on the sites of Mercian burhs before the ninth century has received no substantiated support from archaeology to date. This leaves us with the supposition expressed, or at least allowed in a number of cautious ways, by Martin Biddle, that the burh was an innovation of the later ninth century. The aspects that he established, a rectilinear defended enclosure and a contemporary street grid, may have been intended to signal a town, although I argue above that they could equally mark the lines of a military camp. Either way, this kind of regulation naturally evokes thoughts of Rome. Biddle himself argued that such a design does not need to reflect *Romanitas*, but was simply the logical organisation of a defended space. Although 'some may feel that this is an unduly pragmatic, excessively common-sense of the emergence of the defended planned burh … It is for them to show, for example, how the Classical experience of civil and military planning might have directly and plausibly influenced Anglo-Saxon Mercia and the Wessex of Alfred.'[126]

The Stafford findings urge us to take up this challenge. The argument for the Late Saxon town (Chapter 4) advanced the idea that it had been created in the image of Rome. The layout of the place resembled that of a fort and its *vicus*; its controlled use of space, grain, meat, pottery and the skulls tossed into waster-pits, speak of a military regime. We can add to this from the broader burh repertoire. The Late Saxon pottery industry that sprang up in the late ninth and tenth centuries is well known for the return of wheel-thrown well-finished pottery to England for the first time since the Roman period. In earlier syntheses, this has been credited to the potteries of the Rhineland, and partly inspired by imports from Pingsdorf and Badorf, but these imports do not resemble the early products of the Late Saxon industries very closely.[127] In Chapter

4 a parallel was drawn between the attributes of orange Stafford ware and that of the local Roman pottery – Severn Valley ware – with the implication that imitation was intended. This idea can be applied more widely: dark grey Late Saxon Thetford ware and St Neots ware appear to have ancestry in Roman Nene Valley wares. The yellow- and green-glazed Stamford ware and Winchester ware seem to refer to Roman forum ware. It is not so much an archaising throw-back as a direct homage to products known to belong to Rome, rather than the near continent. It is appreciated that the copy is not exact, any more than Anglo-Saxon sculpture exactly imitates Classical. But the models were to hand. Huge quantities of Roman pottery were discarded in Roman centres, and would have been encountered by Late Saxons, even including whole pots (Chapter 4, p. 60), and the similarities are sufficient to imply that direct references are intended.[128] If the new pottery is not to be tracked to France, it is unlikely to have been simply the serendipitous creation of locals: the supply and distribution of Late Saxon pottery reveal roots of a deeper kind. The zones of influence shown in Fig. 6.2 are broadly collocated with Middle Saxon kingdoms and Roman provinces but also with pottery zones that are Iron Age.[129] It has been proposed that it is the Iron Age too that may have laid down the template for the Late Saxon administrative territories.[130] The significance of such long-term allegiances, and whether due to man or nature, is some way from resolution.

David Hill has suggested that the form of the Late Saxon burh may have taken its inspiration from the military measures put in place by Charles the Bald in the ninth century to defend the western approaches up-river towards Paris. These may have pre-dated Alfred's own initiatives. A double fortification at Pîtres (Pont-de-l'Arche) was recorded as being in the planning stage in 862 and refurbished in 869, and it was still serving to block a Danish advance on Paris in 885. There are enclosures either side of the Seine at its junction with the Eure, and archaeological exploration of the more northerly ('Le Fort') found it to consist of a clay bank and a palisade, which could be assigned by archaeomagnetic dating to a date between 820 and 900. It had subsequently been destroyed by fire.[131] This

---

125 Hutchinson 2006, 99.

126 Biddle 1976, 120–2.

127 Hurst 1976; but the imports will have probably influenced the later products in England.

128 See Tyers 1996. For example, Oxford red/brown slipped bowls (p. 176), south Midlands shell-tempered ware (a possible pre-echo of St Neots ware). Black burnished jars in Dorset and the east (pp. 183–7). Glazed pottery was known in Roman south-east Britain (p. 141). A project which compared the fabrics of the Roman and Late Saxon ceramics in England might resolve the matter of where the Late Saxon potters took their inspiration.

129 Carver, forthcoming.

130 Brooks 2003, 173.

131 Hassall and Hill 1971; Dearden 1988; Dearden and Clark 1990.

precursor of the double-burh just across the Channel is a convenient exemplar, assuming that the house of Wessex required one. But there are others, and they pre-echo more nearly the classical rectilinear style of the fort as advanced here.

The Roman fortresses that have featured throughout this chapter may have been ruins but some at least could be put in working order in an emergency. Danes pursued by Alfred took refuge in Exeter in 877, where they quickly put themselves out of reach.[132] Similarly the Danish army escaped their pursuers by occupying Chester in 893 and were besieged inside the fortress for two days.[133] These must have been extant wall circuits that could be rapidly pressed into service. But there are good reasons for believing that Roman military architecture was emulated more generally and sometimes in detail. In a more recent hypothesis, David Hill surmises a gate and bridge constructed at Winchester and provided with an inscription in 859, tracking it back to Alfred's visits to Vatican City in 853 and 855, where he would have seen the new enclosure wall with its gates and inscriptions. This had been built in 852, following the sack of Rome in 846.[134] Why stop there? England was dotted with Roman forts, baths and temples, many of them still upstanding in the nineteenth century and some (as on Hadrian's Wall) are still visible today after centuries of intensive development. There would have been few more impressive monuments in the landscape of the Late Saxons, and it would be straining credibility to assume they did not understand what they were for. The adoption of the Roman rectilinear shape, and its internal organisation, can be read as more than pragmatic; it is a signal of alignment and agenda. The campaigns of Edward and Æthelflæd even seem to re-run the Roman conquest of Britain with its northward, westward axis, its client kingdoms, buffer states, hostages and acts of fealty. Had the world really progressed so little in five hundred years? Or was there another intellectual force at work?

The suggestion here is not that the spirit of Rome had continued unabated since the time of the province of Britannia, but that it kept revisiting and haunting rulers who attained an appropriate level of power. Nicholas Howe shows how Alfred, after his visit to Rome in 853, began a 'forced program of modernization that sought to reconnect the badly educated and peripheral Anglo-Saxons to the center of Christian belief and culture'. Historically and culturally the later Anglo-Saxons 'found their spiritual empire in Christendom and their capital city in Rome'.[135] Emphasising this verdict, Susan Irvine sees

the adoption of the Roman mantle as a response to papal criticism: England had been portrayed as tolerant towards heathenism, and a desire to make up for it would account for 'a particular concern on the part of Alfred and his advisers to affirm the closeness of the relationship between England and Rome'.[136] An allied motivation might be that Alfred and his successors decided to recreate the province of Britannia not in emulation, but in reaction to the imperial Roman aspirations of France. And while the Roman inspiration was undoubtedly literary and spiritual, there was power in the landscape too. The later Anglo-Saxons were well aware of the might that was Rome and were surrounded by its monuments. The English propensity for choosing Roman sites for monastic foundations can be matched by their evocation of the Roman plan in monasteries in places that had no Roman predecessor, as at Jarrow, and Monkwearmouth.[137] If these monasteries belonged to a first phase of 'romanising' ventures, the creation of the burhs can be seen as a second. Thus Roman places were often chosen to host new towns,[138] and burhs in non-Roman places took the form of Roman forts.

Some of this Roman inspiration no doubt came from books, from Alfred's love of learning, from the tomes stored in the great Middle Anglian and Saxon monastic libraries. Like her father, Æthelflæd was learned and surely inherited something of his mission and sense of historical destiny. Among the books valued by the English upper classes was Cynewulf's history of Helena, Constantine's mother, who recovered the relics of the true cross and its nails and made of them imperial icons. It contains inspirational lines that Æthelflæd may have read: 'Never have I heard far or near of a woman leading a finer force across the seastream on the road of the ocean.'[139]

The banner of Rome may have been *primus inter pares* in the politics of Alfred's heirs, but not exclusively or slavishly. They employed Iron Age methods, not Roman, to construct ramparts, and Æthelflæd expediently served local loyalties by laying a trail of dedications to Mercian saints.[140] But Rome was a symbol of more than a remote historical drama. It had beaten all the peoples of Europe, except perhaps the Anglo-Saxon ancestors. The image of the Roman empire as presented by Bede was not a devouring monster but a story of triumph and resurgence under the Christian cross. Christianity

---

132 Anglo-Saxon Chronicle, s.a. 877; Hill 2003, 223.
133 Anglo-Saxon Chronicle, s.a. 893.
134 Hill 2003, 226–7.
135 Howe 2004, 158, 168.

136 Irvine 2003, 74, 77.
137 Cramp 2005, 352–3.
138 Biddle 1976, 111 and n. 100.
139 Cynewulf, *Elene*, 240b–42. Howe 2004, 164.
140 As mentioned in Chapter 4, and above: Æthelflæd had a fondness for Mercian saints, commemorating Alkmund at Derby, Shrewsbury and Whitchurch, Bertelin at Stafford and Runcorn, Werburgh at Derby and Chester. She transferred relics of Oswald to Gloucester in 909 and founded a chapel dedicated to him at Chester: Thacker 1985; Butler 1986, 47.

had come from Rome and was now the guiding ethos of the English kingdom. For this reason, if for no other, to quote Martin Biddle, 'early Anglo-Saxon history and archaeology are inextricably involved with the Roman world'.[141] Books explained what happened and related it to divine will. But books were not necessarily accurate sources of technical design. For designing forts, pottery and coins, to mention only those products we can still see, the models for the emulation of Roman material culture were on hand and all around. Moreover, the observation that Late Saxon pottery may be copying local Roman types implies that the new craftsmen were working from real models; in short they were archaeologists, looking at Roman walls, and statues, digging up Roman coins and Roman pots. By imitating the forms of Roman culture, Æthelflæd and her family and fellow generals were doing more than saluting an ancient formula; they were making a public statement about the politics of their kingdom and the ultimate status and respect they required. They were determining their future by exercising the martial success and strong government of Rome, and reliving its glory, even at a minor provincial centre like Stafford.

141 Biddle 1976, 112.

Digest A1

Archaeological Interventions at Stafford to 1988

Details in this list are given in the order: intervention number, National Grid reference, date of excavation, location of the intervention, person who did the excavation.

01	SJ 9210 2318, 1954, St Bertelin's Church (Oswald)
02	SJ 9232 2327, 1965, Martin Street (Sherlock)
03	SJ 920 235, 1965, Chell Road (Robinson)
04	SJ 9252 2314, 1961, Clarke Street (Robinson)
05	SJ 918 232, 1969, Tenterbanks (Robinson)
06	SJ 9254 2318, 1970, Clarke Street (Carter)
07	SJ 9260 2315, 1970, South Walls (Celoria)
08	SJ 9209 2305, 1971, Water Street (Robinson)
09	SJ 9202 2344, 1971, Mount Street (Robinson)
10	SJ 9207 2309, 1972, Mill Street (Robinson)
11	SJ 9202 2344, 1972, Mount Street (Robinson)
12	SJ 9191 2394, 1972, Greyfriars (Celoria)
13	SJ 9202 2319, 1973, Earl Street (Robinson/Fisher)
14	SJ 9254 2317, 1974, Clarke Street (Carter)
15	SJ 9253 2314, 1975, Clarke Street (Carver)
16	SJ 9231 2315, 1967?, Tipping Street (SCoFE/SMSAS)
17	SJ 9243 2317, 1977, Tipping Street (Carver)
18	SJ 9209 2327, 1979, 6 St Mary's Grove (Collens)
19	SJ 9237 2321, 1979, Tipping Street (Cane)
20	SJ 9195 2345, 1979, Chell Road (Malam)
21	–
22	SJ 9210 2327, 1979, 7 St Mary's Grove (Graham)
23	SJ 9196 2335, 1979, Sainsbury's development (Malam)
24	SJ 9206 2308, 1979, Almshouses (Cane)
25	SJ 9215 2316, 1979, 11 St Mary's Place (Collens)
25a	SJ 9214 2317, 1979, 11 St Mary's Place (Cane)
26	SJ 9196 2337, 1979, Chell Road (Malam)
27	SJ 919 231 1979, SCoFE (Cane)
28	SJ 9177 2328, 1979, River Sow (Carver)
29	SJ 9212 2327, 1979, St Mary's Grove (Cane)
30/31	SJ 9196 2318, 1981, SCoFE (Taylor)
32/33	SJ 9236 2320, 1981, Tipping Street (Taylor)
34	SJ 9236 2321, 1981, Bath Street (Barnes)
35/36	SJ 9194 2321, 1981, Bath Street (Taylor)
37	SJ 9248 2331, 1981, North Walls (Glazebrook)
38	SJ 9212 2302, 1982, Water Street (Cane)
39	SJ 9213 2317, 1983, St Mary's Place (Cane)
40–41	–
42	SJ 9222 2342, 1983, Vine Hotel (Milne)
43	SJ 9214 2313, 1984, Swan Hotel car-park (Crump)
44	SJ 9183 2323, 1984, Broadeye (Cane)

45   SJ 9234 2323, 1984, Eastgate Street (Cane)
46   SJ 9184 2324, 1984, Broadeye (Milne)
47–52 SJ 920 232, 1985, Albion Place (Darlington)
54   SJ 9204 2308, 1988, Almshouses garden (Cane)
55   SJ 9195 205, 1988, Tenterbanks car park (Cane)

Digest A2

Dendrochronological and Radiocarbon Dates

FR8.7

Dendrochronology
Source: C. Groves, 'Tree-ring Analysis of Timbers from Eastgate Street [sic] Stafford 1982–84', Ancient Monuments Laboratory Report 135/87 (1987)

Tipping Street, ST32:
F142: Well-lining timbers, felling date AD 1255/6
F233: Well-lining timbers felled after AD 1189

St Mary's Grove, ST29:
F608/2270: Well-lining timbers felled late spring/early summer AD 1007
F404/2145: Cess pit-lining timbers felled not before 1173, probably after AD 1183

Archaeomagnetic dates
Source: Jon Cane

Tipping Street, ST32:
Forge: AD 1170

Salter Street kiln:
Kiln 2: AD 1360

Radiocarbon dates

Site	Site code	Lab no.	Sample reference	Radiocarbon age (uncal. BP)	Calibrated date range (1σ) AD	Calibrated date range (2σ) AD
St Bertelin's (see *Radiocarbon* 13 (1971), 152–3)	ST01	Birm 136a	Charcoal ass. with wood believed cruciform coffin of St Bertelin	1105 ± 90	[845]	[800–1000]
		Birm 136b	Ditto	1120 ± 120	[830]	[800–1000]
		Birm 137	Oak believed part of cruciform coffin of St Bertelin	770 ± 78	1180	[1050–1250]
Tipping Street south	ST17	HAR–3039	STS17/8d 29 Nov 78 Wood from firing of kiln	1160 ± 90	770–980	670–1020

St Mary's Grove	ST29	HAR-7039	29/2247/01 Burnt wood and grain from firing of oven F584, S12	1270 ± 70	660–860	640–890
		HAR-7040	29/2247/02	1120 ± 70	820–1000	720–1020
		HAR-7041	29/2247/03	1310 ± 90	640–790	560–890
		HAR-7042	29/2253/01 Burnt wood and grain from post-hole of granary, F596	2290 ± 70	410–250 BC	520–190 BC
Tipping Street north	ST32	HAR-5292	32/1235/01 Wood lining of well F142	690 ± 70 BP	1260–1380	1220–1400
		HAR-8237	32/1516/01 Burnt oak sapwood and heartwood from pottery kiln F246	1150 ± 40 BP	820–960	770–990
		HAR-8238	32/1516/02	1140 ± 40 BP	870–970	780–990
		HAR-8239	32/1753/01 Burnt oak sapwood and heartwood and holly from pottery kiln F238	1140 ± 40 BP	870–970	780–990
		HAR-8240	32/1753/02	1120 ± 40 BP	880–980	800–1000
Bath Street	ST34	HAR-5291	34/1082/01 Charcoal of oak heartwood and hazel from post-hole F58	1320 ± 70	650–780	600–880
King's Pool		HAR-2577	KP 100	960 +/- 80 BP	1030 +/- 80 or 920 +/- 80	
		HAR-2578	KP 140	920 +/- 60 BP	1047–1153 +/- 60	
		HAR-2582	KP 230	1620 +/- 60 BP	420 +/- 60	
Bartley and Morgan 1990, 184		WAT-275	ST9	1370 +/- 70 BP	650	
		WAT-268	ST6	2790 +/- 110	840 BC	
		WAT-849	ST7	2500 +/- 70	600 BC	

Digest A3

Pottery Seriation

Each of the major excavations for which quantification data existed was independently seriated (St Mary's Grove, Bath Street, Tipping Street (north) and Clarke Street)[1]. In each case the best order as determined by stratification formed the Y-axis, and the best order of manufacture of the pottery, as then known, formed the X-axis. The pottery was quantified by Charlotte Cane using EVE (estimated vessel equivalents) expressed as a sum of percentages of the vessel present in a context.

The ordering of the stratification was refined within permitted limits (i.e. where the stratigraphy was unknown or uncertain). The order of manufacture was then improved to produce a less ambiguous or contradictory sequence, the enhancements being argued for in each case (see archive).

The order of pottery manufacture in each of the four seriations was then compared, and a master table prepared. This list of types in chronological order was then reconciled with Deborah Ford's study of the medieval pottery of Staffordshire[2] to produce a concordance between the typology derived by Charlotte Cane and the more general typology resulting from Ford's study.

Since the seriation has been used to refine the arguments for sequence (Chapter 3), given here for reference are the four seriation diagrams and the concordance of pottery types.

Concordance of pottery types
Roman, Late Saxon, medieval and post-medieval pottery was recorded from the Stafford campaign 1975–1985 in large quantities. In general all sherds were recovered by hand and kept from all contexts excavated at recovery level C and finer levels; this means all sherds from all contexts thought to be medieval or earlier on all interventions, plus certain post-medieval contexts at St Mary's Grove where recovery at levels C and D was also applied.

The Roman and Late Saxon types stood out and preliminary studies were made (FR8.2.2 and FR8.2.3). From 1980 Charlotte Cane defined and brought into use a typology for the medieval pottery based on fabrics and forms. The assemblage from ST15 (1975) was later revisited and defined in terms of the new typology. The system used a three-letter code to report the fabric (IWH), denoting, respectively, surface treatment, method of manufacture and hardness. There was a fourth letter or number to report a variant (IWHI K) and a thesaurus to report the form (skillet). Charlotte Cane subsequently gathered these numerous fabrics and forms into thirty-seven groups (FR8.2.4). Unfortunately, not all Ford's examples (above) could be identified among Cane's types, particularly because so little of Cane's assemblage had been drawn. But there were probably sufficient to show where the equivalence was likely to lie (see Table A3.1).

---

1 See FR4.4, FR5.5, FR6.6 and FR7.5; Carver 1985 for the method.
2 Ford 1995.

Table A3.1. Ford/Cane equivalence

Ford 1995	Examples	Cane fabrics	Cane groups
Stafford type		Stafford	Group 8
Iron-rich sandy utilitarian ware (irsw-u) cooking pots/jars	ST34 1126 cp ST34 1363 cp	IWH H/cp AWS F/cp	Group 6
Iron-rich sandy utilitarian ware (irsw-u) jar, bowls, dishes, dripping pans and pipkins			
Iron-rich sandy table ware (irsw-t) *Stafford green glazed pitchers*	ST32 1474, 1503, 1508 Pitcher ST29 I 1301/111 ST29 2146/1 ST29 1872 ST29 1819 ST29 1988	GWH M, GWH I	Group 4, 5?
Iron-rich sandy tableware (irsw-t) jugs and dripping pans *★Audlem*	ST29 1812 ST34 1068 ST29 I 1633 and 2088 ST29 1710/9 ST29 I 1542 ST29 1796 ST29 1871/2★ ST29 1813/33★ ST32 1473/8★	 GWF K/jug GWH E, HWF F GWH D, E	Group 3
Midlands white ware c cooking pots/jars and pipkins			Group 1
Midlands white ware green-glazed jugs *★Chilvers Coton*	ST29 1746, 1778 and 1874 ST29 1930 ST29 1757/24 ST29 1964 ST29 1754/22 ST29 1754/18 ST32 1529/1 ST32 1469 ST29 1746 ST29 1948/5 ST29 1956/1 ST29 1743★ ST29 1762/6		
Midlands white ware jugs, bowls and dishes, mostly red painted	ST29 1857 ST32 1466 ST32 1741 Y2 ST29 2088, 2320, 2322 and 2323	HWH D, E/jug	Group 2
Late medieval orange ware (lmow) and Midlands purple ware (MP) jars, pitchers, jugs and bowls	ST29 1517 ST15 1034 ST29 1716	GWH F/cp	
Late medieval orange ware and Midlands purple cisterns, bowls, pipkins, chafing dishes, 'asparagus boilers', urinals, distillation equipment and industrial vessels, kiln furniture	ST29 1364 Cistern ST29 2091 'Asparagus boiler'		Group 7
Cistercian ware	ST29 I 1257 R9 cup ST29 I 1257 R9		

★ identifies the kiln site.

The Cane types that were identified and quantified at each of the major sites were ordered to give the best fit with the stratification, using a seriation analysis (FR4.4, FR5.5, FR6.6, FR7.5). The types are listed by site below (Table A3.2) in the order in which they came into use, according to the seriation.

Beside each Cane number in this table are 'type numbers' used by Carver in each of the seriation tables. This was mainly to avoid using the cumbersome Cane alphanumeric taxa (e.g. IWH H cp), which can cause the user word-blindness in already overburdened tables. Since the Cane numbers come in many combinations there is no complete set of equivalences between sites. The site with the best stratigraphic sequence and the most pottery types is ST29, and the types are numbered 1–76. The other sites generated additional Cane types and we do not have the equivalence. Each of the other sites was seriated, giving their Cane types Carver numbers. Thus the Carver numbers listed for each site refer only to that site. Naturally the aim is to find equivalence between them, which was done partly on similarity of description and partly by their position in the seriation tables. **Bold** is used for the most convincing concordance. The Ford type is given for each broad family of Cane fabrics. Note that uncertain fabric types occurring in small quantities are omitted from this table. cp = cooking pot.

Table A3.2. *Pottery occurring in Stafford: concordance of seriated order of occurrence for each major excavated sequence*

Ford types	Cane groups	ST15	ST29	ST32	ST34
	Group 15 Group 9 Group 10 Group 21 Group 32 Group 31 Group 33 Group 34	1. Roman	1. Prehistoric 2. Roman Severn Valley ware 3. Roman Black Burnished ware 70. Samian ware 4. Roman Mancetter mortarium 5. Roman Oxford parchment 6. Roman Colour coat	Roman	
Late Saxon wares 10th–11th c.	Group 8 Group 13 Group 17	2. Stafford ware 3. Stamford ware	7. Stafford-ware jar 8. Stafford-ware bowl 9. Stafford-ware lamp 10. Stamford ware 71. St Neots ware	1–2. Stafford ware	1–4. Stafford ware 5. Stamford ware
IRSW–U 11th–12th c.	Group 6	4. **IWH H cp** 5. IW 1 cp	76. IWH C cp 11. **IWH H** cp 13. IWF K cp 26. HWH DE cp 12. IWF I cp	9. **IWH H** 45. AWS F 18. IWF H 17. IWF I 16. IWF J 14. IWF K 12. IWH E 8. IWH I 6. IWH J 3. IWH M	10. **IWH H cp** 7. IWH I cp 14. IWH D cp 16. IWF K jar 19. IWF J cp
IRSW–T Stafford Green-glazed pitchers 12th–13th c.	Group 3 Group 4 Group 5? Group 26?	6. **GW1 pitcher** 7. HW5 pitcher 8. HW1 pitcher 18. AW2 pitcher	24. **GWF K pitcher** 27. GWF E pitcher 17. GWH O pitcher	37. **GWF K pitcher** 40. GWF E pitcher 31. GWH I 33. GWH A 28. HWF B 25. HWH A	34. **GWF K pitcher** 12. IWH D pitcher
IRSW–T				47. AWS C jug	

Midlands White ware 13th – mid 14th c.	Group 1 Group 20?	19. AW5 pitcher 20. GW7 jug 9. HW2 pitcher 10. GW8 jug 11. GW2 jug 14. GW4 jug 15. GW3 jug 12. **GWH L jug** 17. GW6 jug	29. **GWH A jug** 15. IWH I cp 23. IWF J cp 74. AWS C cp 25. IWF K dish 14. IWH I bowl 19. IWH H jar 20. GWH O cp 21. GWH A pitcher 22. GWH I cp 28. GWH A bowl 59. HWF B jug 31. **GWF K jug** 34. **HWH DE jug**	30. GWH J jug 26. HWH A jug 19. **HWH DE jug** 20. HWH DE jar 32. GHW I jug 34. **GWH A jug** 38. **GWF K jug** 61. AWF 3 jug	32. **GWH A jug** 23. **HWH DE jug** 18. IWF J jar 41. AWS cp 36. GWF K jar
Midlands White ware with red stripes	Group 2		40. HWH DE jar 36. IWF B jug 41. GWH I pitcher 44. GWF E skillet 47. AWH J jug 48. AWH E dish 49. GWF K dish		
Midlands Orange/ Purple late 14th c. – 1600	Group 7 Group 11		50. **GWF A jug** Orange ware 51. **IWH J skillet** 53. **GWH I jug** 55. **GWH A dog dish** 30. AWH E jug 35. HWH DE skillet 56. GWF A jar 57. AWH E jar 58. HWF C dish 38. AWF C jug 63. GWH A skillet 72. AWF C cp 66. GWH C jug 65. GWF K cp 69. IWF B cp		40. **GWF A jug** 21. IWF I cp 28. GWH J jug 30. GWH E jug 33. **GWH A bowl** 8. **IWH H skillet** 29. **GWH I jug**
PM After c. 1600	Group 14		61. AWS A cp 32. AWS A jug 60. AWS A bowl		

Unplaced: Groups 12, 18, 19, 22, 23, 24, 25, 29, 36, 37.

Conclusions

It can be seen that, with some minor variations, the pottery types occur in the same order on all four sites. Three sites produced Roman pottery. All sites produced Stafford ware, but only Tipping Street had the full range of forms. The medieval sequence begins abruptly with iron-rich utility wares, mostly cooking pots. There are no hybrids and few candidates for features where Stafford ware is in use with iron-rich cooking pots. Then come the green-glazed pitchers. These dominate table wares in iron-rich fabrics. All sites then receive Midlands white-ware jugs. St Mary's (only) receives a wide range of white-ware cooking pots, pitchers, bowls and dishes as well, and a much wider range of fabrics. Ford describes the 'rich harvest of jugs from ST29' as 'among the finest from Staffordshire'. After the first brief supply of white-ware jugs, Clarke Street and Tipping Street receive no more until the post-medieval period. Accepting Ford's dating for purple and orange wares this ought to mean they ceased to be occupied from the mid fourteenth to sixteenth centuries. St Mary's continued in operation without a break. However, notice that a smaller sample of the St Mary's site (south-west or north-east) would have given a different result. St Mary's north-east sector was unoccupied from the twelfth/thirteenth centuries to the sixteenth century.

There is considerable redundancy in the Cane typology, but it is not clear what this represents – a great variation in fabric or a variation in precision of identification. St Mary's was the site at which the system, designed to be used by completely unskilled workers, was tested, so it would not be surprising if a surplus number of types was created there. The Clarke Street pottery was examined ten years after it was excavated and under different conditions to the other sites, which may explain its dominant GW series.

The principal fabric regimes seem to be consistent: Stafford ware in the tenth to eleventh centuries, iron-rich sandy wares in the twelfth to thirteenth, white wares in the thirteenth to fourteenth, orange and purple (differently fired versions of the same fabric) in fourteenth to fifteenth centuries. The forms of vessels vary more: pitchers (from the twelfth century), jugs (from the late twelfth century) and skillets (from the fourteenth century) seem to be useful markers, but cooking pots and jars make frequent reappearances.

St Mary's Grove seriation

Top half (later)

The X-axis gives the pottery type number. The Y-axis gives the Feature and Context numbers.

F	C	29	28	59	31	34	36	41	46	47	48	49	50	51	53	55	30	35	56	57	58	75	38	63	72	66	65	69	61	32	60
392	2017	5						8					7																8		
	2067																														7
	2056	5			15											6								5							
188	2307												5																		
188	2035				5																										
	2088	10														7															
	2323		12																												
189	1559	15																													
	1314																														
176	1517																									34	60				
	1948	15				10																									
507	1944	5				16	10																								
	1970	68		5	28	30											15													16	
328	1856	5																				5		16							
278	1757	15			15	86									20	5	5														
	1746				76												5										40		10			
	1341	20				20							17					35								50						5
VII																															
294	1800	13																													
469	1845																														
306	1819	25													7		20					10									
306	1820																														
278	1759	10				5																									
321	1857	13			16	30				15	14																				
301	1810	25										43																			
302	1812	5				5			5				35	35	5																
303	1813	40			74									92																	
320	1848	11			15										5																
344	1876	8				54		23																	12						
298	1792			35		30																									
298	1809				18																5								4		
298	1817																														
298	1818																	25	12	5											
[471]	[1929]																														
VI																															

		1	2	3	70	4	5	6	7	8	9	10	71	11	76	24	27	17	13	26	12	29	15	23	74	25	14	19	20	21	22	28	59	31	34	40	41	50
471	1929													18					10																	48			
	1930													20																									20
483	1832													24									114																
	1840													5					20				10															10	
	1937								11	15																													
	1938													7										23															
342	1754									5				5	70				32					17												30	5		
	1874																						124											14	44	30			
	1945																						32																
	1946																																6						
V																																							
435	2116													36		10			5								16												
435	2092													18										22							16	8							
435	2102													36																									
435	2100																																						
435	2155								10																				5	7									
435	2146		10						62	5				86				8	13					10			5	15											
290	1778													40					74					7															
290	1890													14											11	5													
290	1870																																						
290	1871													46																									
290	1887													74									28	28	7														
290	1872								43			10		58					5					28															
426	1769												5	30																									
426	1770																				5																		
555	1638													5																									
404	2113								65			5		92			5		18	7																			
404	2138															7																							
404	2141													12																									
443	2167										5				9																								
608	2217													5																									
449	2178								7																														
IV	1607																																						
557	2196							5	32																														
558	2197							5	44	9																													
136	1611								15	25																													
130	1405												5																										
134	1609																																						
III																																							
	2238		10			5																																	
	2239		5	5	5	5																																	
II																																							

Bath Street seriation

F	C	1	2	3	4	5	7	10	17	14	15	16	19	34	12	32	23	18	41	36	38	22	40	21	24	25	28	30	31	33	35	39	8	29	13
Hor	1104		11					49	5							5								5											9
	1329	30	5	5																								5		5	5				
132	1215							22					5	15			40																		
161	1237		18					12								12	8						5												
	1260						10		10																										
	1263												7																						
	1264																									7									
	1292	27						27																5											
	1293																																	5	
	1294		5																																
189	1336	5						52								20			8						5				5	5		5			
	1337							22					6		12		13																35		
140	1208	23						13									10																		
201	1363		18																																
	1386																																		
	1381					5		10					10				7																		
	1387								20																										
	1432																						10												
179	1376												5			15	5	6	11	12	6	5													
213	1414							10		5			10																						
	1422		5																																
224	1439						7	5																											
	1440							20					11	14				5																	
149	1227							5								7																			
105	1162																																		
73	1103							47	5				5																						
145	1225							8																											
191	1343		5				7	27																											
68	1095											5																							
226	1443										5																								
153	1244		15					7		5				15																					
87	1119							9		5																									
81	1112									10																									
92	1090						6	15	6																										
86	1117						6		6																										
227	1097							5																											
181	1315							11																											
91	1314						5	15	5																		5								
	1224				10																														
74	1105	76																																	
117	1174	12		13																															
76	1107	10																																	
		1	2	3	4	5	7	10	17	14	15	16	19	34	12	32	23	18	41	36	38	22	40	21	24	25	28	30	31	33	35	39	8	29	13

Tipping Street seriation

F	C	1	2	9	48	17	45	3	6	8	12	14	16	18	37	40	25	28	30	20	43	26	19	21	24	27
211	1418												9			16										
216	1426												15													
230	1461											11		10												
207	1411			28													10									
257	1565			7																						
HOR	3																									
185	1380				9																					
191	1367	17			5							13	7													
191	1368	7																								
195	1376	37	4	10					5																	
193	1377	16																								
193	1369	18	28																							
HOR	2			22		26			11			100		11				12						21	13	10
194	1398			19					5				5	11												
194	1399	28					7					7										5				
194	1400				5		10					5														
	1401						23																			
221	1436						7																			
221	1437												5													
232	1468							18																		
259	1572			13																8						
250	1522			5		9	5						10													
251	1531					3	8																			
253	1547																								19	
253	1548						12					16									136					
237	1482												7													
237	1483			11									5													
237	1486								6																	
260	1574											16														
233	1472			10																						
239	1490								18	16				6												
239	1500						7																			
239	1524			7			5						5													
301	1641								6			10														
244	1536						4																			
244	1542			7																						
244	1546					10						10														
276	1595											16														
235	1469			45			32	5	34			32	28	7	15							13			26	
235	1473		22									23										32	11			
249	1527			21	6	5	38					36	43						32	10	10					
249	1529			8					7											10						
249	1538		12																							
234	1474			32																8						
234	1503			122	58		16	14				13	26	14				12	12							
234	1549						10																			
278	1597			5					20	12									22							
278	1600					18	5								21											
305	1645			9																						
318	1678			20	20																					
HOR	1																									
F	C	1	2	9	48	17	45	3	6	8	12	14	16	18	37	40	25	28	30	20	43	26	19	21	24	27

Features beneath Horizon 1 contain only Stafford-ware (types 1 and 2).

Clarke Street seriation

	1	2	3	4	5	6	7	18	8	9	19	20	10	11	14	15	12	17	
1054					31														Cultivation
PERIOD 4																			*Late 14th c.*
1197		40																23	Burning
1109				26	128		10	10		24									Burning
1089	12	35			466			6						8					Burning
1080		32			145	62								37					Burning
1050					58	11								8					Burning
1020		37			2192	5	204	58		6		32		176	5			20	Burning
PERIOD 3D																			*Late 13th–mid 14th c.*
1078		540			615		215							94		147			FENCE
1075		50			53	2								45					Trample
1077	92	425	16		328									146					Dump 4
1087																	335		Dump 4
1183		164			80														Dump 4
1182					19									9					Dump 4
1151																	224		Dump 4
1155					6	9													S2
1153					46											4			S2
1148					18									9	21				S2
1129					21														S2
1117				19															S2
1108					74									6					S2
1152				23	57														S2
1220		102			27											2			Trample
PERIOD 3C																			*13th c.*
1123	5	7022	24		2358	809			29			163		200	53				Clay seal
1122		4327			703	122					18			275	14				Dump 3
1154		2428			165	64								11					Dump 3
1171	30	6040			122		61	9		8			89	6					Dump 3
1192					57	19							18	3					Dump 3
1180	15	568			29		26												Dump 3
1170		329			166		71			17									Dump 3
1172	54	5199	8		770		81			13	17	9							Dump 3
1173	36	816		15						15									hoofprints

PERIOD 3B								*13th c.*
1185					74	59		Dump 3
1189			1581		260		66	Dump 3
1190			382		397		49	Dump 3
1178					42		2	Latrine Pit
1175		5	690		332	7		Latrine Pit
1213		3	666	12	30		82	Dump 2
PERIOD 3A								*12th c.*
1216			4243					Dump 1
1198	★							Dump 1
1214	★							Dump 1
1221	★							Dump 1
1174	★							Dump 1
1230	★							Dump 1
1235		★						Dump 1
1241	★							Dump1
1229		★						Dump 1
1223	★							FENCE
1184	★							Occupation
1236	★							Occupation
1222	★							Ramp
1242	★							Ramp
PERIOD 2								*10th–11th c.*
1177A		★						Ramp
1177B		★						Marsh
1177C		★						Marsh
1232		★						Marsh
1243		★						Marsh
PERIOD 1								*1st–4th c.*

★ pottery recorded but not weighed for seriation

Digest A4

Key to Pottery Illustrations

Roman pottery illustrated

1. Severn Valley ware, jar; from 10 Market Place (Webster 1978, no. 9).
2. Severn Valley ware, rim; from ST15, 1177c (Webster 1978, nos 9, 10 (jar)).
3. Severn Valley ware, rim; from ST15, 1181/84 (Webster 1978, no. 9).
4. Severn Valley ware, rim; from ST15, 1004 (Webster 1978, no. 9).
5. Severn Valley ware, rim; from ST15, 1221 (Webster 1978, no. 31 (or 28) (wide-mouthed jar)).
6. Severn Valley ware, rim; from ST15, 1223 (Webster 1978, no. 37 (wide-mouthed jar)).
7. Severn Valley ware, rim; from ST29, 2238 (Webster 1978, no. 29 (wide-mouthed jar)).
8. Severn Valley ware, rim; from ST15, 1243 (Webster 1978, nos 9, 10 (jar)).
9. Severn Valley ware, rim; from ST29, 2239 (Webster 1978, no. 46 (bowl)).
10. Severn Valley ware, base of tankard; from ST15, 1197 (Walters 1976, nos 1, 2).
11. Severn Valley ware, rim of tankard; from ST15, 1197 (Walters 1976, nos 1, 2).
12. Black burnished ware, rim; from ST15, 1177c (Gillam 1976, nos 10, 13 (jar)).
13. Black burnished ware, rim; from ST15, 1215 (Gillam 1976, nos 8, 10 (jar)).
14. Black burnished ware, rim; from ST15, 1178 (Gillam 1976, no. 10 (jar)).
15. Black burnished ware, base of bowl; from ST29, 2239.
16. Black burnished ware, wall of bowl; from ST15, 1177b (Gillam 1976, nos 75, 80).
17. Black burnished ware, rim and wall of bowl; from ST15, 1177b (Gillam 1976, no. 80).
18. Black burnished ware, rim of bowl; from ST15, 1177c (Gillam 1976, no. 41).
19. Mortarium, rim; from ST15, 1177c (Hartley 1971, no. 13).
20. Mortarium, rim; from ST29, 2238 (Hartley 1971, no. 11).
21. Nene Valley ware, base; from ST29, 2239 (Howe, Perrin and Mackreth 1980, no. 49).

22. Oxford Parchment ware, rim; from ST29, 2240.

Stafford ware illustrated

Type 1: Probable cooking pots

With roll rim (rim types 4, 7, 10)
1. ST15 1221/12
2. ST17 7C/1
3. ST15 1123/2
4. ST17 7C/3
5. ST15 1234/4
6. ST17 7C/5
7. ST15 1235/6
8. ST15 1177/44
9. ST15 1216/45

With flanged rim (rim types 2, 3, 22, 32)
10. ST17 8A/13
11. ST17 7C/15
12. ST17 3/16
13. ST17 7C/18
14. ST17 3/19
15. ST17 7C/20
16. ST17 3/21
17. ST17 3/22
18. ST17 3B/23
19. ST19 1012/24
20. ST19 1005/200
21. ST15 1154/46

With dished/grooved rim (rim type 1)
22. ST15 1123/7
23. ST15 1027/8
24. ST19 1005/9
25. ST15 1216/10
26. ST15 1173/26
27. ST17 8D/25

Type 2: Probable jars

Long jars
28. ST17 3B/201
29. ST32 1753/202

30. ST17 7C/67
31. ST15 1234/11
32. ST17 3/27

Squat jars
33. ST17 8B/39
34. ST17 7C/40
35. ST17 7C/41
36. ST17 7C/42
37. ST17 7C/17

Type 3: Bowls

With flanged rims (rim types 5, 8, 11, 14, 16, 18, 19, 28)
38. ST17 US/32
39. ST17 3B/28
40. ST18 1028/29
41. ST17 7C/52
42. [ST32 US/203 deleted]
43. ST17 7C/204
44. ST17 8B/49
45. ST17 7C/50

With fine-flanged rim
46. ST17 7C/53
47. ST17 7C/38
48. ST17 7C/51
49. ST17 7C/55
50. ST17 7C/56
51. ST17 7C/57
52. ST17 7C/58
53. ST17 7C/59
54. ST17 7C/54

With straight neck (rim types 6, 9, 12, 13, 15, 23, 29, 30, 34)
55. ST15 1123/33
56. ST17 3D/35
57. ST17 8B/36
58. ST17 8D/37
59. ST15 1229/61

Small bowls
60. ST15 1241/34
61. ST17 7C/43
62. ST29 1012/48 [CHECK waster? Meant to be 61??]

Type 4: Probable pitchers

Handles
63. ST15 1275/62
64. ST32 1936/209
65. ST32 1937/210

Body sherd
66. ST15 1171/208

Spouts
67. ST15 1173/63
68. ST17 7C/65
69. ST17 7C/205
70. ST19 1012/206
71. ST19 1012/207

Type 5: Saucepans

72. ST32 1713/211
73. ST32 1936/212

Type 6: Lamps

74. ST32 1343/237
75. ST32 1158/214
76. ST29 1607/118

Type 7: Goblets and pedestals for cups

77. ST32 1936/215 goblet
78. [ST32 1713/11 goblet; lost; deleted]
79. ST19 1004/66 pedestal
80. ST32 1937/213 socketed pedestal

Type 8: Thimble cup

81. ST15 1123/216

Type 9: Bucket or storage vessel

82. ST32 1936/217

Decoration

Incised, linear
83. ST15 1216/218
84. ST29 1633/219
85. ST15 1229/220
86. ST15 1285/221
87. ST15 1154/222
88. ST15 1172/223

Rouletting
89. ST15 1221/14
90. ST19 1004/224
91. ST17 7B/225
92. ST17 8D/226
93. ST17 8A/227
94. ST17 7A/228
95. ST17 7B/229
96. ST19 1012/230
97. ST15 1221/47
98. ST15 1077/60
99. ST17 7B/231

Stamps
100. ST32 1390/232
101. ST32 1390/233
102. ST32 1244/234
103. ST32 1390/49, 235
104. ST32 1994/236

Medieval pottery illustrated

Cooking pots
1. ST32 1902 IWF J/cp
2. ST34 1440 IWH H/cp
3. ST29 1887 IWH H/cp
4. ST29 1517 GWH F/cp

Bowls
5. ST29 1813 IWH H
6. ST29 1746 IWH G

Jugs
7. ST29 1857 HWH DE
8. ST29 1813 GWH E
9. ST15 1072, 1087, 1092, 1113, 1123, 1151.
10. ST29 1874 GWH L
11. ST29 1929 HWH DE

Skillets
12. ST29 1812 IWH J
13. ST29 1818 HWH DE

Digest A5

Excavated Structures

St Bertelin's (ST01; FR3)
S1 Church 1. Timber building of 10th century. F13: Tree-trunk coffin
S2 Church 2. Stone building of 12th century
S3 Church 3. Stone building of 14th century

Clarke Street (ST15; FR4)
S1 Timber fence of 10th century
S2 Timber building of late 12th century
S3 Timber shack of late 12th century
Dump 1 of 10th-century Stafford ware
Dump 2 of 12th-century animal bone
Dump 3 of 12th- to 13th-century animal bone
Dump 4 of 13th century animal bone

St Mary's Grove (ST29; FR5)
S19 Four-post granary (Iron Age)
S20 Four-post granary (Iron Age)
S22 Two posts of structure, probably granary (Iron Age)

S4 Dryer/oven (10/11th century)
S5 Oven (10/11th century)
S12 Oven (10/11th century)
S14 Dryer/oven (10/11th century)
S16 Timber lined cellar (10–11th century)
S17 Fence (10/11th century)
S18 Fence (10/11th century)
S23 Cobbled platform (10/11th century)

F290 Quarry pit of Norman period
F404 Cess pit of Norman period
F608 Well of Late Saxon and Norman period

S7 Stone building of 14/15th century
S8 Grain dryer of 14/15th century
F298 Graveyard boundary ditch of 14/15th century

S3 Timber building of 16th century or later
S10 Timber building of 16th century or later
S15 Brewers' kiln of 16th century or later

Tipping Street north (ST32; FR6)
S1 Pottery kiln (10/11th century)
S2 Pottery kiln (10/11th century)
S4 East fence of potters' enclosure

S5, 5A South fence of potters' enclosure (10/11th century)
S6 West fence of potters' enclosure (10/11th century)

S3 Forge (12/13th century)
S7, 8 Medieval house, west side
S9, 10 Medieval house, east side

Bath Street (ST34; FR7)
F92 Shoulder of ditch (10–14th century)
S1 Fence or palisade (10th century)
S2 Structure ('tower') (10th century)
S3 House platform (medieval)

Digest A6

Contents of the Stafford Online Archive

http://ads.ahds.ac.uk/catalogue/archive/stafford_eh_2009

5.3 Excavations at St Mary's Grove. Revised report by M. O. H. Carver

5.4 Contexts, Features and Assemblages

    5.4.1   By Period

    5.4.2   In Numerical Order

5.5 Seriation

FR6. ST32 Excavations at Tipping Street, 1982–83

6.1 Summary and Contents

6.2 Notes by the Excavator, Mark Taylor

6.3 Report by Jon Cane based on Mark Taylor's notes

6.4 Revised report by M. O. H. Carver, 2007

6.5 List of Defined Contexts, Features and Structures

6.6 Seriation Analysis

FR7. ST34 Excavations at Bath Street, 1981–82

7.1 Summary and Contents

7.2 Report by Jon Cane, Roy Barnes and Jenny Glazebrook

7.3 Revised report by M. O. H. Carver, 2007

7.4 List of Features, Contexts and Assemblages

7.5 Seriation Analysis

FR8. Artefacts

8. 1 Table of Contents

8.2 Pottery Typology

    8.2.1   Roman Pottery

    8.2.2   Stafford Ware

    8.2.3   Medieval Pottery

8.3 Wood and Charcoal

8.4 Bone and Stone

8.5 Cu Alloy

    8.51   Coins

8.6 Iron

    8.6.1   Assemblage from Pit F234

8.7 Chronology

    8.7.1   Dendrochronology

    8.7.2   Radiocarbon Dating

FR9. Bone

9.1 Human Bone by Alison Cameron

9.2 Animal Bone by James Rackham, Madeleine Hummler and Rebecca Nicholson

FR10. Plant Remains

10.1   Plant Macrofossils by Lisa Moffett

10.2   Pollen Sequence from the King's Pool by James Greig

FR11. The Stafford Hinterland

An essay by Lawrence Bowkett

BIBLIOGRAPHY

For a list of works about Stafford archaeology please refer to FR1.5

Amorosi, T. 1992. 'Climate Impact and Human Response in Northeast Iceland: Archaeological Investigations at Svalbard, 1986–1988', in C. D. Morris and D. J. Rackham (eds), *Norse and Later Settlement and Subsistence in the North Atlantic* (Glasgow), 103–48

Armstrong, P., D. Tomlinson and D. H. Evans 1991. *Excavations at Lurk Lane, Beverley, 1979–82*, Sheffield Excavation Report 1 (Sheffield)

Ashby, S. P. 2006. 'Time, Trade and Identity: Bone and Antler Combs in Northern Britain c. AD700–1400' (unpublished Ph.D. thesis, Department of Archaeology, York)

———— 2007. 'Bone and Antler Combs', *Finds Research Group Datasheet* 40

———— 2009. 'Combs, Contact and Chronology: Reconsidering Hair Combs in Early-historic and Viking-Age Atlantic Scotland', *Medieval Archaeology* 53, 1–34

Astill, Grenville 2000. 'General Survey 600–1300', in Palliser, 27–49

———— 2006. 'Community, Identity and the Later Anglo-Saxon Town', in W. Davies, G. Halsall and A. Reynolds (eds), *People and Space in the Middle Ages, 300–1300* (Turnhout), 233–54

———— 2009a. 'Anglo-Saxon Attitudes: How should post-AD 700 Burials be Interpreted?' in D. Sayer and H. Williams (eds), *Mortuary Practices and Social Identities in the Middle Ages* (Exeter), 222–35

———— 2009b. 'Medieval Towns and Urbanization', in R. Gilchrist and A. Reynolds (eds), *Reflections: 50 Years of Medieval Archaeology 1957–2007*, Society for Medieval Archaeology Monograph 30 (Leeds), 255–70

Ayers, B. 1985. *Excavations within the North-East Bailey of Norwich Castle, 1979*, East Anglian Archaeology 28 (Gressinghall)

Baker, Nigel, Hal Dalwood, Richard Holt, Charles Mundy and Gary Taylor 1992. 'From Roman to Medieval Worcester: Development and Planning in the Anglo-Saxon City', *Antiquity* 66, 65–74

Baker, Nigel and Richard Holt 2004. *Urban Growth and the Medieval Church: Gloucester and Worcester* (Aldershot)

Barker, Philip 1970. *The Origins of Worcester*, Transactions of the Worcester Archaeological Society

Barlow, Frank, Martin Biddle, Olof von Feilitzen and D. J. Keene 1976. *Winchester in the Early Middle Ages: An Edition and Discussion of the Winton Domesday* (Oxford)

Barnes, R., L. Bowkett, C. B. K. Cane, J. Cane, M. O. H. Carver and M. Taylor 1982. 'Excavations in Central Stafford', *West Midlands Archaeology* 25, 96–105

Bartley, D. D. and A. V. Morgan 1990. 'The Palynological Record of the King's Pool, Stafford, England', *New Phytologist* 116, 177–94

Bassett, Steven 2008. 'The Middle and Late Anglo-Saxon Defences of West Mercian Towns', *Anglo-Saxon Studies in Archaeology and History* 15, 180–239

Batey, C. E. 1987. *Freswick Links, Caithness: A Reappraisal of the Late Norse Site in its Context*, British Archaeological Reports, British Series 179 (Oxford)

Biddle, Martin 1975. '*Felix Urbs Winthonia*: Winchester in the Age of Monastic Reform', in D. Parsons (ed.), *Tenth-Century Studies* (Chichester), 123–40

———— 1976. 'Towns', in David M. Wilson (ed.), *The Archaeology of Anglo-Saxon England* (London), 99–150

———— 1986. 'Archaeology, Architecture, and the Cult of the Saints in Anglo-Saxon England', in L. A. S. Butler and R. K. Morris (eds), *The Anglo-Saxon Church: Papers on History, Architecture and Archaeology in honour of Dr H. M. Taylor*, Council for British Archaeology, Research Report 60, 1–31

———— (ed.) 1990. *Object and Economy in Medieval Winchester*, Winchester Studies 7, vol. II (Oxford)

———— and David Hill 1971. 'Late Saxon Planned Towns', *Ant.J.* 51, 70–85

Birbeck, V. 2005. *The Origins of Mid-Saxon Southampton* (Wessex Archaeology)

Blair, J. 2005. *The Church in Anglo-Saxon Society* (Oxford)

Bonnet, Charles 1993. *Les fouilles de l'ancien groupe épiscopal de Genève (1976–1993)* (Geneva)

Bourdillon, Jennifer 1994. 'The animal provisioning of Saxon Southampton' in Rackham: 120–125

Bowker, C. 1982. 'Environmental Research at Wasperton: Procedure and Assessment', *West Midlands Archaeology* 25, 45–51

Brooks, Nicholas 1971. 'The Development of Military Obligations in Eighth- and Ninth-Century England', in Peter Clemoes and Kathleen Hughes (eds), *England before the Conquest: Studies in Primary Sources presented to Dorothy Whitelock* (London), 69–84

———— 1996. 'The Administrative Background to the Burghal Hidage', in Hill and Rumble, 128–50

———— 2003. 'Administrative Government: the West Saxon Inheritance', in Reuter, 153–173.

Brühl, C. 1977. 'The Town as a Political Centre: General Survey', in M. W. Barley (ed.), *European Towns: Their Archaeology and Early History* (London), 419–30

Butler, L. A. S. 1986. 'Church Dedications and the Cults of Anglo-Saxon Saints in England', in L. A. S. Butler and R. K. Morris (eds), *The Anglo-Saxon Church: Papers on History, Architecture and Archaeology in honour of Dr H. M.*

Taylor, Council for British Archaeology, Research Report 60, 44–50

Butler, L.A.S. 1991. *Sandal Castle, Wakefield, the History and Archaeology of a Medieval Castle* (Wakefield)

Cane, C. B. K., J. Cane, M. O. H. Carver, J. Glazebrook and M. Taylor 1981. 'Stafford, Staffordshire', *West Midlands Archaeology* 24, 101–10

———, J. Cane and M. O. H. Carver 1983. 'Saxon and Medieval Stafford, New Results and Theories', *West Midlands Archaeology* 26, 48–65

Carver, M. O. H. 1975. 'Clarke St., Stafford', *West Midlands Archaeology* 18, 55

——— 1977. 'Stafford, Eastgate Street', *West Midlands Archaeology* 20, 73

——— 1978. 'Early Shrewsbury: an Archaeological Definition in 1975', *Transactions of the Shropshire Archaeological Society* 59 (1973/4 iss. 1978), 225–63

——— 1979. 'Stafford Town', *West Midlands Archaeological News Sheet* 22, 7–13

——— 1980a. *Underneath Stafford Town* (Stafford)

——— (ed.) 1980b. *Medieval Worcester: An Archaeological Framework. Reports, Surveys, Texts and Essays*, Transactions of the Worcestershire Archaeological Society 3S, 7

——— 1981. 'The Archaeology of Early Lichfield: an Inventory and Recent Results', *Transactions of the South Staffordshire Archaeology and History Society* 22, 1–12

——— 1985. 'Theory and Practice in Urban pottery seriation' *J. Archaeol. Sci.* 12: 353–66

——— 1987. *Underneath English Towns* (London)

——— 1993. *Arguments in Stone: Archaeological Research and the European Town in the First Millennium*, Oxbow Monographs 29 (Oxford)

——— 1995. 'Roman to Norman at York Minster', in Derek Phillips and Brenda Heywood, *Excavations at York Minster*, vol. I (London), chapter 4

——— 1996. 'Transitions to Islam: Urban Rôles in the East and South Mediterranean, Fifth to Tenth Centuries AD', in N. Christie and S. T. Loseby (eds), *Towns in Transition: Urban Evolution in Late Antiquity and the Early Middle Ages* (Aldershot), 159–83

——— 2003. *Archaeological Value and Evaluation* (SAP Società Archeologica, Mantua)

——— 2005. *Sutton Hoo. A Seventh Century Princely Burial Ground and its Context* (London)

——— 2008. *Portmahomack, Monastery of the Picts* (Edinburgh)

——— 2009. *Archaeological Investigation* (London)

Carver, Martin, Catherine Hills and Jonathan Scheschkewitz 2009. *Wasperton. A Roman, British and Anglo-Saxon Community in central England* (Boydell Press)

Carver, Martin forthcoming. 'What were they Thinking? Intellectual Territories in Anglo-Saxon England', in D. Hinton and H. Hamerow (eds), *Oxford Handbook of Anglo-Saxon Archaeology*

Chadwick, H. M. 1905. *Studies on Anglo-Saxon Institutions* (Cambridge)

Clark, J. (ed.) 2004. *The Medieval Horse and its Equipment c.1150–1450* (London)

Clarke, D. and A. Heald 2002. 'Beyond Typology: Combs, Economics, Symbolism and Regional Identity in Late Norse Scotland', *Norwegian Archaeological Review* 35, 81–93

Clarke, H. and A. Carter 1977. *Excavations at Kings Lynn 1963–70*, Society for Medieval Archaeology Monograph Series 7 (London)

Collingwood, W. G. 1927 [1989]. *Northumbrian Crosses of the Pre-Norman Period* (Lampeter)

Cowgill, J., M. de Neergard, and N. Griffiths 2000. *Knives and Scabbards* (London)

Cramp, Rosemary 1976. 'Monastic Sites', in D. M. Wilson (ed), *The Archaeology of Anglo-Saxon England* (London), 201–52

——— 2005. *Monkwearmouth and Jarrow Monastic Sites* (London)

Cunliffe, Barry 1976. *Excavations at Porchester Castle, Vol. II: Saxon*, Society of Antiquaries Research Report 33

——— 1978. *Iron Age Communities in Britain* (London)

——— 1979. 'Some Concluding Thoughts', in B. C. Burnham and H. B. Johnson (eds), *Invasion and Response: The Case of Roman Britain*, British Archaeological Reports, British Series 73 (Oxford)

Currie, C. R. J. 1988. 'Early Vetches in Medieval England: A Note', *Economic History Review*, Second Series 41 (1) (February 1988), 114–16

Curtis, Robert 2001. *Ancient Food Technology* (Leiden)

——— 2008. 'Food Processing and Preparation', in J. P. Oleson (ed.), *The Oxford Handbook of Engineering and Technology in the Classical World* (Oxford)

Curwen, E. C. and G. Hatt 1953. *Plough and Pasture: The Early History of Farming* (New York)

Cuttler, Richard, John Hunt and Stephanie Rátkai 2009. 'Saxon Burh and Royal Castle: Re-thinking Early Urban Space in Stafford', *Transactions of the Staffordshire Archaeological Society* 43, 39–85

Dallas, C. 1993. *Excavations in Thetford by B. K. Davison between 1964 and 1970*, East Anglian Archaeology Report 62 (Norfolk Museums Service)

Dalwood, Hal and Rachel Edwards 2004. *Excavations at Deansway, Worcester, 1988–89: Romano-British Small Town to Late Medieval City*, Council for British Archaeology Research Report 139 (York)

Darlington, J. 1985. 'Approaches to Iron Artefact Analysis: A Guide and Appraisal' (unpublished MA dissertation, University of Birmingham)

Darlington, John (ed.) 2001. *Stafford Castle: Survey, Excavation and Research 1978–1998, Volume 1: The Surveys* (Stafford Borough Council)

Dearden, Brian 1988. 'Charles the Bald's Fortified Bridge at Pîtres (Seine): Recent Archaeological Investigations', in R. Allen Brown (ed.), *Anglo-Norman Studies XI* (Woodbridge), 107–12

——— and Anthony Clark 1990. 'Pont-de-1'Arche or Pitres? A Location and Archaeomagnetic Dating for Charles the Bald's Fortifications on the Seine', *Antiquity* 64, 567–71

Dobson, Barrie 2000. 'General Survey 1300–1540', in Palliser, 273–90

Dodd, Anne (ed.) 2003. *Oxford before the University: The Late Saxon and Norman Archaeology of the Thames Crossing, the Defences and the Town* (Oxford)

Dulley, A. J. F. 1967. 'Excavations at Pevensey, Sussex, 1962–6', *Medieval Archaeology* 11, 209–32

Dunlevy, M. M. 1988. 'A Classification of Early Irish Combs', *Proceedings of the Royal Irish Academy* 88, 341–422

Dyer, C. C. and T. Slater 2000. 'The Midlands', in Palliser, 609–37

Edees, E.S. 1972. *Flora of Staffordshire* (Newton Abbot)

Edwards, Matthew John 2004. 'The Anglo-Saxon Origins of Stafford and its Churches' (unpublished M.Phil. thesis, University of Birmingham)

Egan, G. and F. Pritchard 2002. *Dress Accessories c.1150–1450* (London)

Evans, E. 1957. *Irish Folk Ways* (London)

Fenton, A. 1978. *The Northern Isles* (Edinburgh)

—— 1999. *Scottish Country Life* (East Linton)

Flodin, L. 1989. *Kammakeriet i Trondheim ca. 1000–1600* (Trondheim)

Ford, Deborah A. 1995. *Medieval Pottery in Staffordshire, AD800–1600: A Review*, Staffordshire Archaeological Studies 7 (Stoke on Trent)

—— 1999. 'A Late Saxon Pottery Industry in Staffordshire: A Review', *Medieval Ceramics* 22–23 (1998–99), 11–36

Foreman, M. 1991. 'The Bone and Antler', in Armstrong et al., 183–196

Galloway, P. 1990. 'Toilet Equipment: Combs of Bone, Antler, and Ivory', in Biddle, 665–678

Gillam, J. P. 1976. 'Coarse Fumed Ware in Northern Britain', *Glasgow Archaeological Journal* 4, 57–80

Glazebrook, Jenny 1983. 'Stafford – A Survey of the Urban Fabric' (unpublished MA dissertation, University of Birmingham)

Goodhall, I. H. 1973. 'Appendix 6: Iron Objects', in Huggins and Huggins, 168–75

—— 1983. 'Iron Objects', in Mayes and Butler, 240–52

—— 1990. 'Horseshoes', in Biddle, 1053–67

Gould, J. 1968. 'Excavations at Tamworth 1967', *Lichfield and South Staffordshire Archaeological and Historical Society Transactions* 9, 18–23

—— 1969. 'The Western Entrance to the Saxon Borough', *Lichfield and South Staffordshire Archaeological and Historical Society Transactions* 10, 31–41

Greig, J. R. A. 1982a. 'Past and Present Lime Woods in Europe', in S. Limbrey and M. Bell (eds), *Archaeological Aspects of Woodland Ecology*, British Archaeological Reports, International Series 146, 23–55

—— 1982b. 'The Interpretation of Pollen Spectra from Urban Archaeological Deposits', in A. R. Hall and H. K. Kenward (eds), *Environmental Archaeology in the Urban Context*, Council for British Archaeology Research Report 43 (York), 47–65

—— 1983. 'Plant Foods in the Past: A Review of the Evidence from Northern Europe', *Journal of Plant Foods* 5, 179–214

Griffiths, David 2001. 'The North-West Frontier', in Higham and Hill: 167–87

Haase, C. 1960. *Die Entstehung der westfälischen Städte* (Münster)

Hansen, G. 2005. *Bergen c.800–1170: The Emergence of a Town* (Bergen)

Hartley, K. F. 1971. 'Mortaria from Mancetter, 1964', *Transactions of the Birmingham and Warwickshire Archaeological Society* 84, 28–34

—— and G. Webster 1961. 'A Romano-British Kiln at Manduessedum', *TBWAS* 77

Haslam, J. 1987. 'Market and Fortress in England in the Reign of Offa', *World Archaeology* 19.1, 76–93

—— 2003. 'Excavations at Cricklade 1975', *Internet Archaeology* 14

—— 2005. 'King Alfred and the Vikings: Strategies and Tactics, 876–886 AD', *Anglo-Saxon Studies in Archaeology and History* 13, 122–54

—— 2009. 'The Development of Late-Saxon Christchurch, Dorset, and the Burghal Hidage', *Medieval Archaeology* 53, 95–118

Hassall, J. and D. Hill 1971. 'Pont-de-L'Arche. Frankish Influence on the West Saxon burh?' *Archaeological Journal* 127, 188–95

Heighway, C. M., A. P. Garrod and A. G. Vince 1979. 'Excavations at 1 Westgate Street, Gloucester, 1975', *Medieval Archaeology* 23, 159–213

Higham, N. J. and D. H. Hill (eds) 2001. *Edward the Elder 899–924* (London)

Hill, David 1969. 'The Burghal Hidage: the Establishment of a Text', *Medieval Archaeology* 13, 84–92

—— 1981. *An Atlas of Anglo-Saxon England* (Oxford)

—— 2001. 'The Shiring of Mercia – Again', in Higham and Hill, 144–59

—— 2003. 'The Origins of Alfred's Urban Policies', in Reuter, 219–33

—— and Alexander Rumble (eds) 1996. *The Defence of Wessex: The Burghal Hidage and Anglo-Saxon Fortifications* (Manchester)

Hill, Peter 1997. *Whithorn and St Ninian: The Excavation of a Monastic Town 1984–91* (Stroud)

Hillman, G. C. 1981. 'Reconstructing Crop Processing from Charred Remains of Crops', in R. Mercer (ed.), *Farming Practice in British Prehistory* (Edinburgh), 123–62

Hinton, D.A. 1990. 'Buckles and Buckle Plates', in Biddle, 502–26

Holdsworth, P. (ed) 1987. *Excavations in the Medieval Burgh of Perth 1979–1981*, Society of Antiquaries of Scotland Monograph Series 5 (London)

Hope-Taylor, B. 1977. *Yeavering: An Anglo-British Centre of Early Northumbria* (London)

Horn, Walter and Ernst Born 1979. *The Plan of St. Gall*, 2 vols (Berkeley, California)

Horne, J. S. 1937. 'Portrait of Mathew Cradock, 1520–1592', *Transactions of the Old Stafford Society*, 27–33

Howe, M. D., J. R. Perrin and D. F. Mackreth 1980. *Roman Pottery from the Nene Valley: A Guide*, Peterborough City Museum Occasional Paper No. 2

Howe, N. 2004. 'Rome: Capital of Anglo-Saxon England', *Journal of Medieval and Early Modern Studies* 34.1, 147–72

Huggins, P. J. and R. M. Huggins 1973. 'Excavations of Monastic Forge and Saxo-Norman Enclosure, Waltham Abbey, Essex', *Essex Archaeology and History* 5, 127–84

Hurley, M. F. and O. M. B. Scully 1997. *Late Viking Age and Medieval Waterford: Excavations 1986–1992* (Waterford)

Hurst, H. R. 1986. *Gloucester: The Roman and Later Defences* (Gloucester)

Hurst, J. 1976. 'The Pottery', in David M. Wilson (ed.), *The Archaeology of Anglo-Saxon England* (London), 283–348

Hutchinson, A. R. J. 2006. 'The Origins of King's Lynn? Control of Wealth on the Wash prior to the Norman Conquest', *Medieval Archaeology* 50, 71–104

Irvine, Susan 2003. 'The Anglo-Saxon Chronicle and the Idea of Rome', in Reuter, 63–78

James, Heather F. and Peter Yeoman 2008. *Excavations at St Ethernan's Monastery, Isle of May, Fife 1992–7* (Perth)

Jarvis, Keith S. 1983. *Excavations in Christchurch 1969–1980* (Dorchester)

Jones, G. 1984. 'Interpretation of Archaeological Plant Remains: Ethnographic Models from Greece', in W. van Zeist and W.A. Casparie (eds), *Plants and Ancient Man* (Rotterdam), 43–61

Jones, Michael J., David Stocker and Alan Vince 2003. *The City by the Pool: Assessing the Archaeology of the City of Lincoln* (Oxford)

Kemp, R. 1996. *Anglian Settlement at 46–54 Fishergate*, The Archaeology of York 7/1 (York)

Kent, Charles W. 1988. 'The Anglo-Saxon burh and byrig', *Modern Language Notes* 3.6, 176–7

Keynes, Simon 2001. 'Edward, King of the Anglo-Saxons', in Higham and Hill, 40–66

Lambert, L. 1923. *A Short History of the College of Stafford with its Collegiate Church of St Mary* (Stafford)

———— 1925. *St Mary's and the College Quarter of Stafford* (Birmingham)

———— 1939. *The Queen Elizabeth Grant and the College Estate in the Town of Stafford* (Stafford)

Long, C.D. 1975. 'Excavations in the Medieval City of Trondheim, Norway', *Medieval Archaeology* 19, 1–32

Lowe, Christopher 2006. *Excavations at Hoddom, Dumfriesshire: An Early Ecclesiastical Site in South-West Scotland* (Edinburgh)

———— 2008. *Inchmarnock: An Early Historic Island Monastery and its Archaeological Landscape* (Edinburgh)

Luik, H. 1998. *Muinas- ja keskaegsed luukammid Eestis, Muinasaja Teadus 6.* (Tallinn)

Lyon, Stewart 2001. 'The Coinage of Edward the Elder', in Higham and Hill, 67–78

MacGregor, A. 1985. *Bone, Antler, Ivory and Horn: The Technology of Skeletal Materials since the Roman Period* (London)

————, A. J. Mainman et al. 1999. *Craft, Industry and Everyday Life: Bone, Antler, Ivory and Horn from Anglo-Scandinavian and Medieval York*, The Archaeology of York 17/2 (York)

Mayes, P. and L. A. S. Butler 1983. *Sandal Castle Excavations 1964–73* (Wakefield)

Moffett, L. 1986a. 'The Medieval Cereals and Weeds from School Road, Alcester (AL 13)', *Ancient Monuments Laboratory Report* 16/86

———— 1986b. 'Charred Plant Remains from a Medieval Tenement at Warwick, Bridge End', *Ancient Monuments Laboratory Report* 17/86

———— 1986c. 'Crops and Crop Processing in a Romano-British Village at Tiddington: the Evidence from the Charred Plant Remains', *Ancient Monuments Laboratory Report* 15/86

———— 1987. 'Cultivated Plants and Domestic Activities: the Evidence from the Charred Plant Remains from Dean Court Farm, Oxon.', *Ancient Monuments Laboratory Report* 202/87

———— 1994. 'Charred Cereals from Some Ovens/Kilns in Late Saxon Stafford and the Botanical Evidence for the Pre-burh Economy', in James Rackham (ed.), *Environment and Economy in Anglo-Saxon England*, Council for British Archaeology Research Report 89 (York), 55–64

Morris, C. A. 2000. *Wood and Wood-Working in Anglo-Scandinavian and Medieval York*, Archaeology of York 17/13 (York)

Murphy, P. 1983a. 'Iron Age to Late Saxon Land Use in the Breckland', in M. Jones (ed.), *Integrating the Subsistence Economy*, British Archaeological Reports, International Series 181, 177–209

———— 1983b. 'Plant Macrofossils', in B. Ayers and P. Murphy, *A Waterfront Excavation at Whitefriars Street Car Park, Norwich, 1979*, East Anglian Archaeology 17, 40–4

———— 1985. 'The Cereals and Crop Weeds', in S. West, *West Stow: The Anglo-Saxon Village*, vol. 1, East Anglian Archaeology, 100–8

Musty, J. 1974. 'Medieval Pottery Kilns', in V. I. Evison, H. Hodges and J.G. Hurst (eds), *Medieval Pottery from Excavations: Studies presented to Gerald Clough Dunning* (London), 41–65

O'Connor, Terence 1994. '8–11th century economy and environment in York' in Rackham, 136–47

O'Sullivan, Jerry and Tomás Ó Carragáin 2008. *Inishmurray: Monks and Pilgrims in an Atlantic Landscape, Vol. 1: Archaeological Survey and Excavations 1997–2000* (Cork)

Oswald, A. 1955a. *The Church of St Bertelin at Stafford and its Cross* (Birmingham)

Oswald, A. 1955b. 'Excavation of a Saxon Chapel at St Bertelin at Stafford', *Archaeological News Letter* 5, 152–4

———— 1962–3. 'Excavation of a Thirteenth-Century Wooden Building at Weoley Castle, Birmingham, 1960–61', *Medieval Archaeology* 6–7, 109–34

Ottaway, P. J. 1992. *Anglo-Scandinavian Ironwork from Coppergate*, The Archaeology of York 17/6 (York)

———— and N. S. H. Rogers 2002. *Craft, Industry and Everyday Life: Finds from Medieval York*, Archaeology of York 17/15 (York)

Palliser, D. M. (ed.) 2000. *The Cambridge Urban History of Britain* (Cambridge)

Persson, J. 1976. 'Kammar', in A. V. Mårtensson (ed.), *Uppgrävt förflutet för PK-banken i Lund* (Malmö), 317–32

Phillips, Derek and Brenda Heywood 1995. *Excavations at York Minster, Vol. 1: From Roman Fortress to Norman Cathedral* (London)

Rackham, James (ed.) 1994. *Environment and Economy in Anglo-Saxon England* (CBA Research Report 89)

———— 1994. 'Economy and environment in Saxon London' in Rackham: 126–35

Rahtz, Philip 1977. 'The Archaeology of West Mercian Towns', in Ann Dornier (ed.), *Mercian Studies* (Leicester), 107–30

———— and Robert Meeson 1992. *An Anglo-Saxon Watermill at Tamworth*, Council for British Archaeology Research Report 83 (York)

Ralegh Radford, C. 1970. 'The Later Pre-Conquest Boroughs and their Defences', *Medieval Archaeology* 14, 83–103

Reuter, Timothy (ed.) 2003. *Alfred the Great: Papers from the Eleventh-Centenary Conferences* (Aldershot)

Reynolds, A. J. 1999. *Later Anglo-Saxon England: Life and Landscape* (Stroud)

———— 2001. 'Avebury: A Late Anglo-Saxon burh?' *Antiquity* 75, 29–30

Robinson, P. H. 1968–70. 'The Stafford Moneyers, AD924–1165', *Transactions of the Stafford History and Civic Society*, 10–22

Rogerson, A. and C. Dallas 1984. 'Excavations at Thetford 1948–59 and 1973–1977', *East Anglian Archaeology* 22, 77–106

RCHM(E): Royal Commission on Historical Monuments

(England) 1959. 'Whareham West Walls', *Medieval Archaeology* 3, 120–38

Rytter, J. 1991. 'Kamme fra Kungahälla', *Kungahälla arkeologi 1989. Fornlämning 53 Ytterby socken.* ed. (Göteborg), 39–51

Shoesmith, R. 1980. *Excavations at Castle Green* [Hereford], Council for British Archaeology Research Report 36 (York)

——— 1982. *Excavations on and close to the Defences* [Hereford], Council for British Archaeology Research Report 46 (York)

Shotton, F. and R. E. G. Williams 1971. in *Radiocarbon* 13, 152–3

Smirnova, L. 2005. *Comb-Making in Medieval Novgorod (950–1450): An Industry in Transition* (Oxford)

Spall, C. A. and N. J. Toop 2005. *Excavations at Blue Bridge Lane and Fishergate House*, www.archaeologicalplanningconsultancy.co.uk/mono/001

Spall, Cecily and Nicola Toop 2008. 'Before Eoforwic: New Light on York in the 6th–7th Centuries', *Medieval Archaeology* 52, 1–26

Stenton, F. M. 1971. *Anglo-Saxon England*, 3rd edn (Oxford)

Thacker. Alan 1985. 'Kings, Saints, and Monasteries in Pre-Viking Mercia', *Midland History* 10, 1–25

Thomas, A. and A. Boucher (eds) 2002. *Hereford City Excavations, Vol. IV. 1976–1990: Further Sites and Evolving Interpretations* (Hereford City and County Archaeological Trust)

Tusser, T. 1580 [1984]. *Five Hundred Points of Good Husbandry*, introduction by Geoffrey Grigson (Oxford)

Tweddle, D., J. Moulden and E. Logan 1999. *Anglian York: A Survey of the Evidence*, The Archaeology of York 7/2 (York)

Tyers, Paul 1996. *Roman Pottery in Britain* (London)

Ulbricht, I. 1980. 'Middelalderlig kamproduktion i Slesvig', *Hikuin* 6, 147–52

Vince, A. G. 1985. 'The Saxon and Medieval Pottery of London: A Review', *Medieval Archaeology* 19, 25–93

——— 1994. 'Saxon Urban Economies: An Archaeological Perspective', in James Rackham (ed.), *Environment and Economy in Anglo-Saxon England*, Council for British Archaeology Research Report 89 (York), 108–119

Wainwright, F. T. 1959. 'Æthelflæd, Lady of the Mercians', in Peter Clemoes (ed.), *The Anglo-Saxons: Studies in Some Aspects of their History and Culture presented to Bruce Dickins* (London), 53–69

Walker, Alison Jill 1976. 'The Archaeology of Stafford to 1600 AD' (unpublished MA dissertation, University of Bradford)

Walker, I. W. 2000. *Mercia and the Making of England* (Stroud)

Walters, P. L. 1976. 'Romano-British Pottery Site at Great Buckman's Farm', *Transactions of the Worcestershire Archaeological Society* 3rd series 5, 63–72

Ward, Simon 2001. 'Edward the Elder and the Re-establishment of Chester', in Higham and Hill, 160–6

Ward Perkins, J. B. 1940. *London Museum Medieval Catalogue* (London)

Watson, Bruce, Trevor Brigham and Tony Dyson 2001. *London Bridge: 2000 Years of a River Crossing*, Museum of London Archaeology Service monograph 8 (London)

Webster, G. et al. 1953. 'A Saxon Treasure Hoard Found at Chester, 1950', *Antiquaries Journal* 33, 22–32

Webster, Leslie E. and John Cherry 1972. 'Medieval Britain in 1971', *Medieval Archaeology* 16, 147–212

——— 1973. 'Medieval Britain in 1973', *Medieval Archaeology* 17, 138–88

——— 1980. 'Medieval Britain in 1979', *Medieval Archaeology* 24, 218–64

Webster, P. V. 1978. 'Severn Valley Ware: A Preliminary Study', *Transactions of the Bristol and Gloucestershire Archaeological Society* 94, 18–46

Whitelock, D. (ed.) 1961. *The Anglo-Saxon Chronicle* (London)

Wiberg, C. 1977. 'Horn og Beinmaterialet fra "Mindets tomt"', in H. I. Høeg, H.-E. Lidén, A. Liestøl, P. B. Molaug, E. Schia and C. Wiberg (eds), *De arkeologiske utgravninger i Gamlebyen, Oslo. Bind 1* (Oslo), 202–13

——— 1979. 'Beinmaterialet', in E. Schia (ed.), *De arkeologiske utgravninger i Gamlebyen, Oslo. Bind 2: Feltene "Oslogate 3 og 7"* (Oslo), 59

Wiberg, T. 1987. 'Kammer', in E. Schia (ed.), *De Arkeologiske utgravninger i Gamlebyen, Oslo. Bind 3* (Oslo)

Williams, D. F. 1985. 'The Petrology of Chester Ware', in D. J. P. Mason, *Excavations at Chester* (Chester City Council), 55–6

Williams, J. H. 1979. *St Peter Street, Northampton: Excavations 1973–76* (Northampton)

Young, Deborah and Philip Morgan 2001. 'Stafford Castle 1066–1563', in Darlington, 32–82

Youngs, Susan M., John Clark and Terry Barry 1985. 'Medieval Britain and Ireland in 1984', *Medieval Archaeology* 29, 158–230

INDEX

Page numbers in **bold** refer to illustrated matter